Elasticsearch 5.x Cookbook

Third Edition

Over 170 advanced recipes to search, analyze, deploy, manage, and monitor data effectively with Elasticsearch 5.x

Alberto Paro

Pack<t>

BIRMINGHAM - MUMBAI

Elasticsearch 5.x Cookbook

Third Edition

First published: December 2013

Second edition: January 2015

Third edition: February 2017

Production reference: 1310117

Published by Packt Publishing Ltd.
Livery Place
35 Livery Street
Birmingham
B3 2PB, UK.
ISBN 978-1-78646-558-0

www.packtpub.com

Credits

Author

Alberto Paro

Reviewer

Marcelo Ochoa

Commissioning Editor

Amey Varangaonkar

Acquisition Editor

Divya Poojari

Content Development Editor

Amrita Noronha

Technical Editor

Deepti Tuscano

Copy Editor

Safis Editing

Project Coordinator

Shweta H Birwatkar

Proofreader

Safis Editing

Indexer

Rekha Nair

Production Coordinator

Arvindkumar Gupta

About the Author

Alberto Paro is an engineer, project manager, and software developer. He currently works as freelance trainer/consultant on big data technologies and NoSQL solutions. He loves to study emerging solutions and applications mainly related to big data processing, NoSQL, natural language processing, and neural networks. He began programming in BASIC on a Sinclair Spectrum when he was eight years old, and to date, has collected a lot of experience using different operating systems, applications, and programming languages.

In 2000, he graduated in computer science engineering from Politecnico di Milano with a thesis on designing multiuser and multidevice web applications. He assisted professors at the university for about a year. He then came in contact with The Net Planet Company and loved their innovative ideas; he started working on knowledge management solutions and advanced data mining products. In summer 2014, his company was acquired by a big data technologies company, where he worked until the end of 2015 mainly using Scala and Python on state-of-the-art big data software (Spark, Akka, Cassandra, and YARN). In 2013, he started freelancing as a consultant for big data, machine learning, Elasticsearch and other NoSQL products. He has created or helped to develop big data solutions for business intelligence, financial, and banking companies all over the world. A lot of his time is spent teaching how to efficiently use big data solutions (mainly Apache Spark), NoSql datastores (Elasticsearch, HBase, and Accumulo) and related technologies (Scala, Akka, and Playframework). He is often called to present at big data or Scala events. He is an evangelist on Scala and Scala.js (the transcompiler from Scala to JavaScript).

In his spare time, when he is not playing with his children, he likes to work on open source projects. When he was in high school, he started contributing to projects related to the GNOME environment (gtkmm). One of his preferred programming languages is Python, and he wrote one of the first NoSQL backends on Django for MongoDB (Django-MongoDB-engine). In 2010, he began using Elasticsearch to provide search capabilities to some Django e-commerce sites and developed PyES (a Pythonic client for Elasticsearch), as well as the initial part of the Elasticsearch MongoDB river. He is the author of *Elasticsearch Cookbook* as well as a technical reviewer of *Elasticsearch Server-Second Edition, Learning Scala Web Development*, and the video course, *Building a Search Server with Elasticsearch*, all of which are published by *Packt Publishing*.

It would have been difficult for me to complete this book without the support of a large number of people.

First, I would like to thank my wife, my children and the rest of my family for their support.

A personal thanks to my best friends, Mauro and Michele, and to all the people that helped me and my family.

I'd like to express my gratitude to everyone at Packt Publishing who are involved in the development and production of this book. I'd like to thank Amrita Noronha for guiding this book to completion and Deepti Tuscano and Marcelo Ochoa for patiently going through the first draft and providing their valuable feedback. Their professionalism, courtesy, good judgment, and passion for books are much appreciated.

About the Reviewer

Marcelo Ochoa works at the system laboratory of Facultad de Ciencias Exactas of the Universidad Nacional del Centro de la Provincia de Buenos Aires and is the CTO at Scotas.com, a company that specializes in near real-time search solutions using Apache Solr and Oracle. He divides his time between university jobs and external projects related to Oracle and big data technologies. He has worked on several Oracle-related projects, such as the translation of Oracle manuals and multimedia CBTs. His background is in database, network, web, and Java technologies. In the XML world, he is known as the developer of the DB Generator for the Apache Cocoon project. He has worked on the open source projects DBPrism and DBPrism CMS, the Lucene-Oracle integration using the Oracle JVM Directory implementation, and the Restlet.org project, where he worked on the Oracle XDB Restlet Adapter, which is an alternative to writing native REST web services inside a database-resident JVM.

Since 2006, he has been part of an Oracle ACE program. Oracle ACEs are known for their strong credentials as Oracle community enthusiasts and advocates, with candidates nominated by ACEs in the Oracle technology and applications communities.

He has coauthored *Oracle Database Programming using Java and Web Services* by *Digital Press* and *Professional XML Databases* by *Wrox Press*, and has been the technical reviewer for several books by Packt Publishing such as *Apache Solr 4 Cookbook* and *ElasticSearch Server*.

www.PacktPub.com

eBooks, discount offers, and more

Did you know that Packt offers eBook versions of every book published, with PDF and ePub files available? You can upgrade to the eBook version at www.PacktPub.com and as a print book customer, you are entitled to a discount on the eBook copy. Get in touch with us at customercare@packtpub.com for more details.

At www.PacktPub.com, you can also read a collection of free technical articles, sign up for a range of free newsletters and receive exclusive discounts and offers on Packt books and eBooks.

⋀⋀Mapt

https://www2.packtpub.com/books/subscription/packtlib

Do you need instant solutions to your IT questions? PacktLib is Packt's online digital book library. Here, you can search, access, and read Packt's entire library of books.

Why subscribe?

- Fully searchable across every book published by Packt
- Copy and paste, print, and bookmark content
- On demand and accessible via a web browser

Customer Feedback

Thank you for purchasing this Packt book. We take our commitment to improving our content and products to meet your needs seriously—that's why your feedback is so valuable. Whatever your feelings about your purchase, please consider leaving a review on this book's Amazon page. Not only will this help us, more importantly it will also help others in the community to make an informed decision about the resources that they invest in to learn.

You can also review for us on a regular basis by joining our reviewers' club. **If you're interested in joining, or would like to learn more about the benefits we offer, please contact us**: customerreviews@packtpub.com.

To Giulia and Andrea, my extraordinary children.

Table of Contents

Preface

The most common requirements of today standard applications are the search and analytics capabilities. On the market we can find a lot of solutions to answer to these need both in commercial and in open source world. One of the most used libraries for searching is Apache Lucene. This library is the base of a large number of search solutions such as Apache Solr, Indextank, and Elasticsearch.

Elasticsearch is one of the most powerful solution, written with the cloud and distributed computing in mind. Its main author, Shay Banon, famous for having developed Compass (http://www.compass-project.org), released the first version of Elasticsearch in March 2010.

Thus the main scope of Elasticsearch is to be a search engine; it also provides a lot of features that allows using it also as data-store and analytic engine via its aggregation framework.

Elasticsearch contains a lot of innovative features: JSON REST based, natively distributed in a map/reduce approach for both search and analytics, easy to set up and extensible with plugins. From 2010 when it started to be developed, to last version (5.x) there is a big evolution of the product becoming one of the most used datastore for a lot of markets. In this book we will go in depth on these changes and features and many others capabilities available in Elasticsearch.

Elasticsearch is also a product in continuous evolution and new functionalities are released both by the Elasticsearch Company (the company founded by Shay Banon to provide commercial support for Elasticsearch) and by Elasticsearch users as plugin (mainly available on GitHub). Today a lot of the major world players in IT industry (see some use cases at https://www.elastic.co/use-cases) are using Elasticsearch for its simplicity and advanced features.

In my opinion, Elasticsearch is probably one of the most powerful and easy-to-use search solution on the market. In writing this book and these recipes, I and the book reviewers have tried to transmit our knowledge, our passion, and best practices to better manage it.

What this book covers

Chapter 1, *Getting Started,* The goal of this chapter is to give the reader an overview of the basic concepts of Elasticsearch and the ways to communicate with it.

Chapter 2, *Downloading and Setup,* covers the basic steps to start using Elasticsearch from the simple install to a cloud ones.

Chapter 3, *Managing Mappings,* covers the correct definition of the data fields to improve both indexing and searching quality.

Chapter 4, *Basic Operations,* teaches the most common actions that are required to ingest data in Elasticsearch and to manage it.

Chapter 5, *Search,* talks about executing search, sorting and related API calls. The API discussed in this chapter are the main

Chapter 6, *Text and Numeric Queries,* talks about Search DSL part on text and numeric fields —the core of the search functionalities of Elasticsearch.

Chapter 7, *Relationships and Geo Queries,* talks about queries that works on related document (child/parent, nested) and geo located fields.

Chapter 8, *Aggregations,* covers another capability of Elasticsearch, the possibility to execute analytics on search results to improve both the user experience and to drill down the information contained in Elasticsearch.

Chapter 9, *Scripting,* shows how to customize Elasticsearch with scripting and use the scripting capabilities in different part of Elasticsearch (search, aggregation, and ingest) using different languages. The chapter is mainly focused on Painless the new scripting language developed by Elastic Team.

Chapter 10, *Managing Clusters and Nodes,* shows how to analyze the behavior of a cluster/node to understand common pitfalls.

Chapter 11, *Backup and Restore,* covers one of the most important component in managing data: Backup. It shows how to manage a distributed backup and restore of snapshots.

Chapter 12, *User Interfaces,* describes two of the most common user interfaces for Elasticsearch 5.x: Cerebro, mainly used for admin activities, and Kibana with X-Pack as a common UI extension for Elasticsearch.

Chapter 13, *Ingest,* talks about the new ingest functionality introduced in Elasticsearch 5.x to import data in Elasticsearch via an ingestion pipeline.

Chapter 14, *Java Integration,* describes how to integrate Elasticsearch in Java application using both REST and native protocols.

Chapter 15, *Scala Integration,* describes how to integrate Elasticsearch in Scala using elastic4s: an advanced type-safe and feature rich Scala library based on native Java API.

Chapter 16, *Python Integration,* covers the usage of the official Elasticsearch Python client.

Chapter 17, *Plugin Development,* describes how to create native plugins to extend Elasticsearch functionalities. Some examples show the plugin skeletons, the setup process, and their building.

Chapter 18, *Big Data Integration,* covers how to integrate Elasticsearch in common big data tools such as Apache Spark and Apache Pig.

What you need for this book

For this book you will need a computer, of course. In terms of software required you don't have to be worried, all the components we use are open source and available for every platform.

For all the REST example, the CURL software (http://curl.haxx.se/) is used to simulate the command from command line. It's common preinstalled in Linux and Mac OS X operative systems. For Windows, it can be downloaded from its site and put in a PATH that can be called from command-line.

For the Chapter 14, *Java Integration* and and Chapter 17, *Plugin Development,* it is required the Maven build tool (http://maven.apache.org/), which is a standard for managing build, packaging and deploy in Java. It is natively supported in Java IDEs such as Eclipse and Intellij IDEA.

For Chapter 15, *Scala Integration,* SBT, (http://www.scala-sbt.org/) is required to compile Scala projects, but it can be also used with IDE that supports Scala such as Eclipse and Intellij IDEA.

The Chapter 16, *Python Integration,* requires the Python interpreter installed. By default it's available on Linux and Mac OS X , for Windows can be downloaded from the official python site (http://www.python.org). For the current examples the version 2.X is used.

Who this book is for

This book is for developers who want to start using both Elasticsearch and at the same time improve their Elasticsearch knowledge. The book covers all the aspects of using Elasticsearch and provides solutions and hints for everyday usage. The recipes are reduced in complexity to easy focus the reader on the discussed Elasticsearch aspect and to easily memorize the Elasticsearch functionalities.

The latter chapters that discuss the Elasticsearch integration in JAVA, Scala, Python, and Big Data tools show the user how to integrate the power of Elasticsearch in their applications.

The chapter, that talks about plugin development, shows an advanced usage of Elasticsearch and its core extension, so some skilled Java know-how is required.

Sections

In this book, you will find several headings that appear frequently (Getting ready, How to do it, How it works, There's more, and See also).

To give clear instructions on how to complete a recipe, we use these sections as follows:

Getting ready

This section tells you what to expect in the recipe, and describes how to set up any software or any preliminary settings required for the recipe.

How to do it...

This section contains the steps required to follow the recipe.

How it works...

This section usually consists of a detailed explanation of what happened in the previous section.

There's more...

This section consists of additional information about the recipe in order to make the reader more knowledgeable about the recipe.

See also

This section provides helpful links to other useful information for the recipe.

Conventions

In this book, you will find a number of styles of text that distinguish between different kinds of information. Here are some examples of these styles, and an explanation of their meaning.

Code words in text are shown as follows: "After the name and the type parameters, usually a river requires an extra configuration that can be passed in the _meta property"

A block of code is set as follows:

```
cluster.name: elasticsearch
node.name: "My wonderful server"
network.host: 192.168.0.1
discovery.zen.ping.unicast.hosts: ["192.168.0.2","192.168.0.3[9300-9400]"]
```

Any command-line input or output is written as follows:

```
curl -XDELETE 'http://127.0.0.1:9200/_river/my_river/'
```

> Warnings or important notes appear in a box like this.

> Tips and tricks appear like this.

Reader feedback

Feedback from our readers is always welcome. Let us know what you think about this book—what you liked or may have disliked. Reader feedback is important for us to develop titles that you really get the most out of.

To send us general feedback, simply send an e-mail to feedback@packtpub.com, and mention the book title via the subject of your message.

If there is a topic that you have expertise in and you are interested in either writing or contributing to a book, see our author guide on http://www.packtpub.com/authors.

Customer support

Now that you are the proud owner of a Packt book, we have a number of things to help you to get the most from your purchase.

Downloading the example code

You can download the example code files for this book from your account at http://www.packtpub.com. If you purchased this book elsewhere, you can visit http://www.packtpub.com/support and register to have the files e-mailed directly to you.

You can download the code files by following these steps:

1. Log in or register to our website using your e-mail address and password.
2. Hover the mouse pointer on the SUPPORT tab at the top.
3. Click on Code Downloads & Errata.
4. Enter the name of the book in the Search box.
5. Select the book for which you're looking to download the code files.
6. Choose from the drop-down menu where you purchased this book from.
7. Click on Code Download.

You can also download the code files by clicking on the Code Files button on the book's webpage at the Packt Publishing website. This page can be accessed by entering the book's name in the Search box. Please note that you need to be logged in to your Packt account.

Once the file is downloaded, please make sure that you unzip or extract the folder using the latest version of:

- WinRAR / 7-Zip for Windows
- Zipeg / iZip / UnRarX for Mac
- 7-Zip / PeaZip for Linux

The code bundle for the book is also hosted on GitHub at `https://github.com/PacktPubl ishing/Elasticsearch-5x-Cookbook-Third-Edition`. We also have other code bundles from our rich catalog of books and videos available at `https://github.com/PacktPublish ing/`. Check them out!

Errata

Although we have taken every care to ensure the accuracy of our content, mistakes do happen. If you find a mistake in one of our books—maybe a mistake in the text or the code—we would be grateful if you would report this to us. By doing so, you can save other readers from frustration and help us improve subsequent versions of this book. If you find any errata, please report them by visiting `http://www.packtpub.com/submit-errata`, selecting your book, clicking on the errata submission form link, and entering the details of your errata. Once your errata are verified, your submission will be accepted and the errata will be uploaded on our website, or added to any list of existing errata, under the Errata section of that title. Any existing errata can be viewed by selecting your title from `http://w ww.packtpub.com/support`.

Piracy

Piracy of copyright material on the Internet is an ongoing problem across all media. At Packt, we take the protection of our copyright and licenses very seriously. If you come across any illegal copies of our works, in any form, on the Internet, please provide us with the location address or website name immediately so that we can pursue a remedy.

Please contact us at `copyright@packtpub.com` with a link to the suspected pirated material.

We appreciate your help in protecting our authors, and our ability to bring you valuable content.

Questions

You can contact us at `questions@packtpub.com` if you are having a problem with any aspect of the book, and we will do our best

1
Getting Started

In this chapter, we will cover the following recipes:

- Understanding node and cluster
- Understanding node services
- Managing your data
- Understanding cluster, replication, and sharding
- Communicating with Elasticsearch
- Using the HTTP protocol
- Using the native protocol

Introduction

To efficiently use **Elasticsearch**, it is very important to understand its design and working.

The goal of this chapter is to give the readers an overview of the basic concepts of Elasticsearch and to be a quick reference for them. It's essential to better understand them to not fall in common pitfalls due to the lack of know-how about Elasticsearch architecture and internals.

The key concepts that we will see in this chapter are node, index, shard, type/mapping, document, and field.

Elasticsearch can be used in several ways such as:

- Search engine, which is its main usage
- Analytics framework via its powerful aggregation system
- Data store, mainly for log

A brief description of the Elasticsearch logic helps the user to improve performance, search quality and decide when and how to optimize the infrastructure to improve scalability and availability. Some details on data replications and base node communication processes are also explained in the upcoming section, *Understanding cluster, replication, and sharding*.

At the end of this chapter, the protocols used to manage Elasticsearch are also discussed.

Understanding node and cluster

Every instance of Elasticsearch is called **node**. Several nodes are grouped in a cluster. This is the base of the cloud nature of Elasticsearch.

Getting ready

To better understand the following sections, knowledge of the basic concepts such as application node and cluster are required.

How it work…

One or more Elasticsearch nodes can be setup on physical or a virtual server depending on the available resources such as RAM, CPUs, and disk space.

A default node allows us to store data in it and to process requests and responses. (In Chapter 2, *Downloading and Setup*, we will see details on how to set up different nodes and cluster topologies).

When a node is started, several actions take place during its startup: such as:

- Configuration is read from the environment variables and from the `elasticsearch.yml` configuration file
- A node name is set by config file or chosen from a list of built-in random names
- Internally, the Elasticsearch engine initializes all the modules and plugins that are available in the current installation

After node startup, the node searches for other cluster members and checks its index and shard status.

To join two or more nodes in a cluster, these rules must be matched:

- The version of Elasticsearch must be the same (2.3, 5.0, and so on), otherwise the join is rejected
- The cluster name must be the same

The network must be configured to support broadcast discovery (default) and they can communicate with each other. (Refer to *How to setup networking* recipe `Chapter 2, Downloading and Setup`).

A common approach in cluster management is to have one or more master nodes, which is the main reference for all cluster-level actions, and the other ones called secondary, that replicate the master data and actions.

To be consistent in write operations, all the update actions are first committed in the master node and then replicated in secondary ones.

In a cluster with multiple nodes, if a master node dies, a master-eligible one is elected to be the new master. This approach allows automatic failover to be setup in an Elasticsearch cluster.

There's more...

In Elasticsearch, we have four kinds of nodes:

- Master nodes that are able to process **REST** (`https://en.wikipedia.org/wiki/Representational_state_transfer`) responses and all other operations of search. During every action execution, Elasticsearch generally executes actions using a MapReduce approach (`https://en.wikipedia.org/wiki/MapReduce`): the non data node is responsible for distributing the actions to the underlying shards (map) and collecting/aggregating the shard results (reduce) to send a final response. They may use a huge amount of RAM due to operations such as aggregations, collecting hits, and caching (that is, scan/scroll queries).
- Data nodes that are able to store data in them. They contain the indices shards that store the indexed documents as Lucene indexes.
- Ingest nodes that are able to process ingestion pipeline (new in Elasticsearch 5.x).
- Client nodes (no master and no data) that are used to do processing in a way; if something bad happens (out of memory or bad queries), they are able to be killed/restarted without data loss or reduced cluster stability. Using the standard configuration, a node is both master, data container and ingest node.

In big cluster architectures, having some nodes as simple client nodes with a lot of RAM, with no data, reduces the resources required by data nodes and improves performance in search using the local memory cache of them.

See also

- The *Setting up a single node*, *Setting a multi node cluster* and *Setting up different node types* recipes in `Chapter 2`, *Downloading and Setup*.

Understanding node services

When a node is running, a lot of services are managed by its instance. Services provide additional functionalities to a node and they cover different behaviors such as networking, indexing, analyzing, and so on.

Getting ready

Starting an Elasticsearch node, a lot of output will be prompted; this output is provided during services start up. Every Elasticsearch server, that is running, provides services.

How it works...

Elasticsearch natively provides a large set of functionalities that can be extended with additional plugins.

During a node startup, a lot of required services are automatically started. The most important ones are:

- **Cluster services**: This helps you to manage the cluster state and intra node communication and synchronization
- **Indexing service**: This helps you to manage all the index operations, initializing all active indices and shards
- **Mapping service**: This helps you to manage the document types stored in the cluster (we'll discuss mapping in `Chapter 3`, *Managing Mappings*)

- **Network services**: This includes services such as HTTP REST services (default on port 9200), and internal ES protocol (port 9300), if the thrift plugin is installed
- **Plugin service**: (We will discuss in Chapter 2, *Downloading and Setup*, for installation andChapter 12, *User Interfaces* for detail usage)
- **Aggregation services**: This provides advanced analytics on stored Elasticsearch documents such as statistics, histograms, and document grouping
- **Ingesting services**: This provides support for document preprocessing before ingestion such as field enrichment, NLP processing, types conversion, and automatic field population
- **Language scripting services**: This allows adding new language scripting support to Elasticsearch

> Throughout the book, we'll see recipes that interact with Elasticsearch services. Every base functionality or extended functionality is managed in Elasticsearch as a service.

Managing your data

If you'll be using Elasticsearch as a search engine or a distributed data store, it's important to understand concepts on how Elasticsearch stores and manages your data.

Getting ready

To work with Elasticsearch data, a user must have basic knowledge of data management and JSON (https://en.wikipedia.org/wiki/JSON) data format that is the *lingua franca* for working with Elasticsearch data and services.

How it works…

Our main data container is called **index** (plural **indices**) and it can be considered similar to a database in the traditional SQL world. In an index, the data is grouped in data types called **mappings** in Elasticsearch. A mapping describes how the records are composed (**fields**). Every record, that must be stored in Elasticsearch, must be a JSON object.

Natively, Elasticsearch is a schema-less data store: when you put records in it, during insert it processes the records, splits it in fields, and updates the schema to manage the inserted data.

To manage huge volumes of records, Elasticsearch uses the common approach to split an index into multiple parts (**shards**) so that they can be spread on several nodes. The shard management is transparent to user usage: all common record operations are managed automatically in Elasticsearch's application layer.

Every record is stored in only a shard; the sharding algorithm is based on record ID, so many operations, that require loading and changing of records/objects, can be achieved without hitting all the shards, but only the shard (and their replicas) that contains your object.

The following schema compares Elasticsearch structure with SQL and MongoDB ones:

Elasticsearch	SQL	MongoDB
Index (indices)	Database	Database
Shard	Shard	Shard
Mapping/Type	Table	Collection
Field	Column	Field
Object (JSON object)	Record (tuples)	Record (BSON object)

The following screenshot is a conceptual representation of an Elasticsearch cluster with three nodes, one index with four shards and replica set to 1 (primary shards are in bold):

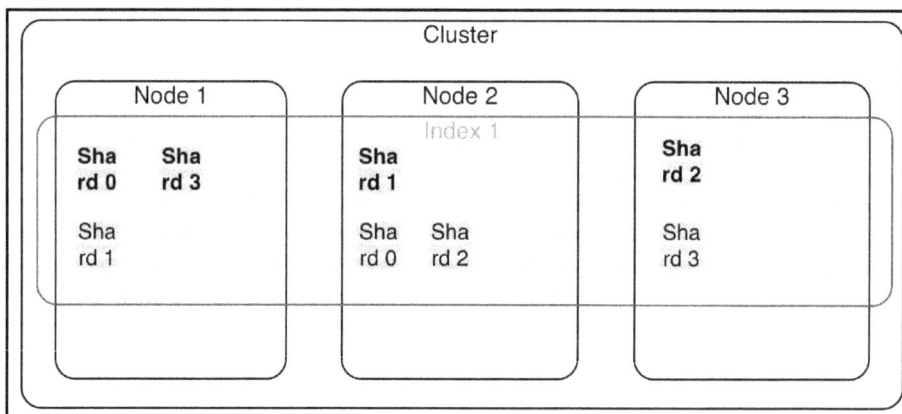

There's more...

Elasticsearch, to ensure safe operations on index/mapping/objects, internally has rigid rules about how to execute operations.

In Elasticsearch the operations are divided into:

- **Cluster/Index operations**: All write actions are locking, first they are applied to the master node and then to the secondary one. The read operations are typically broadcasted to all the nodes.
- **Document operations**: All write actions are locking only for the single hit shard. The read operations are balanced on all the shard replicas.

When a record is saved in Elasticsearch, the destination shard is chosen based on:

- The **unique identifier (ID)** of the record. If the ID is missing, it is auto generated by Elasticsearch
- If **routing** or **parent** (we'll see it in the parent/child mapping) parameters are defined, the correct shard is chosen by the hash of these parameters

Splitting an index in a shard allows you to store your data in different nodes, because Elasticsearch tries to balance the shard distribution on all the available nodes.

Every shard can contain up to 2^{32} records (about 4.9 Billions), so the real limit to shard size it is the storage size.

Shards contain your data, and during the search process all the shards are used to calculate and retrieve results: so Elasticsearch performance in big data scales horizontally with the number of shards.

All native records operations (that is, index, search, update, and delete) are managed in shards.

The shard management is completely transparent to the user. Only advanced users tend to change the default shard routing and management to cover their custom scenarios, for example, if there is a requirement to put customer data in the same shard to speed up his operations (search/index/analytics).

Best practices

It's best practice not to have too big in size shard (over 10Gb) to avoid poor performance in indexing due to continuous merging and resizing of index segments.

While indexing (a record update is equal to indexing a new element) Lucene, the Elasticsearch engine, writes the indexed documents in blocks (segments/files) to speed up the write process. Over time the small segments are deleted and their sum up is written as a new fragment. Having big fragments due to big shards with a lot of data slows down the indexing performance.

It is not good to over-allocate the number of shards to avoid poor search performance because Elasticsearch works in a map and reduce way due to native distribute search. Shards consist of the worker that does the job of indexing/searching and the master/client nodes do the redux part (collect the results from shards and compute the result to be sent to the user). Having a huge number of empty shards in indices consumes only memory and increases search times due to an overhead on network and results aggregation phases.

See also

- You can also view more information about Shard at
  `http://en.wikipedia.org/wiki/Shard_(database_architecture)`

Understanding cluster, replication, and sharding

Related to shards management, there are key concepts of **replication and cluster status**.

Getting ready

You need one or more nodes running to have a cluster. To test an effective cluster, you need at least two nodes (that can be on the same machine).

How it works...

An index can have one or more replicas (full copies of your data, automatically managed by Elasticsearch): the shards are called **primary** ones if they are part of the primary replica, and **secondary** ones if they are part of other replicas.

To maintain consistency in write operations, the following workflow is executed:

- The write is first executed in the primary shard
- If the primary write is successfully done, it is propagated simultaneously in all the secondary shards
- If a primary shard becomes unavailable, a secondary one is elected as primary (if available) and the flow is re-executed

During search operations, if there are some replicas, a valid set of shards is chosen randomly between primary and secondary to improve performances. Elasticsearch has several allocation algorithms to better distribute shards on nodes. For reliability, replicas are allocated in a way that if a single node becomes unavailable, there is always at least one replica of each shard that is still available on the remaining nodes.

The following figure shows some example of possible shards and replica configuration:

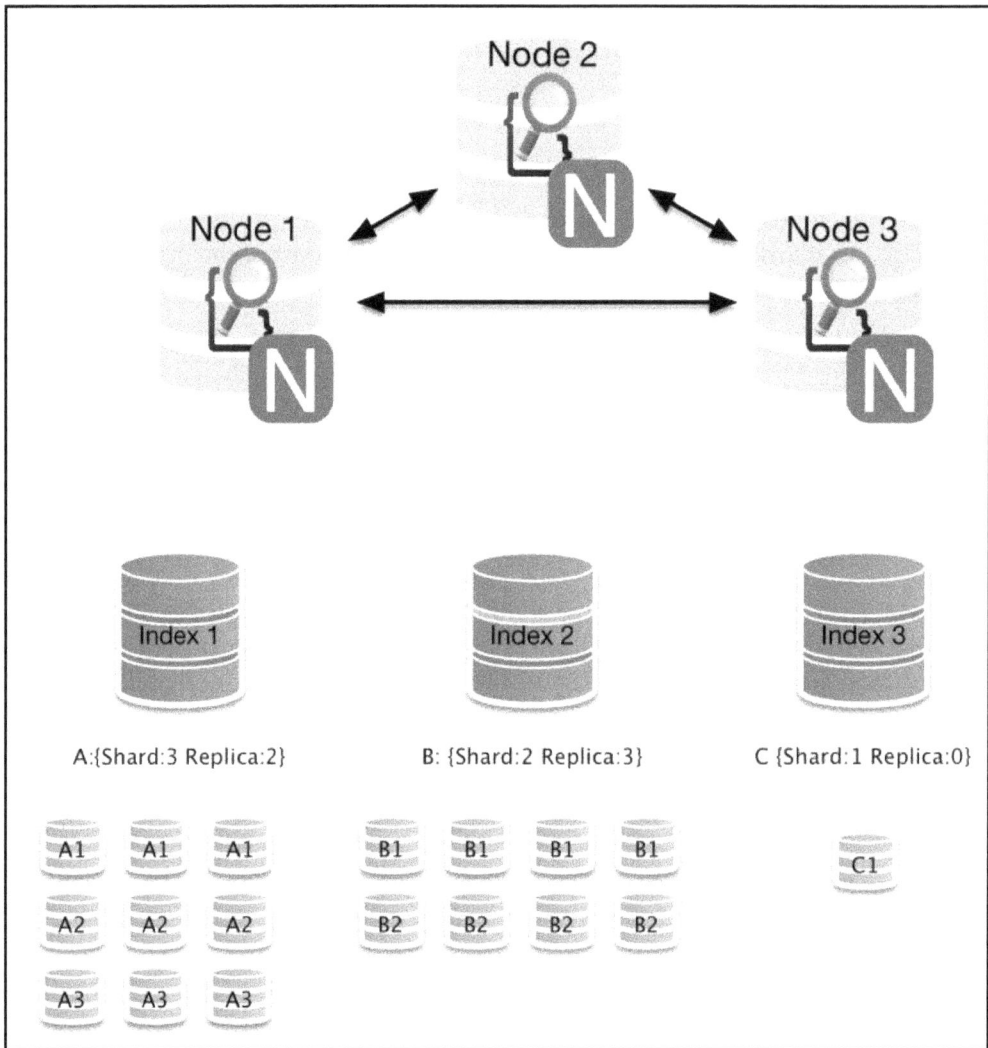

The replica has a cost to increase the indexing time due to data node synchronization and also the time spent to propagate the message to the slaves (mainly in an asynchronous way).

Best practice

To prevent data loss and to have high availability, it's good to have at least one replica; so, your system can survive a node failure without downtime and without loss of data.

A typical approach for scaling performance in search when your customer number is to increase the replica number.

There's more…

Related to the concept of replication, there is the **cluster status** indicator of the health of your cluster.

It can cover three different states:

- **Green**: This state depicts that everything is ok.
- **Yellow**: This state depicts that some shards are missing but you can work.
- **Red**: This state depicts that, "Houston we have a problem". Some primary shards are missing. The cluster will not accept writing and errors and stale actions may happen due to missing shards. If the missing shard cannot be restored, you have lost your data.

Solving the yellow status

- Mainly yellow status is due to some shards that are not allocated.
- If your cluster is in "recovery" status (this means that it's starting up and checking the shards before we put them online), just wait so that the shards start up process ends.
- After having finished the recovery, if your cluster is always in yellow state, you may not have enough nodes to contain your replicas (because, for example, the number of replicas is bigger than the number of your nodes). To prevent this, you can reduce the number of your replicas or add the required number of nodes.

> The total number of nodes must not be lower than the maximum number of replicas.

Solving the red status

- You have loss of data. This is when you have one or more shards missing.
- You need to try to restore the node(s) that are missing. If your nodes restart and the system goes back to yellow or green status, you are safe. Otherwise, you have lost data and your cluster is not usable: delete the index/indices and restore them from backups or snapshots (if you have already done it) or from other sources.

To prevent data loss, I suggest having always at least two nodes and a replica set to 1.

> Having one or more replicas on different nodes on different machines allows you to have a live backup of your data, always updated.

See also

- We'll see replica and shard management in the *Managing index settings* recipe in Chapter 4, *Basic Operations*.

Communicating with Elasticsearch

In Elasticsearch 5.x, there are only two ways to communicate with the server using HTTP protocol or the native one. In this recipe, we will take a look at these main protocols.

Getting ready

The standard installation of Elasticsearch provides access via its web services on port 9200 for HTTP and 9300 for native Elasticsearch protocol. Simply starting an Elasticsearch server, you can communicate on these ports with it.

How it works...

Elasticsearch is designed to be used as a RESTful server, so the main protocol is the HTTP usually on port 9200 and above. This is the only protocol that can be used by programming languages that don't run on a **Java Virtual Machine (JVM)**.

Every protocol has advantages and disadvantages. It's important to choose the correct one depending on the kind of applications you are developing. If you are in doubt, choose the **HTTP protocol** layer that is the most standard and easy to use.

Choosing the right protocol depends on several factors, mainly architectural and performance related. This schema factorizes the advantages and disadvantages related to them:

Protocol	Advantages	Disadvantages	Type
HTTP	This is more frequently used. It is API safe and has general compatibility for different ES versions. Suggested. JSON. It is easy to proxy and to balance with HTTP balancers.	This is an HTTP overhead. HTTP clients don't know the cluster topology, so they require more hops to access data.	Text
Native	This is a fast network layer. It is programmatic. It is best for massive index operations.	The API changes and breaks applications. It depends on the same version of ES Server. Only on JVM. It is more compact due to its binary nature. It is faster because the clients know the cluster topology. The native serializer/deserializer are more efficient than the JSON ones.	Binary

Using the HTTP protocol

This recipe shows some samples of using the HTTP protocol.

Getting ready

You need a working Elasticsearch cluster. Using the default configuration, Elasticsearch enables the 9200 port on your server to communicate in HTTP.

How to do it…

The standard RESTful protocol is easy to integrate because it is the lingua franca for the Web and can be used by every programming language.

Now, I'll show how easy it is to fetch the Elasticsearch greeting API on a running server at 9200 port using several programming languages.

In Bash or Windows prompt, the request will be:

```
curl -XGET http://127.0.0.1:9200
```

In Python, the request will be:

```
import urllib
result = urllib.open("http://127.0.0.1:9200")
```

In Java, the request will be:

```
import java.io.BufferedReader;
import java.io.InputStream;
import java.io.InputStreamReader;
import java.net.URL;

...
try {
// get URL content
  URL url = new URL("http://127.0.0.1:9200");
  URLConnection conn = url.openConnection();
// open the stream and put it into BufferedReader
  BufferedReader br = new BufferedReader(new
InputStreamReader(conn.getInputStream()));

String inputLine;
while ((inputLine = br.readLine()) != null){
System.out.println(inputLine);
}
br.close();
System.out.println("Done");
} catch (MalformedURLException e) {
e.printStackTrace();
} catch (IOException e) {
e.printStackTrace();
}
```

In Scala, the request will be:

```
scala.io.Source.fromURL("http://127.0.0.1:9200",
"utf-8").getLines.mkString("\n")
```

For every language sample, the response will be the same:

```
{
  "name" : "elasticsearch",
  "cluster_name" : "elasticsearch",
  "cluster_uuid" : "rbCPXgcwSM6CjnX8u3oRMA",
  "version" : {
  "number" : "5.1.1",
  "build_hash" : "5395e21",
  "build_date" : "2016-12-06T12:36:15.409Z",
  "build_snapshot" : false,
  "lucene_version" : "6.3.0"
  },
  "tagline" : "You Know, for Search"
}
```

How it works...

Every client creates a connection to the server index / and fetches the answer. The answer is a JSON object.

You can call Elasticsearch server from any programming language that you like. The main advantages of this protocol are:

- **Portability**: It uses web standards so it can be integrated in different languages (Erlang, JavaScript, Python, or Ruby) or called from command-line applications such as `curl`
- **Durability**: The REST APIs don't often change. They don't break for minor release changes as native protocol does
- **Simple to use**: It speaks JSON to JSON
- **More supported than others protocols**: Every plugin typically supports a REST endpoint on HTTP
- **Easy cluster scaling**: Simply put your cluster nodes behind an HTTP load balancer to balance the calls such as HAProxy or NGINX

In this book, a lot of examples are done calling the HTTP API via the command-line `curl` program. This approach is very fast and allows you to test functionalities very quickly.

There's more...

Every language provides drivers to best integrate Elasticsearch or RESTful web services. The Elasticsearch community provides official drivers that support the most used programming languages.

Using the native protocol

Elasticsearch provides a native protocol, used mainly for low-level communication between nodes, but is very useful for fast importing of huge data blocks. This protocol is available only for JVM languages and is commonly used in Java, Groovy, and Scala.

Getting ready

You need a working Elasticsearch cluster–the standard port for native protocol is `9300`.

How to do it...

The steps required to use the native protocol in a Java environment are as follows (in `Chapter 14`, *Java Integration* we'll discuss it in detail):

1. Before starting, we must be sure that Maven loads the Elasticsearch JAR adding to the `pom.xml` lines:

   ```
   <dependency>
      <groupId>org.elasticsearch</groupId>
      <artifactId>elasticsearch</artifactId>
      <version>5.0</version>
   </dependency>
   ```

2. Depending on Elasticsearch JAR, creating a Java client, it's quite easy:

   ```
   import org.elasticsearch.common.settings.Settings;
   import org.elasticsearch.client.Client;
   import org.elasticsearch.client.transport.TransportClient;
   ...
   Settings settings = Settings.settingsBuilder()
   .put("client.transport.sniff", true).build();
    // we define a new settings
    // using sniff transport allows to autodetect other nodes
   Client client = TransportClient.builder()
   ```

```
.settings(settings).build().addTransportAddress
(new InetSocketTransportAddress("127.0.0.1", 9300));
// a client is created with the settings
```

How it works...

To initialize a native client, some settings are required to properly configure it. The important ones are:

- `cluster.name`: It is the name of the cluster
- `client.transport.sniff`: It allows to sniff the rest of the cluster topology and adds discovered nodes into the client list of machines to use

With these settings, it's possible to initialize a new client giving an IP address and port (default `9300`).

There's more...

This is the internal protocol used in Elasticsearch: it's the fastest protocol available to talk with Elasticsearch.

The native protocol is an optimized binary one and works only for JVM languages. To use this protocol, you need to include `elasticsearch.jar` in your JVM project. Because it depends on Elasticsearch implementation, it must be the same version of the Elasticsearch cluster.

> Every time you update Elasticsearch, you need to update the elasticsearch.jar on which it depends, and if there are internal API changes, you need to update your code.

To use this protocol, you also need to study the internals of Elasticsearch, so it's not so easy to use as HTTP protocol.

Native protocol is very useful for massive data import. But as Elasticsearch is mainly thought as a REST HTTP server to communicate with, it lacks support for everything is not standard in Elasticsearch core, such as plugins entry points. Using this protocol, you are unable to call entry points made by external plugins in an easy way.

The native protocol seems easier to integrate in a Java/JVN project, but due to its nature that follows the fast release cycles of Elasticsearch, its API could change often even for minor release upgrades and your code will be broken.

See also

The native protocol is the most used in the Java world and it will be deeply discussed in `Chapters 14`, *Java Integration,* `Chapters 15`, *Scala Integration,* and `Chapter 17`, *Plugin Development.*

For further details on Elasticsearch Java API, they are available on Elasticsearch site at `http s://www.elastic.co/guide/en/elasticsearch/client/java-api/current/index.html`.

2
Downloading and Setup

In this chapter, we will cover the following recipes:

- Downloading and installing Elasticsearch
- Setting up networking
- Setting up a node
- Setting up for Linux systems
- Setting up different node types
- Setting up a client node
- Setting up an ingest node
- Installing plugins in Elasticsearch
- Installing plugins manually
- Removing a plugin
- Changing logging settings
- Setting up a node via Docker

Introduction

This chapter explains the installation process and the configuration from a single developer machine to a big cluster, giving you hints on how to improve performance and skip misconfiguration errors.

There are different options in installing Elasticsearch and setting up a working environment for development and production.

When testing out Elasticsearch for a development cluster, the tool requires almost no configuration. However, when moving to production, it is important to properly configure the cluster based on your data, use cases, and your product architecture. The setup step is very important because a bad configuration can lead to bad results, poor performances, and kill your servers.

In this chapter, the management of Elasticsearch plugins is also discussed: installing, configuring, updating, and removing.

Downloading and installing Elasticsearch

Elasticsearch has an active community and the release cycles are very fast.

Because Elasticsearch depends on many common Java libraries (Lucene, Guice, and Jackson are the most famous ones), the Elasticsearch community tries to keep them updated and fixes bugs that are discovered in them and in Elasticsearch core. The large user base is also source of new ideas and features for improving Elasticsearch use cases.

For these reasons, if it's possible, the best practice is to use the latest available release (usually the more stable one and the less bugs free).

Getting ready

A supported Elasticsearch operative system (Linux/MacOSX/Windows) with a Java JVM 1.8 (the Oracle one is the preferred `http://www.oracle.com/technetwork/java/javase/downloads/jdk8-downloads-2133151.html`) or above installed. A web browser is required to download the Elasticsearch binary release. At least 1GB of free disk space is required to install Elasticsearch.

How to do it...

For downloading and installing an Elasticsearch server, we will perform the steps given as follows:

We download Elasticsearch from the Web. The latest version is always downloadable at the web address `https://www.elastic.co/downloads/elasticsearch`. The three versions that are available for different operative systems are as follows:

- `elasticsearch-{version-number}.zip` is for both Linux/Mac OSX and Windows operative systems
- `elasticsearch-{version-number}.tar.gz` is for Linux/Mac
- `elasticsearch-{version-number}.deb` is for Debian-based Linux distributions (this also covers the Ubuntu family); it is installable with the Debian command `dpkg -i elasticsearch-*.deb`
- `elasticsearch-{version-number}.rpm` is for RedHat-based Linux distributions (this also covers the Centos family). It is installable with the `rpm -i elasticsearch-*.rpm` command.

> **TIP**
>
> The preceding packages contain everything to start Elasticsearch. This book targets version 5.x or above, the latest and most stable version of Elasticsearch was 5.1.1. To check out whether it's latest or not, visit `https://www.elastic.co/downloads/elasticsearch`.

We extract the binary content. After downloading the correct release for your platform, the installation involves expanding the archive in a working directory.

> **TIP**
>
> Choose a working directory that is safe to charset problems and it has not a long path to prevent problems when Elasticsearch creates its directories to store index data.

For Windows platform, a good directory could be `c:\es`, on Unix and MacOSX `/opt/es`.

To run Elasticsearch, you need a Java Virtual Machine 1.8 or above installed. For better performances, I suggest you to use the latest Sun/Oracle 1.8 version.

If you are a Mac OS X user and you have installed Homebrew (`http://brew.sh/`), the first and the second step are automatically managed by the command `brew install elasticsearch`.

We start Elasticsearch to check if everything is working. To start your Elasticsearch server, just install the directory and type for Linux and MacOsX:

```
# bin/elasticsearch
```

Alternatively, you can type the following for Windows:

```
# bin\elasticserch.bat
```

Your server should now start up as shown in the following screenshot:

How it works...

The Elasticsearch package generally contains three directories:

- `bin`: This contains the script to start and manage Elasticsearch. The most important ones are and follows:
    - elasticsearch(`.bat`): This is the main script to start Elasticsearch
    - plugin(`.bat`): This is a script to manage plugins
- `config`: This contains the Elasticsearch configs. The most important ones are as follows:
    - `elasticsearch.yml`: This is the main config file for Elasticsearch
    - `log4j2.properties`: This is the logging config file

- `lib`: This contains all the libraries required to run Elasticsearch
- `modules`: This contains the Elasticsearch default module extensions
- `plugins`: This contains the installed plugins

There's more...

During Elasticsearch start up a lot of events happened:

- A node name is chosen automatically (for example, Robert Kelly) if not provided in elasticsearch.yml. The name is randomly taken from an in-code embedded Elasticsearch text file (`src/main/resources/config/names.txt`).
- A node name hash is generated for this node (for example, `whqVp_4zQGCgMvJ1CXhcWQ`).
- If the modules are loaded, the default installed modules are:
    - `aggs-matrix-stats`: This acts as a good support for aggregation matrix stats
    - `ingest-common`: These include common functionalities for ingesting
    - `lang-expression`: This acts as a good support for Expression language
    - `lang-groovy`: This acts as a good support for Groovy language
    - `lang-mustache`: This acts as a good support for Mustacle language
    - `lang-painless`: This acts as a good support for Painless language
    - `percolator`: This acts as a good support for percolator capabilities
    - `reindex`: This acts as a good support for reindex action
- If there are plugins, they are loaded.
- Automatically, if not configured, Elasticsearch binds on all network addresses available, two ports:
    - Port `9300` is used for internal intranode communication
    - Port `9200` is used for HTTP rest API
- After starting, if indices are available, they are restored and ready to be used.

If these port numbers are already bound, Elasticsearch automatically increments the port number and tries to bind on them until a port is available (that is, `9201`, `9202`, and so on). This feature is very useful when you want to fire up several nodes on the same machine mainly for testing and developing.

There are more events that are fired during Elasticsearch start-up. We'll see them in detail in other recipes.

See also

- The *Setting up networking* recipe will help you for initial network setup
- Check the official Elasticsearch download page at `https://www.elastic.co/downloads/elasticsearch` to get the latest version

Setting up networking

Correctly setting up networking is very important for your nodes and cluster.

There are a lot of different installation scenarios and networking issues: the first step for configuring the nodes to build a cluster is to correctly set the node discovery.

Getting ready

You need a working Elasticsearch installation and know your current networking configuration (that is, IP).

How to do it…

For configuring networking, we will perform the following steps:

- Open the Elasticsearch configuration file with your favorite text editor.
- Using standard Elasticsearch configuration `config/elasticsearch.yml` file, your node is configured to bind on all your machine interfaces and does discovery broadcasting events to the nodes listed in `discovery.zen.ping.unicast.hosts`. This means that it sends signals to the machine in unicast list and waits for a response. If a node responds to it, they can join in a cluster.

- If another node is available in the same LAN, they join the cluster.

> Only nodes with the same Elasticsearch version and same cluster name
> (`cluster.name` option in `elasticsearch.yml`) can join each other.

- To customize the network preferences, you need to change some parameters in
  the `elasticsearch.yml` file, as follows:

```
cluster.name: ESCookBook
node.name: "Node1"
network.host: 192.168.1.35
discovery.zen.ping.unicast.hosts:
["192.168.1.35","192.168.1.36[9300-9400]"]
```

This configuration sets the cluster name to Elasticsearch, the node name, the network
address, and it tries to bind the node to the address given in the discovery section:

- We can check the configuration during node loading.
- We can now start the server and check whether the networking is configured:

```
[...][INFO ][o.e.p.PluginsService ] [PARO] loaded plugin
[ingest-geoip]  [...][INFO ][o.e.p.PluginsService ] [PARO] loaded
plugin [lang-python]  [...][INFO ][o.e.p.PluginsService ] [PARO]
loaded plugin [sql]  [...][INFO ][o.e.n.Node ] [PARO] initialized
[...][INFO ][o.e.n.Node ] [PARO] starting ...  [...][INFO ]
[o.e.t.TransportService ] [PARO] publish_address
{192.168.1.35:9300}, bound_addresses {[fe80::1]:9300},
{[::1]:9300}, {192.168.1.35:9300}  [...][INFO ]
[o.e.c.s.ClusterService ] [PARO] new_master {PARO}{7kRRhYpeQx-
fub3-1h3sWQ}{EtRxMnNnTJGvp2giGuAxkQ}{127.0.0.1}{192.168.1.35:9300},
reason: zen-disco-elected-as-master ([0] nodes joined)  [...]
[INFO ][o.e.h.HttpServer ] [PARO] publish_address
{192.168.1.35:9200}, bound_addresses {[fe80::1]:9200},
{[::1]:9200}, {192.168.1.35:9200}  [...][INFO ][o.e.n.Node ] [PARO]
started
```

In this case, we have:

- The transport bound to `0:0:0:0:0:0:0:0:9300` and `192.168.1.35:9300`
- The REST HTTP interface bound to `0:0:0:0:0:0:0:0:9200` and
  `192.168.1.35:9200`

How it works...

The main important configuration keys for networking management are:

- `cluster.name` sets up the name of the cluster. Only nodes with the same name can join together
- `node.name`: if not defined, it is automatically assigned by Elasticsearch

It allows defining a name for the node. If you have a lot of nodes on different machine, it is useful to set this name meaningful to easy locate them. Using a valid name is more easy to remember than a generate name such as `whqVp_4zQGCgMvJ1CXhcWQ`. You always must set up a `node.name` if you need to monitor your server. Generally, node name is the same of host server name for easy maintenance.

The `network.host` defines the IP of your machine to be used in bind the node. If your server is on different LANs or you want to limit the bind on only a LAN, you must set this value with your server IP.

The `discovery.zen.ping.unicast.hosts` allows you to define a list of hosts (with ports or port range) to be used to discover other nodes to join the cluster. This setting allows using the node in LAN where broadcasting is not allowed or auto discovery is not working (that is, packet filtering routers). The referred port is the transport one, usually `9300`. The addresses of the hosts list can be a mix of:

- host name, that is, `myhost1`
- IP address, that is, `192.168.1.2`
- IP address or hostname with the port, that is, `myhost1:9300`, `192.168.168.1.2:9300`
- IP address or hostname with a range of ports, that is, `myhost1:[9300-9400]`, `192.168.168.1.2:[9300-9400]`

Before Elasticsearch 5.x, the default network configuration was the auto discovery with broadcast: this behavior is deprecated and removed in version 5.x or above because it generates a lot of issues during cluster management and it doesn't work in cloud deployment and generally in corporate networking due to the block on broadcasting protocol.

See also

- The *Setting up a node* recipe

Setting up a node

Elasticsearch allows customizing several parameters in an installation. In this recipe, we'll see the most used ones to define where to store our data and to improve the overall performances.

Getting ready

You need a working Elasticsearch installation as we described in the *Downloading and installing Elasticsearch* recipe and a simple text editor to change configuration files.

How to do it...

The steps required for setting up a simple node are as follows:

- Open `config/elasticsearch.yml` with an editor of your choice.
- Setup the directories that store your server data.
- For Linux or Mac OS X type the following command:

```
path.conf: /opt/data/es/conf
path.data: /opt/data/es/data1,/opt2/data/data2
path.work: /opt/data/work
path.logs: /opt/data/logs
path.plugins: /opt/data/plugins
```

- For Windows type the following command:

```
path.conf: c:\Elasticsearch\conf
path.data: c:\Elasticsearch\data
path.work: c:\Elasticsearch\work
path.logs: c:\Elasticsearch\logs
path.plugins: c:\Elasticsearch\plugins
```

- Set up parameters to control the standard index creation. These parameters are:

```
index.number_of_shards: 5
index.number_of_replicas: 1
```

How it works...

The `path.conf` defines the directory that contains your configuration: mainly `elasticsearch.yml` and `logging.yml`. This is default `$ES_HOME/config` with `ES_HOME` to install directory.

> It's useful to set up the `config` directory outside your application directory, so you don't need to copy the configuration files every time you update your version or change the Elasticsearch installation directory.

The `path.data` is the most important one: it allows us to define one or more directories (in different disk) where you can store your index data. When you define more than one directory, they are managed a la RAID 0 (their space is sum up), favoring locations with most free space.

The `path.work` is a location when Elasticsearch stores temporary files.

The `path.log` is where log files are put. The control how to log is managed in `logging.yml`.

The `path.plugins` allows you to override the plugins path (the default is `$ES_HOME/plugins`). It's useful to put system-wide plugins.

The main parameters used to control index and shards in `index.number_of_shards` that controls the standard number of shards for a new created index and `index.number_of_replicas` that controls the initial number of replicas.

There's more...

There are a lot of other parameters that can be used to customize your Elasticsearch installation and new ones are added with new releases. The most important ones are described in this and the next recipe.

See also

- The *Setting up for Linux Systems* recipe
- The official Elasticsearch documentation at `https://www.elastic.co/guide/en/elasticsearch/reference/current/setup.html`

Setting up for Linux systems

If you are using a Linux system, you need to manage extra setup to improve performance or to resolve production problems with many indices.

This recipe covers two common errors that happened in production:

- Too many open files that can corrupt your indices and your data
- Slow performance in search and indexing due to garbage collector

> The other possible big troubles arise when you go out of disk space. In this scenario, some files can get corrupted. To prevent your indices from corruption and possible data loss, it is best practice to monitor the storage spaces.

Getting ready

You need a working Elasticsearch installation as we described in the *Downloading and installing Elasticsearch* recipe in this chapter and a simple text editor to change configuration files.

How to do it...

For improving the performances on Linux systems, we will perform the following steps:

1. First you need to change the current limit for the user that runs the Elasticsearch server. In these examples, we call it `elasticsearch`.
2. For allowing Elasticsearch to manage a large number of files, you need to increment the number of file descriptors (number of files) that a user can manage. To do so, you must edit your `/etc/security/limits.conf` and add these lines at the end:

    ```
    elasticsearch - nofile 65536
    elasticsearch - memlock unlimited
    ```

3. Then, a machine restart is required to be sure that the changes are taken.

4. The new version of Ubuntu (that is, version 16.04 or more) could skip the `/etc/security/limits.conf` in `init.d` scripts; in these cases you need to edit `/etc/pam.d/su` and uncomment the following line:

   ```
   # session    required    pam_limits.so
   ```

5. For controlling memory swapping, you need to set up this parameter in `elasticsearch.yml`:

   ```
   bootstrap.memory_lock
   ```

6. To fix the memory usage size of Elasticsearch server, we need to set up up to the same value `ES_MIN_MEM` and `ES_MAX_MEM` in `$ES_HOME/bin/elasticsearch.in.sh`. You can otherwise setup `ES_HEAP_SIZE` that automatically initializes the min and max values to the same.

How it works...

The standard limit of file descriptors (max number of open files for user) is typically `1024`. When you store a lot of records in several indices, you run out of file descriptors very quickly, so your Elasticsearch server becomes unresponsive and your indices may become corrupted and as a result make you lose your data.

Changing the limit to a very high number, your Elasticsearch doesn't hit the maximum number of open files.

The other settings for memory prevent Elasticsearch swapping memory and give a performance boost in a production environment. This setting is required because during indexing and searching Elasticsearch creates and destroys a lot of objects in memory. This large number of create/destroy actions fragments the memory reducing performances: the memory becomes full of holes and when the system needs to allocate more memory it suffers an overhead to find compacted memory. If you don't set `bootstrap.memory_lock: true`, Elasticsearch dumps the whole process memory on disk and defragments it back in memory, freezing the system. With this setting, the defragmentation step is done all in memory, with a huge performance boost.

Setting up different node types

Elasticsearch is natively designed for the cloud, so when you need to release a production environment with a huge number of records and you need high availability and good performances, you need to aggregate more nodes in a cluster.

Elasticsearch allows defining different type of nodes to balance and improve overall performances.

Getting ready

You need a working Elasticsearch installation as we described in the *Downloading and installing Elasticsearch* recipe and a simple text editor to change the configuration files.

How to do it...

For advance, set up a cluster. There are some parameters that must be configured to define different node types.

These parameters are in `config/elasticsearch.yml` file and they can be set with the following steps:

1. Set up whether the node can be master or not:

        node.master: true

2. Set up whether a node must contain data or not:

        node.data: true

How it works...

The `node.master` parameter defines that the node can become master for the cloud. The default value for this parameter is `true`.

A master node is an arbiter for the cloud: it takes decisions about shard management, it keeps the cluster status, and it's the main controller of every index action. If your master nodes are on overload, all the clusters will have penalty performances.

The optimum number of master nodes is given by the following equation:

$$NumberofMasterNodes = \frac{Numberofnodes}{2} + 1$$

The `node.data` allows you to store data in the node. The default value for this parameter is `true`. This node will be a worker that index and search data.

By mixing these two parameters, it's possible to have different node types as shown in the following table:

node.master	node.data	Node description
true	true	This is the default node. It can be the master, which contains data.
false	true	This node never becomes a master node, it only holds data. It can be defined as a workhorse of your cluster.
true	false	This node only serves as a master: to not store any data and to have free resources. This will be the coordinator of your cluster.
false	false	This node acts as a search load balancer (fetching data from nodes, aggregating results, and so on).

The more frequently used node type is the first one, but if you have a very big cluster or special needs, you can differentiate the scopes of your nodes to better serve searches and aggregations.

Setting up a client node

The master nodes that we have seen previously are the most important for cluster stability. To prevent the queries and aggregations from creating instability in your cluster, client nodes can be used to provide safe communication with the cluster.

Getting ready

You need a working Elasticsearch installation as we described in the *Downloading and installing Elasticsearch* recipe in this chapter and a simple text editor to change configuration files.

How to do it...

For advance set up of a cluster, there are some parameters that must be configured to define different node types.

These parameters are in the `config/elasticsearch.yml` file and they can set up a client node with the following steps:

1. Set up the node as a no master:

    ```
    node.master: false
    ```

2. Set up the node to not contain data:

    ```
    node.data: false
    ```

How it works...

The client node is a special node that works as a proxy/pass thought for the cluster.

Its main advantages are:

- It can easily kill or remove the cluster without problems, that's not a master, so it doesn't participate in cluster functionalities and it doesn't contain data so there are no data relocations/replication due to its failure
- Prevent the instability of the cluster due to developers'/users' bad queries. Sometimes a user executes too large aggregations (that is, date histograms with range some years and interval 10 seconds), the Elasticsearch node could crash. The client node is not a master and its overload doesn't give problem to cluster stability.
- If the client node is embedded in the application, there are less round trips for the data and speeding up the application.
- You can add them to balance the search and aggregation throughput without generating changes and data relocation in the cluster.

Setting up an ingestion node

The main goals of Elasticsearch are indexing, searching, and analytics, but it's often required to modify or enhance the documents before storing in Elasticsearch.

The most common scenarios in this case are:

- Preprocessing the log string to extract meaningful data.
- Enrich the content of some textual fields with **Natural Language Processing (NLP)** tools.
- Add some transformation during ingestion such as convert IP in geolocalization or build custom fields at ingest time

Getting ready

You need a working Elasticsearch installation as we described in the *Downloading and installing Elasticsearch* recipe and a simple text editor to change configuration files.

How to do it...

To set up an ingest node, you need to edit the `config/elasticsearch.yml` file and set up the `ingest` property to `true`:

```
node.ingest: true
```

How it works...

The default configuration for Elasticsearch is to set the node as ingest node (refer to `Chapter 13`, *Ingest*, for more info on ingestion pipeline).

As the client node, using the ingest node is a way to provide functionalities to Elasticsearch without suffering cluster safety.

> If you want preventing node to be used for ingestion, you need to disable it with `node.ingest: false`. It's best practice to disable it in master and data node to prevent ingestion error issues and to protect the cluster. The client node is the best candidate to be also ingest ones.

The best practice if you are using NLP, attachment extraction (via attachment ingest plugin) or logs ingestion, is to have a pool of client nodes (no master, no data) with ingestion active.

The attachment plugin and NLP ones, in the previous version of Elasticsearch, were available in standard data node or master node. They give a lot of problems to Elasticsearch due to:

- High CPU usage for NLP algorithms that saturates all CPU on Data node giving bad indexing and searching performances
- Instability due to bad format of attachment and/or Tika (the library used for managing document extraction) bugs

> The best practice is to have a pool of client nodes with ingestion enabled to provide the best safety for the cluster and ingestion pipeline.

Installing plugins in Elasticsearch

One of the main features of Elasticsearch is the possibility to extend it with plugins. Plugins extend Elasticsearch features and functionalities in several ways.

In Elasticsearch 5.x, the plugins are **native plugins**–they are jars files that contain application code. They are used for:

- ScriptEngine (JavaScript, Python, Scala, and Ruby)
- Custom Analyzers, tokenizers, and scoring
- REST entry points
- Ingestion pipeline stages
- Supporting new storages (Hadoop)

Getting ready

You need a working Elasticsearch installation as we described in the *Downloading and installing Elasticsearch* recipe and a prompt/shell to execute commands in Elasticsearch install directory.

How to do it...

Elasticsearch provides a script for automatic download and for installation of plugins in `bin/directory` called `plugin`.

The steps required to install a plugin are:

- Call the plugin and `install` Elasticsearch command with the plugin name reference.
- For installing an administrative interface for Elasticsearch simply call:

  On Linux type the following command:

  ```
  bin/elasticsearch-plugin install lang-python
  ```

  On Windows type the following command:

  ```
  elasticsearch-plugin.bat install lang-python
  ```

- If the plugin needs to change security permission, a warning is prompted and you need to accept if you want to continue.
- Check starting the node that the plugin is correctly loaded.

In the following screenshot, you can see the installation and the starting of Elasticsearch server along with the installed plugin:

```
alberto  MacParoBacon    21:24    elasticsearch/5.1.1
         bin/elasticsearch-plugin install lang-python
Warning: Ignoring JAVA_TOOL_OPTIONS=-Dfile.encoding=UTF8
-> Downloading lang-python from elastic
[=============================================] 100%??
@@@@@@@@@@@@@@@@@@@@@@@@@@@@@@@@@@@@@@@@@@@@@@@@@@@@@@@@@@@@@@@@@
@      WARNING: plugin requires additional permissions      @
@@@@@@@@@@@@@@@@@@@@@@@@@@@@@@@@@@@@@@@@@@@@@@@@@@@@@@@@@@@@@@@@@
* java.lang.RuntimePermission createClassLoader
* java.lang.RuntimePermission getClassLoader
* org.elasticsearch.script.ClassPermission <<STANDARD>>
See http://docs.oracle.com/javase/8/docs/technotes/guides/security/permissions.html
for descriptions of what these permissions allow and the associated risks.

Continue with installation? [y/N]y
-> Installed lang-python

alberto  MacParoBacon    21:26    elasticsearch/5.1.1
```

Remember that a plugin installation requires an Elasticsearch server restart.

How it works...

The elasticsearch-plugin `plugin[.bat]` script is a wrapper for Elasticsearch plugin manager. It can be used to install or remove a plugin with the `remove` options.

There are several ways to install the plugin:

- Passing the URL of the plugin (ZIP archive):

  ```
  bin/elasticsearch-plugin install
  http://mywoderfulserve.com/plugins/awesome-plugin.zip
  ```

- Using the `install` parameter with the GitHub repository of the plugin.
- The install parameter, that must be given, is formatted in this way:

  ```
  <username>/<repo>[/<version>]
  ```

During the install process, Elasticsearch plugin manager is able to:

- Download the plugin
- Create a plugins directory in `ES_HOME`, if it's missing
- Unzip the plugin content in the plugin directory
- Remove temporary files

The installation process is completely automatic, no further actions are required. The user must only pay attention that the process ends with an Installed message to be sure that the install process is completed correctly.

Restarting the server is always required to be sure that the plugin is correctly loaded by Elasticsearch.

There's more...

If your current Elasticsearch application depends on one or more plugins, a node can be configured to fire up only if these plugins are installed and available. To achieve this behavior, you can provide the `plugin.mandatory` directive in the `elasticsearch.yml` configuration file.

For the previous example (Elasticsearch-lang-python), the config line to be added is:

```
plugin.mandatory: python
```

There are also some hints to remember while installing plugins.

Updating some plugins in a node environment can bring malfunction due to different plugin versions in different nodes. If you have a big cluster for safety, it's better to check for updates in a separate environment to prevent problems.

To prevent that updating an Elasticsearch version server could also break your custom binary plugins due to some internal API changes, in Elasticsearch 5.x the plugins need to have the same version of Elasticsearch server in their manifest.

> Upgrading an Elasticsearch server version means upgrading all the installed plugins.

See also

- On Elasticsearch site there is an updated list of available plugins (https://www.elastic.co/guide/en/elasticsearch/plugins/master/index.html)
- The *Installing plugin manually* recipe

Installing plugins manually

Sometimes your plugin is not available online or standard installation fails, so you need to install your plugin manually.

Getting ready

You need a working Elasticsearch installation as we described in the *Downloading and installing Elasticsearch* recipe and a prompt/shell to execute commands in Elasticsearch install directory.

How to do it...

We assume that your plugin is named `awesome` and it's packed in a file called `awesome.zip`.

The steps required to manually install a plugin are:

- Copy your zip file in the plugins directory in your Elasticsearch home installation
- If the directory named `plugins` doesn't exist, create it
- Unzip the content of the plugin in the plugins directory
- Remove the zip archive to clean up unused files

How it works...

Every Elasticsearch plugin is contained in a directory (usually named as the plugin name). The plugin directory should be filled with one or more JAR files.

When Elasticsearch starts, it scans the plugins directory and loads them.

If a plugin is corrupted or broken, the server doesn't start.

Removing a plugin

You have installed some plugins and now you need to remove a plugin because it's not required. Removing an Elasticsearch plugin is easy to uninstall if everything goes right, otherwise you need to manually remove it.

This recipe covers both cases.

Getting ready

You need a working Elasticsearch installation as we described in the *Downloading and installing Elasticsearch* recipe and a prompt/shell to execute commands in Elasticsearch install directory. Before removing a plugin, it is safer to stop Elasticsearch server to prevent error due to the deletion of plugin JAR.

How to do it...

The steps to remove a plugin are as follows:

1. Stop your running node to prevent exceptions caused due to removal of a file.
2. Using the Elasticsearch plugin manager, which comes with its script wrapper (plugin).

    On Linux and MacOSX, type the following command:

    ```
    elasticsearch-plugin remove lang-python
    ```

    On Windows, type the following command:

    ```
    elasticsearch-plugin.bat remove lang-python
    ```

3. Restart the server.

How it works...

The plugin manager's `remove` command tries to detect the correct name of the plugin and to remove the directory of the installed plugin.

If there are undeletable files on your plugin directory (or strange astronomical events that hits your server), the plugin script might fail to manually remove a plugin you need to follow these steps:

- Go into the plugins directory
- Remove the directory with your plugin name

Changing logging settings

Standard logging settings work very well for general usage.

Changing the log level can be useful to check for bugs or understanding malfunctions due to bad configuration or strange plugin behaviors. A verbose log can be used from Elasticsearch community to cover problems.

If you need to debug your Elasticsearch server or change how the logging works (that is, remoting send events), you need to change the `log4j2.properties` parameters.

Getting ready

You need a working Elasticsearch installation as we described in the *Downloading and installing Elasticsearch* recipe and a simple text editor to change configuration files.

How to do it...

In the `config` directory in your Elasticsearch install directory, there is a `log4j2.properties` file, which controls the working settings.

The steps required for changing the logging settings are:

1. To emit every kind of logging Elasticsearch has, you can change the current root level logging which is:

```
rootLogger.level = info
```

2. This needs to be changed to the following:

```
rootLogger.level = debug
```

3. Now, if you start Elasticsearch from command-line (with `bin/elasticsearch -f`), you should see a lot of garbage:

```
[2017-01-11T21:34:16,369][DEBUG][o.e.b.Seccomp] BSD RLIMIT_NPROC
initialization successful[2017-01-11T21:34:16,377][DEBUG]
[o.e.b.Seccomp] OS X seatbelt initialization successful
[2017-01-11T21:34:16,404][DEBUG][o.e.b.JarHell]
java.class.path:
/usr/local/Cellar/elasticsearch/5.1.1/libexec/lib/elasticsearch-
5.1.1.jar:/usr/local/Cellar/elasticsearch/5.1.1/libexec/lib
/elasticsearch5.1.1.jar:/usr/local/Cellar/elasticsearch/5.1.1/
libexec/lib/HdrHistogram2.1.6.jar:/usr/local/Cellar/
elasticsearch/5.1.1/libexec/lib/hppc-0.7.1.jar:/usr
/local/Cellar/
... (truncated)...
```

How it works...

Elasticsearch logging system is based on the `log4j` library (`http://logging.apache.org/log4j/`).

Log4j is a powerful library to manage logging, covering all of its functionalities is outside the scope of this book. If a user needs advanced usage, there are a lot of books and articles on the Internet about it.

Setting up a node via Docker

Docker (`https://www.docker.com/`) has become a common way to deploy for testing or production some application server.

Docker is a container system that allows to easily deploy replicable installations of server applications. With Docker, you don't need to set up a host, configure it, download the Elasticsearch server, unzip it, or start the server–everything is done automatically by Docker.

Getting ready

You need a working Docker installation to be able to execute docker commands (`https://www.docker.com/products/overview`).

How to do it...

1. If you want to start a vanilla server, just execute:

```
docker pull docker.elastic.co/elasticsearch/elasticsearch:5.1.1
```

2. An output similar to the following screenshot will be shown:

```
alberto  MacParoBacon   21:44  ⚫ ~/.docker
  docker pull docker.elastic.co/elasticsearch/elasticsearch:5.1.1
5.1.1: Pulling from elasticsearch/elasticsearch

3690ec4760f9: Pull complete
f52154c3d3fc: Downloading [======>                    ] 6.286 MB/51.83 MB
4075cc5db14a: Download complete
93889b68d3f9: Downloading [=========>                 ] 6.194 MB/33.29 MB
33720f77e849: Download complete
d1ddd1420cac: Downloading [=====>                     ] 1.562 MB/15.41 MB
61d61543041b: Waiting
4c746b62ddf3: Waiting
2246369d1afe: Waiting
81ea6699fce5: Waiting
```

3. After downloading the Elasticsearch image, we can start a develop instance via:

```
docker run -p 9200:9200 -p 9300:9300 -e "http.host=0.0.0.0" -e
"transport.host=0.0.0.0"
docker.elastic.co/elasticsearch/elasticsearch:5.1.1
```

4. To check if Elasticsearch server is running, execute the following command:

```
docker ps
```

5. The default exported ports are 9200 and 9300.

How it works...

The Docker container provides a Debian Linux installation with Elasticsearch installed.

Elasticsearch Docker installation is easily repeatable and does not require a lot of editing and configuration.

The default installation can be tuned into in several ways:

1. You can pass a parameter to Elasticsearch via command line using the –e flags:

```
docker run -d docker.elastic.co/elasticsearch/elasticsearch:5.1.1
elasticsearch -e "node.name=NodeName"
```

2. You can customize the default settings of the environment providing custom Elasticsearch configuration providing a volume mount point at `/usr/share/elasticsearch/config`.

```
docker run -d -v "$PWD/config":/usr/share/elasticsearch/config
docker.elastic.co/elasticsearch/elasticsearch:5.1.1
```

3. You can persist the data between docker reboots configuring a local data mount point to store index data. The path to be used as mount point is `/usr/share/elasticsearch/config`.

```
docker run -d -v "$PWD/esdata":/usr/share/elasticsearch/data
docker.elastic.co/elasticsearch/elasticsearch:5.1.1
```

There's more...

The official Elasticsearch images are not only provided by Docker. There are several customized images for custom purpose. Some of these are optimized for large cluster deploy or more complex Elasticsearch cluster topologies than the standard ones.

Docker is very handy also to test several versions of Elasticsearch in a clean way without installing too much stuff on the host machine.

See also

You can further refer to:

- The official Elasticsearch Docker documentation at
  `https://www.elastic.co/guide/en/elasticsearch/reference/5.1/docker.htm`
  `l`
- All the ELK (Elasticsearch, Logstash, and Kibana) Stack via Docker at
  `https://hub.docker.com/r/sebp/elk/`
- The Docker documentation at `https://docs.docker.com/`

3
Managing Mappings

In this chapter, will cover the following recipes:

- Using explicit mapping creation
- Mapping base types
- Mapping arrays
- Mapping an object
- Mapping a document
- Using dynamic templates in document mapping
- Managing nested objects
- Managing a child document
- Adding a field with multiple mappings
- Mapping a GeoPoint field
- Mapping a GeoShape field
- Mapping an IP field
- Mapping an attachment field
- Adding metadata to a mapping
- Specifying different analyzers
- Mapping a completion field

Introduction

Mapping is a very important concept in Elasticsearch, as it defines how the search engine should process a document.

Search engines perform two main operations:

- **Indexing**: This is the action to receive a document and store/index/process in an index
- **Searching**: This is the action to retrieve the data from the index

These two parts are strictly connected. An error in the indexing step leads to unwanted or missing search results.

Elasticsearch has explicit mapping on an index/type level. When indexing, if a mapping is not provided, a default one is created, guessing the structure from the data fields that compose the document; then, this new mapping is automatically propagated to all cluster nodes.

The default type mapping has sensible default values, but when you want to change their behavior or you want to customize several other aspects of indexing (storing, ignoring, completion, and so on), you need to provide a new mapping definition.

In this chapter, we'll see all the possible types that compose the mappings.

Using explicit mapping creation

If we consider the index as a database in the SQL world, the mapping is similar to the table definition.

Elasticsearch is able to understand the structure of the document that you are indexing (reflection) and create the mapping definition automatically (explicit mapping creation).

Getting ready

You need an up-and-running Elasticsearch installation as we described in the *Downloading and installing Elasticsearch* recipe in `Chapter 2`, *Downloading and Setup*.

To execute `curl` via command-line, you need to install `curl` for your operative system.

To better understand examples and code in this recipe, basic knowledge of JSON is required.

How to do it...

You can explicitly create a mapping by adding a new document in Elasticsearch. We will perform the following steps:

1. Create an index:

   ```
   curl -XPUT http://127.0.0.1:9200/test
   ```

   The answer will be as follows:

   ```
   {acknowledged":true}
   ```

2. Put a document in the index:

   ```
   curl -XPUT http://127.0.0.1:9200/test/mytype/1 -d
   '{"name":"Paul", "age":35}'
   ```

   The answer will be as follows:

   ```
   {
   "_index":"test",
   "_type":"mytype",
   "_id":"1",
   "_version":1,
   "forced_refresh":false,
   "_shards":{"total":2,"successful":1,"failed":0},
   "created":true
   }
   ```

3. Get the mapping and pretty print it:

   ```
   curl -XGET http://127.0.0.1:9200/test/mytype/_mapping?
   pretty=true
   ```

4. The result mapping autocreated by Elasticsearch should be:

```
{
  "test" : {
    "mappings" : {
      "mytype" : {
        "properties" : {
          "age" : {
            "type" : "long"
          },
          "name" : {
            "type" : "text",
            "fields" : {
              "keyword" : {
                "type" : "keyword",
                "ignore_above" : 256
              }
            }
          }
        }
      }
    }
  }
}
```

How it works…

The first command line creates an index where we'll configure the type/mapping and insert the documents.

The second command inserts a document in the index. (We'll see the index creation in the *Creating an index* recipe in `Chapter 4`, *Basic Operations* and record indexing in the *Indexing a document* recipe in `Chapter 4`, *Basic Operations*)

During the document index phase, Elasticsearch checks if the type `mytype` exists, otherwise it creates one dynamically.

Elasticsearch reads all the default properties for the field of the mapping and starts to process them:

- If the field is already present in the mapping and the value of the field is valid (it matches the correct type), Elasticsearch does not need to change the current mappings.

- If the field is already present in the mapping, but the value of the field is of a different type, it tries to upgrade the field type (that is, from integer to long). If the types are not compatible, it throws an exception and the index process fails.
- If the field is not present, it tries to auto detect the type of field. It updates the mappings with a new field mapping.

There's more...

In Elasticsearch, the separation of documents in types is logical not physical. The Elasticsearch core engine transparently manages it. Physically, all the document types go in the same Lucene index, so there is no full separation between them. The concept of types is purely logical and enforced by Elasticsearch. The user is not bothered about this internal management, but in some cases with huge amount of records; this has an impact on the performances in reading and writing records because all the records are stored in the same index files.

> Mapping types are used to group fields, but the fields in each mapping type are not independent of each other. Fields with the same name and in the same index in different mapping types map to the same field internally: they must have the same mapping.

Every document has a unique identifier called UID for index, stored in the special field _uid of the document. It is automatically calculated adding the type of the document to the _id. In our example the _uid will be mytype#1.

The _id can be provided at index time or can be assigned automatically by Elasticsearch, if it is missing.

When a mapping type is created or changed, Elasticsearch automatically propagates mapping changes to all nodes in the cluster, so that all the shards are aligned in how to process that particular type.

See also

- Refer to *How to create and customize mapping during index creation* and *Creating an index, How to put new mappings in an index*, and *Putting mapping* recipes in Chapter 4, *Basic Operations*

Mapping base types

Using explicit mapping allows to be faster in starting to insert the data using a schema less approach without being concerned of the field types, so as to achieve better results and performance in indexing, it's required to manually define a mapping.

Fine-tuning mapping brings some advantages such as:

- Reducing the index size on the disk (disabling functionalities for custom fields)
- Indexing only interesting fields (general speed up)
- Precooking data for fast search or real-time analytics (such as facets)
- Correctly defining whether a field must be analyzed in multiple tokens or considered as a single token

Elasticsearch allows using base fields with a wide range of configurations.

Getting ready

You need an up-and-running Elasticsearch installation as we described in the *Downloading and installing Elasticsearch* recipe in `Chapter` 2, *Downloading and Setup*.

To execute `curl` via the command line, you need to install `curl` for your operative system.

To execute this recipe's examples, you need to create an index with the name `test` where to put mappings as explained in the *Using explicit mapping creation* recipe.

How to do it...

Let's use a semi real-world example of a shop order for our ebay-like shop.

We initially define an order such as:

Name	Type	Description
id	identifier	Order identifier
date	date(time)	Date of order
customer_id	id reference	Customer ID reference
name	string	Name of the item

quantity	integer	How many items?
vat	double	VAT for item
sent	boolean	The order was sent

Our `order` record must be converted to an Elasticsearch mapping definition:

```
{
    "order" : {
        "properties" : {
            "id" : {"type" : "keyword"},
            "date" : {"type" : "date"},
            "customer_id" : {"type" : "keyword"},
            "sent" : {"type" : "boolean"},
            "name" : {"type" : "keyword"},
            "quantity" : {"type" : "integer"},
            "vat" : {"type" : "double", "index":"false"}
        }
    }
}
```

Now the mapping is ready to be put in the index. We will see how to do it in the *Putting a Mapping in an Index* recipe in `Chapter 4`, *Basic Operations*.

How it works...

Field type must be mapped to one of the Elasticsearch base types, adding options about how the field must be indexed.

The following table is a reference of the mapping types:

Type	ES-Type	Description
String, VarChar	keyword	This is a text field that is not tokenizable: CODE0011
String, VarChar, Text	text	This is a text field to be tokenized: a nice text
Integer	integer	This is an Integer (32 bit): 1,2,3,or 4
long	long	This is a long value (64 bit)
float	float	This is a floating point number (32 bit): 1.2, or 4.5
double	double	This is a floating point number (64 bit)

boolean	boolean	This is a Boolean value: true or false
date/datetime	date	This is a date or datetime value: 2013-12-25, 2013-12-25T22:21:20
bytes/binary	binary	This includes some bytes that are used for binary data such as file or stream of bytes.

Depending on the data type, it's possible to give explicit directives to Elasticsearch on processing the field for better management. The most used options are:

- `store` (default `false`): This marks the field to be stored in a separate index fragment for fast retrieving. Storing a field consumes disk space, but reduces computation if you need to extract it from a document (that is, in scripting and aggregations). The possible values for this option are `false` and `true`.

> The stored fields are faster than others in aggregations.

- `index` : This defines if the field should be indexed. The possible values for this parameter are `true` and `false`. No, index fields are not searchable (default `true`).
- `null_value`: This defines a default value if the field is null.
- `boost` : This is used to change the importance of a field (default `1.0`).

> Boost works only a term level so it's mainly used in term, terms and match queries.

- `search_analyzer`: This defines an analyzer to be used during the search. If not defined, the analyzer of the parent object is used (default `null`).
- `analyzer`: This sets the default analyzer to be used (default `null`).
- `include_in_all`: This marks the current field to be indexed in the special `_all` field (a field that contains the concatenated text of all fields) (default `true`).

- norms : This controls the Lucene norms. This parameter is used to better score queries. If the field is used only for filtering, it's best practice to disable it to reduce resource usage (default true for analyzed fields and false for not_analyzed ones).
- copy_to: This allows you to copy the content of a field to another one to achieve functionalities similar to the _all field.
- ignore_above: This allows you to skip the indexing string bigger than its value. It is useful for processing fields for exact filtering, aggregations, and sorting. It also prevents to have a single term token too big and prevent errors due to Lucene term byte-length limit of 32766 (default 2147483647).

There's more...

In the previous version of Elasticsearch, the standard mapping for string was string. In version 5.x, the string mapping is deprecated and migrated to keyword and text mappings.

In Elasticsearch version 5.x, as shown in the *Using explicit mapping creation* recipe, the explicit inferred type for a string is a multifield mapping:

- The default processing is text. This mapping allows textual queries (that is, term, match, and span queries). In the example provided in the *Using explicit mapping creation* recipe, it was name.
- The keyword subfield is used for keyword mapping. This field can be used for exact term match and for aggregation and sorting. In the example provided in the *Using explicit mapping creation* recipe, it was name.keyword.

Another important parameter, available only for text mapping, is the term_vector (the vector of terms that compose a string, refer to the Lucene documentation for further details at http://lucene.apache.org/core/6_1_0/core/org/apache/lucene/index/Terms.html) for details defining:

- no: This is the default value, skip term vector
- yes: This is the store term vector
- with_offsets: This is the store term vector with token offset (start, end position in a block of characters)
- with_positions: This is the store the position of the token in the term vector
- with_positions_offsets: This stores all term vector data

> **TIP**
>
> Term vectors allow fast highlighting, but consume disk space due to storing of additional text information. It's best practice to activate only in fields that require highlighting such as title or document content.

See also

The online documentation on Elasticsearch provides the full description of all the properties for the different mapping fields at `https://www.elastic.co/guide/en/elasticsearch/reference/master/mapping-params.html`.

The *Specifying a different Analyzer* recipe shows alternative analyzers to the standard one.

For newcomers who want to explore the concepts of tokenization, I would suggest to read official Elasticsearch documentation at `https://www.elastic.co/guide/en/elasticsearch/reference/current/analysis-tokenizers.html`.

Mapping arrays

An array or multivalue fields are very common in data models (such as multiple phone numbers, addresses, names, alias, and so on), but not natively supported in traditional SQL solutions.

In SQL, multivalue fields require the creation of accessory tables that must be joined to gather all the values, leading to poor performance when the cardinality of records is huge.

Elasticsearch, which works natively in JSON, provides support for multivalue fields transparently.

Getting ready

You need an up-and-running Elasticsearch installation as we described in the *Downloading and installing Elasticsearch* recipe in `Chapter 2`, *Downloading and Setup*.

To execute `curl` via the command line, you need to install `curl` for your operative system.

How to do it...

Every field is automatically managed as an array. For example, to store tags for a document, the mapping will be:

```
{
    "document" : {
        "properties" : {
    "name" : {"type" : "keyword"},
    "tag" : {"type" : "keyword", "store" : "yes"},
    ...
        }
    }
}
```

This mapping is valid for indexing both the documents. The following is the code for `document1`:

```
{"name": "document1", "tag": "awesome"}
```

The following is the code for `document2`:

```
{"name": "document2", "tag": ["cool", "awesome", "amazing"] }
```

How it works...

Elasticsearch transparently manages the array: there is no difference if you declare a single value or a multivalue due to its Lucene core nature.

Multivalues for field are managed in Lucene adding them to a document with the same field name. For people with SQL background, this behavior may be quite strange, but this is a key point in NoSQL world as it reduces the need for the join query and creating different tables to manage multivalues. An array of embedded objects has the same behavior as of simple fields.

Mapping an object

The object is the base structure (analogous to a record in SQL). Elasticsearch extends the traditional use of objects allowing recursive embedded objects.

Getting ready

You need an up-and-running Elasticsearch installation as we described in the *Downloading and installing Elasticsearch* recipe in this `Chapter 2`, *Downloading and Setup*.

To execute `curl` via the command line, you need to install `curl` for your operative system.

How to do it...

We can rewrite the mapping of order type form of the mapping the base types recipe using an array of items:

```
{
    "order" : {
    "properties" : {
    "id" : {"type" : "keyword"},
    "date" : {"type" : "date"},
    "customer_id" : {"type" : "keyword", "store" : "yes"},
    "sent" : {"type" : "boolean"},

    "item" : {
    "type" : "object",
    "properties" : {
    "name" : {"type" : "text"},
    "quantity" : {"type" : "integer"},
    "vat" : {"type" : "double"}
     }
    }
        }
    }
}
```

How it works...

Elasticsearch speaks native JSON, so every complex JSON structure can be mapped into it.

When Elasticsearch is parsing an object type, it tries to extract fields and processes them as its defined mapping; otherwise, it learns the structure of the object using reflection.

The most important attributes for an object are:

- `properties`: This is a collection of fields or objects (we can consider them as columns in the SQL world).
- `enabled`: This is if the object should be processed. If it's set to false, the data contained in the object is not indexed and it could not be searched (default `true`).
- `dynamic`: This allows Elasticsearch to add new field names to the object using a reflection on values of the inserted data. If it's set to `false`, when you try to index an object contained a new field type, it'll be rejected silently. If it's set to `strict`, when a new field type is present in the object, an error is raised skipping the index process. Control dynamic parameter allows being safe about change in the document structure (default `true`).
- `include_in_all`: This adds the object values to the special `_all` field (used to aggregate the text of all document fields) (default `true`).

The most used attribute is `properties` that allows mapping the fields of the object in Elasticsearch fields.

Disabling the indexing part of the document reduces the index size; however, the data cannot be searched. In other words, you end up with a smaller file on disk, but there is a cost in functionality.

See also

There are special objects that are described in the following recipes:

- The *Mapping a document* recipe
- The *Managing a child document* recipe
- The *Mapping nested objects* recipe

Mapping a document

The document is also referred as the root object. It has special parameters to control its behavior, mainly used internally to do special processing, such as routing or time-to-live of documents.

In this recipe, we'll take a look at these special fields and learn how to use them.

Getting ready

You need an up-and-running Elasticsearch installation as we described in the *Downloading and installing Elasticsearch* recipe in `Chapter 2`, *Downloading and Setup*.

To execute `curl` via the command line, you need to install `curl` for your operative system.

How to do it...

We can extend the preceding order example adding some of the special fields, for example:

```
{
  "order": {
  "_id": {
  "index": true
  },
  "_type": {
  "store": "yes"
  },
  "_source": {
  "store": "yes"
  },
  "_all": {
  "enable": false
  },
  "_routing": {
  "required": true
  },
  "_index": {
  "enabled": true
  },
  "_size": {
  "enabled": true,
  "store": "yes"
  },
  "properties": {
  ... truncated ....
        }
     }
  }
}
```

How it works...

Every special field has its own parameters and value options, such as:

- _id: This allows indexing only the ID part of the document. All the ID queries will have a speed up using the ID value (default not indexed and not stored).
- _type: This allows indexing the type of the document (default indexed and not stored).
- _index: This controls if the index must be stored as part of the document. It can be enabled by setting the parameter "enabled": true (default enabled=false).
- _size: This controls if it stores the size of the source record. (It requires the size mapping plugin installed) (default enabled=false).
- _all: This controls the creation of the _all field (a special field that aggregates all the text of all the document fields). Because this functionality requires a lot of CPU and storage; if it is not required, it is better to disable it (default enabled=true).
- _source: This controls the storage of the document source. Storing the source, it is very handful, but it's a storage overhead, so it is not required; it's better to turn it off (default enabled=true).
- _parent: This defines the parent document (refer to the *Mapping Child Document* recipe).
- _routing: This defines the shard that will store the document. It supports additional parameters required (true/false): to force the presence of the routing value, raising an exception if not provided.

The power of control how to index and process a document is very important and allows resolving issues related to complex data types.

Every special field has parameters to set particular configuration and some of their behavior could change in different releases of Elasticsearch.

See also

- You can refer recipes *Using Dynamic Templates in Document Mapping* in this chapter and *Putting a Mapping in an Index* in Chapter 4, *Basic Operations*

Using dynamic templates in document mapping

In the *Using explicit mapping creation* recipe, we have seen how Elasticsearch is able to guess the field type using reflection. In this recipe, we'll see how to help it to improve its guessing capabilities via dynamic templates.

Dynamic template feature is very useful, for example, if you need to create several indices, with similar types, because it allows moving the need to define mappings from coded initial routines to automatic index-document creation. A typical usage is to define types for Logstash log indices.

Getting ready

You need an up-and-running Elasticsearch installation as we described in the *Downloading and installing Elasticsearch* recipe in `Chapter 2`, *Downloading and Setup*.

To execute `curl` via the command line, you need to install `curl` for your operative system.

How to do it...

We can extend the previous mapping adding document-related settings:

```
{
    "order" : {
    "dynamic_date_formats":["yyyy-MM-dd", "dd-MM-yyyy"],
    "date_detection":true,
    "numeric_detection":true,
    "dynamic_templates":[
    {"template1":{
    "match":"*",
    "match_mapping_type":"long",
    "mapping":{"type":" {dynamic_type}", "store":true}
    }}
    ],
    "properties" : {...}
    }
}
```

How it works...

The root object (document) controls the behavior of its fields and all its children object fields. In document mapping we can define the following:

- `date_detection`: This enables the extraction of a date from a string (default `true`)
- `dynamic_date_formats`: This is a list of valid date formats, it's used if `date_detection` is active
- `numeric_detection`: This enables you to convert strings in number, if it is possible (default `false`)
- `dynamic_templates`: This is a list of templates used to change the explicit mapping and if one of these templates is matched, the rules defined in it are used for build the final mapping

A dynamic template is composed of two parts: the matcher and the mapping one.

To match a field to activate the template, several types of matchers are available, such as:

- `match`: This allows defining a match on the field name. The expression is a standard GLOB pattern (`http://en.wikipedia.org/wiki/Glob_(programming)`).
- `unmatch`: This allows defining the expression to be used to exclude matches (optional).
- `match_mapping_type` : This controls the types of the matched fields, for example, string, integer, and so on (optional)
- `path_match`: This allows matching the dynamic template against the full dot notation of the field, for example, `obj1.*.value` (optional)
- `path_unmatch`: This will do the opposite of `path_match`, excluding the matched fields (optional)
- `match_pattern`: This allows switching the matchers to `regex` (regular expression); otherwise, the glob pattern match is used (optional)

The dynamic template mapping part is a standard one, but with the ability to use special placeholders such as:

- `{name}`: This will be replaced with the actual dynamic field name
- `{dynamic_type}`: This will be replaced with the type of the matched field

> The order of the dynamic templates is very important, only the first one that is matched is executed. It is good practice to order first the ones with more strict rules, and then the others.

There's more...

The dynamic template is very handy when you need to set a mapping configuration to all the fields. This action can be done adding a dynamic template similar to this one:

```
"dynamic_templates" : [
    {
        "store_generic" : {
            "match" : "*",
            "mapping" : {
                "store" : "yes"
            }
        }
    }
]
```

In this example, all the new fields, which will be added with explicit mapping, will be stored.

See also

- You can see the default Elasticsearch behavior in creating mapping in the *Using explicit mapping creation* recipe and the base way to define a mapping in the *Mapping a document* recipe
- The glob pattern is available at `http://en.wikipedia.org/wiki/Glob_pattern`

Managing nested objects

There is a special type of embedded object, the nested one. This resolves a problem related to Lucene indexing architecture, in which all the fields of embedded objects are viewed as a single object. During search, in Lucene, it is not possible to distinguish values between different embedded objects in the same multivalued array.

If we consider the previous order example, it's not possible to distinguish an item name and its quantity with the same query, as Lucene puts them in the same Lucene document object. We need to index them in different documents and then join them. This "entire trip" is managed by nested objects and nested queries.

Getting ready

You need an up-and-running Elasticsearch installation as we described in the *Downloading and installing Elasticsearch* recipe in chapter 2, *Downloading and Setup*.

How to do it…

A nested object is defined as the standard object with the type nested.

From the example in the *Mapping an object* recipe, we can change the type from object to nested:

```
{
    "order" : {
        "properties" : {
            "id" : {"type" : "keyword"},
            "date" : {"type" : "date"},
            "customer_id" : {"type" : "keyword", "store" : "yes"},
            "sent" : {"type" : "boolean"},
            "item" : {"type" : "nested",
                "properties" : {
                "name" : {"type" : "keyword"},
                "quantity" : {"type" : "long"},
                "vat" : {"type" : "double"}
            }
        }
    }
}
```

How it works...

When a document is indexed, if an embedded object is marked as `nested`, it's extracted by the original document and indexed in a new external document.

In the preceding example, we have reused mapping of the *Mapping an Object* recipe, but we have changed the type of the item from `object` to `nested`. No other required action must be taken to convert an embedded object to a nested one.

The nested objects are special Lucene documents that are saved in the same block of data of its parent: this approach allows fast joining with the parent document.

Nested objects are not searchable with standard queries, but only with nested ones. They are not shown in standard query results.

The lives of nested objects are related to their parents: deleting/updating a parent automatically deletes/updates all nested children. Changing the parent means Elasticsearch will:

- Mark old document deleted
- Mark all nested documents deleted
- Index the new document version
- Index all nested documents

There's more...

Sometimes, it is required to propagate information of nested objects to their parent or root objects, mainly to build simpler queries about their parents (such as terms queries without using nested ones). To achieve this goal, there are two special properties of nested objects:

- `include_in_parent`: This allows to automatically add the nested fields to the immediate parent
- `include_in_root`: This adds the nested object fields to the root object
- These settings add data redundancy, but they reduce the complexity of some queries improving performance

See also

- Nested objects require special query to search for them: they will be discussed in the *Using nested Query* recipe in `Chapter 7`, *Relationships and Geo Queries*

- The *Managing child document* recipe shows another way to manage child/parent relations between documents

Managing child document

In the previous recipe, we have seen how it's possible to manage relations between objects with the nested object type. The disadvantage of nested objects is their dependence from their parent. If you need to change a value of a nested object, you need to reindex the parent (this brings a potential performance overhead if the nested objects change too quickly). To solve this problem, Elasticsearch allows defining child documents.

Getting ready

You need an up-and-running Elasticsearch installation as we described in the *Downloading and installing Elasticsearch* recipe in `Chapter 2`, *Downloading and Setup*.

How to do it...

We can modify the mapping of the `order` example indexing the items as separated child documents.

We need to extract the `item` object and create a new type document item with the `_parent` property set.

```
{
    "order": {
        "properties": {
            "id": {
                "type": "keyword",
                "store": "yes"
            },
            "date": {
                "type": "date"
            },
```

```
            "customer_id": {
                "type": "keyword",
                "store": "yes"
            },
            "sent": {
                "type": "boolean"
            }
        }
    },
    "item": {

    "_parent": {
    "type": "order"
     },
        "properties": {
            "name": {
                "type": "text"
            },
            "quantity": {
                "type": "integer"
            },
            "vat": {
                "type": "double"
            }
        }
    }
}
```

The preceding mapping is similar to the one in the previous recipe. The item object is extracted from the order (in the previous example, it was nested) and added as a new mapping. The only difference is that "type": "nested" has become "type": "object" (it can be omitted) and the new special field _parent that defines the parent/child relation.

How it works...

The child object is a standard root object (document) with an extra property defined: _parent.

The type property of _parent refers to the type of the parent document.

The child document must be indexed in the same shard of the parent: so when indexed an extra parameter must be passed: the parent id. (We'll see how to do it in the *Indexing a document* recipe in the next chapter.)

Child document doesn't require reindexing the parent document when we want to change its values: so it's fast in indexing, reindexing (updating), and deleting.

There's more...

In Elasticsearch, we have different ways to manage relations between objects:

- Embedding with `type=object`: This is implicitly managed by Elasticsearch and it considers the embedded as part of the main document. It's fast, but you need to reindex the main document for changing a value of the embedded object.
- Nesting with `type=nested`: This allows more accurate search and filtering of the parent using nested query on children. Everything works as for embedded object except for query.
- External children documents: Here, the children are the external document, with a property `_parent` to bind them to the parent. They must be indexed in the same shard of the parent. The join with the parent is a bit slower than the nested one, because the nested objects are in the same data block of the parent in Lucene index and they are loaded with the parent, otherwise the child document requires more read operations.

Choosing how to model the relation from objects depends on your application scenario.

There is also another approach that can be used, but on big data documents, it brings poor performances: it's decoupling join relation. You do the join query in two steps: first you collect the ID of the children/other documents and then you search them in a field of their parent.

See also

- You can refer *Using the has_child query*, *Using the top_children query* and *Using the has_parent query* in `Chapter 7`, *Relationships and Geo Queries* for more details on child/parent queries

Adding a field with multiple mapping

Often a field must be processed with several core types or in different ways. For example, a string field must be processed `tokenized` for search and `not-tokenized` for sorting. To do this, we need to define a multifield special property `fields`.

The `fields` property is a very powerful feature of mappings because it allows you to use the same field in different ways.

Getting ready

You need an up-and-running Elasticsearch installation as we described in the *Downloading and installing Elasticsearch* recipe in `Chapter 2`, *Downloading and Setup*.

How to do it...

To define a multifield property, we need to define a dictionary containing the subfields called `fields`. The subfield with the same name of parent field is the default one.

If we consider the item of our `order` example, we can index the name in this way:

```
"name": {
        "type": "keyword",
        "fields": {
        "name": {
        "type": "keyword"},
        "tk": {
        "type": "text"
                },
        "code": {
        "type": "text",
        "analyzer": "code_analyzer"
          }
      }
    },
```

If we already have a mapping stored in Elasticsearch and we want to migrate the fields in a multi-field property, it's enough to save a new mapping with a different type and Elasticsearch provides the merge automatically. New subfields in the `fields` property can be added without problems at any moment, but the new subfields will be available only to newly indexed documents.

How it works...

During indexing when Elasticsearch processes a `fields` property of type multifield, it reprocesses the same field for every subfield defined in the mapping.

To access the subfields of a multifield, we have a new path built on the base field plus the subfield name. If we consider the preceding example, we have:

- `name`: This points to the default multifield subfield-field (the keyword one)
- `name.tk`: This points to the standard analyzed (tokenized) field
- `name.code`: This points to a field analyzed with a code extractor analyzer

If you notice in the preceding example, we have changed the analyzer to introduce a code extractor analyzer that allows extracting the item code from a string.

Using the multifield if we index a string such as `Good Item to buy - ABC1234` we'll have:

- `name = Good Item to buy - ABC1234` (useful for sorting)
- `name.tk= ["good", "item", "to", "buy", "abc1234"]` (useful for searching)
- `name.code = ["ABC1234"]` (useful for searching and faceting)

There's more...

The `fields` property is very useful in data processing, because it allows defining several ways to process a field data.

For example, if we are working for document content, we can define as subfields analyzers to extract names, places, date/time, geo location, and so on.

The subfields of a multifield are standard core type fields: we can do every process we want on them such as search, filter, aggregation, and scripting.

See also

- The *Specifying different analyzers* recipe

Mapping a GeoPoint field

Elasticsearch natively supports the use of geolocation types: special types that allow localizing your document in geographic coordinates (latitude and longitude) around the world.

There are two main types used in geographic world: the point and the shape. In this recipe, we'll see geo point–the base element of geo location.

Getting ready

You need an up-and-running Elasticsearch installation as we described in the *Downloading and installing Elasticsearch* recipe in `Chapter 2`, *Downloading and Setup*.

How to do it...

The type of the field must be set to `geo_point` to define a GeoPoint.

We can extend the order example adding a new field that stores the location of a customer. This will be the result:

```
{
    "order": {
        "properties": {
            "id": {
                "type": "keyword",
                "store": "yes"
            },
            "date": {
                "type": "date"
            },
            "customer_id": {
                "type": "keyword",
                "store": "yes"
            },
            "customer_ip": {
                "type": "ip",
                "store": "yes"
            },

            "customer_location": {
            "type": "geo_point"
            },
```

```
    "sent": {
        "type": "boolean"
      }
    }
  }
}
```

How it works...

When Elasticsearch indexes a document with a geo point field (`lat,lon`), it processes the latitude and longitude coordinates and creates special accessory field data to fast query on these coordinates.

Depending on properties, given a latitude and a longitude, it's possible to compute the `geohash` value (`http://en.wikipedia.org/wiki/Geohash`) and the index process also optimizes these values for special computation such as distance, ranges, and in shape match.

Geo point has special parameters that allow storing additional geographic data:

- `lat_lon`: This allows storing the latitude and longitude as the `.lat` and `.lon` fields. Storing these values improves the performance in many memory algorithms used in distance and in shape calculus (default `false`).

> It makes sense to set `lat_lon` to `true` so that you store them if there is a single point value for field to improve speed up search and reduce memory usage during computation.

- `geohash`: This allows storing the computed geohash value (default `false`).
- `geohash_precision`: This defines the precision to be used in geohash calculus. For example, given a geo point value `[45.61752, 9.08363]`, it will store (default `12`):
  - `customer_location = 45.61752, 9.08363`
  - `customer_location.lat = 45.61752`
  - `customer_location.lon = 9.08363`
  - `customer_location.geohash = u0n7w8qmrfj`

There's more...

GeoPoint is a special type and can accept several formats as input:

- `lat` and `lon` as properties:

```
{
  "customer_location": {
  "lat": 45.61752,
  "lon": 9.08363
  },
```

- `lan` and `lon` as string:

```
"customer_location": "45.61752,9.08363",
```

- geohash string:

```
"customer_location": "u0n7w8qmrfj",
```

- as a GeoJSON array (note in it `lat` and `lon` are reversed):

```
"customer_location": [9.08363, 45.61752]
```

Mapping a GeoShape field

An extension to the concept of point is the shape. Elasticsearch provides a type that facilitates the management of arbitrary polygons: the GeoShape.

Getting ready

You need an up-and-running Elasticsearch installation as we described in the *Downloading and installing Elasticsearch* recipe in `Chapter 2`, *Downloading and Setup*.

To be able to use advanced shape management, Elasticsearch requires two JAR libraries in its `classpath` (usually the `lib` directory):

- Spatial4J (v0.3)
- JTS (v1.13)

How to do it

To map a `geo_shape` type, a user must explicitly provide some parameters:

- `tree`: This is the name of the PrefixTree implementation: geohash for `GeohashPrefixTree` and quadtree for `QuadPrefixTree` (default `geohash`)
- `precision`: This is used instead of `tree_levels` to provide a more human value to be used in the tree level. The precision number can be followed by the unit, that is, 10m, 10km, 10miles, and so on
- `tree_levels`: This is the maximum number of layers to be used in the prefix tree
- `distance_error_pct`: This sets the maximum errors allowed in prefix tree (default `0,025%` – `max 0,5%`).

The `customer_location` mapping, that we have seen in the previous recipe using `geo_shape`, will be as follows:

```
"customer_location": {
    "type": "geo_shape",
    "tree": "quadtree",
    "precision": "1m"
},
```

How it works...

When a shape is indexed or searched internally, a path tree is created and used.

A path tree is a list of terms that contains geographic information, computed to improve performance in evaluating geo calculus.

The path tree also depends on the shape type: point, linestring, polygon, multipoint, and multipolygon.

See also

To understand the logic behind the GeoShape, some good resources are the Elasticsearch page that tells you about GeoShape and the sites of the libraries used for geographic calculus (`https://github.com/spatial4j/spatial4j` and `http://central.maven.org/maven2/com/vividsolutions/jts/1.13/`).

Mapping an IP field

Elasticsearch is used in a lot of systems to collect and search logs such as Kibana (`https://w
ww.elastic.co/products/kibana`) and LogStash (`https://www.elastic.co/products/lo
gstash`). To improve search in these scenarios, it provides the IPv4 and IPv6 type that can
be used to store IP address in an optimized way.

Getting ready

You need an up-and-running Elasticsearch installation as we described in the *Downloading
and installing Elasticsearch* recipe in `Chapter 2`, *Downloading and Setup*.

How to do it...

You need to define the type of the field that contains IP address as `ip` as follows:

Using the preceding order example, we can extend it adding the customer IP with:

```
"customer_ip": {
"type": "ip",
"store": "yes"
  }
```

The IP must be in the standard point notation form, that is:

```
"customer_ip":"19.18.200.201"
```

How it works...

When Elasticsearch is processing a document, if a field is an IP one, it tries to convert its
value to a numerical form and generate tokens for fast value searching.

The IP has special properties:

- `index`: This defines whether the field must be indexed. Otherwise, `false` must
  be used (default `true`)
- `doc_values`: This defines whether the field values should be stored in a column-
  stride fashion to speed up sorting and aggregations (default `true`)

The other properties (`store`, `boost`, `null_value`, and `include_in_all`) work as other base types.

The advantage of using IP fields over the string is the faster speed in every range and filter and lower resource usage (disk and memory).

Mapping an attachment field

Elasticsearch allows extending its core types to cover new requirements with native plugins that provide new mapping types. A most used custom field type is the attachment one.

It allows indexing and searching the contents of common documental files, that is, Microsoft office formats, open document formats, PDF, ePub, and many others.

Getting ready

You need an up-and-running Elasticsearch installation as we described in the *Downloading and installing Elasticsearch* recipe in `Chapter 2`, *Downloading and Setup* with the ingest attachment plugin installed.

It can be installed from the command line with the following command:

```
bin/elasticsearch-plugin install ingest-attachment
```

How to do it...

To map a field as attachment, it's required to set the `type` to `attachment`.

Internally, the attachment field defines the `fields` property as a multi-field that takes some binary data (encoded base64) and extracts several useful information such as `author`, `content`, `title`, `date`, and so on.

If we want to create a mapping for an e-mail storing attachment, it will be:

```
{
    "email": {
        "properties": {
            "sender": {
                "type": "keyword"
            },
            "date": {
```

```
            "type": "date"
        },
        "document": {
            "type": "attachment",
            "fields": {
                "file": {
                    "store": "yes",
                    "index": "analyzed"
                },
                "date": {
                    "store": "yes"
                },
                "author": {
                    "store": "yes"
                },
                "keywords": {
                    "store": "yes"
                },
                "content_type": {
                    "store": "yes"
                },
                "title": {
                    "store": "yes"
                }
            }
        }
            }
        }
    }
}
```

How it works...

The attachment plugin internally uses Apache Tika, a library specialized in text extraction from documents. The list of supported document types is available in the Apache Tika site (`http://tika.apache.org/1.9/formats.html`), but it covers all the common file types.

The attachment type field receives a base64 binary stream that is processed by Tika metadata and text extractor. The field can be seen as a multi-field that stores different contents in his subfields:

- `file`: This stores the content of the file
- `date`: This stores the file creation data, extracted by Tika metadata

- `author`: This stores the file author, extracted by Tika metadata
- `keywords`: This stores the file keywords, extracted by Tika metadata
- `content_type`: This stores the file content type
- `title`: This stores the file title, extracted by Tika metadata

The default settings for attachment plugin is to extract 100,000 chars. This value can be changed globally by setting the index settings `index.mappings.attachment.indexed_chars` or when indexing the element passing a value to `_indexed_chars` property.

There's more...

The attachment type is not a mapping provided in a vanilla installation of Elasticsearch. It is a good example of how it's possible to extend Elasticsearch with custom types and mappings to provide new functionalities that natively are not available in Elasticsearch.

The attachment plugin is very useful for indexing documents, e-mails and every type of unstructured document.

See also

- For more information, you can check the official attachment plugin page at `https://www.elastic.co/guide/en/elasticsearch/plugins/master/ingest-attachment.html` and the Tika library page at `http://tika.apache.org`.

Adding metadata to a mapping

Sometimes when we are working with our mapping, it is required to store some additional data to be used for display purpose, ORM facilities, permissions, or simply to track them in the mapping.

Elasticsearch allows storing every kind of JSON data we want in the mapping with the special field `_meta`.

Getting ready

You need an up-and-running Elasticsearch installation as we described in the *Downloading and installing Elasticsearch* recipe in `Chapter 2`, *Downloading and Setup*.

How to do it...

1. The `_meta` mapping field can be populated with any data we want. Consider the following example:

```
{
    "order": {
        "_meta": {
            "attr1": ["value1", "value2"],
            "attr2": {
                "attr3": "value3"
            }
        }
    }
}
```

How it works...

When Elasticsearch processes a new mapping and finds a `_meta` field, it stores it in the global mapping status and propagates the information to all the cluster nodes.

The `_meta` is only for storing purpose; it's not indexed and searchable.

It can be used for:

- Storing type metadata
- Storing **Object Relational Mapping (ORM)** related information
- Storing type permission information
- Storing extra type information (that is, icon filename used to display the type)
- Storing template parts for rendering web interfaces

Specifying a different analyzer

In the previous recipes, we have seen how to map different fields and objects in Elasticsearch and we have described how it's easy to change the standard analyzer with the `analyzer` and `search_analyzer` properties.

In this recipe, we will see several analyzers and how to use them to improve the indexing and searching quality.

Getting ready

You need an up-and-running Elasticsearch installation as we described in the *Downloading and installing Elasticsearch* recipe in `Chapter 2`, *Downloading and Setup*.

How to do it...

Every core type field allows you to specify custom analyzer for indexing and for searching as field parameters.

For example, if we want that the name field uses a standard analyzer for indexing and a simple analyzer for searching, the mapping will be as follows:

```
{
    "name": {
        "type": "string",
        "index_analyzer": "standard",
        "search_analyzer": "simple"
    }
}
```

How it works...

The concept of analyzer comes from Lucene (the core of Elasticsearch). An analyzer is a Lucene element that is composed by a tokenizer, that splits a text in tokens, and one or more token filter, that do token manipulation such as lowercasing, normalization, removing stop words, stemming, and so on.

During indexing phase, when Elasticsearch processes a field that must be indexed, an analyzer is chosen, looking first if it is defined in the `index_analyzer` field, then in document, and finally in the index.

> Choosing the correct analyzer is essential to have good results during the query phase.

Elasticsearch provides several analyzers in its standard installation. In the following table, the most common ones are described:

Name	Description
standard	It divides the text using a standard tokenizer–normalize tokens, lowercase tokens and remove unwanted tokens.
simple	It divides text at non-letter and converts them to lowercase.
whitespace	It divides text at spaces.
stop	It processes the text with standard analyzer, then applies custom stopwords.
keyword	It considers the all text as a token.
pattern	It divides text using a regular expression.
snowball	It works as a standard analyzer plus a stemming at the end of processing.

For special language purposes, Elasticsearch supports a set of analyzers aimed at analyzing specific language text, such as Arabic, Armenian, Basque, Brazilian, Bulgarian, Catalan, Chinese, Cjk, Czech, Danish, Dutch, English, Finnish, French, Galician, German, Greek, Hindi, Hungarian, Indonesian, Italian, Norwegian, Persian, Portuguese, Romanian, Russian, Spanish, Swedish, Turkish, and Thai.

See also

There are several Elasticsearch plugins that extend the list of available analyzers. The most famous ones are:

- ICU analysis plugin
  (https://www.elastic.co/guide/en/elasticsearch/plugins/master/analysis-icu.html)
- Phonetic analysis plugin
  (https://www.elastic.co/guide/en/elasticsearch/plugins/master/analysis-phonetic.html)
- Smart chinese analysis plugin
  (https://www.elastic.co/guide/en/elasticsearch/plugins/master/analysis-smartcn.html)
- Japanese (kuromoji) analysis plugin
  (https://www.elastic.co/guide/en/elasticsearch/plugins/master/analysis-kuromoji.html)

Mapping a completion field

For providing search functionalities for our user, one of the most common requirements is to provide text suggestion for our query.

Elasticsearch provides a helper for archiving this functionality via a special type mapping called **completion**.

Getting ready

You need an up-and-running Elasticsearch installation as we described in the *Downloading and installing Elasticsearch* recipe in Chapter 2, *Downloading and Setup*.

How to do it...

The definition of a completion field is similar to the previous core type fields. For example, to provide suggestion for a name with alias, we can write a similar mapping:

```
{
    "name": {"type": "string", "copy_to":["suggest"]},
    "alias": {"type": "string", "copy_to":["suggest"]},
    "suggest": {
        "type": "completion",
        "payloads": true,
        "analyzer": "simple",
        "search_analyzer": "simple"
    }
}
```

In this example, we have defined two string fields `name` and `alias` and a `suggest` completer for them.

How it works...

There are several ways in Elasticsearch for providing a suggestion. You can have the same functionality also using some queries with wildcards or prefix, but the completion fields are much faster due to natively optimized structures used.

Internally, Elasticsearch builds a **Finite State Transducer** (**FST**) structure for suggesting terms. (The topic is described in great detail at the following Wikipedia page `http://en.wikipedia.org/wiki/Finite_state_transducer`.)

The most important properties that can be configured to use the `completion` field are:

- `analyzer`: This defines the analyzer to be used for indexing within this document. The default is simple for keeping stopwords in suggested terms such as at, the, of, and so (default `simple`).
- `search_analyzer`: This defines the analyzer to be used for searching (default `simple`).
- `preserve_separators`: This controls how tokens are processed . If disabled, the `spaces` are trimmed in suggestion and allows to match `fightc` as `fight club` (default `true`).
- `max_input_length`: This property reduces the characters in the input string to reduce the suggester size. Try to suggest that the longest text is nonsense because it is against usability (default `50`) .

- `payloads`: This allows storing payloads (additional item values to be returned) (default `false`). For example, if you are searching for a book, it will be useful as it not only returns the book title, but also it's ISBN. This is shown in the below example:

```
curl -X PUT 'http://localhost:9200/myindex/mytype/1' -d '{
    "name" : "Elasticsearch Cookbook",      "suggest" : {
    "input": ["ES", "Elasticsearch", "Elastic Search", "Elastic
    Search Cookbook" ],
    "output": "Elasticsearch Cookbook",
    "payload" : { "isbn" : "1782166629" },
    "weight" : 34
  }
}'
```

In the preceding example, we are able to see some functionalities that are available during indexing time for the `completion` field and they are:

- `input`: This manages a list of provided values usable for suggesting. If you are able to enrich your data, this can improve the quality of your suggester.
- `output`: This is the wished suggester result to be shown (optional).
- `payload`: This includes some extra data to be returned (optional).
- `weight`: This is a weight boost to be used to score suggester (optional).

At the start of the recipe, I've used a shortcut using the `copy_to` field property to populate the completion field from several fields. The `copy_to` property simply copies the content of one field in one or more other fields.

See also

- In this recipe, we have discussed only the mapping and indexing functionality of completion, the search part will be discussed in the *Suggesting a Correct Query* recipe in `Chapter 5`, *Search*

4
Basic Operations

In this chapter, we will cover the following recipes:

- Creating an index
- Deleting an index
- Opening/closing an index
- Putting a mapping in an index
- Getting a mapping
- Reindexing an index
- Refreshing an index
- Flushing an index
- ForceMerge an index
- Shrinking an index
- Checking if an index or type exists
- Managing index settings
- Using index aliases
- Rollover an index
- Indexing a document
- Getting a document
- Deleting a document
- Updating a document
- Speeding up atomic operations (bulk operations)
- Speeding up GET operations (multi GET)

Introduction

Before starting with indexing and searching in Elasticsearch, we need to cover how to manage indices and perform operations on documents. In this chapter, we'll start discussing different operations on indices such as `create`, `delete`, `update`, `open`, and `close`. These operations are very important because they allow you to better define the container (index) that will store your documents. The index `create`/`delete` actions are similar to the SQL `create`/`delete` database commands.

After the indices management part, we'll learn how to manage mappings to complete the discussion started in the previous chapter and to lay the basis for the next chapter which is mainly centered on search.

A large portion of this chapter is dedicated to **Create–Read–Update–Delete** (**CRUD**) operations on records that are the **core** of records storing and management in Elasticsearch.

To improve indexing performance, it's also important to understand bulk operations and avoid their common pitfalls.

This chapter doesn't cover operations involving queries, as this is the main theme of the following chapters such as `Chapter 5`, *Search*, `Chapter 6`, *Text and Numeric Queries* and `Chapter 7`, *Relationships and Geo Queries*, and cluster operations that will be discussed in `Chapter 10`, *Managing Clusters and Nodes* because they are mainly related to control and monitoring the cluster.

Creating an index

The first operation to do before starting indexing data in Elasticsearch is to create an index–the main container of our data.

An index is similar to the concept of a database in SQL, a container for types (tables in SQL) and documents (records in SQL).

Getting ready

You need an up-and-running Elasticsearch installation, as used in the *Downloading and installing Elasticsearch* recipe in `Chapter 2`, *Downloading and Setup*.

To execute `curl` via the command line, you need to install `curl` for your operative system.

How to do it...

The HTTP method to create an index is PUT (but also POST works); the REST URL contains the index name:

```
http://<server>/<index_name>
```

For creating an index, we will perform the following steps:

1. From the command line, we can execute a PUT call:

```
curl -XPUT http://127.0.0.1:9200/myindex -d '{
    "settings" : {
    "index" : {
    "number_of_shards" : 2,
    "number_of_replicas" : 1
  }
 }
}'
```

2. The result returned by Elasticsearch should be:

```
{"acknowledged":true,"shards_acknowledged":true}
```

3. If the index already exists, a 400 error is returned:

```
{
"error" : {
"root_cause" : [
  {
    "type" : "index_already_exists_exception",
    "reason" : "index [myindex/YJRxuqvkQWOe3VuTaTbu7g] already
    exists",
    "index_uuid" : "YJRxuqvkQWOe3VuTaTbu7g",
    "index" : "myindex"
  }
 ],
"type" : "index_already_exists_exception",
"reason" : "index [myindex/YJRxuqvkQWOe3VuTaTbu7g] already
exists",
"index_uuid" : "YJRxuqvkQWOe3VuTaTbu7g",
"index" : "myindex"
  },
"status" : 400
}
```

How it works...

During index creation, the replication can be set with two parameters in the `settings/index` object:

- `number_of_shards`, which controls the number of shards that compose the index (every shard can store up to 2^{32} documents)
- `number_of_replicas`, which controls the number of replications (how many times your data is replicated in the cluster for high availability)

- A good practice is to set this value at least to `1`

The API call initializes a new index, which means:

- The index is created in a primary node first and then its status is propagated to all nodes of the cluster level
- A default mapping (empty) is created
- All the shards required by the index are initialized and ready to accept data

The index creation API allows defining the mapping during creation time. The parameter required to define a mapping is `mapping` and accepts multi mappings. So in a single call it is possible to create an index and put the required mappings.

There are also some limitations to the index name; the only accepted characters are as follows:

- ASCII letters `[a-z]`
- Numbers `[0-9]`
- point `.`, minus `-`, `&` and `_`

There's more...

The `create index` command allows passing also the mappings section, which contains the mapping definitions. It is a shortcut to creating an index with mappings, without executing an extra `PUT` mapping call.

A common example of this call, using the mapping from the *Putting a mapping in an index* recipe, is as follows:

```
curl -XPOST localhost:9200/myindex -d '{
    "settings" : {
        "number_of_shards" : 2,
        "number_of_replicas" : 1
    },
    "mappings" : {
      "order" : {
          "properties" : {
              "id" : {"type" : "keyword", "store" : "yes"},
              "date" : {"type" : "date", "store" : "no" ,
              "index":"not_analyzed"},
              "customer_id" : {"type" : "keyword", "store" :
                               "yes"},
              "sent" : {"type" : "boolea+n",
                        "index":"not_analyzed"},
              "name" : {"type" : "text", "index":"analyzed"},
              "quantity" : {"type" : "integer",
                            "index":"not_analyzed"},
              "vat" : {"type" : "double", "index":"no"}
          }
      }
    }
}'
```

See also

- All the main concepts related to index are discussed in the *Understanding clusters, replication, and sharding* recipe in `Chapter 1`, *Getting Started*
- After having created an index, you generally need to add a mapping as described in the *Putting a mapping in an index* recipe in this chapter

Deleting an index

The counterpart of creating an index is deleting one. Deleting an index means deleting its shards, mappings, and data. There are many common scenarios when we need to delete an index, such as:

- Removing the index to clean unwanted/obsolete data (for example, old Logstash indices).
- Resetting an index for a scratch restart.
- Deleting an index that has some missing shards, mainly due to some failures, to bring the cluster back in a valid state. (If a node dies and it's storing a single replica shard of an index, this index is missing a shard so the cluster state becomes red. In this case, you'll bring back the cluster to a green status, but you lose the data contained in the deleted index.)

Getting ready

You need an up-and-running Elasticsearch installation, as used in the *Downloading and installing Elasticsearch* recipe in `Chapter 2`, *Downloading and Setup*.

To execute `curl` via the command line, you need to install `curl` for your operative system.

The index created in the previous recipe is required to be deleted.

How to do it...

The HTTP method used to delete an index is `DELETE`. The following URL contains only the index name:

```
http://<server>/<index_name>
```

For deleting an index, we will perform the steps given as follows:

1. Execute a `DELETE` call, by writing the following command:

```
curl -XDELETE http://127.0.0.1:9200/myindex
```

2. We check the result returned by Elasticsearch. If everything is all right, it should be:

```
{"acknowledged":true}
```

3. If the index doesn't exist, a `404` error is returned:

```
{
    "error" : {
    "root_cause" : [
    {
        "type" : "index_not_found_exception",
        "reason" : "no such index",
        "resource.type" : "index_or_alias",
        "resource.id" : "myindex",
        "index_uuid" : "_na_",
        "index" : "myindex"
      }
    ],
        "type" : "index_not_found_exception",
        "reason" : "no such index",
        "resource.type" : "index_or_alias",
        "resource.id" : "myindex",
        "index_uuid" : "_na_",
        "index" : "myindex"
    },
    "status" : 404
}
```

How it works...

When an index is deleted, all the data related to the index is removed from the disk and is lost.

During the delete processing, first the cluster is updated, and then the shards are deleted from the storage. This operation is very fast; in a traditional filesystem it is implemented as a recursive delete.

It's not possible restore a deleted index if there is no backup.

Also, calling using the special `_all index_name` can be used to remove all the indices. In production it is good practice to disable the *all indices deletion* by adding the following line to `elasticsearch.yml`:

```
action.destructive_requires_name:true
```

See also

- The previous recipe, *Creating an index*, is strongly related to this recipe.

Opening/closing an index

If you want to keep your data but save resources (memory/CPU), a good alternative to deleting indexes is to close them.

Elasticsearch allows you to open/close an index putting it into online/offline mode.

Getting ready

You need an up-and-running Elasticsearch installation, as used in the *Downloading and installing Elasticsearch* recipe in `Chapter 2`, *Downloading and Setup*.

To execute `curl` via the command line, you need to install `curl` for your operative system.

To correctly execute the following commands, the index created in the *Creating an index* recipe is required.

How to do it...

For opening/closing an index, we will perform the following steps:

1. From the command line, we can execute a `POST` call to close an index using:

```
curl -XPOST http://127.0.0.1:9200/myindex/_close
```

2. If the call is successful, the result returned by Elasticsearch should be:

```
{,"acknowledged":true}
```

3. To open an index from the command line, type the following command:

```
curl -XPOST http://127.0.0.1:9200/myindex/_open
```

4. If the call is successful, the result returned by Elasticsearch should be:

```
{"acknowledged":true}
```

How it works...

When an index is closed, there is no overhead on the cluster (except for metadata state): the index shards are switched off and they don't use file descriptors, memory, or threads.

There are many use cases when closing an index:

- Disabling date-based indices (indices that store their records by date), for example, when you keep an index for a week, month, or day and you want to keep a fixed number of old indices (that is, two months) online and some offline (that is, from two months to six months).
- When you do searches on all the active indices of a cluster and don't want to search in some indices (in this case, using an alias is the best solution, but you can achieve the same concept as an alias with closed indices).

> An alias cannot have the same name as an index.

When an index is closed, calling open restores its state.

See also

- In the *Using index aliases* recipe in this chapter, we will discuss advanced usage of indices references in a time-based index to simplify management on opened indices.

Putting a mapping in an index

In the previous chapter, we saw how to build mapping by indexing documents. This recipe shows how to put a type mapping in an index. This kind of operation can be considered as the Elasticsearch version of an SQL-created table.

Getting ready

You need an up-and-running Elasticsearch installation,as used in the *Downloading and installing Elasticsearch* recipe in `Chapter 2`, *Downloading and Setup*.

To execute `curl` via the command line, you need to install `curl` for your operative system.

To correctly execute the following commands, the index created in the *Creating an index* recipe is required.

How to do it...

The HTTP method to put a mapping is PUT (also POST works). The URL format for putting a mapping is:

```
http://<server>/<index_name>/<type_name>/_mapping
```

For putting a mapping in an index, we will perform the steps given as follows:

1. If we consider the type order of the previous chapter, the call will be as follows:

```
curl -XPUT 'http://localhost:9200/myindex/order/_mapping' -d '{
     "order" : {
     "properties" : {
     "id" : {"type" : "keyword", "store" : "yes"},
     "date" : {"type" : "date", "store" : "no" ,
             "index":"not_analyzed"},
     "customer_id" : {"type" : "keyword", "store" : "yes"},
     "sent" : {"type" : "boolean", "index":"not_analyzed"},
     "name" : {"type" : "text", "index":"analyzed"},
     "quantity" : {"type" : "integer",
                "index":"not_analyzed"},
     "vat" : {"type" : "double", "index":"no"}
     }
   }
 }'
```

2. In case of success, the result returned by Elasticsearch should be:

```
{"acknowledged":true}
```

How it works...

This call checks if the index exists and then it creates one or more type mapping as described in the definition. To learn how to define a mapping description, see `Chapter 3, Managing Mappings`.

During mapping insert, if there is an existing mapping for this type, it is merged with the new one. If there is a field with a different type and the type could not be updated, an exception expanding `fields` property is raised. To prevent an exception during the merging mapping phase, it's possible to specify the `ignore_conflicts` parameter to `true` (default is `false`).

The `PUT` mapping call allows you to set the type for several indices in one shot; list the indices separated by commas or to apply all indexes using the _all alias.

There's more...

There is not a delete operation for mapping. It's not possible to delete a single mapping from an index. To remove or change a mapping you need to manage the following steps:

1. Create a new index with the new/modified mapping
2. Reindex all the records
3. Delete the old index with incorrect mapping

In Elasticsearch 5.x there is also a new operation to speed up this process: the reindex command that we will see in the *Reindex an index* recipe in this chapter.

See also

- Strongly related to this recipe is the *Getting a mapping* recipe, which allows you to control the exact result of the put mapping command

Getting a mapping

After having set our mappings for processing types, we sometimes need to control or analyze the mapping to prevent issues. The action to get the mapping for a type helps us to understand the structure or its evolution due to some merge and implicit type guessing.

Getting ready

You need an up-and-running Elasticsearch installation, as used in the *Downloading and installing Elasticsearch* recipe in `Chapter 2`, *Downloading and Setup*.

To execute `curl` via the command line, you need to install `curl` for your operative system.

To correctly execute the following commands, the mapping created in the *Putting a mapping in an index* recipe is required.

How to do it...

The HTTP method to get a mapping is `GET`. The URL formats for getting mappings are:

`http://<server>/_mapping`

`http://<server>/<index_name>/_mapping`

`http://<server>/<index_name>/<type_name>/_mapping`

To get a mapping from the type of an index, we will perform the following steps:

1. If we consider the type `order` of the previous chapter, the call will be as follows:

   ```
   curl -XGET 'http://localhost:9200/myindex/order/_mapping?
   pretty=true'
   ```

   The pretty argument in the URL is optional, but very handy to pretty print the response output.

2. The result returned by Elasticsearch should be as follows:

```
{
    "myindex" : {
        "mappings" : {
            "order" : {
                "properties" : {
                    "customer_id" : {
                        "type" : "keyword",
            "store" : true
            },
    ... truncated
            }
        }
    }
}
}
```

How it works...

The mapping is stored at the cluster level in Elasticsearch. The call checks both index and type existence and then it returns the stored mapping.

The returned mapping is in a reduced form, which means that the default values for a field are not returned.

Elasticsearch, to reduce network and memory consumption, returns only not default values.

Retrieving a mapping is very useful for several purposes:

- Debugging template level mapping
- Checking if implicit mapping was derivated correctly by guessing fields
- Retrieving the mapping metadata, which can be used to store type-related information
- Simply checking if the mapping is correct

If you need to fetch several mappings, it is better to do it at index level or cluster level to reduce the numbers of API calls.

See also

- To insert a mapping in an index, refer to the *Putting a mapping in an index* recipe in this chapter
- To manage dynamic mapping in an index, refer to the *Using dynamic templates in document mapping* recipe in `Chapter 3`, *Managing Mappings*

Reindexing an index

There are a lot of common scenarios that involve changing your mapping. Due to limitation to Elasticsearch mapping, that is, it not being possible to delete a defined one, you often need to reindex index data. The most common scenarios are:

- Changing an analyzer for a mapping
- Adding a new subfield to a mapping and you need to reprocess all the records to search for the new subfield
- Removing an unused mapping
- Changing a record structure that requires a new mapping

Getting ready

You need an up-and-running Elasticsearch installation, as used in the *Downloading and installing Elasticsearch* recipe in `Chapter 2`, *Downloading and Setup*.

To execute `curl` via the command line, you need to install `curl` for your operative system.

To correctly execute the following commands, the index created in the *Creating an index* recipe is required.

How to do it...

The HTTP method to reindex an index is `POST`. The URL formats to get mapping is `http://<server>/_reindex`.

To get a mapping from the type of an index, we will perform the steps given as follows:

1. If we want to reindex data from `myindex` to the `myindex2` index, the call will be:

```
curl -XPOST 'http://localhost:9200/_reindex?pretty=true' -d '{
  "source": {
    "index": "myindex"
  },
  "dest": {
    "index": "myindex2"
  }
}'
```

2. The result returned by Elasticsearch should be:

```
{
  "took" : 66,
  "timed_out" : false,
  "total" : 2,
  "updated" : 0,
  "created" : 2,
  "deleted" : 0,
  "batches" : 1,
  "version_conflicts" : 0,
  "noops" : 0,
  "retries" : {
    "bulk" : 0,
    "search" : 0
  },
  "throttled_millis" : 0,
  "requests_per_second" : "unlimited",
  "throttled_until_millis" : 0,
  "failures" : [ ]
}
```

How it works...

The reindex functionality introduced in Elasticsearch 5.x provides an efficient way to reindex a document.

In the previous Elasticsearch version, this functionality was to be implemented at a client level. The advantages of the new Elasticsearch implementations are as follows:

- Fast copy of data because it is completely managed to server side.
- Better management of the operation due to the new task API.
- Better error handling support as it is done at server level. This allows us to better manage failover during the reindex operation.

At server level, this action is composed of the following steps:

1. Initialization of an Elasticsearch task to manage the operation.
2. Creation of the target index and copying the source mappings if required.
3. Executing a query to collect the documents to be reindexed.
4. Reindex all the documents via bulk operations until all documents are reindexed.

The main parameters that can be provided to this action are:

- The `source` section that manages how to select source documents. The most important sub sections are as follows:
    - `index`, which is the source index to be used. It can also be a list of indices.
    - `type` (optional), which is the source type to be reindexed. It can also be a list of types.
    - `query` (optional), which is an Elasticsearch query to be used to select parts of the document.
    - `sort` (optional), which can be used to provide a way of sorting the documents.
- The `dest` section that manages how to control the target written documents. The most important parameters in this section are:
    - `index`, which is the target index to be used. If it is not available, it's created.
    - `version_type` (optional), if it is set to external, the external version is preserved.
    - `routing` (optional), which controls the routing in the destination index. It can be:
    - `keep` (the default), which preserves the original routing

- `discard`, which discards the original routing
- `=<text>`, which uses the text value for the routing
- `pipeline` (optional), which allows you to define a custom pipeline for ingestion. We will see more about the ingestion pipeline in `Chapter 13`, *Ingest*.
- `size` (optional), the number of documents to be reindexed.
- `script` (optional), which allows you to define a scripting for document manipulation. This case will be discussed in the *Reindex with a custom script* recipe in `Chapter 9`, *Scripting*.

See also

- In this chapter, check out the *Speeding up atomic operation* recipe, which will talk about using the bulk operation to quickly ingest data. The bulk actions are used under the hood by the reindex functionality.
- To manage task execution, please refer to the *Using the task management API* recipe in `Chapter 10`, *Managing Clusters and Nodes*.
- The *Reindex with a custom script* recipe in `Chapter 9`, *Scripting*, which will show several common scenarios for reindexing documents with a custom script.
- `Chapter 13`, *Ingest* will discuss how to use the ingestion pipeline.

Refreshing an index

Elasticsearch allows the user to control the state of the searcher using forced refresh on an index. If not forced, the newly indexed document will be only searchable after a fixed time interval (usually one second).

Getting ready

You need an up-and-running Elasticsearch installation, as used in the *Downloading and installing Elasticsearch* recipe in `Chapter 2`, *Downloading and Setup*.

To execute `curl` via the command line, you need to install `curl` for your operative system.

To correctly execute the following commands, use the index created in the *Creating an index* recipe.

How to do it...

The HTTP method used for both operations is POST. The URL formats for refreshing an index, are:

```
http://<server>/<index_name(s)>/_refresh
```

The URL formats, for refreshing all the indices in a cluster, are:

```
http://<server>/_refresh
```

For refreshing an index, we will perform the following steps:

1. If we consider the type order of the previous chapter, the call will be:

   ```
   curl -XPOST 'http://localhost:9200/myindex/_refresh'
   ```

2. The result returned by Elasticsearch should be as follows:

   ```
   {"_shards":{"total":4,"successful":2,"failed":0}}
   ```

How it works...

Near Real-Time (**NRT**) capabilities are automatically managed by Elasticsearch, which automatically refreshes the indices every second if data is changed in them.

To force a refresh before the internal Elasticsearch interval, you can call the refresh API on one or more indices (more indices are comma separated) or on all the indices.

Elasticsearch doesn't refresh the state of an index at every inserted document as to prevent poor performance due to the excessive I/O required in closing and reopening file descriptors.

> You must force the refresh to have your last index data available for searching.

Generally, the best time to call the refresh is after having indexed a lot of data to be sure that your records are searchable instantly. It's also possible to force a refresh during a document indexing, adding `refresh=true` as a query parameter. For example:

```
curl -XPOST
'http://localhost:9200/myindex/order/2qLrAfPVQvCRMe7Ku8r0Tw?
refresh=true' -d '{
    "id" : "1234",
    "date" : "2013-06-07T12:14:54",
    "customer_id" : "customer1",
    "sent" : true,
  "in_stock_items" : 0,
  "items":[
        {"name":"item1", "quantity":3, "vat":20.0},
        {"name":"item2", "quantity":2, "vat":20.0},
        {"name":"item3", "quantity":1, "vat":10.0}
    ]
}'
```

See also

- Refer to the *Flushing an index* recipe in this chapter to force indexed data writing on disk and the *ForceMerge an index* recipe to optimize an index for searching

Flushing an index

Elasticsearch for performance reasons stores some data in memory and on a transaction log. If we want to free memory, empty the transaction log, and be sure that our data is safely written on disk, we need to flush an index.

Elasticsearch automatically provides periodic flush on disk, but forcing flush can be useful, for example:

- When we need to shut down a node to prevent stale data
- To have all the data on a safe state (for example, after a big indexing operation to have all the data flushed and refreshed)

Getting ready

You need an up-and-running Elasticsearch installation, as used in the *Downloading and installing Elasticsearch* recipe in `Chapter 2`, *Downloading and Setup*.

To execute `curl` via the command line, you need to install `curl` for your operative system.

To correctly execute the following commands, use the index created in the *Creating an index* recipe.

How to do it...

The HTTP method used for both operations is `POST`. The URL format for flushing an index, is:

```
http://<server>/<index_name(s)>/_flush[?refresh=True]
```

The URL format for flushing all the indices in a cluster, is:

```
http:///_flush[?refresh=True]
```

1. For flushing an index, we will perform the steps given as follows: if we consider the type order of the previous chapter, the call will be as follows:

   ```
   curl -XPOST 'http://localhost:9200/myindex/_flush?refresh=true'
   ```

2. If everything is all right, the result returned by Elasticsearch should be:

   ```
   {"_shards":{"total":4,"successful":2,"failed":0}}
   ```

The result contains the shard operation status.

How it works...

To reduce writing, Elasticsearch tries not to put overhead in I/O operations and it caches in memory some data until refresh to execute a multi-documents single write to improve performance.

To clean up memory and force this data on disk, the `flush` operation is required.

In the flush call, it is possible to give an extra request parameter, `refresh`, to also force the index refresh.

> Flushing too often affects index performance. Use it wisely!

See also

- In this chapter, refer to the *Refreshing an index* recipe to search for more recently indexed data and the *ForceMerge an index* recipe to optimize an index for searching

ForceMerge an index

The Elasticsearch core is based on Lucene, which stores the data in segments on disk. During the life of an index, a lot of segments are created and changed. With the increase of segment number, the speed of search is decreased due to the time required to read all of them. The ForceMerge operation allows us to consolidate the index for faster search performance and reducing segments.

Getting ready

You need an up-and-running Elasticsearch installation, as used in the *Downloading and installing Elasticsearch* recipe in `Chapter 2`, *Downloading and Setup*.

To execute `curl` via the command line, you need to install `curl` for your operative system.

To correctly execute the following commands, use the index created in the *Creating an index* recipe.

How to do it...

The HTTP method used is POST. The URL format for optimizing one or more indices, is:

```
http://<server>/<index_name(s)>/_flush[?refresh=True]
```

The URL format for optimizing all the indices in a cluster, is:

```
http://<server>/_flush[?refresh=True]
```

For optimizing or to ForceMerge an index, we will perform the steps given as follows:

1. If we consider the index created in the *Creating an index* recipe, the call will be:

    ```
    curl -XPOST 'http://localhost:9200/myindex/_forcemerge'
    ```

2. The result returned by Elasticsearch should be:

    ```
    {
      "_shards" : {
        "total" : 10,
        "successful" : 5,
        "failed" : 0
      }
    }
    ```

The result contains the shard operation status.

How it works...

Lucene stores your data in several segments on disk. These segments are created when you index a new document/record or when you delete a document.

In Elasticsearch the deleted document is not removed from disk, but marked deleted (tombstone), to free up space you need to ForceMerge to purge deleted documents.

Due to all these factors the segment number can be large. (For this reason, in the setup we have increased the file description number for Elasticsearch processes.)

Internally Elasticsearch has a merger, which tries to reduce the number of segments, but it's designed to improve the index performances rather than search performances. The ForceMerge operation in Lucene tries to reduce the segments in an IO-heavy way, removing unused ones, purging deleted documents, and rebuilding the index with the minor number of segments.

The main advantages are:

- Reducing both file descriptors
- Freeing memory used by the segment readers
- Improving performance in search due to less segments management

> ForceMerge is a very IO-heavy operation. The index can be unresponsive during this optimization. It is generally executed on indices that rarely are modified, such as Logstash previous days.

There's more...

You can pass several additional parameters to the ForceMerge call, such as:

- `max_num_segments`: The default value is `autodetect`. For full optimization, set this value to 1.
- `only_expunge_deletes`: The default value is `false`. Lucene does not delete documents from segments, but it marks them as deleted. This flag only merges segments that have been deleted.
- `flush`: The default value is `true`. Elasticsearch performs a flush after force merge.
- `wait_for_merge`: The default value is `true`. If the request needs to wait then the merge ends.

See also

- In this chapter, refer to the *Refreshing an index* recipe to search for more recent indexed data and the *Flushing an index* recipe to force indexed data writing on disk

Shrinking an index

The latest version of Elasticsearch provides a new way to optimize the index, via the shrink API it's possible to reduce the number of shards of an index.

This feature targets several common scenarios:

- The wrong number of shards during the initial design sizing. Often sizing the shards without knowing the correct data/text distribution tends to oversize the number of shards
- Reducing the number of shards to reduce memory and resource usage
- Reducing the number of shards to speed up searching

Getting ready

You need an up-and-running Elasticsearch installation, as used in the *Downloading and installing Elasticsearch* recipe in `Chapter 2`, *Downloading and Setup*.

To execute `curl` via the command line, you need to install `curl` for your operative system.

To correctly execute the following commands, use the index created in the *Creating an index* recipe.

How to do it...

The HTTP method used is `POST`. The URL format for optimizing one or more indices, is:

```
http://<server>/<source_index_name>/_shrink/<target_index_name>
```

To shrink an index, we will perform the steps given as follows:

1. We need all the primary shards of the index to be shrinking in the same node. We need the name of the node that will contain the shrink index. We can retrieve it via the `_nodes` API:

   ```
   curl -XGET 'http://localhost:9200/_nodes?pretty'
   ```

   In the result there will be a similar section:

   ```
   ....
   "nodes" : {
       "5Sei9ip8Qhee3J0o9dTV4g" : {
   ```

```
        "name" : "Gin Genie",
        "transport_address" : "127.0.0.1:9300",
        "host" : "127.0.0.1",
        "ip" : "127.0.0.1",
        "version" : "5.0.0-alpha4",
    ....
```

The name of my node is `Gin Genie`

2. Now we can change the index settings, forcing allocation to a single node for our index, and disabling the writing for the index. This can be done via:

```
curl -XPUT 'http://localhost:9200/myindex/_settings' -d '
{
  "settings": {
  "index.routing.allocation.require._name": "Gin Genie",
  "index.blocks.write": true
  }
}'
```

3. We need to check if all the shards are relocated. We can check for the green status:

```
curl -XGET 'http://localhost:9200/_cluster/health?pretty'
```

The result will be:

```
{
  "cluster_name" : "ESCookBook3",
  "status" : "green",
  "timed_out" : false,
  "number_of_nodes" : 2,
  "number_of_data_nodes" : 2,
  "active_primary_shards" : 15,
  "active_shards" : 15,
  "relocating_shards" : 0,
  "initializing_shards" : 0,
  "unassigned_shards" : 15,
  "delayed_unassigned_shards" : 0,
  "number_of_pending_tasks" : 0,
  "number_of_in_flight_fetch" : 0,
  "task_max_waiting_in_queue_millis" : 0,
  "active_shards_percent_as_number" : 50.0
}
```

4. The index should be in a read-only state to shrink. We need to disable the writing for the index via:

```
curl -XPUT 'http://localhost:9200/myindex/_settings?
index.blocks.write=true'
```

5. If we consider the index created in the *Creating an index* recipe, the shrink call for creating the `reduced_index`, will be:

```
curl -XPOST
'http://localhost:9200/myindex/_shrink/reduced_index' -d '{
"settings": {
"index.number_of_replicas": 1,
"index.number_of_shards": 1,
"index.codec": "best_compression"
    },
"aliases": {
"my_search_indices": {}
  }
}'
```

6. The result returned by Elasticsearch should be:

```
{"acknowledged":true}
```

7. We can also wait for a `yellow` status if the index it is ready to work:

```
curl -XGET 'http://localhost:9200/_cluster/health?
wait_for_status=yellow'
```

8. Now we can remove the read-only by changing the index settings:

```
curl -XPUT 'http://localhost:9200/myindex/_settings?
index.blocks.write=true'
```

How it works...

The shrink API reduces the number of shards, executing the following steps:

1. Elasticsearch creates a new target index with the same definition as the source index, but with a smaller number of primary shards.
2. Elasticsearch hard-links (or copies) segments from the source index into the target index.

If the filesystem doesn't support hard-linking, then all segments are copied into the new index, which is a much more time consuming process.

Elasticsearch recovers the target index as though it were a closed index that has just been reopened. On a Linux system the process is very fast due to hard-links.

The prerequisites for executing a shrink are as follows:

- All the primary shards must be on the same node
- The target index must not exist
- The target number of shards must be a factor of the number of shards in the source index

There's more...

This Elasticsearch functionality provides support for new scenarios in Elasticsearch usage.

The first scenario is when you over estimate the number of shards. If you don't know your data, it's difficult to choose the correct number of shards to be used. So often a Elasticsearch user tends to oversize the number of shards.

Another interesting scenario is to use shrinking to provide a boost at indexing time. The main way to speed up Elasticsearch writing capabilities to a high number of documents is to create indices with a lot of shards (in general, the ingestion speed is about equal to the number of shards multiplied for document/second ingested by a single shard). The standard allocation moves the shards on different nodes, so generally the more shards you have, the faster the writing speed: so to achieve fast writing speed you create 15 or 30 shards for index. After the indexing phase, the index doesn't receive new records (such as time-based indices): the index is only searched, so to speed up the search you can shrink your shards.

See also

- In this chapter, refer to the *ForceMerge an index* recipe to optimize your indices for searching

Checking if an index or type exists

A common pitfall error is to query for indices and types that don't exist. To prevent this issue, Elasticsearch gives the user the ability to check the index and type existence.

This check is often used during an application startup to create indices and types that are required for correct working.

Getting ready

You need an up-and-running Elasticsearch installation, as used in the *Downloading and installing Elasticsearch* recipe in `Chapter 2`, *Downloading and Setup*.

To execute `curl` via the command line, you need to install `curl` for your operative system.

To correctly execute the following commands, use the index created in the *Creating an index* recipe.

How to do it...

The HTTP method to check existence is `HEAD`. The URL format for checking an index is:

`http://<server>/<index_name>/`

The URL format for checking a type is:

`http://<server>/<index_name>/<type>/`

To check if an index exists, we will perform the steps given as follows:

1. If we consider the index created in the *Creating an index* recipe, the call will be:

   ```
   curl -i -XHEAD 'http://localhost:9200/myindex/'
   ```

2. The `-i curl options` allows dumping the server headers.

3. If the index exists, an HTTP status code 200 is returned, if missing, a 404. For checking if a type exists, we will perform the steps given as follows:

4. If we consider the mapping created in the *Putting a mapping in an index* recipe, the call will be as follows:

```
curl -i -XHEAD 'http://localhost:9200/myindex/order/'
```

5. If the index exists, an HTTP status code 200 is returned, if missing, a 404.

How it works...

This is a typical HEAD REST call to check existence. It doesn't return body response, but only the status code, which is the result status of the operation.

The most common status codes are:

- 20X family if everything is okay
- 404 if the resource is not available
- 50X family if there are server errors

> **TIP**
> Before every action involved in indexing, generally on application startup, it's good practice to check if an index or type exists to prevent future failures.

Managing index settings

Index settings are more important because they allow you to control several important Elasticsearch functionalities such as sharding/replica, caching, term management, routing, and analysis.

Getting ready

You need an up-and-running Elasticsearch installation, as used in the *Downloading and installing Elasticsearch* recipe in Chapter 2, *Downloading and Setup*.

To execute `curl` via the command line, you need to install `curl` for your operative system.

To correctly execute the following commands, use the index created in the *Creating an index* recipe.

How to do it…

For managing the index settings, we will perform the following steps:

1. To retrieve the settings of your current index, use the following URL format:
   ```
   http://<server>/<index_name>/_settings
   ```

2. We are reading information via the REST API, so the method will be `GET` and an example of call, using the index created in the *Creating an index* recipe, is as follows:
   ```
   curl -XGET 'http://localhost:9200/myindex/_settings?
   pretty=true'
   ```

3. The response will be something similar:
   ```
   {
     "myindex" : {
       "settings" : {
         "index" : {
           "uuid" : "pT65_cn_RHKmg1wPX7BGjw",
           "number_of_replicas" : "1",
           "number_of_shards" : "2",
           "version" : {
             "created" : "1020099"
           }
         }
       }
     }
   }
   ```

4. The response attributes depend on the index settings set. In this case, the response will be the number of replicas (1), shards (2), and the index creation version (1020099). The UUID represents the unique ID of the index.

5. To modify the index settings, we need to use the `PUT` method. A typical settings change is to increase the replica number:

```
curl -XPUT 'http://localhost:9200/myindex/_settings' -d '
{"index":{ "number_of_replicas": "2"}}'
```

How it works...

Elasticsearch provides a lot of options to tune the index behaviors, such as:

- **Replica management**:
    - `index.number_of_replicas`: The number of replicas each shard has
    - `index.auto_expand_replicas`: This allows you to define a dynamic number of replicas related to the number of shards

> Using `set index.auto_expand_replicas` to `0-all` allows creating an index that is replicated in every node (very useful for settings or cluster propagated data such as language options/stopwords).

- **Refresh interval (default 1s)**: In the *Refreshing an index* recipe, we saw how to manually refresh an index. The index settings `index.refresh_interval` control the rate of automatic refresh.
- **Write management**: Elasticsearch provides several settings to block read/write operation in the index and to change metadata. They live in the `index.blocks` settings.
- **Shard Allocation Management**: These settings control how the shards must be allocated. They live in the `index.routing.allocation.*` namespace.

There are other index settings that can be configured for very specific needs. In every new version of Elasticsearch, the community extends these settings to cover new scenarios and requirements.

There's more…

The `refresh_interval` parameter allows several tricks to optimize the indexing speed. It controls the rate of refresh and refreshing and reduces the index performances due to opening and closing of files. A good practice is to disable the refresh interval *(set -1)* during a big bulk indexing and restore the default behavior after it. This can be done with these steps:

1. Disable the refresh:

   ```
   curl -XPOST 'http://localhost:9200/myindex/_settings' -d '
   {"index":{"index_refresh_interval": "-1"}}'
   ```

2. Bulk index millions of documents.
3. Restore the refresh:

   ```
   curl -XPOST 'http://localhost:9200/myindex/_settings' -d '
   {"index":{"index_refresh_interval": "1s"}}'
   ```

4. Optionally, you can optimize index for search performances:

   ```
   curl -XPOST 'http://localhost:9200/myindex/_optimize'
   ```

See also

- In this chapter, refer to the *Refreshing an index* recipe to search for more recent indexed data and the *ForceMerge an index* recipe to optimize an index for searching.

Using index aliases

Real-world applications have a lot of indices and queries that span on more indices. This scenario requires defining all the indices names on which queries; aliases allow grouping them in a common name.

Some common scenarios of this usage are as follows:

- Log indices divided by date (that is, log_YYMMDD) for which we want to create an alias for *the last week, the last month, today, yesterday,* and so on. This pattern is commonly used in log applications such as Logstash (http://logstash.net/).
- Collecting website contents in several indices (*New York Times, The Guardian, …*) for those we want refers as an index alias called *sites.*

Getting ready

You need an up-and-running Elasticsearch installation, as used in the *Downloading and installing Elasticsearch* recipe in Chapter 2, *Downloading and Setup.*

To execute curl via the command line, you need to install curl for your operative system.

How to do it...

The URL format for control aliases is:

http://<server>/_aliases

http://<server>/<index>/_alias/<alias_name>

For managing the index aliases, we will perform the steps given as follows:

1. We are reading the aliases, status for all indices via the REST API, so the method will be GET and an example of call is:

   ```
   curl -XGET 'http://localhost:9200/_aliases'
   ```

2. Giving a response similar to this one:

   ```
   {
       "myindex": {
           "aliases": {}
       },
       "test": {
           "aliases": {}
       }
   }
   ```

3. Aliases can be changed with add and delete commands.
4. To read an alias for a single index, we use the `_alias` endpoint:

```
curl -XGET 'http://localhost:9200/myindex/_alias'
```

The result should be as follows:

```
{
    "myindex" : {
    "aliases" : {
    "myalias1" : { }
    }
  }
}
```

5. To add an alias, type the following command:

```
curl -XPUT 'http://localhost:9200/myindex/_alias/myalias1'
```

The result should be as follows:

```
{"acknowledged":true}
```

This action adds the `myindex` index to the `myalias1` alias.

6. To delete an alias, type the following command:

```
curl -XDELETE 'http://localhost:9200/myindex/_alias/myalias1'
```

The result should be:

```
{"acknowledged":true}
```

The *delete action* removed `myindex` from the `myalias1` alias.

How it works...

Elasticsearch, during search operations, automatically expands the alias, so the required indices are selected.

The alias metadata is kept in the cluster state. When an alias is added/deleted, all the changes are propagated to all the cluster nodes.

Aliases are mainly functional structures to simply manage indices when data is stored in multiple indices.

There's more...

Aliases can also be used to define a filter and routing parameter.

Filters are automatically added to the query to filter out data. Routing via an alias allows us to control which shards to hit during searching and indexing.

An example of this call is:

```
curl -XPOST 'http://localhost:9200/myindex/_aliases/user1alias' -d '
  {
    "filter" : {
      "term" : { "user" : "user_1" }
    },
    "search_routing" : "1,2",
    "index_routing" : "2"
  }'
```

In this case, we are adding a new alias, *user1alias*, to a `myindex` index, adding:

- A filter to select only documents that match a field user with a `user_1` term.
- A list and a routing key to select the shards to be used during a search.
- A routing key to be used during indexing. The routing value is used to modify the destination shard of the document.

> The `search_routing` parameter allows multi value routing keys.
> The `index_routing` parameter is single value only.

Rollover an index

When using a system that manages logs, it is very common to use rolling files for your log entries. Taking this idea, we can have indices that are similar to rolling files.

We can define some conditions to be checked and leave it to Elasticsearch to automatically roll new indices and refer via an alias to only a **virtual** index.

Getting ready

You need an up-and-running Elasticsearch installation, as used in the *Downloading and installing Elasticsearch* recipe in Chapter 2, *Downloading and Setup*.

To execute curl via the command line, you need to install curl for your operative system.

How to do it...

To enable a rolling index, we need an index with an alias that only points to it. For example, to set a log rolling index we follow these steps:

1. We need an index with a logs_write alias that only points to it:

```
curl  -XPUT 'http://127.0.0.1:9200/mylogs-000001' -d '
{
  "aliases": {
    "logs_write": {}
  }
}'
```

The result will be an acknowledgement:

```
{"acknowledged":true}
```

2. We can add the rolling to the logs_write alias:

```
curl -XPOST 'http://127.0.0.1:9200/logs_write/_rollover?
pretty'-d '
{
  "conditions": {
    "max_age":    "7d",
    "max_docs":   100000
  },
  "settings": {
    "index.number_of_shards": 3
  }
}'
```

The result will be as follows:

```
{
   "old_index" : "mylogs-000001",
   "new_index" : "mylogs-000001",
   "rolled_over" : false,
   "dry_run" : false,
```

```
        "conditions" : {
          "[max_docs: 100000]" : false,
          "[max_age: 7d]" : false
        }
      }
```

3. In case your alias doesn't point to a single index, a similar error is returned:

```
{
  "error" : {
    "root_cause" : [
      {
        "type" : "illegal_argument_exception",
        "reason" : "source alias maps to multiple indices"
      }
    ],
    "type" : "illegal_argument_exception",
    "reason" : "source alias maps to multiple indices"
  },
  "status" : 400
}
```

How it works...

The rolling index is a special alias that manages the auto-creation of new indices when one of the conditions is matched.

This is a very convenient functionality because it is completely managed by Elasticsearch, reducing a lot of user custom backend code.

The information of creating the new index is taken from the source, but you can also apply custom settings on index creation.

The name convention is automatically managed by Elasticsearch, automatically incrementing the numeric part of the index name (by default, it uses six ending digits).

See also

- Refer to the *Using index aliases* recipe in this chapter to manage aliases for indices.

Indexing a document

In Elasticsearch there are two vital operations: **index** and **search**.

Indexing means storing one or more documents in an index: a similar concept of inserting records in a relational database.

In Lucene, the core engine of Elasticsearch, inserting or updating a document has the same cost: in Lucene and Elasticsearch update means replace.

Getting ready

You need an up-and-running Elasticsearch installation, as used in the *Downloading and installing Elasticsearch* recipe in `Chapter 2`, *Downloading and Setup*.

To execute `curl` via the command line, you need to install `curl` for your operative system.

To correctly execute the following commands, use the index and mapping created in the *Putting a mapping in an index* recipe.

How to do it...

To index a document, several REST entry points can be used:

Method	URL
POST	`http://<server>/<index_name>/<type>`
PUT/POST	`http://<server>/<index_name>/<type> /<id>`
PUT/POST	`http://<server>/<index_name>/<type> /<id>/_create`

To index a document, we need to perform the following steps:

1. If we consider the type `order` of the previous chapter, the call to index a document will be as follows:

   ```
   curl -XPOST
   'http://localhost:9200/myindex/order/2qLrAfPVQvCRMe7Ku8r0Tw' -d
   '{
       "id" : "1234",
       "date" : "2013-06-07T12:14:54",
   ```

```
        "customer_id" : "customer1",
        "sent" : true,
    "in_stock_items" : 0,
    "items":[
            {"name":"item1", "quantity":3, "vat":20.0},
            {"name":"item2", "quantity":2, "vat":20.0},
            {"name":"item3", "quantity":1, "vat":10.0}
        ]
    }'
```

2. If the index operation was successful, the result returned by Elasticsearch should be as follows:

```
{
    "_index" : "myindex",
    "_type" : "order",
    "_id" : "2qLrAfPVQvCRMe7Ku8r0Tw",
    "_version" : 1,
    "forced_refresh" : false,
    "_shards" : {
        "total" : 2,
        "successful" : 1,
        "failed" : 0
    },
    "created" : true
}
```

Some additional information is returned from the index operation, such as:

- An auto generated ID if it's not specified (in this example: 2qLrAfPVQvCRMe7Ku8r0Tw)
- The version of the indexed document per the Optimistic Concurrency Control (the version is 1 because it was the first time to save/update the document)
- Whether the record has been created ("create":true in this example)

How it works...

One of the most used APIs in Elasticsearch is the index. Basically, indexing a JSON document consists internally in the following steps:

1. Routing the call to the correct shard based on the ID or routing/parent metadata. If the ID is not supplied by the client, a new one is created (see the *Managing your data* recipe in Chapter 1, *Getting Started* for details).

2. Validating the sent JSON.
3. Processing the JSON according to the mapping. If new fields are present in the document (and the mapping can be updated), new fields are added in the mapping.
4. Indexing the document in the shard. If the ID already exists, it is updated.
5. If it contains nested documents, it extracts them and it processes them separately.
6. Returning information about the saved document (ID and versioning).

It's important to choose the correct ID for indexing your data. If you don't provide an ID, Elasticsearch during the indexing phase will automatically associate a new one to your document. To improve performances, the ID should generally be of the same character length to improve balancing of the data tree that stores them.

Due to the REST call nature, it's better to pay attention when not using ASCII characters due to URL encoding and decoding (or be sure that the client framework you use correctly escapes them).

Depending on the mappings, other actions take place during the indexing phase: propagation on replica, nested processing, and percolator.

The document will be available for standard search calls after a refresh (forced with an API call or after the time slice of 1 second, Neal Real-Time): every GET API on the document doesn't require a refresh and can be instantly available.

The refresh can also be forced by specifying the `refresh` parameter during indexing.

There's more...

Elasticsearch allows passing the index API URL several query parameters to control how the document is indexed. The most used ones are as follows:

- `routing`: Which controls the shard to be used for indexing, that is:

    ```
    curl -XPOST 'http://localhost:9200/myindex/order?routing=1'
    ```

- `parent`: Which defines the parent of a child document and uses this value to apply routing. The parent object must be specified in the mappings:

    ```
    curl -XPOST 'http://localhost:9200/myindex/order?parent=12'
    ```

- `timestamp`: The timestamp to be used in indexing the document. It must be activated in the mappings:

```
curl -XPOST 'http://localhost:9200/myindex/order?timestamp=
2013-01-25T19%3A22%3A22'
```

- `consistency(one/quorum/all)`: By default, an index operation succeeds if a quorum (>replica/2+1) of active shards are available. The right consistency value can be changed for index action:

```
curl -XPOST 'http://localhost:9200/myindex/order?
consistency=one'
```

- `replication (sync/async)`: Elasticsearch returns from an index operation when all the shards of the current replication group have executed the index operation. Setting the replication async, allows us to execute the index action synchronous only on the primary shard and asynchronous on secondary shards. In this way, the API call returns the response action faster:

```
curl -XPOST 'http://localhost:9200/myindex/order?
replication=async' ...
```

- `version`: The version allows us to use the **Optimistic Concurrency Control** (http://en.wikipedia.org/wiki/Optimistic_concurrency_control). The first time index of a document, the version 1, is set on the document. At every update this value is incremented. Optimistic Concurrency Control is a way to manage concurrency in every insert or update operation. The passed version value is the last seen version (usually returned by a get or a search). The index happens only if the current index version value is equal to the passed one:

```
curl -XPOST 'http://localhost:9200/myindex/order?version=2' ...
```

- `op_type`: Which can be used to force a create on a document. If a document with the same ID exists, the index fails:

```
curl -XPOST 'http://localhost:9200/myindex/order?
op_type=create'...
```

- `refresh`: Which forces a refresh after having indexed the document. It allows having documents ready for search after indexing them:

```
curl -XPOST 'http://localhost:9200/myindex/order?
refresh=true'...
```

- `timeout`: Which defines a time to wait for the primary shard to be available. Sometimes the primary shard is not in a writable status (relocating or recovering from a gateway) and a timeout for the write operation is raised after one minute:

  ```
  curl -XPOST 'http://localhost:9200/myindex/order?timeout=5m'
  ...
  ```

See also

- The *Getting a document* recipe in this chapter to learn how to retrieve a stored document
- The *Deleting a document* recipe in this chapter to learn how to delete a document
- The *Updating a document* recipe in this chapter to learn how to update fields in a document
- For Optimistic Concurrency Control, the Elasticsearch way to manage concurrency on a document, a good reference can be found at `http://en.wikipedia.org/wiki/Optimistic_concurrency_control`

Getting a document

After having indexed a document, during your application life it must probably be retrieved.

The GET REST call allows us to get a document in real time without the need of a refresh.

Getting ready

You need an up-and-running Elasticsearch installation, as used in the *Downloading and installing Elasticsearch* recipe in `Chapter 2`, *Downloading and Setup*.

To execute `curl` via the command line, you need to install `curl` for your operative system.

To correctly execute the following commands, use the indexed document in the *Indexing a document* recipe.

How to do it…

The GET method allows us to return a document given its index, type, and ID.

The REST API URL is:

```
http://<server>/<index_name>/<type_name>/<id>
```

To get a document, we will perform the following steps:

1. If we consider the document, which we had indexed in the previous recipe, the call will be:

   ```
   curl -XGET
   'http://localhost:9200/myindex/order/2qLrAfPVQvCRMe7Ku8r0Tw?
   pretty=true'
   ```

2. The result returned by Elasticsearch should be the indexed document:

   ```
   {
   "_index":"myindex",
   "_type":"order",
   "_id":"2qLrAfPVQvCRMe7Ku8r0Tw",
   "_version":1,
   "found":true,
   "_source" : {
       "id" : "1234",
       "date" : "2013-06-07T12:14:54",
       "customer_id" : "customer1",
       "sent" : true,
       "items":[
           {"name":"item1", "quantity":3, "vat":20.0},
           {"name":"item2", "quantity":2, "vat":20.0},
           {"name":"item3", "quantity":1, "vat":10.0}
       ]
   }}
   ```

3. Our indexed data is contained in the _source parameter, but other information is returned:
   - _index: The index that stores the document
   - _type: The type of the document

- `_id`: The ID of the document
- `_version`: The version of the document
- `found`: Whether the document has been found
- If the record is missing, an error `404` is returned as status code and the return JSON will be:

```
{
  "_id": "2qLrAfPVQvCRMe7Ku8r0Tw",
  "_index": "myindex",
  "_type": "order",
  "found": false
}
```

How it works...

The Elasticsearch GET API on the document doesn't require a refresh: all the GET calls are in real time.

This call is very fast because Elasticsearch redirects the search only on the shard that contains the document without an other overhead, and the document IDs are often cached in memory for fast look up.

The source of the document is only available if the `_source` field is stored (default settings in Elasticsearch).

There are several additional parameters that can be used to control the get call:

- `fields` allow us to retrieve only a subset of fields. This is very useful to reduce bandwidth or to retrieve calculated fields such as the attachment mapping ones:

```
curl 'http://localhost:9200/myindex/order/
2qLrAfPVQvCRMe7Ku8r0Tw?fields=date,sent'
```

- `routing` allows us to specify the shard to be used for the get operation. To retrieve a document, the routing used in indexing time must be the same as the search time:

```
curl 'http://localhost:9200/myindex/order/
2qLrAfPVQvCRMe7Ku8r0Tw?routing=customer_id'
```

- `refresh` allows us to refresh the current shard before doing the get operation (it must be used with care because it slows down indexing and introduces some overhead):

```
curl http://localhost:9200/myindex/order/
2qLrAfPVQvCRMe7Ku8r0Tw?refresh=true
```

- `preference` allows us to control which shard replica is chosen to execute the `GET` method. Generally, Elasticsearch chooses a random shard for the `GET` call. The possible values are as follows:
    - `_primary` for the primary shard.
    - `_local`, first trying the local shard and then falling back to a random choice. Using the local shard reduces the bandwidth usage and should generally be used with autoreplicating shards (replica set to 0-all).
    - `custom value` for selecting a shard related value such as `customer_id` and `username`.

There is more...

The GET API is very fast, so a good practice for developing applications is to try to use as much as possible. Choosing the correct ID form during application development can bring a big boost in performance.

If the shard, which contains the document, is not bound to an ID, to fetch the document a query with an ID filter (we will see them in `Chapter 6`, *Text and Numeric Queries* in the *Using a IDS query* recipe) is required.

If you don't need to fetch the record, but only check the existence, you can replace `GET` with `HEAD` and the response will be status code `200` if it exists, or `404` if it is missing.

The `GET` call has also a special endpoint `_source` that allows fetching only the source of the document.

The GET source REST API URL is:

```
http://<server>/<index_name>/<type_name>/<id>/_source
```

To fetch the source of the previous order, we will call:

```
curl -XGET
http://localhost:9200/myindex/order/2qLrAfPVQvCRMe7Ku8r0Tw/_source
```

See also

- Refer to the *Speeding up the GET operation* recipe in this chapter to learn how to execute multiple GET in one shot to reduce fetching time.

Deleting a document

Deleting documents in Elasticsearch is possible in two ways: using the DELETE call or the delete_by_query call, which we'll see in the next chapter.

Getting ready

You need an up-and-running Elasticsearch installation, as used in the *Downloading and installing Elasticsearch* recipe in Chapter 2, *Downloading and Setup*.

To execute curl via the command line, you need to install curl for your operative system.

To correctly execute the following commands, use the indexed document in the *Indexing a document* recipe.

How to do it...

The REST API URL is the same as the GET calls, but the HTTP method is DELETE:

```
http://<server>/<index_name>/<type_name>/<id>
```

To delete a document, we will perform the following steps:

1. If we consider the `order` indexed in the *Indexing a document* recipe, the call to delete a document will be:

```
curl -XDELETE
'http://localhost:9200/myindex/order/2qLrAfPVQvCRMe7Ku8r0Tw'
```

2. The result returned by Elasticsearch should be:

```
{
  "found" : true,
  "_index" : "myindex",
  "_type" : "order",
  "_id" : "2qLrAfPVQvCRMe7Ku8r0Tw",
  "_version" : 4,
  "result" : "deleted",
  "_shards" : {
    "total" : 2,
    "successful" : 1,
    "failed" : 0
  }
}
```

3. If the record is missing, an error `404` is returned as status code and the return JSON will be:

```
{
  "found" : false,
  "_index" : "myindex",
  "_type" : "order",
  "_id" : "2qLrAfPVQvCRMe7Ku8r0Tw",
  "_version" : 5,
  "result" : "not_found",
  "_shards" : {
    "total" : 2,
    "successful" : 1,
    "failed" : 0
  }
}
```

How it works…

Deleting records only hits shards that contain documents, so there is no overhead. If the document is a child, the parent must be set to look for the correct shard.

There are several additional parameters that can be used to control the delete call. The most important ones are:

- `routing` allows specifying the shard to be used for the delete operation
- `version` allows defining a version of the document to be deleted to prevent modification on this document
- `parent`, similar to routing, is required if the document is a child one

> The `DELETE` operation has to restore functionality. Every document that is deleted is lost forever.

Deleting a record is a fast operation, very easy to use if the IDs of the document to delete are available. Otherwise, we must use the `delete_by_query` call, which we will see in the next chapter.

See also

- Refer to the *Deleting by query* recipe in `Chapter 5`, *Search* to delete a bunch of documents that match a query

Updating a document

Documents stored in Elasticsearch can be updated during their lives. There are two available solutions to do this operation in Elasticsearch: adding a new document or using the update call.

The update call can work in two ways:

- Providing a script that uses the update strategy
- Providing a document that must be merged with the original one

The main advantage of an update versus an index is the networking reduction.

Getting ready

You need an up-and-running Elasticsearch installation, as used in the *Downloading and installing Elasticsearch* recipe in `Chapter 2`, *Downloading and Setup*.

To execute `curl` via the command line, you need to install `curl` for your operative system.

To correctly execute the following commands, use the indexed document in the *Indexing a document* recipe.

To use dynamic scripting languages, they must be enabled: see `Chapter 9`, *Scripting*.

How to do it…

As we are changing the state of the data, the HTTP method is `POST` and the REST URL is:

```
http://<server>/<index_name>/<type_name>/<id>/_update
```

To update a document, we will perform the following steps:

1. If we consider the type order of the previous recipe, the call to update a document will be:

```
curl -XPOST
'http://localhost:9200/myindex/order/2qLrAfPVQvCRMe7Ku8r0Tw/
_update?pretty' -d '{
    "script" : {
      "inline":"ctx._source.in_stock_items += params.count",
      "params" : {
        "count" : 4
    }
  }
}'
```

2. If the request is successful, the result returned by Elasticsearch should be:

```
{
  "_index" : "myindex",
  "_type" : "order",
  "_id" : "2qLrAfPVQvCRMe7Ku8r0Tw",
  "_version" : 2,
  "result" : "updated",
  "_shards" : {
    "total" : 2,
    "successful" : 1,
    "failed" : 0
  }
}
```

3. The record will be as follows:

```
{
    "_id": "2qLrAfPVQvCRMe7Ku8r0Tw",
    "_index": "myindex",
    "_source": {
        "customer_id": "customer1",
        "date": "2013-06-07T12:14:54",
        "id": "1234",
  "in_stock_items": 4,
....
        "sent": true
    },
    "_type": "order",
    "_version": 3,
    "exists": true
}
```

4. The visible changes are:

    The scripted field is changed

    The version is incremented

If you are using Elasticsearch (1.2 or above) and you have disabled scripting support (default configuration), an error will be raised:

```
{
  "error" : {
    "root_cause" : [
      {
        "type" : "remote_transport_exception",
        "reason" : "[Gin Genie][127.0.0.1:9300]
        [indices:data/write/update[s]]"
      }
    ],
    "type" : "illegal_argument_exception",
    "reason" : "failed to execute script",
    "caused_by" : {
      "type" : "illegal_state_exception",
      "reason" : "scripts of type [inline], operation
      [update] and lang [painless] are disabled"
    }
  },
  "status" : 400
}
```

How it works...

The update operation takes a document, it applies to this document the changes required in the script or in the update document, and it will reindex the changed document. In Chapter 9, *Scripting* a we will explore the scripting capabilities of Elasticsearch.

The standard language for scripting in Elasticsearch is **Painless** and it's used in these examples.

The script can operate on the ctx._source: the source of the document (it must be stored to work) and it can change the document in place. It's possible to pass parameters to a script passing a JSON object. These parameters are available in the execution context.

A script can control the Elasticsearch behavior after the script execution via setting the `ctx.op` value of the context. Available values are as follows:

- `ctx.op="delete"` the document will be deleted after the script execution.
- `ctx.op="none"` the document will skip the indexing process. A good practice to improve performances it is to set the `ctx.op="none"` if the script doesn't update the document to prevent a reindexing overhead.

The `ctx` also manages the timestamp of the record in `ctx._timestamp`. It's possible to also pass an additional object in the `upsert` property to be used if the document is not available in the `index`:

```
curl -XPOST
'http://localhost:9200/myindex/order/2qLrAfPVQvCRMe7Ku8r0Tw/_update' -d '{
"script" : {
"inline":"ctx._source.in_stock_items += params.count",
"params" : {
"count" : 4
}
},
"upsert" : {"in_stock_items":4}}'
```

If you need to replace some field values, a good solution is not to write complex update script, but to use the special property `doc`, which allows us to *overwrite* the values of an object. The document provided in the `doc` parameter will be merged with the original one. This approach is easier to use, but it cannot set the `ctx.op`, so if the update doesn't change the value of the original document, the next successive phase will always be executed:

```
curl -XPOST
'http://localhost:9200/myindex/order/2qLrAfPVQvCRMe7Ku8r0Tw/_update'
-d '{"doc" : {"in_stock_items":10}}'
```

If the original document is missing, it is possible to provide a `doc` value (the document to be created) for an `upsert` as a `doc_as_upsert` parameter:

```
curl -XPOST
'http://localhost:9200/myindex/order/2qLrAfPVQvCRMe7Ku8r0Tw/_update'
-d '{"doc" : {"in_stock_items":10}, "doc_as_upsert":true}'
```

Using Painless scripting, it is possible to apply an advanced operation on fields, such as:

- Remove a field, that is:

    ```
    "script" : {"inline": "ctx._source.remove("myfield"}}
    ```

- Add a new field, that is:

    ```
    "script" : {"inline": "ctx._source.myfield=myvalue"}}
    ```

The update REST call is very useful because it has some advantages:

- It reduces the bandwidth usage, because the update operation doesn't need a round trip to the client of the data
- It's safer, because it automatically manages the optimistic concurrent control: if a change happens during script execution, the script it's reexecuted with updates the data
- It can be bulk executed

See also

- Refer to the following recipe, *Speeding up atomic operations*, to learn how to use bulk operations to reduce the networking load and speed up ingestion

Speeding up atomic operations (bulk operations)

When we are inserting/deleting/updating a large number of documents, the HTTP overhead is significant. To speed up the process Elasticsearch allows executing the bulk of CRUD calls.

Getting ready

You need an up-and-running Elasticsearch installation, as used in the *Downloading and installing Elasticsearch* recipe in Chapter 2, *Downloading and Setup*.

To execute curl via the command line, you need to install curl for your operative system.

How to do it...

As we are changing the state of the data, the HTTP method is POST and the REST URL is:

```
http://<server>/<index_name/_bulk
```

To execute a bulk action, we will perform the following steps:

1. We need to collect the create/index/delete/update commands in a structure made of bulk JSON lines, composed by a line of action with metadata and another optional line of data related to the action. Every line must end with a new line \n. A bulk data file should be, for example:

```
{ "index":{ "_index":"myindex", "_type":"order", "_id":"1" } }
{ "field1" : "value1",  "field2" : "value2"  }
{ "delete":{ "_index":"myindex", "_type":"order", "_id":"2" } }
{ "create":{ "_index":"myindex", "_type":"order", "_id":"3" } }
{ "field1" : "value1",  "field2" : "value2"  }
{ "update":{ "_index":"myindex", "_type":"order", "_id":"3" } }
{ "doc":{"field1" : "value1",  "field2" : "value2"  }}
```

2. This file can be sent with this POST:

```
curl -s -XPOST localhost:9200/_bulk --data-binary @bulkdata;
```

3. The result returned by Elasticsearch should collect all the responses of the actions.

How it works...

The bulk operation allows aggregating different calls as a single one: a header part with the action to be performed and a body for some operations as index, create, and update.

The header is composed by the action name and the object of parameters. Looking at the previous index example, we have:

```
{ "index":{ "_index":"myindex", "_type":"order", "_id":"1" } }
```

For indexing and creating, an extra body is required with the data:

```
{ "field1" : "value1",  "field2" : "value2"  }
```

The delete action doesn't require optional data, so only the header composes it:

```
{ "delete":{ "_index":"myindex", "_type":"order", "_id":"1" } }
```

In the 0.90 or upper, Elasticsearch allows us to execute also bulk update:

```
{ "update":{ "_index":"myindex", "_type":"order", "_id":"3" } }
```

The header accepts all the common parameters of the update action such as `doc`, `upsert`, `doc_as_upsert`, `lang`, `script`, and `params`. For controlling the number of retries in case of concurrency, the bulk update defines the `_retry_on_conflict` parameter set to the number of retries to be performed before raising an exception.

And a possible body for the update, is:

```
{ "doc":{"field1" : "value1",  "field2" : "value2"  }}
```

The bulk item can accept several parameters, such as:

- `routing` to control the routing shard.
- `parent` to select a parent item shard. This is required if you are indexing some child documents. Global bulk parameters that can be passed via query arguments are:
- `consistency` (`one`, `quorum`, `all`) (default `quorum`), which controls the number of active shards before executing write operations.
- `refresh` (default `false`), which forces a refresh in the shards involved in bulk operations. The new indexed document will be available immediately without waiting for the standard refresh interval (1s).
- `pipeline`, which forces an index using the provided ingest pipeline.

Usually, Elasticsearch client libraries that use Elasticsearch REST API, automatically implement a serialization of bulk commands.

The correct number of commands to serialize in a bulk is a user choice, but there are some things to consider:

- In standard configuration, Elasticsearch limits the HTTP call to 100 MB in size. If the size is over the limit, the call is rejected.
- Multiple complex commands take a lot of time to be processed so pay attention to client timeout.
- The small size of commands in a bulk doesn't improve performance.

If the documents aren't big, 500 commands in a bulk can be a good number to start with, and it can be tuned depending on data structures (number of fields, number of nested objects, complexity of fields, and so on).

Speeding up GET operations (multi GET)

The standard GET operation is very fast, but if you need to fetch a lot of documents by ID, Elasticsearch provides the multi GET operation.

Getting ready

You need an up-and-running Elasticsearch installation, as used in the *Downloading and installing Elasticsearch* recipe in Chapter 2, *Downloading and Setup*.

To execute curl via the command line, you need to install curl for your operative system.

To correctly execute the following commands, use the indexed document in the *Indexing a document* recipe.

How to do it...

The multi GET REST URLs are:

```
http://<server</_mget

http://<server>/<index_name>/_mget
http://<server>/<index_name>/<type_name>/_mget
```

To execute a multi GET action, we will perform the following steps:

1. The method is POST with a body that contains a list of document IDs and the index/type if they are missing. As an example, using the first URL, we need to provide the index, type, and ID:

```
curl -XPOST 'localhost:9200/_mget' -fd '{
    "docs" : [
        {
            "_index" : "myindex",
            "_type" : "order",
            "_id" : "2qLrAfPVQvCRMe7Ku8r0Tw"
        },
        {
            "_index" : "myindex",
            "_type" : "order",
            "_id" : "2"
        }
    ]
}'
```

This kind of call allows us to fetch documents in several different indices and types.

2. If the index and the type is fixed, a call should also be in the form of:

```
curl 'localhost:9200/test/type/_mget' -d '{
    "ids" : ["1", "2"]
}'
```

The multi get result is an array of documents.

How it works...

Multi GET call is a shortcut for executing many get commands in one shot.

Elasticsearch internally spreads the get in parallel on several shards and collects the results to return to the user.

The `get` object can contain the following parameters:

- `_index`: The index that contains the document. It can be omitted if passed in the URL.
- `_type`: The type of the document. It can be omitted if passed in the URL.
- `_id`: The document ID.
- `stored_fields`: (optional) a list of fields to retrieve.
- `_source`: (optional) source filter object.
- `routing`: (optional) the shard routing parameter.

The advantages of a multi GET are as follows:

- Reduced networking traffic, both internally and externally of Elasticsearch
- Speed up if used in an application: the time of processing a multi get is quite similar to a standard get

See also...

- Refer to the *Getting a document* recipe in this chapter to learn how to execute a simple get and general parameters for a GET call

5
Search

In this chapter, we will cover the following recipes:

- Executing a search
- Sorting results
- Highlighting results
- Executing a scrolling query
- Using the search_after functionality
- Returning inner hits in results
- Suggesting a correct query
- Counting matched results
- Explaining a query
- Query profiling
- Deleting by query
- Updating by query
- Matching all the documents
- Using a Boolean query

Introduction

Now we have set the mappings and put the data in the indices, we can search.

In this chapter, we will cover the search using different factors: sorting, highlighting, scrolling, suggesting, counting, and deleting. These actions are the core part of Elasticsearch: ultimately, everything in Elasticsearch is about serving the query and returning good-quality results.

This chapter is divided in two parts: the first part shows how to perform an API call-related search, the last part will look at two special query operators that are the basis for building complex queries in the next chapters.

All the recipes in this chapter require us to prepare and populate the required indices: the online code is available on the PacktPub website (`https://www.packtpub.com/big-data-and-business-intelligence/elasticsearch-cookbook`) or via GitHub (`https://github.com/aparo/elasticsearch-cookbook-third-edition`). There are scripts to initialize all the required data.

Executing a search

Elasticsearch was born as a search engine: its main purpose is to process queries and give results.

In this recipe, we'll see that a search in Elasticsearch is not only limited to matching documents, but it can also calculate additional information required to improve the search quality.

Getting ready

You will need an up-and-running Elasticsearch installation as used in the *Downloading and installing Elasticsearch* recipe in `Chapter 2`, *Downloading and Setup*.

To execute `curl` via a command line, you need to install `curl` for your operating system.

To correctly execute the following commands you will need an index populated with the
`chapter_05/populate_query.sh` script available in the online code.

The mapping used in all these chapter queries and searches is the following:

```
{
  "mappings": {
    "test-type": {
      "properties": {
        "pos": {
          "type": "integer",
          "store": "yes"
        },
        "uuid": {
          "store": "yes",
          "type": "keyword"
        },
        "parsedtext": {
          "term_vector": "with_positions_offsets",
          "store": "yes",
          "type": "text"
        },
        "name": {
          "term_vector": "with_positions_offsets",
          "store": "yes",
          "fielddata": true,
          "type": "text",
          "fields": {
            "raw": {
              "type": "keyword"
            }
          }
        },
        "title": {
          "term_vector": "with_positions_offsets",
          "store": "yes",
          "type": "text",
          "fielddata": true,
          "fields": {
            "raw": {
              "type": "keyword"
            }
          }
        }
      }
    },
    "test-type2": {
      "_parent": {
```

```
            "type": "test-type"
        }
      }
    }
  }
```

How to do it…

To execute the search and view the results, we will perform the following steps:

1. From the command line, we can execute a search as follows:

```
curl -XGET 'http://127.0.0.1:9200/test-index/test-type/_search'
-d '{"query":{"match_all":{}}}'
```

> In this case, we have used a `match_all` query that means *return all the documents*. We'll discuss this kind of query in the *Matching all the documents* recipe in this chapter.

2. If everything works, the command will return the following:

```
{
  "took" : 2,
  "timed_out" : false,
  "_shards" : {
    "total" : 5,
    "successful" : 5,
    "failed" : 0
  },
  "hits" : {
    "total" : 3,
    "max_score" : 1.0,
    "hits" : [ {
      "_index" : "test-index",
      "_type" : "test-type",
      "_id" : "1",
      "_score" : 1.0, "_source" : {"position": 1, "parsedtext":
"Joe Testere nice guy", "name": "Joe Tester", "uuid": "11111"}
    }, {
      "_index" : "test-index",
      "_type" : "test-type",
      "_id" : "2",
      "_score" : 1.0, "_source" : {"position": 2, "parsedtext":
"Bill Testere nice guy", "name": "Bill Baloney", "uuid":
"22222"}
    }, {
```

```
        "_index" : "test-index",
        "_type" : "test-type",
        "_id" : "3",
        "_score" : 1.0, "_source" : {"position": 3, "parsedtext":
        "Bill is not\n
        nice guy", "name": "Bill Clinton", "uuid": "33333"}
    } ]
  }
}
```

3. These results contain a lot of information:
    - took is the milliseconds of time required to execute the query.
    - time_out indicates whether a timeout occurred during the search. This is related to the timeout parameter of the search. If a timeout occurs, you will get partial or no results.
    - _shards is the status of shards divided into:
        - total, which is the number of shards.
        - successful, which is the number of shards in which the query was successful.
        - failed, which is the number of shards in which the query failed, because some error or exception occurred during the query.
    - hits are the results which are composed of the following:
        - total is the number of documents that match the query.
        - max_score is the match score of first document. It is usually one, if no match scoring was computed, for example in sorting or filtering.
        - Hits which is a list of result documents.

The resulting document has a lot of fields that are always available and others that depend on search parameters. The most important fields are as follows:

- _index: The index field contains the document
- _type: The type of the document
- _id: This is the ID of the document
- _source (this is the default field returned, but it can be disabled): the document source

- `_score`: This is the query score of the document
- `sort`: If the document is sorted, values that are used for sorting
- `highlight`: Highlighted segments if highlighting was requested
- `fields`: Some fields can be retrieved without needing to fetch all the source objects

How it works...

The HTTP method to execute a search is `GET` (although `POST` also works); the REST endpoints are as follows:

```
http://<server>/_search
http://<server>/<index_name(s)>/_search
http://<server>/<index_name(s)>/<type_name(s)>/_search
```

> Not all the HTTP clients allow you to send data via a `GET` call, so the best practice, if you need to send body data, is to use the `POST` call.

Multi indices and types are comma separated. If an index or a type is defined, the search is limited only to them. One or more aliases can be used as index names.

The core query is usually contained in the body of the `GET`/`POST` call, but a lot of options can also be expressed as URI **query parameters**, such as the following:

- `q`: This is the query string to do simple string queries, as follows:

  ```
  curl -XGET 'http://127.0.0.1:9200/test-index/test-type/_search?
  q=uuid:11111'
  ```

- `df`: This is the default field to be used within the query, as follows:

  ```
  curl -XGET 'http://127.0.0.1:9200/test-index/test-type/_search?
  df=uuid&q=11111'
  ```

- `from` (the default value is 0): The start index of the hits.
- `size` (the default value is 10): The number of hits to be returned.
- `analyzer`: The default analyzer to be used.
- `default_operator` (the default value is OR): This can be set to AND or OR.
- `explain`: This allows the user to return information about how the score is calculated, as follows:

```
curl -XGET 'http://127.0.0.1:9200/test-index/test-type/_search?
q=parsedtext:joe&explain=true'
```

- `stored_fields`: These allows the user to define fields that must be returned, as follows:

```
curl -XGET 'http://127.0.0.1:9200/test-index/test-type/_search?
q=parsedtext:joe&stored_fields=name'
```

- `sort` (the default value is score): This allows the user to change the documents in order. Sort is ascendant by default; if you need to change the order, add desc to the field, as follows:

```
curl -XGET 'http://127.0.0.1:9200/test-index/test-type/_search?
sort=name.raw:desc'
```

- `timeout` (not active by default): This defines the timeout for the search. Elasticsearch tries to collect results until a timeout. If a timeout is fired, all the hits accumulated are returned.
- `search_type`: This defines the search strategy. A reference is available in the online Elasticsearch documentation at https://www.elastic.co/guide/en/elasticsearch/reference/current/search-request-search-type.html.
- `track_scores` (the default value is false): If true, this tracks the score and allows it to be returned with the hits. It's used in conjunction with sort, because sorting by default prevents the return of a match score.
- `pretty` (the default value is false): If true, the results will be pretty printed.

Generally, the query, contained in the body of the search, is a JSON object. The body of the search is the core of Elasticsearch's search functionalities; the list of search capabilities extends in every release. For the current version (5.x) of Elasticsearch, the available parameters are as follows:

- `query`: This contains the query to be executed. Later in this chapter, we will see how to create different kinds of queries to cover several scenarios.
- `from`: This allows the user to control pagination. The `from` parameter defines the start position of the hits to be returned (default 0) and `size` (default 10).

> **TIP**
>
> The pagination is applied to the currently returned search results. Firing the same query can bring different results if a lot of records have the same score or a new document is ingested. If you need to process all the result documents without repetition, you need to execute scan or scroll queries.

- `sort`: This allows the user to change the order of the matched documents. This option is fully covered in the *Sorting results* recipe.
- `post_filter`: This allows the user to filter out the query results without affecting the aggregation count. It's usually used for filtering by facet values.
- `_source`: This allows the user to control the returned source. It can be disabled (`false`), partially returned (`obj.*`) or use multiple exclude/include rules. This functionality can be used instead of fields to return values (for complete coverage of this, take a look at the online Elasticsearch reference at `http://www.elasticsearch.org/guide/en/elasticsearch/reference/current/search-request-source-filtering.html`).
- `fielddata_fields`: This allows the user to return a field data representation of the field.
- `stored_fields`: This controls the fields to be returned.

> **TIP**
>
> Returning only the required fields reduces the network and memory usage, improving the performance. The suggested way to retrieve custom fields is to use the `_source` filtering function because it doesn't need to use Elasticsearch's extra resources.

- `aggregations/aggs`: These control the aggregation layer analytics. These will be discussed in the next chapter.
- `index_boost`: This allows the user to define the per-index boost value. It is used to increase/decrease the score of results in boosted indices.

- `highlighting`: This allows the user to define fields and settings to be used for calculating a query abstract (see the *Highlighting results* recipe in this chapter).
- `version` (the default value `false`) This adds the version of a document in the results.
- `rescore`: This allows the user to define an extra query to be used in the score to improve the quality of the results. The `rescore` query is executed on the hits that match the first query and filter.
- `min_score`: If this is given, all the result documents that have a score lower than this value are rejected.
- `explain`: This returns information on how the TD/IF score is calculated for a particular document.
- `script_fields`: This defines a script that computes extra fields via scripting to be returned with a hit. We'll look at Elasticsearch scripting in `Chapter 9`, *Scripting*.
- `suggest`: If given a query and a field, this returns the most significant terms related to this query. This parameter allows the user to implement the Google-like *do you mean* functionality (see the *Suggesting a correct query* recipe).
- `search_type`: This defines how Elasticsearch should process a query. We'll see the scrolling query in the *Executing a scrolling query* recipe in this chapter.
- `scroll`: This controls the scrolling in scroll/scan queries. The scroll allows the user to have an Elasticsearch equivalent of a DBMS cursor.
- `_name`: This allows returns for every hit that matches the named queries. It's very useful if you have a Boolean and you want the name of the matched query.
- `search_after`: This allows the user to skip results using the most efficient way of scrolling. We'll see this functionality in the *Using search_after functionality* recipe in this chapter.
- `preference`: This allows the user to select which shard/s to use for executing the query.

There's more...

To improve the quality of the results score, Elasticsearch provides the `rescore` functionality. This capability allows the user to reorder a top number of documents with another query that's generally much more expensive (CPU/time consuming), for example, if the query contains a lot of match queries or scripting. This approach allows the user to execute the `rescore` query on just a small subset of results, reducing overall computation time and resources.

The `rescore` query, as for every query, is executed at shard level so it's automatically distributed.

> The best candidates to be executed in the `rescore` query are complex queries with a lot of nested options and everything that is used is scripting (due to the massive overhead of scripting languages).

The following example will show you how to execute a fast query (a boolean one) in the first phase and then to `rescore` query it with a `match` query in the `rescore` section:

```
curl -s -XPOST 'localhost:9200/_search' -d '{
    "query" : {
        "match" : {
            "parsedtext" : {
                "operator" : "or",
                "query" : "nice guy joe",
                "type" : "boolean"
            }
        }
    },
    "rescore" : {
        "window_size" : 100,
        "query" : {
            "rescore_query" : {
                "match" : {
                    "parsedtext" : {
                        "query" : "joe nice guy",
                        "type" : "phrase",
                        "slop" : 2
                    }
                }
            },
            "query_weight" : 0.8,
            "rescore_query_weight" : 1.5
        }
    }
}
'
```

The `rescore` parameters are as follows:

- `window_size`: The example is `100`. This controls how many results per shard must be considered in the rescore functionality.
- `query_weight`: The default value is `1.0` and `rescore_query_weight` default value is `1.0`. These are used to compute the final score using the following formula:

final_score=query_score*query_weight + rescore_score*rescore_query_weight

If a user wants to only keep the rescore score, he can set the `query_weight` to 0.

See also

- The *Executing an aggregation* recipe in `Chapter 8`, *Aggregations* explains how to use the aggregation framework during queries
- The *Highlighting results* recipe in this chapter explains how to use the highlighting functionality for improving the user experience in results
- The *Executing a scrolling query* recipe in this chapter covers how to efficiently paginate results
- The *Suggesting terms for a query* recipe in this chapter helps to correct text queries

Sorting results

When searching for results, the most common criterion for sorting in Elasticsearch is the relevance to a text query.

Real-world applications often need to control the sorting criteria in scenarios, such as the following:

- Sorting a user by last name and first name
- Sorting items by stock symbols, price (ascending, descending)
- Sorting documents by size, file type, source

Getting ready

You need an up-and-running Elasticsearch installation as used in the *Downloading and installing Elasticsearch* recipe in Chapter 2, *Downloading and Setup*.

To execute curl via the command line, you need to install curl for your operating system.

To correctly execute the following commands, you will need an index populated with the chapter_05/populate_query.sh script available in the online code.

How to do it...

In order to sort the results, we will perform the following steps:

1. Add a sort section to your query as follows:

```
curl -XGET 'http://127.0.0.1:9200/test-index/test-type/_search?
pretty' -d'{
  "query": {
    "match_all": {}
  },
  "sort": [
    {
      "price": {
        "order": "asc",
        "mode": "avg",
        "unmapped_type" : "double",
        "missing": "_last"
      }
    },
    "_score"
  ]
}'
```

2. The returned result should be similar to the following:

```
...,
  "hits" : {
    "total" : 3,
    "max_score" : null,
    "hits" : [ {
      "_index" : "test-index",
      "_type" : "test-type",
      "_id" : "1",
      "_score" : 1.0, "_source" :{ ... "price":4.0},
```

```
    "sort" : [
        4.0,
        1.0
    ]
}, {
    . . . .
```

The sort result is very special: an extra field `sort` is created to collect the value used for sorting.

How it works...

The `sort` parameter can be defined as a list that can contain both simple strings and JSON objects.

The sort strings are the name of the field (such as `field1`, `field2`, `field3` or `field4`, and so on) used for sorting and are similar to the SQL function `order by`.

The JSON object allows users extra parameters as follows:

- `order` (asc/desc): This defines whether the order must be considered ascendant (default) or descendent.
- `unmapped_type` (long/int/double/string/...): This defines the type of the `sort` parameter if the value is missing. It's best practice to define it to prevent sorting errors due to missing values.
- `missing` (_last/_first): This defines how to manage missing values – whether to put them at the end (_last) of the results or at the start (_first).
- mode: This defines how to manage multi-value fields. Possible values are:
    - min: The minimum value is chosen (that is to say that in the case of multi-price on an item, it chooses the lowest for comparison).
    - max: The maximum value is chosen.
    - sum: The sort value will be computed as the sum of all the values. This mode is only available on numeric array fields.
    - avg: The sort value will be the average of all the values. This mode is only available on numeric array fields.
    - median: The sort value will be the median of all the values. This mode is only available on numeric array fields.

> **TIP**
> If we want to add the relevance score value to the sort list, we must use the special sort field _score.

In case you are sorting for a nested object, there are two extra parameters that can be used, as follows:

- nested_path: This defines the nested object to be used for sorting. The field defined for sorting will be relative to the nested_path. If not defined, then the sorting field is related to the document root.
- nested_filter: This defines a filter that is used to remove nested documents that don't match from the sorting value extraction. This filter allows a better selection of values to be used in sorting.

For example, if we have an address object nested in a person document and we can sort for the city.name, we can use the following:

- address.city.name without defining the nested_path
- city.name if we define a nested_path address

> **TIP**
> The sorting process requires that the sorting fields of all the matched query documents are fetched to be compared. To prevent high memory usage, its better to sort numeric fields, and in case of string sorting, choose short text fields processed with an analyzer that doesn't tokenize the text.

There's more...

If you are using sort, pay attention to the tokenized fields, because the sort order depends on the lower-order token if ascendant and the higher order token if descendent. In case of tokenized fields, this behavior is not similar to a common sort because we execute it at term level.

For example, if we sort by the descending name field, we use the following:

```
curl -XGET 'http://127.0.0.1:9200/test-index/test-type/_search?
sort=name:desc'
```

In the preceding example, the results are as follows:

```
...
"hits" : [ {
     "_index" : "test-index",
     "_type" : "test-type",
     "_id" : "1",
     "_score" : null, "_source" : {"position": 1, "parsedtext": "Joe
Testere nice guy", "name": "Joe Tester", "uuid": "11111"},
     "sort" : [ "tester" ]
   }, {
     "_index" : "test-index",
     "_type" : "test-type",
     "_id" : "3",
     "_score" : null, "_source" : {"position": 3, "parsedtext": "Bill is
not\n            nice guy", "name": "Bill Clinton", "uuid": "33333"},
     "sort" : [ "clinton" ]
   }, {
     "_index" : "test-index",
     "_type" : "test-type",
     "_id" : "2",
     "_score" : null, "_source" : {"position": 2, "parsedtext": "Bill
Testere nice guy", "name": "Bill Baloney", "uuid": "22222"},
     "sort" : [ "bill" ]
   }
```

The expected SQL results can be obtained using a not-tokenized field, in this case
name.raw, as follows:

```
curl -XGET 'http://127.0.0.1:9200/test-index/test-type/_search?
sort=name.raw:desc'
```

The results are as follows:

```
{
  ...
  "hits" : {
    "total" : 3,
    "max_score" : null,
    "hits" : [
      {
        ..."_id" : "1",...
        "sort" : [
          "Joe Tester"
        ]
      },
      {
        ..."_id" : "3",
```

```
      ..."sort" : [
         "Bill Clinton"
      ]
   },
   {
      ..."_id" : "2",
      ..."sort" : [
         "Bill Baloney"
      ]
   }
   ]
   }
}
```

There are two special sorting types: **geo distance** and **scripting**.

Geo distance sorting uses the distance from a geo point (location) as metric to compute the ordering. A sorting example could be as follows:

```
...
"sort" : [
      {
         "_geo_distance" : {
            "pin.location" : [-70, 40],
            "order" : "asc",
            "unit" : "km"
         }
      }
   ], ...
```

It accepts special parameters such as the following:

- unit: This defines the metric to be used to compute the distance.
- distance_type (sloppy_arc/arc/plane): This defines the type of distance to be computed. The name _geo_distance for the field is mandatory.

The point of reference for the sorting can be defined in several ways as we have already discussed in the *Mapping a geo point field* recipe in Chapter 3, *Managing Mappings*.

Using the scripting for sorting will be discussed in *Sorting data using scripts* recipe in Chapter 9, *Scripting* after we introduce the scripting capabilities of Elasticsearch.

See also

- The *Mapping a GeoPoint field* recipe in Chapter 3, *Managing Mappings*. This explains how to correct create a mapping for a geo point field
- The *Sorting with scripts* recipe in Chapter 9, *Scripting* will explain the use of custom script for computing values to sort on

Highlighting results

Elasticsearch performs a good job of finding matching results also in big text documents. It's useful for searching text in very large blocks, but to improve user experience, you need to show users the abstract: a small portion of the text that has matched the query. The abstract is a common way to help users to understand how the matched document is relevant to them.

The highlight functionality in Elasticsearch is designed to do this job.

Getting ready

You will need an up-and-running Elasticsearch installation as used in the *Downloading and installing Elasticsearch recipe* in Chapter 2, *Downloading and Setup*.

To execute curl via a command line you need to install curl for your operating system.

To correctly execute the following commands, you will need an index populated with the chapter_05/populate_query.sh script available in the online code.

How to do it...

For searching and highlighting the results, we will perform the following:

1. From the command line, we can execute a search with a highlight parameter as follows:

```
curl -XGET 'http://127.0.0.1:9200/test-index/_search?
pretty&from=0&size=10' -d '
{
"query": {"query_string": {"query": "joe"}},
"highlight": {
"pre_tags": ["<b>"],
"fields": {
"parsedtext": {"order": "score"},
"name": {"order": "score"}},
    "post_tags": ["</b>"]}}'
```

2. If everything works, the command will return the following result:

```
{
  ... truncated ...
  "hits" : {
    "total" : 1,
    "max_score" : 0.44194174,
    "hits" : [ {
      "_index" : "test-index",
      "_type" : "test-type",
      "_id" : "1",
      "_score" : 0.44194174, "_source" : {"position": 1,
"parsedtext": "Joe Testere nice guy", "name": "Joe Tester",
"uuid": "11111"},
      "highlight" : {
        "name" : [ "<b>Joe</b> Tester" ],
        "parsedtext" : [ "<b>Joe</b> Testere nice guy" ]
      }
    } ]
  }
}
```

As you can see, in the standard results there is a new field called `highlight`, which contains the highlighted fields within an array of fragments.

How it works...

When the `highlight` parameter is passed to the search object, Elasticsearch tries to execute the highlight on the document results.

The highlighting phase, which is after the document fetch one, tries to extract the highlight using the following steps:

1. It collects the terms available in the query.
2. It initializes the highlighter with the parameters given during the query.
3. It extracts the interested fields and tries to load them if they are stored, otherwise they are taken from the source.
4. It executes the query on single fields to detect the more relevant parts.
5. It adds the found highlighted fragments to the hit.

Using the highlighting functionality is very easy, but there are some important factors to pay attention to, as follows:

- The field that must be used for highlighting must be available in one of these forms: stored, in source, or in stored term vector

  > **TIP**
  >
  > The Elasticsearch highlighter checks the presence of the data field first as the term vector (this is a faster way to execute the highlighting). If the field does not use the term vector (a special indexing parameter that allows to store in index additional positional text data), it tries to load the field value from the stored fields. If the field is not stored, it finally loads the JSON source, interprets it, and extracts the data value if available. Obviously, the last approach is the slowest and most resource intensive.

- If a special analyzer is used in the search, it should also be passed to the highlighter (this is often automatically managed)

When executing highlighting on a large number of fields, you can use the wildcard to multi select them (that is to say `name*`).

The common properties for controlling highlighting field usage are as follows:

- `order`: This defines the matched fragments selection order.
- `force_source`: This skips the term vector or stored field and takes the field from the source (default `false`).
- `type` (optional, valid values are `plain`, `postings`, and `fvh`): This is used to force a specific highlight type.
- `number_of_fragment`: The default value is 5. This parameter controls how many fragments return. It can be configured globally or for field.
- `fragment_size`: The default value is 100. This is the number of characters that the fragments must contain. It can be configured globally or for field.

There are several optional parameters that can be passed in the highlight object to control the highlighting markup, and these are as follows:

- `pre_tags`/`post_tags`: A list of tags to be used for marking the highlighted text.
- `tags_schema="styled"`: This allows the user to define a tag schema that marks highlighting with different tags with ordered importance. This is a helper to reduce the definition of a lot of `pre_tags`/`post_tags` tags.
- `encoder`: The default value is `html`. If this is set to `html`, it will escape HTML tags in the fragments.
- `require_field_match`: The default value is `true`. If this is set to false, it allows the highlighting also on fields that don't match the query.
- `boundary_chars`: This is a list of characters that are used for phrase boundaries (that is , ; : /).
- `boundary_max_scan`: The default value is 20. This controls how many characters the highlighting must scan for boundaries in a match. It's used to provide better fragment extraction.

- `matched_fields`: This allows the user to combine multi fields to execute the highlighting. This is very useful if the field that you use for highlighting is a multi field analyzed with different analyzers (such as standard, linguistic, and so on). It can only be used when the highlighter is a **Fast Vector Highlighter** (**FVH**). An example of this usage could be as follows:

```
{
    "query": {
        "query_string": {
            "query": "content.plain:some text",
            "fields": ["content"]
        }
    },
    "highlight": {
        "order": "score",
        "fields": {
            "content": {
                "matched_fields": ["content", "content.plain"],
                "type" : "fvh"
            }
        }
    }
}
```

See also

- Refer to the *Executing a search* recipe in this chapter to understand how to structure a search

Executing a scrolling query

Every time a query is executed, the results are calculated and returned to the user. In Elasticsearch, there is not a deterministic order for records: pagination on a big block of values can bring inconsistency between results due to added and deleted documents and also documents with the same score. The scrolling query tries to resolve this kind of problem, giving a special cursor that allows the user to uniquely iterate all the documents.

Getting ready

You will need an up-and-running Elasticsearch installation as used in the *Downloading and installing Elasticsearch* recipe in `Chapter 2`, *Downloading and Setup*.

To execute `curl` via a command line, you need to install `curl` for your operating system.

To correctly execute the following commands, you will need an index populated with the `chapter_05/populate_query.sh` script available in the online code.

How to do it...

In order to execute a scrolling query, we will perform the following steps:

1. From the command line, we can execute a search of type scan, as follows:

   ```
   curl -XGET 'http://127.0.0.1:9200/test-index/test-type/_search?
   pretty&scroll=10m&size=1' -d '{"query": {
       "match_all": {}
     }}'
   ```

2. If everything works, the command will return the following result:

   ```
   {
     "_scroll_id" :
   "DnF1ZXJ5VGhlbkZldGNoBQAAAAAAAAGFkxOZU5IaDh3U19TSEs3QWZ
     CempKMEEAAAAAAAABxZMTmVOSGg4d1NfU0hLN0FmQnpqSjBBAAAAAAAAAg
     WTE5lTkhoOHdTX1NISzdBZkJ6akowQQAAAAAAAAJFkxOZU5IaDh3U19TS
     Es3QWZCempKMEEAAAAAAAAChZMTmVOSGg4d1NfU0hLN0FmQnpqSjBB",
     "took" : 10,
     "timed_out" : false,
     "_shards" : {
     "total" : 5,
     "successful" : 5,
     "failed" : 0
   },
     "hits" : {
     "total" : 3,
     "max_score" : 1.0,
     "hits" : [
   {
       "_index" : "test-index",
       "_type" : "test-type",
       "_id" : "2",
       "_score" : 1.0,
   ```

```
                "_source" : {...}
            }
        ]
    }
}
```

3. The result is composed of the following:

   - scroll_id: The value to be used for scrolling records
   - took: The time required to execute the query
   - timed_out: Whether the query was timed out
   - _shards: This query status is the information about the status of shards during the query
   - hits: An object that contains the total count and the result hits

4. With a scroll_id, you can use scroll to get the results, as follows:

```
curl -XGET 'localhost:9200/_search/scroll?scroll=10m' -d
'DnF1ZXJ5VGhlbkZldGNoBQAAAAAAAAGFkxOZU5IaDh3U19TSEs3QWZCemp
KMEEAAAAAAAABxZMTmVOSGg4d1NfU0hLN0FmQnpqSjBBBAAAAAAAAAg
WTE51TkhoOHdTX1NISzdBZkJ6akowQQAAAAAAAAJFkxOZU5IaDh3U19TSEs
3QWZCempKMEEAAAAAAAAChZMTmVOSGg4d1NfU0hLN0FmQnpqSjBB'
```

5. The result should be something similar to the following:

```
{
  "_scroll_id" :
  "DnF1ZXJ5VGhlbkZldGNoBQAAAAAAAAGFkxOZU5IaDh3U19TSEs3QWZ
  CempKMEEAAAAAAAABxZMTmVOSGg4d1NfU0hLN0FmQnpqSjBBBAAAAAAAAAg
  WTE51TkhoOHdTX1NISzdBZkJ6akowQQAAAAAAAAJFkxOZU5IaDh3U19TSEs
  3QWZCempKMEEAAAAAAAAChZMTmVOSGg4d1NfU0hLN0FmQnpqSjBB",
    "took" : 20,
    "timed_out" : false,
    "_shards" : {
    "total" : 5,
    "successful" : 0,
    "failed" : 5
  },
    "hits" : {
    "total" : 3,
    "max_score" : 0.0,
  ...}
```

How it works…

The scrolling query is interpreted as a standard search. This kind of search is designed to iterate on a large set of results, so the score and the order are not computed.

During the query phase, every shard stores the state of the IDs in the memory until the timeout. Processing a scrolling query is done in two steps, as follows:

1. The first part executes a query and returns a `scroll_id` used to fetch the results.
2. The second part executes the document scrolling. You iterate the second step, getting the new `scroll_id`, and fetch other documents.

> If you need to iterate on a big set of records, the scrolling query must be used, otherwise you could have duplicated results.

The scrolling query is similar to every executed standard query, but there is a special parameter that must be passed in the query string.

The `scroll=(your timeout)` parameter allows the user to define how long the hits should live. The time can be expressed in seconds using the s postfix (that is to say 5s, 10s, 15s, and so on) or in minutes using the m postfix (that is to say 5m, 10m, and so on). If you are using a long timeout, you must be sure that your nodes have a lot of RAM to keep the resulting ID live. This parameter is mandatory and must be always provided.

There's more…

Scrolling is very useful for executing re-indexing actions or iterating on very large result sets, and the best approach for this kind of action is to use the sort by the special field _doc to obtain all the matched documents, and to be more efficient.

So, if you need to iterate on a large bucket of documents for re-indexing, you should execute a similar query, as follows:

```
curl -XGET 'http://127.0.0.1:9200/test-index/test-type/_search?
pretty&scroll=10m&size=1' -d '  {
  "query": {
    "match_all": {}
  },
  "sort": [
    "_doc"
  ]
}'
```

The scroll result values are kept in the memory until the scroll timeout. It's best practice to clean this memory if you don't use the scroller any more: to delete a scroll from the Elasticsearch memory, the commands are as follows:

- If you know your scroll ID/IDs, you can provide them to the delete call as follows:

```
curl -XDELETE localhost:9200/_search/scroll -d '
{
    "scroll_id" : ["DnF1ZXJ5VGhlbkZldGNoBQAA..."]
}'
```

- If you want to clean all the scrolls, you can use the special _all keyword, as follows:

```
curl -XDELETE localhost:9200/_search/scroll/_all
```

See also

- The *Executing a search* recipe in this chapter for structuring a search
- The official documentation about scrolling that gives examples on using slice for mapping scrolling on multiple slices is
  at https://www.elastic.co/guide/en/elasticsearch/reference/master/search-request-scroll.html

Using the search_after functionality

Elasticsearch standard pagination using `from` and `size` performs very poorly on large datasets because for every query you need to compute and discard all the results before the from value. The scrolling doesn't have this problem, but it consumes a lot, due to memory search contexts, so it cannot be used for frequent user queries.

To bypass these problems, Elasticsearch 5.x provides the `search_after` functionality that provides a fast skipping for scrolling results.

Getting ready

You will need an up-and-running Elasticsearch installation as used in the *Downloading and installing Elasticsearch* recipe in `Chapter 2`, *Downloading and Setup.*

To execute `curl` via a command line, you need to install `curl` for your operating system.

To correctly execute the following commands, you will need an index populated with the `chapter_05/populate_query.sh` script available in the online code.

How to do it...

In order to execute a scrolling query, we will perform the following steps:

1. From the command line, we can execute a search which will provide a sort for your value and use the `_uid` of the document as the last sort parameter, as follows:

```
curl -XGET 'http://127.0.0.1:9200/test-index/test-type/_search?
pretty' -d '
{
    "size": 1,
    "query": {
        "match_all" : {}
    },
    "sort": [
        {"price": "asc"},
        {"_uid": "desc"}
    ]
}'
```

2. If everything works, the command will return the following:

```
{
  "took" : 52,
  "timed_out" : false,
  "_shards" : {...},
  "hits" : {
    "total" : 3,
    "max_score" : null,
    "hits" : [
      {
        "_index" : "test-index",
        "_type" : "test-type",
        "_id" : "1",
        "_score" : null,
        "_source" : {...},
        "sort" : [
          4.0,
          "test-type#1"
        ]
      }
    ]
  }
}
```

3. To use the search_after functionality, you need to keep track of your last sort result, which in this case is as follows: [4.0, "test-type#1"].

4. To fetch the next result, you must provide the search_after functionality with the last sort value of your last record, as follows:

```
curl -XGET 'http://127.0.0.1:9200/test-index/test-type/_search?
pretty' -d '
{
    "size": 1,
    "query": {
        "match_all" : {}
    },
      "search_after": [4.0, "test-type#1"],
    "sort": [
        {"price": "asc"},
        {"_uid": "desc"}
    ]
}'
```

How it works...

Elasticsearch uses Lucene for indexing data. In Lucene indices, all the terms are sorted and stored in an ordered way, so it's natural for Lucene to be extremely fast in skipping to a term value. This operation is managed in the Lucene core with the `skipTo` method. This operation doesn't consume memory and in the case of `search_after`, a query is built using `search_after` values to fast skip in Lucene search and to speed up the result pagination.

The `search_after` functionality is introduced in Elasticsearch 5.x, but it must be kept as an important focal point to improve the user experience in search scrolling/pagination results.

See also

- Refer to the *Executing a search* recipe in this chapter to learn how to structure a search for size pagination and *The executing a scrolling query recipe* for scrolling values in a query

Returning inner hits in results

In Elasticsearch, via nested and child documents, we can have complex data models. Elasticsearch, by default, returns only documents that match the searched type and not the nested/children one that matches the query.

The `inner_hits` function is introduced in Elasticsearch 5.x to provide this functionality.

Getting ready

You will need an up-and-running Elasticsearch installation as used in the *Downloading and installing Elasticsearch* recipe in Chapter 2, *Downloading and Setup*.

To execute `curl` via a command line, you need to install `curl` for your operating system.

To correctly execute the following commands, you will need an index populated with the `chapter_05/populate_query.sh` script available in the online code.

How to do it...

To return inner hits during a query, we will perform the following steps:

1. From the command line, we can execute a call adding `inner_hits` as follows:

```
curl -XPOST 'http://127.0.0.1:9200/test-index/test-
type/_search?pretty' -d '{
    "query": {
            "has_child" : {
                "type" : "test-type2",
                "query" : {
                    "term" : {
                        "value" : "value1"
                    }
                },
                "inner_hits":{}
            }
        }
    }
}'
```

2. The result returned by Elasticsearch, if everything works, should be as follows:

```
{
  "took" : 82,
  "timed_out" : false,
  "_shards" : {
    "total" : 5,
    "successful" : 5,
    "failed" : 0
  },
  "hits" : {
    "total" : 1,
    "max_score" : 1.0,
    "hits" : [
      {
        "_index" : "test-index",
        "_type" : "test-type",
        "_id" : "1",
        "_score" : 1.0,
        "_source" : {
          "position" : 1,
          "parsedtext" : "Joe Testere nice guy",
          "name" : "Joe Tester",
          "uuid" : "11111",
          "price" : 4.0
```

```
                },
                "inner_hits" : {
                  "test-type2" : {
                    "hits" : {
                      "total" : 1,
                      "max_score" : 0.2876821,
                      "hits" : [
                        {
                          "_type" : "test-type2",
                          "_id" : "1",
                          "_score" : 0.2876821,
                          "_routing" : "1",
                          "_parent" : "1",
                          "_source" : {
                            "name" : "data1",
                            "value" : "value1"
                          }
                        }
                      ]
                    }
                  }
                }
              }
            ]
          }
        }
```

How it works...

When executing nested/children queries, Elasticsearch executes a two-step query as follows:

1. It executes the nested/children query and returns the IDs of the referred values.
2. It executes the other part of the query filtering by the returned IDs of step 1.

Generally, the results of the nested/children query are not taken, because they require memory. Using the inner_hits, the nested/children query intermediate hits are kept and returned to the user.

To control the inner_hits returned documents, standard parameters for the search are available such as from, size, sort, highlight, _source, explain, scripted_fields, docvalues_fields, and version.

There is also a special property name used to name inner_hits, which allows the user to easily determine it in case of multiple inner_hits returning sections.

See also

- The *Executing a search* recipe in this chapter for all the standard parameters in searches for controlling returned hits
- The *Using a has_child query, Using a top_children query, Using a has_parent query* and *Using a nested query* recipes in `Chapter 7`, *Relationships and Geo Queries* is useful for queries that can be used for inner hits

Suggesting a correct query

It's very common for users to commit typing errors or to require suggestions for words that they are writing. These issues are solved by Elasticsearch with the suggest functionality.

Getting ready

You will need an up-and-running Elasticsearch installation as used in the *Downloading and installing Elasticsearch* recipe in `Chapter 2`, *Downloading and Setup*.

To execute `curl` via a command line, you need to install `curl` for your operating system.

To correctly execute the following commands, you will need an index populated with the `chapter_05/populate_query.sh` script available in the online code.

How to do it...

To suggest relevant terms by query, we will perform the following steps:

1. From the command line, we can execute a suggest call, as follows:

```
curl -XGET 'http://127.0.0.1:9200/test-index/_suggest?
pretty' -d '{
    "suggest1" : {
      "text" : "we find tester",
      "term" : {
      "field" : "parsedtext"
    }
  }
}'
```

2. The result returned by Elasticsearch, if everything works, should be as follows:

```
{
  "_shards" : {
    "total" : 5,
    "successful" : 5,
    "failed" : 0
  },
  "suggest1" : [
    {
      "text" : "we",
      "offset" : 0,
      "length" : 2,
      "options" : [ ]
    },
    {
      "text" : "find",
      "offset" : 3,
      "length" : 4,
      "options" : [ ]
    },
    {
      "text" : "tester",
      "offset" : 8,
      "length" : 6,
      "options" : [
        {
          "text" : "testere",
          "score" : 0.8333333,
          "freq" : 2
        }
      ]
    }
  ]
}
```

The result is composed of the following:

- The shards' status at the time of the query
- The list of tokens with their available candidates

How it works...

The suggested API call works by collecting terms stats on all the index shards. Using the Lucene field statistics, it is possible to detect the correct term or complete term.

The HTTP method to execute a suggest is GET (but POST also works); the REST endpoints are as follows:

```
http://<server>/_suggest
```

```
http://<server>/<index_name(s)>/_suggest
```

> **TIP**
>
> This call can also be embedded in the standard search API call.

There are two types of suggester term and phrase as follows:

- The simpler suggester to use is the term suggester. It requires only the text and the field to work. It also allows the user to set a lot of parameters such as the minimum size for a word, how to sort results, and the suggester strategy. A complete reference is available on the Elasticsearch website.
- The phrase suggester is able to keep relations between terms that it needs to suggest. The phrase suggester is less efficient than the term one, but it provides better results.

The suggest API is a new feature that allows parameters and options to change between releases, and allows new suggesters to be added via plugins.

See also

- The *Executing a search* recipe in this chapter for how to structure a search
- The phrase suggester online documentation is available at https://www.elastic.co/guide/en/elasticsearch/reference/current/search-suggesters-phrase.html
- The completion suggester online documentation is available at https://www.elastic.co/guide/en/elasticsearch/reference/current/search-suggesters-completion.html
- The context suggester online documentation is available at https://www.elastic.co/guide/en/elasticsearch/reference/current/suggester-context.html

Counting matched results

It is often required to return only the count of the matched results and not the results themselves.

There are a lot of scenarios involving counting, such as the following:

- To return the number of something (how many posts for a blog, how many comments for a post)
- Validating whether some items are available. Are there posts? Are there comments?

Getting ready

You will need an up-and-running Elasticsearch installation as used in the *Downloading and installing Elasticsearch* recipe in Chapter 2, *Downloading and Setup*.

To execute curl via a command line, you need to install curl for your operating system.

To correctly execute the following commands, you will need an index populated with the chapter_05/populate_query.sh script available in the online code.

How to do it...

In order to execute a counting query, we will perform the following steps:

1. From the command line, we will execute a count query, as follows:

```
curl -XGET 'http://127.0.0.1:9200/test-index/test-type/_count?
pretty' -d '{"query":{"match_all":{}}}'
```

2. The result returned by ElasticSearch, if everything works, should be as follows:

```
{
   "count" : 3,
   "_shards" : {
   "total" : 5,
      "successful" : 5,
      "failed" : 0
   }
}
```

The result is composed of the count result (a long type) and the shard status at the time of the query.

How it works...

The query is interpreted in the same way as for searching. The count action is processed and distributed in all the shards, in which is executed as a low-level Lucene count call. Every hit shard returns a count that is aggregated and returned to the user.

> In Elasticsearch, counting is faster than searching. In the case that the result source hits are not required, it's good practice to use the count API because it's faster and requires less resources.

The HTTP method to execute a count is GET (but also POST works), and the REST endpoints are as follows:

```
http://<server>/_count
http://<server>/<index_name(s)>/_count
http://<server>/<index_name(s)>/<type_name(s)>/_count
```

Multi indices and types are comma separated. If an index or a type is defined, the search is limited only to them. An alias can be used as an index name.

Typically, a body is used to express a query, but for simple queries, the q (query argument) can be used. For example, look at the following code:

```
curl -XGET 'http://127.0.0.1:9200/test-index/test-type/_count?
q=uuid:11111'
```

There's more...

In a previous version of Elasticsearch, the count API call (_count REST entrypoint) was implemented as a custom action, but in Elasticsearch version 5.x, it's removed. Internally the previous count API is implemented as a standard search with the size set to 0.

Using this trick, it not only speeds up the searching, but reduces networking.

You can use this approach to execute aggregations (we will see them in `Chapter 8,` *Aggregations*) without returning hits.

The previous query can be also executed as follows:

```
curl -XGET 'http://127.0.0.1:9200/test-index/test-type/_search?
pretty&size=0' -d '{"query":{"match_all":{}}}'
```

And the result returned by Elasticsearch, if everything works, should be as follows:

```
{
  "took" : 32,
  "timed_out" : false,
  "_shards" : {
    "total" : 5,
    "successful" : 5,
    "failed" : 0
  },
  "hits" : {
    "total" : 3,
    "max_score" : 0.0,
    "hits" : [ ]
  }
}
```

The count result (a long type) is available in the `hits.total`.

See also

- *The Executing a search* recipe in this chapter on using size to paginate
- `Chapter 8,` *Aggregations* on how to use the aggregations

Explaining a query

When executing searches, it's very common to have documents that don't match the query as expected. To easily debug these scenarios, Elasticsearch provides the explain query call.

Getting ready

You will need an up-and-running Elasticsearch installation as used in the *Downloading and installing Elasticsearch* recipe in `Chapter 2`, *Downloading and Setup*.

To execute `curl` via a command line, you need to install `curl` for your operating system.

To correctly execute the following commands, you will need an index populated with the `chapter_05/populate_query.sh` script available in the online code.

How to do it...

The steps required to execute the explain query call are as follows:

1. From the command line, we will execute an explain query against a document as follows:

```
curl -XGET 'http://127.0.0.1:9200/test-index/test-
type/1/_explain?pretty' -d '{
    "query": {
        "term": {
            "uuid": "11111"
        }
    }
}'
```

2. The result returned by Elasticsearch, if everything works, should be as follows:

```
{
  "_index" : "test-index",
  "_type" : "test-type",
  "_id" : "1",
  "matched" : true,
  "explanation" : {
    "value" : 0.2876821,
    "description" : "sum of:",
    "details" : [
      {
        "value" : 0.2876821,
        "description" : "weight(uuid:11111 in 0)
        [PerFieldSimilarity], result of:",
        "details" : [
  {
          "value" : 0.2876821,
          "description" : "score(doc=0,freq=1.0 =
```

```
                              termFreq=1.0\n), product of:",
                         "details" : [
                            {
                              "value" : 0.2876821,
                              "description" : "idf(docFreq=1, docCount=1)",
                              "details" : [ ]
                            },
                            ....
              }
                  ]
          },
          {
            "value" : 0.0,
            "description" : "match on required clause,product of:",
            "details" : [
               {
                 "value" : 0.0,
                 "description" : "# clause",
                 "details" : [ ]
               },
               {
                 "value" : 1.0,
                 "description" : "_type:test-type, product of:",
                 "details" : [....]
               }
            ]
          }
        ]
      }
    }
```

The important parts of the result are the following:

- matched: Whether the documents match or not in the query
- explanation: This section is composed of objects made of:
  - value: A double score of that query section
  - description: A string representation of the matching token (in case of wildcards or multi-terms, it can give information about the matched token)
  - details: An optional list of explanation objects

In this case, the details show two query parts:

- The first is the query that we have provided.
- The second one is automatically added by Elasticsearch to filter the document type (in Elasticsearch, there is no physical separation of document types, they are all stored in the same index and are filtered out at the time of the query). The score for this filter query is 0.0 to prevent changing the relevance.

How it works...

The explain call is a view of how Lucene computes the results. In the description section of the explain object, there are the Lucene representations of that part of the query.

A user doesn't need to be a Lucene expert to understand the explain descriptions, but they provide a highlight of how the query is executed and the terms are matched.

Query profiling

A new feature available in Elasticsearch 5.x is the profile API. This allows the user to track the time spent by Elasticsearch in executing a search or an aggregation.

Getting ready

You will need an up-and-running Elasticsearch installation as used in the *Downloading and installing Elasticsearch* recipe in Chapter 2, *Downloading and Setup*.

To execute curl via a command line, you need to install curl for your operating system.

To correctly execute the following commands, you will need an index populated with the chapter_05/populate_query.sh script available in the online code.

How to do it…

The steps to profile a query are as follows:

1. From the command line, we will execute a search with the profile set to `true`, as follows:

```
curl -XGET 'http://127.0.0.1:9200/test-index/test-type/_search?
pretty' -d '{
    "profile": true,
    "query": {
        "term": {
            "uuid": "11111"
        }
    }
}'
```

2. The result returned by Elasticsearch, if everything works, should be as follows:

```
{
  "took" : 14,
  "timed_out" : false,
  "_shards" : {...},
  "hits" : {...},
  "profile" : {
    "shards" : [
      {
        "id" : "[LNeNHh8wS_SHK7AfBzjJ0A][test-index][1]",
        "searches" : [
          {
            "query" : [
              {
                "type" : "BooleanQuery",
                "description" : "+uuid:11111 #
                (ConstantScore(_type:test-type))^0.0",
                "time" : "0.4339050000ms",
                "breakdown" : {
                  "score" : 0,
                  "build_scorer_count" : 0,
                  "match_count" : 0,
                  "create_weight" : 433904,
                  "next_doc" : 0,
                  "match" : 0,
                  "create_weight_count" : 1,
                  "next_doc_count" : 0,
                  "score_count" : 0,
                  "build_scorer" : 0,
```

```
                    "advance" : 0,
                    "advance_count" : 0
                },
                "children" : [
                    {
                    "type" : "TermQuery",
                    "description" : "uuid:11111",
                    "time" : "0.3952920000ms",
                     "breakdown" : {
                     "score" : 0,
                     "build_scorer_count" : 0,
                     "match_count" : 0,
                     "create_weight" : 395291,
                     "next_doc" : 0,
                     "match" : 0,
                     "create_weight_count" : 1,
                     "next_doc_count" : 0,
                     "score_count" : 0,
                     "build_scorer" : 0,
                     "advance" : 0,
                     "advance_count" : 0
                     }
                },
                 ...
            ]
        }
    ],
    "rewrite_time" : 229995,
    "collector" : [
    {
        "name" : "SimpleTopScoreDocCollector",
        "reason" : "search_top_hits",
        "time" : "0.004353000000ms"
    }
    ]
    }
  ],
  "aggregations" : [ ]
}...
    ]
  }
}
```

The output is very verbose. It's divided for shard and for single hit.

How it works...

The profile APIs are introduced in Elasticsearch 5.x for tracking times in executing queries and aggregations.

When a query is executed, if profiling is activated, all the internal calls are tracked using the internal instrumental API. For this reason, the profile API adds an overhead to the computation.

The output is also very verbose and depends on the internal components of both Elasticsearch and Lucene, so the format of the result can change in the future.

Deleting by query

We saw how to delete a document in the recipe *Deleting a document* in Chapter 4, *Basic Operations*. Deleting a document is very fast but it requires knowing the document ID.

Elasticsearch provides a call to delete all the documents that match a query via an additional module called **reindex,** which is installed by default.

Getting ready

You will need an up-and-running Elasticsearch installation as used in the *Downloading and installing Elasticsearch* recipe in Chapter 2, *Downloading and Setup*.

To execute curl via a command-line you need to install curl for your operating system.

To correctly execute the following commands you will need an index populated with the chapter_05/populate_query.sh script available in the online code.

How to do it...

In order to delete by query, we will perform the following steps:

1. From the command line, we will execute a query as follows:

```
curl -XPOST 'http://127.0.0.1:9200/test-index/test-
type/_delete_by_query?pretty' -d '{"query":{"match_all":{}}}'
```

2. The result returned by Elasticsearch, if everything works, should be as follows:

```
{
  "took" : 71,
  "timed_out" : false,
  "total" : 3,
  "deleted" : 3,
  "batches" : 1,
  "version_conflicts" : 0,
  "noops" : 0,
  "retries" : {
   "bulk" : 0,
   "search" : 0
  },
  "throttled_millis" : 0,
  "requests_per_second" : -1.0,
  "throttled_until_millis" : 0,
  "failures" : [ ]
}
```

3. The main components of the result are as follows:
   - `total`: The number of documents that match the query
   - `deleted`: The number of documents deleted
   - `batches`: The number of bulk actions executed to delete the documents
   - `version_conflicts`: The number of documents not deleted due to a version conflict during the bulk action
   - `noops`: The number of deleted not executed to a noop event
   - `retries.bulk`: The number of bulk actions that are retried
   - `retries.search`: The number of searches that are retried

How it works...

The `delete_by_query` function is executed automatically using the following steps:

1. In a master node, the query is executed and the results are scrolled.
2. For every bulk size element (default 1,000), a bulk is executed.
3. The bulk results are checked for conflicts. If no conflicts exist, a new bulk is executed until all the matched documents are deleted.

The `delete_by_query` call automatically manages back pressure (it reduces the delete command rate if the server has a high load).

> **TIP**
>
> When you want to remove all the documents without re-indexing a new index, a `delete_by_query` with a `match_all_query` allows you to clean your mapping of all the documents. This call is analogous to the `truncate_table` of the SQL language.

The HTTP method to execute a `delete_by_query` command is `POST`; the REST endpoints are as follows:

```
http://<server>/_delete_by_query
```

```
http://<server>/<index_name(s)>/_delete_by_query
http://<server>/<index_name(s)>/<type_name(s)>/_delete_by_query
```

Multi indices and types are comma separated. If an index or a type is defined, the search is limited only to them.

An alias can be used as the index name.

Typically, a body is used to express a query, but for simple queries the `q` (query argument) can be used. For example, look at the following code:

```
curl -XDELETE
'http://127.0.0.1:9200/test-index/test-type/_delete_by_query?q=uuid:11111'
```

There's more...

Further query arguments are as follows:

- `conflicts`: If it is set to `proceed`, when there is a version conflict, the call doesn't exit, it skips the error and it finishes execution
- `routing`: This is used to target only some shards
- `scroll_size`: This controls the size of the scrolling and the bulk (default `1000`)

See also

- The *Deleting a document* recipe in Chapter 4, *Basic Operations* is useful for executing a delete for a single document
- The *Delete by query task* recipe in Chapter 10, *Managing Clusters and Nodes* is useful for monitoring asynchronous delete by query actions

Updating by query

In the previous chapter, we saw how to update a document (Chapter 4, *Basic Operations*, *Update a document* recipe).

The update_by_query API call allows the user to execute the update on all the documents that match a query. It is very useful if you need to do the following:

- Reindex a subset of your records that match a query. It's common if you change your document mapping and need the documents to be reprocessed.
- Update values of your records the match a query.

This functionality is provided by an additional module called reindex that is installed by default.

Getting ready

You will need an up-and-running Elasticsearch installation as used in the *Downloading and installing Elasticsearch* recipe in Chapter 2, *Downloading and Setup*.

To execute curl via a command line, you need to install curl for your operating system.

To correctly execute the following commands, you will need an index populated with the chapter_05/populate_query.sh script available in the online code.

How to do it...

In order to execute an update from a query that simply reindexes your documents, we will perform the following steps:

1. From the command line, we will execute a query as follows:

```
curl -XPOST 'http://127.0.0.1:9200/test-index/test-
type/_update_by_query?pretty' -d '{"query":{"match_all":{}}}'
```

2. The result returned by Elasticsearch, if everything works, should be as follows:

```
{
  "took" : 117,
  "timed_out" : false,
  "total" : 3,
  "updated" : 3,
  "deleted" : 0,
  "batches" : 1,
  "version_conflicts" : 0,
  "noops" : 0,
  "retries" : {
    "bulk" : 0,
    "search" : 0
  },
  "throttled_millis" : 0,
  "requests_per_second" : -1.0,
  "throttled_until_millis" : 0,
  "failures" : [ ]
}
```

The most important components of the result are:

- `total`: The number of documents that match the query
- `updated`: The number of documents updated
- `batches`: The number of bulk actions executed to update the documents
- `version_conflicts`: The number of documents not deleted due to a version conflict during bulk action
- `noops`: The number of deleted documents not executed to a noop event
- `retries.bulk`: The number of bulk actions that are retried
- `retries.search`: The number of searches that are retried

How it works...

The `update_by_query` function works in a very similar way to the `delete_by_query` API, and is executed automatically using the following steps:

1. In a master node, the query is executed and the results are scrolled.
2. For every bulk size element (default 1,000), a bulk with the update command is executed.
3. The bulk results are checked for conflicts. If there are no conflicts, a new bulk is executed and the action search/bulk are executed until all the matched documents are deleted.

The HTTP method to execute an `update_by_query` is `POST`, and the REST endpoints are as follows:

```
http://<server>/_update_by_query
http://<server>/<index_name(s)>/_update_by_query
http://<server>/<index_name(s)>/<type_name(s)>/_update_by_query
```

Multi indices and types are comma separated. If an index or a type is defined, the search is limited only to them.

An alias can be used as an index name.

The additional query arguments are as follows:

- `conflicts`: If it is set to `proceed`, when there is a version conflict, the call doesn't exit, it skips the error and it finishes execution
- `routing`: This is used to target only some shards
- `scroll_size`: This controls the size of the scrolling and the bulk (the default size is `1000`)

There's more...

The `update_by_query` API can accept a script section in its body. In this way, it can become a powerful tool for executing custom updates on a subset of documents. (We will see scripting in detail in `Chapter 9`, *Scripting*.) It can be considered similar to the SQL Update command.

With this facility, we can add a new field and initialize its value with a script as follows:

```
curl -XPOST 'http://127.0.0.1:9200/test-index/test-
type/_update_by_query?pretty' -d '
{
"script": {
    "inline": "ctx._source.hit=4",
    "lang": "painless"
  },
"query":{"match_all":{}}
}'
```

With the preceding example, we add a `hit` field set to 4 for every document that matches the query. This is similar to the SQL command, as follows:

```
update test-type set hit=4
```

> The `update_by_query` API is one of the more powerful tools that Elasticsearch provides.

See also

- The *Update a document* recipe in `Chapter 4`, *Basic Operations* is useful for executing an update for a single document

Matching all the documents

One of the most common queries, usually in conjunction with a filter, is the `match_all` query. This kind of query allows the user to return all the documents. It's often used in conjunction with filters.

Getting ready

You will need an up-and-running Elasticsearch installation as used in the *Downloading and installing Elasticsearch* recipe in `Chapter 2`, *Downloading and Setup*.

To execute `curl` via a command line, you need to install `curl` for your operating system.

To correctly execute the following commands, you will need an index populated with the `chapter_05/populate_query.sh` script available in the online code.

How to do it...

In order to execute a `match_all` query, we will perform the following steps:

1. From the command line, we execute the query, as follows:

```
curl -XPOST 'http://127.0.0.1:9200/test-index/test-
type/_search?pretty' -d '{"query": {"match_all" : {}}}'
```

2. The result returned by Elasticsearch, if everything works, should be as follows:

```
{
  "took" : 52,
  "timed_out" : false,
  "_shards" : {
    "total" : 5,
    "successful" : 5,
    "failed" : 0
  },
  "hits" : {
    "total" : 3,
    "max_score" : 1.0,
    "hits" : [ {
      "_index" : "test-index",
      "_type" : "test-type",
      "_id" : "1",
      "_score" : 1.0, "_source" : {"position": 1, "parsedtext":
      "Joe Testere nice guy", "name": "Joe Tester", "uuid":
      "11111"}
    }, {
      "_index" : "test-index",
      "_type" : "test-type",
      "_id" : "2",
      "_score" : 1.0, "_source" : {"position": 2, "parsedtext":
      "Bill Testere nice guy", "name": "Bill Baloney",
      "uuid": "22222"}
    }, {
      "_index" : "test-index",
      "_type" : "test-type",
      "_id" : "3",
      "_score" : 1.0, "_source" : {"position": 3, "parsedtext":
```

```
             "Bill is not\n
              nice guy", "name": "Bill Clinton", "uuid": "33333"}
          } ]
      }
   }
```

The result is a standard query result as we have seen in the *Executing a search* recipe.

How it works…

The `match_all` query is one of the most common ones. It's faster because it doesn't require the score calculus (it's wrapped in a Lucene `ConstantScoreQuery`).

> If no query is defined in the search object, the default query will be a `match_all`.

See also

- Refer to the *Executing a search* recipe in this chapter for further reference

Using a boolean query

Most people using a search engine have at sometime used the syntax with minus (–) and plus (+) to include or exclude query terms. The Boolean query allows the user to programmatically define queries to include, exclude, optionally include (`should`), or filter in the query.

This kind of query is one of the most important ones because it allows the user to aggregate a lot of simple queries/filters that we will see in this chapter to build a big complex one.

Two main concepts are important in searches: **query** and **filter**. The query means that the matched results are scored using an internal Lucene scoring algorithm; for the filter, the results are matched without scoring. Because the filter doesn't need to compute the score, it is generally faster and can be cached.

Getting ready

You will need an up-and-running Elasticsearch installation as used in the *Downloading and installing Elasticsearch* recipe in `Chapter 2`, *Downloading and Setup*.

To execute `curl` via a command line, you need to install `curl` for your operating system.

To correctly execute the following commands, you will need an index populated with the `chapter_05/populate_query.sh` script available in the online code.

How to do it...

For executing a Boolean query, we will perform the following steps:

1. We execute a Boolean query from the command line as follows:

```
curl -XPOST 'http://127.0.0.1:9200/test-index/test-
type/_search?pretty' -d '{
    "query": {
        "bool" : {
        "must" : [{
            "term" : { "parsedtext" : "joe" }
        }],
        "must_not" : [{
            "range" : {
                "position" : { "from" : 10, "to" : 20 }
            }
        }],
        "should" : [
            {
                "term" : { "uuid" : "11111" }
            },
            {
                "term" : { "uuid" : "22222" }
            }
        ],
        "filter" : [{
            "term" : { "parsedtext" : "joe" }
        }],
    "minimum_number_should_match" : 1,
        "boost" : 1.0
        }
    }
}'
```

2. The result returned by Elasticsearch is similar to the previous recipes, but in this case it should return one record (`id:1`).

How it works...

The `bool` query is often one of the most used because it allows the user to compose a large query using a lot of simpler ones. One of the following four parts is mandatory:

- `must`: A list of queries that must be satisfied. All the `must` queries must be verified to return the hits. It can be seen as an `AND` filter with all its sub queries.
- `must_not`: A list of queries that must not be matched. It can be seen as not filter of an `AND` query.
- `should`: A list of queries that can be verified. The minimum number of these queries that must be verified and this value is controlled by `minimum_number_should_match` (default 1).
- `filter`: A list of queries to be used as the filter. They allow the user to filter out results without changing the score and relevance. The filter queries are faster than standard ones because they don't need to compute the score.

> **TIP**
>
> The Boolean filter is much faster than a group of And/Or/Not queries because it is optimized for executing fast Boolean bitwise operations on document bitmap results.

6
Text and Numeric Queries

In this chapter, we will cover the following recipes:

- Using a term query
- Using a terms query
- Using a prefix query
- Using a wildcard query
- Using a regexp query
- Using span queries
- Using a match query
- Using a query string query
- Using a simple query string query
- Using the range query
- The common terms query
- Using IDs query
- Using the function score query
- Using the exists query
- Using the template query

Introduction

In this chapter, we will see queries that are used for searching text and numeric values. They are simpler and the most common ones to be used in Elasticsearch.

The first part of the chapter covers the text queries from the simple term and terms query to the complex query string query. We'll understand how the queries are strongly related to the mapping for choosing the correct query based on mapping.

In the last part of the chapter, we will see some special query that covers fields, helpers for building complex queries from strings, and query templates.

Using a term query

Searching or filtering for a particular term is very frequent. Term queries work with exact value matches and are generally very fast.

The term queries can be compared to the equal "=" query in the SQL world (for not tokenized fields).

Getting ready

You need an up-and-running Elasticsearch installation as we described in the *Downloading and installing Elasticsearch* recipe in Chapter 2, *Downloading and Setup*.

To execute `curl` via the command line, you need to install `curl` for your operative system.

To correctly execute the following commands, you need an index populated with the `chapter_05/populate_query.sh` script available in the online code.

How to do it...

To execute a term query, we will perform the following steps:

1. We execute a term query from the command line:

```
curl -XPOST 'http://127.0.0.1:9200/test-index/test-
type/_search?pretty=true' -d '{
  "query": {
      "term": {
          "uuid": "33333"
      }
  }
}'
```

2. The result returned by Elasticsearch, if everything is alright, should be as follows:

```
{
  "took" : 58,
  "timed_out" : false,
  "_shards" : {
    "total" : 5,
    "successful" : 5,
    "failed" : 0
  },
  "hits" : {
    "total" : 1,
    "max_score" : 0.30685282,
    "hits" : [ {
      "_index" : "test-index",
      "_type" : "test-type",
      "_id" : "3",
      "_score" : 0.30685282, "_source" : {"position": 3,
      "parsedtext": "Bill is not\n
      nice guy", "name": "Bill Clinton", "uuid": "33333"}
    } ]
  }
}
```

3. For executing a term query as a filter, we need to use it wrapped in a Boolean query. The preceding term query will be executed in this way:

```
curl -XPOST 'http://127.0.0.1:9200/test-index/test-
type/_search?pretty=true' -d '{
  "query": {
    "bool": {
      "filter": {
        "term": {
          "uuid": "33333"
        }
      }
    }
  }
}'
```

4. The result returned by Elasticsearch, if everything is alright, should be:

```
{
  "took" : 46,
  "timed_out" : false,
  "_shards" : {
    "total" : 5,
    "successful" : 5,
```

```
      "failed" : 0
    },
    "hits" : {
      "total" : 1,
      "max_score" : 0.0,
      "hits" : [
        {
          "_index" : "test-index",
          "_type" : "test-type",
          "_id" : "3",
          "_score" : 0.0,
          "_source" : {
            "hit" : 4,
            "price" : 6.0,
            "name" : "Bill Clinton",
            "position" : 3,
            "parsedtext" : "Bill is not\n
             nice guy",
            "uuid" : "33333"
          }
        }
      ]
    }
  }
```

The result is a standard query result as we have seen in the *Executing a Search* recipe in `Chapter 5`, *Search*.

How it works...

Lucene, due to its inverted index, is one of the fastest engines at searching for a term/value in a field.

Every field that is indexed in Lucene is converted in a fast search structure for its particular type:

- The text is split in tokens if analyzed or saved as a single token
- The numeric fields are converted in their fastest binary representation
- The date and datetime fields are converted in binary forms

In Elasticsearch, all these conversion steps are automatically managed. Search for a term, independent from the value, which is archived by Elasticsearch using the correct format for the field.

Internally, during a term query execution, all the documents matching the term are collected, then they are sorted by score (the scoring depends on the Lucene, similarity algorithm chosen by default BM25. For more details about Elasticsearch similarity algorithms

see `https://www.elastic.co/guide/en/elasticsearch/reference/5.x/index-modules-si milarity.html`).

If we look for the results of the previous searches, for the term query the hit has `0.30685282` as the score, the filter has `1.0`. The time required for scoring if the sample is very small is not so relevant, but if you have thousands or millions of documents it takes much more time.

> If the score is not important, prefer to use the term filter.

The filter is preferred to the query when the score is not important. The typical scenarios are:

- Filtering permissions
- Filtering numerical values
- Filtering ranges

> In filtered query, the filter applies first, narrowing the number of documents to be matched against the query, then the query is applied.

There's more...

Matching a term is the basis of Lucene and Elasticsearch. To correctly use these queries, you need to pay attention to how the field is indexed.

As we saw in `Chapter 3`, *Managing Mappings*, the terms of an indexed field depend on the analyzer used to index it. To better understand this concept, there is a representation of a phrase depending on several analyzers in the following table. For standard string analyzers, if we have a similar phrase `Phrase: Peter's house is big`, the results will be similar to the following table:

Mapping index	Analyzer	Tokens
`"index": false`	(No index)	(No tokens)
`"type": "keyword"`	KeywordAnalyzer	["Peter's house is big"]
`"type": "text"`	StandardAnalyzer	["peter", "s", "house", "is", "big"]

The common pitfalls in searching are related to misunderstanding the analyzer/mapping configuration.

`KeywordAnalyzer`, which is used as the default for the `not tokenized` field, saves the string unchanged as a single token.

`StandardAnalyzer`, the default for the `type="text"` field, tokenizes on whitespaces and punctuation; every token is converted into lowercase. You should use the same analyzer for indexing to analyze the query (the default settings).

In the preceding example, if the phrase is analyzed with `StandardAnalyzer`, you cannot search for the term "Peter", but rather for "peter" because the StandardAnalyzer executes lowercase on terms.

> When the same field requires one or more search strategies, you need to use the `fields` property via the different analyzers that you need.

Using a terms query

The previous type of search works very well for single term search. If you want search for multiple terms, you can process it in two ways: using a boolean query or using a multi-term query.

Getting ready

You need an up-and-running Elasticsearch installation as we described in the *Downloading and installing Elasticsearch* recipe in `Chapter 2`, *Downloading and Setup*.

To execute `curl` via the command line, you need to install `curl` for your operative system.

To correctly execute the following commands, you need an index populated with the `chapter_05/populate_query.sh` script available in the online code.

How to do it...

For executing a terms query, we will perform the following steps:

1. We execute a terms query, from the command line:

```
curl -XPOST 'http://127.0.0.1:9200/test-index/test-
type/_search?pretty=true' -d '{
    "query": {
        "terms": {
            "uuid": ["33333", "32222"]
        }
    }
}'
```

2. The result returned by Elasticsearch, if everything is alright, should be:

```
{
  "took" : 16,
  "timed_out" : false,
  "_shards" : {
    "total" : 5,
    "successful" : 5,
    "failed" : 0
  },
  "hits" : {
    "total" : 1,
    "max_score" : 0.2876821,
    "hits" : [
      {
        "_index" : "test-index",
        "_type" : "test-type",
        "_id" : "3",
        "_score" : 0.2876821,
        "_source" : {
```

```
            "hit" : 4,
            "price" : 6.0,
            "name" : "Bill Clinton",
            "position" : 3,
            "parsedtext" : "Bill is not\n
            nice guy",
            "uuid" : "33333"
          }
        }
      ]
    }
  }
}
```

How it works...

The terms query is related to the previous kind of query; it extends the term query to support multivalues.

This call is very useful because it is very common to the concept of filtering on multivalues. In traditional SQL, this operation is achieved with the in keyword in the where clause, that is, Select * from *** where color in ("red", "green").

In the preceding samples, the query searches for uuid with value 33333 or 22222.

The terms query is not a merely helper for the term matching function.

The terms query allows you to define extra parameters to control the query behavior such as:

- minimum_match/minimum_should_match: This controls how many matched terms are required to validate the query, as follows:

```
"terms": {
"color": ["red", "blue", "white"],
    "minimum_should_match":2
    }
```

- The preceding query matches all the documents where the color field has at least two values among red, blue and white.

- boost: This is the standard query boost value used to modify the query weight. This can be very useful if you want to give more relevance to the terms matched to increase the final document score.

There's more...

Because terms filtering is very powerful, to give some speedup in searching, the terms can be fetched by other documents during the query.

This is a very common scenario. Think, for example, a user that contains the list of groups in which he is associated and you want to filter documents that can be seen only by some groups. The pseudocode should be:

```
curl -XGET localhost:9200/my-index/document/_search?pretty=true -d '{
    "query" : {
        "terms" : {
            "can_see_groups" : {
                "index" : "my-index",
                "type" : "user",
                "id" : "1bw71LaxSzSp_zV6NB_YGg",
                "path" : "groups"
            }
        }
    }
}'
```

In this example, the list of groups is fetched at runtime from a document (which is always identified by an index, type, and ID) and the path (`field`) that contains the values to put in it. The `routing` parameter is also supported.

This is a similar pattern to SQL:

```
select * from xxx where can_see_group in (select groups from user where
user_id='1bw71LaxSzSp_zV6NB_YGg')
```

Generally, NoSQL datastores do not support join, so the data must be optimized to searching via denormalization or other techniques.

Elasticsearch does not provide something similar to the SQL joins, but it provides similar alternatives, such as:

- Child/parent queries
- Nested queries
- Terms filtered with external document term fetching.

See also

- The *Executing a search* recipe in `Chapter 5`, *Search*
- The *Using a term query* in this chapter
- The *Using a boolean query* recipe in `Chapter 5`, *Search*
- The *Using the nested query, Using the has_child query* and *Using the has_parent query* recipes in `Chapter 7`, *Relationships and Geo Queries*.

Using a prefix query

The prefix query is used when only the starting part of a term is known. It allows completing truncated or partial terms.

Getting ready

You need an up-and-running Elasticsearch installation as we described in the *Downloading and installing Elasticsearch* recipe in `Chapter 2`, *Downloading and Setup*.

To execute `curl` via the command line, you need to install `curl` for your operative system.

To correctly execute the following commands, you need an index populated with the `chapter_05/populate_query.sh` script available in the online code.

How to do it...

For executing a prefix query, we will perform the following steps:

1. We execute a prefix query from the command line:

```
curl -XPOST 'http://127.0.0.1:9200/test-index/test-
type/_search?pretty=true' -d '{
    "query": {
        "prefix": {
            "uuid": "222"
        }
    }
}'
```

2. The result returned by Elasticsearch, if everything is alright, should be:

```
{
  "took" : 1,
  "timed_out" : false,
  "_shards" : {
    "total" : 5,
    "successful" : 5,
    "failed" : 0
  },
  "hits" : {
    "total" : 1,
    "max_score" : 1.0,
    "hits" : [
      {
        "_index" : "test-index",
        "_type" : "test-type",
        "_id" : "2",
        "_score" : 1.0,
        "_source" : {
          "hit" : 4,
          "price" : 5.0,
          "name" : "Bill Baloney",
          "position" : 2,
          "parsedtext" : "Bill Testere nice guy",
          "uuid" : "22222"
        }
      }
    ]
  }
}
```

How it works...

When a prefix query is executed, Lucene has a special method to skip to terms that start with a common prefix: so the execution of a prefix query is very fast.

The prefix query is used in general in scenarios where term completion is required as follows:

- Name completion
- Code completion
- On type completion

When you design a tree structure in Elasticsearch, if the ID of the item contains the hierarchic relation, it can speed up the application filtering very much. As example is to have:

Id	Element
001	Fruit
00102	Apple
0010201	Green Apple
0010202	Red Apple
00103	Melon
0010301	White Melon
002	Vegetables

In the preceding example, we have structured the ID that contains information about the tree structure, which allows us to create such queries:

- Filter by all the fruits:

    ```
    "prefix": {"fruit_id": "001" }
    ```

- Filter by all apple types:

    ```
    "prefix": {"fruit_id": "001002" }
    ```

- Filter by all the vegetables:

    ```
    "prefix": {"fruit_id": "002" }
    ```

If it's compared to a standard SQL `parent_id` table on a very large dataset, the reduction in join and the fast search performance of Lucene can filter the results in some milliseconds compared to some seconds/minutes.

> Structuring the data in the correct way can give impressive performance boost!

There's more...

The prefix query can be very handy when you are searching for ending text.

For example, a user must match document with a field `filename` with ending extension `png`. Usually, users tend to execute a poor performance regex query similar to `.*png`. The regex needs to check every term of the fields, so the computation time is very long.

The best practice is to index the filename field with a reverse analyzer.

To achieve this, perform the following steps:

1. We define `reverse_analyzer` to index level, putting this in the settings:

```
{
  "settings": {
    "analysis": {
      "analyzer": {
        "reverse_analyzer": {
          "type": "custom",
          "tokenizer": "keyword",
          "filter": [
            "lowercase",
            "reverse"
          ]
        }
      }
    }
  }
}
```

2. When we define the `filename` field, we use `reverse_analyzer` for its subfield.

```
"filename" : {
  "type" : "keyword",
  "fields":{
    "rev":{
        "type" : "text",
        "analyzer": "reverse_analyzer"
    }
  }
},
```

3. Now we can search using a prefix query, using a similar query:

```
"query": {
        "prefix": {
                "filename.rev": ".png"
        }
}
```

Using this approach, for example, when you index a file named `myTest.png`, the internal Elasticsearch data will be similar to the following ones:

```
filename:"myTest.png"
filename.rev:"gnp.tsetym"
```

Because the text analyzer is used both for indexing and searching the prefix text `.png` will be automatically processed in `gnp` when the query is executed.

Moving from regex to prefix for ending match can bring down your execution time from several seconds to several milliseconds!!

See also

- The *Using a term query* recipe

Using a wildcard query

The wildcard query is used when a part of a term is known. It allows completing truncated or partial terms. They are very famous because they are often for commands on files on system shells (that is, `ls *.jpg`).

Getting ready

You need an up-and-running Elasticsearch installation as we described in the *Downloading and installing Elasticsearch* recipe in `Chapter 2`, *Downloading and Setup*.

To execute `curl` via the command line, you need to install `curl` for your operative system.

To correctly execute the following commands, you need an index populated with the `chapter_05/populate_query.sh` script available in the online code.

How to do it...

For executing a wildcard query, we will perform the following steps:

1. We execute a wildcard query from the command line:

```
curl -XPOST 'http://127.0.0.1:9200/test-index/test-
type/_search?pretty=true' -d '{
    "query": {
        "wildcard": {
            "uuid": "22?2*"
        }
    }
}'
```

2. The result returned by Elasticsearch, if everything is alright, should be:

```
{
  "took" : 1,
  "timed_out" : false,
  "_shards" : {
    "total" : 5,
    "successful" : 5,
    "failed" : 0
  },
  "hits" : {
    "total" : 1,
    "max_score" : 1.0,
    "hits" : [
      {
        "_index" : "test-index",
        "_type" : "test-type",
        "_id" : "2",
        "_score" : 1.0,
        "_source" : {
          "price" : 5.0,
          "name" : "Bill Baloney",
          "position" : 2,
          "parsedtext" : "Bill Testere nice guy",
          "uuid" : "22222"
        }
      }
    ]
  }
}
```

How it works...

The wildcard is very similar to a regular expression, but it has only two special characters:

- `*` : This means match zero or more characters
- `?`: This means match one character

During the query execution, all the terms of the searched field are matched against the wildcard query. So, the performance of the wildcard query depends on the cardinality of your terms. To improve performance, it's suggested to not execute the wildcard query that starts with `*` or `?`.

To speed up search, it's best practice to have some starting characters to use the `skipTo` Lucene method in order to reduce the processed terms.

See also

- The *Using a regexp query* recipe
- The *Using a prefix query* recipe

Using a regexp query

In the previous recipes, we have seen different term queries (terms, prefix, and wildcard); another powerful term query is the regexp (regular expression) one.

Getting ready

You need an up-and-running Elasticsearch installation as we described in the *Downloading and installing Elasticsearch* recipe in `Chapter 2`, *Downloading and Setup*.

To execute `curl` via the command line, you need to install `curl` for your operative system.

To correctly execute the following commands, you need an index populated with the
chapter_05/populate_query.sh script available in the online code.

How to do it...

For executing a regexp query, we will perform the following steps:

1. We can execute a regexp term query from the command line:

```
curl -XPOST 'http://127.0.0.1:9200/test-index/test-
type/_search?pretty=true' -d '{
    "query": {
        "regexp": {
            "parsedtext": {
                "value": "j.*",
                "flags" : "INTERSECTION|COMPLEMENT|EMPTY"
            }
        }
    }
}'
```

2. The query result will be:

```
{
  "took" : 68,
  "timed_out" : false,
  "_shards" : {
    "total" : 5,
    "successful" : 5,
    "failed" : 0
  },
  "hits" : {
    "total" : 1,
    "max_score" : 1.0,
    "hits" : [
      {
        "_index" : "test-index",
        "_type" : "test-type",
        "_id" : "1",
        "_score" : 1.0,
        "_source" : {
          "hit" : 4,
          "price" : 4.0,
          "name" : "Joe Tester",
          "position" : 1,
          "parsedtext" : "Joe Testere nice guy",
```

```
            "uuid" : "11111"
        }
      }
    ]
  }
}
```

The score for a matched regex result is always 1.0.

How it works...

The regexp query executes the regular expression against all terms of the documents. Internally, Lucene compiles the regular expression in an automaton to improve performances. Thus, generally, the performance of this query is not fast, as the performance depends on the regular expression used.

To speed up regexp query, a good approach is to have a regular expression that doesn't start with a wildcard.

The parameters that are used to control this process are as follows:

- `boost` (default `1.0`): This includes the values used for boosting the score for this query.
- `flags`: This is a list of one or more flags pipe | delimited. The available flags are:
    - `ALL`: This enables all the optional regexp syntax
    - `ANYSTRING`: This enables anystring (`@`)
    - `AUTOMATON`: This enables named automata (`<identifier>`)
    - `COMPLEMENT`: This enables complement (`~`)
    - `EMPTY`: This enables empty language (`#`)
    - `INTERSECTION`: This enables intersection (`&`)
    - `INTERVAL`: This enables numerical intervals (`<n-m>`)
    - `NONE`: This enables no optional regexp syntax

> To avoid poor performance in search don't execute regex starting with . *. Prefer to use prefix query on string processed with a reverse analyzer.

See also

- The official documentation for regexp query at https://www.elastic.co/guide/en/elasticsearch/reference/master/query-dsl-regexp-query.html for the regular expression syntax used by Lucene
- The *Using a prefix query* recipe
- The *Using a wildcard query* recipe

Using span queries

The big difference between standard databases (SQL, but also many NoSQL such as MongoDB, Riak, or CouchDB) and Elasticsearch is the number of facilities to express text queries.

The span query family is a group of queries that control a sequence of text tokens via their positions: the standard queries don't take care of positional presence of text tokens.

Span queries allow defining several kinds of queries:

- The exact phrase query
- The exact fragment query (that is, take off and give up)
- Partial exact phrase with a "slop" (other tokens between the searched terms, that is, "the man" with slop 2 can also match "the strong man", "the old wise man", and so on)

Getting ready

You need an up-and-running Elasticsearch installation as we described in the *Downloading and installing Elasticsearch* recipe in Chapter 2, *Downloading and Setup*.

To execute curl via the command line, you need to install curl for your operative system.

To correctly execute the following commands, you need an index populated with the chapter_05/populate_query.sh script available in the online code.

How to do it...

For executing span queries, we will perform the following steps:

1. The main element in span queries is span_term whose usage is similar to the term of the standard query. One or more span_term can be aggregated to formulate a span query.

2. The span_first query defines a query in which the span_term must match in the first token or near it. The following is an example:

```
curl -XPOST 'http://127.0.0.1:9200/test-index/test-
type/_search?pretty=true' -d '{
    "query": {
        "span_first" : {
            "match" : {
                "span_term" : { "parsedtext" : "joe" }
            },
            "end" : 5
        }
    }
}'
```

3. The span_or query is used to define multivalues in a span query. This is very handy for simple synonym search.

```
curl -XPOST 'http://127.0.0.1:9200/test-index/test-
type/_search?pretty=true' -d '{
    "query": {
        "span_or" : {
            "clauses" : [
                { "span_term" : { "parsedtext" : "nice" } },
                { "span_term" : { "parsedtext" : "cool" } },
                { "span_term" : { "parsedtext" : "wonderful"}}
            ]
        }
    }
}'
```

The list of clauses is the core of `span_or` query, because it contains the span terms that should match.

5. Similar to `span_or`, there is a `span_multi` query, which wraps multi term queries such as prefix, wildcard, and so on. Consider the following code, for example:

```
curl -XPOST 'http://127.0.0.1:9200/test-index/test-
type/_search?pretty=true' -d '{
    "query": {
        "span_multi":{
            "match":{
                "prefix" : { "parsedtext" :  { "value" : "jo" }
            }
        }
    }
}'
```

6. Queries can be used to create the `span_near` query that allows controlling the token sequence of the query:

```
curl -XPOST 'http://127.0.0.1:9200/test-index/test-
type/_search?pretty=true' -d '{
    "query": {
        "span_near" : {
            "clauses" : [
                { "span_term" : { "parsedtext" : "nice" } },
                { "span_term" : { "parsedtext" : "joe" } },
                { "span_term" : { "parsedtext" : "guy" } }
            ],
            "slop" : 3,
            "in_order" : false,
            "collect_payloads" : false
        }
    }
}'
```

7. For complex queries, skipping matching given positional tokens is very important. This can be achieved with the `span_not` query:

```
curl -XPOST 'http://127.0.0.1:9200/test-index/test-
type/_search?pretty=true' -d '{
    "query": {
        "span_not" : {
            "include" : {
                "span_term" : { "parsedtext" : "nice" }
```

```
            },
            "exclude" : {
                "span_near" : {
                    "clauses" : [
                        { "span_term" : { "parsedtext" : "not"
                        } },
                        { "span_term" : { "parsedtext" : "nice"
                        } }
                    ],
                    "slop" : 1,
                    "in_order" : true
                }
            }
        }
    }
}'
```

The `include` section contains the span that must be matched, `exclude` contains the span that must not be matched. It matches documents with the term `nice`, but not `not nice`. This can be very useful to exclude negative phrases!!!

8. For searching with a span query that is "surrounded" by other terms, we can use the `span_containing`.

```
curl -XPOST 'http://127.0.0.1:9200/test-index/test-
type/_search?pretty=true' -d '{
    "query": {
        "span_containing" : {
            "little" : {
                "span_term" : { "parsedtext" : "nice" }
            },
            "big" : {
                "span_near" : {
                    "clauses" : [
                        { "span_term" : { "parsedtext" : "not"
                        } },
                        { "span_term" : { "parsedtext" : "guy"
                        } }
                    ],
                    "slop" : 5,
                    "in_order" : true
                }
            }
        }
    }
}'
```

The `little` section contains the span that must be matched. The `big` section contains the span that contains the `little` matches. In the preceding case, the matched expression will be something similar to `not * nice * guy`.

10. For searching with a span query that is enclosed by other span terms, we can use `span_within`.

```
curl -XPOST 'http://127.0.0.1:9200/test-index/test-
type/_search?pretty=true' -d '{
    "query": {
        "span_within" : {
            "little" : {
                "span_term" : { "parsedtext" : "nice" }
            },
            "big" : {
                "span_near" : {
                    "clauses" : [
                        { "span_term" : { "parsedtext" : "not"
                        } },
                        { "span_term" : { "parsedtext" : "guy"
                        } }
                    ],
                    "slop" : 5,
                    "in_order" : true
                }
            }
        }
    }
}'
```

The `little` section contains the span that must be matched. The `big` section contains the span that contains the `little` matches.

How it works...

Lucene provides the span queries available in Elasticsearch.

The base span query is the `span_term` that works exactly as the term query. The goal of this span query is to match an exact term (field plus text). It can be composed to formulate other kind of span queries.

The main usage of span query is a proximity search: terms that are close to each other.

Using `span_term` in `span_first` means to match a term, which must be in the first position. If the end parameter (integer) is defined, it extends the first token matching to the passed value.

One of the most powerful span queries is `span_or` that allows defining multiple terms in the same position. It covers several scenarios such as:

- Multinames
- Synonyms
- Several verbal forms

The `span_or` query does not have the counterpart `span_and`, which should have no meaning, because span queries are positional.

If the number of terms that must be passed to a `span_or` is huge, it can be reduced with a `span_multi` query with a prefix or a wildcard. This approach allows matching, for example, all the term play, playing, plays, player, players, and so on using a prefix query with `play`.

Otherwise, the most powerful span query is `span_near`, which allows defining a list of span queries (`clauses`) to be matched in sequence or not. The parameters that can be passed to this span query are:

- `in_order`: This defines that the term matched in the clauses must be executed in order. If you define two span near queries with two span terms to match `joe` and `black`, and `in_order` is `true`, you will not be able to match `black` `joe` text (default `true`).
- `slop`: This defines the distance between terms that must be matched from the clauses (default `0`).

For settings slop to 0 and `in_order` to `true`, you are creating an `exact phrase` match.

The `span_near` query and slop can be used to create a phrase matching that is able to have some terms that are unknown. For example, consider matching an expression such as `the house`. If you need to execute an exact match, you need to write a similar query:

```
{
    "query": {
        "span_near" : {
            "clauses" : [
                { "span_term" : { "parsedtext" : "the" } },
                { "span_term" : { "parsedtext" : "house" } }
            ],
            "slop" : 0,
            "in_order" : true
        }
    }
}
```

Now, if you have, for example, an adjective between `the` article and `house` (that is, the wonderful house, the big house, and so on), the previous query never matches them. To achieve this goal is required to set the slop to 1.

Usually, slop is set to 1, 2, or 3 as values: high values (> `10`) have no meaning.

See also

- The *Using a match query* recipe

Using a match query

Elasticsearch provides a helper to build complex span queries that depend on simple preconfigured settings. This helper is called **match query**.

Getting ready

You need an up-and-running Elasticsearch installation as we described in the *Downloading and installing Elasticsearch* recipe in `Chapter 2`, *Downloading and Setup*.

To execute `curl` via the command line, you need to install `curl` for your operative system.

To correctly execute the following commands, you need an index populated with the `chapter_05/populate_query.sh` script available in the online code.

How to do it...

For executing match queries, we will perform the following steps:

1. The standard usage of a match query simply requires the field name and the query text. Consider the following example:

```
curl -XPOST 'http://127.0.0.1:9200/test-index/test-
type/_search?pretty=true' -d '{
    "query": {
        "match" : {
            "parsedtext" : {
                "query": "nice guy",
                "operator": "and"
            }
        }
    }
}'
```

2. If you need to execute the same query as a phrase query, the type from match changes in `match_phrase`:

```
curl -XPOST 'http://127.0.0.1:9200/test-index/test-
type/_search?pretty=true' -d '{
    "query": {
        "match_phrase" : {
            "parsedtext" : "nice guy"
        }
    }
}'
```

3. An extension of the previous query used in text completion or `search as you type` functionality is `match_phrase_prefix`:

```
curl -XPOST 'http://127.0.0.1:9200/test-index/test-
type/_search?pretty=true' -d '{
    "query": {
        "match_phrase_prefix" : {
            "parsedtext" : "nice gu"
        }
    }
}'
```

4. A common requirement is the possibility to search for several fields with the same query. The `multi_match` parameter provides this capability:

```
curl -XPOST 'http://127.0.0.1:9200/test-index/test-
type/_search?pretty=true' -d '{
    "query": {
        "multi_match" : {
            "fields":["parsedtext", "name"],
            "query": "Bill",
            "operator": "and"
        }
    }
}'
```

How it works...

The match query aggregates several frequent-used query types that cover standard query scenarios.

The standard match query creates a boolean query that can be controlled by these parameters:

- `operator`: This defines how to store and process the terms. If it's set to OR, all the terms are converted in a boolean query with all the terms in *should clauses*. If it's set to AND, the terms build a list of *must clauses* (default OR).
- `analyzer`: This allows overriding the default analyzer of the field (default based on mapping or set in searcher).
- `fuzziness`: This allows defining fuzzy term. Related to this parameter, `prefix_length` and `max_expansion` are available.
- `zero_terms_query` (none/all): This allows you to define a tokenizer filter that removes all terms from the query, the default behavior is to return nothing or all the documents. This is the case when you build an English query searching for the or a that means it could match all the documents (default none).
- `cutoff_frequency`: This allows handling dynamic stopwords (very common terms in text) at runtime. During query execution, terms over the `cutoff_frequency` are considered stopwords. This approach is very useful as it allows converting a general query to a domain-specific query, because terms to skip depend on text statistics. The correct value must be defined empirically.

The boolean query created from the match query is very handy, but it suffers from some common problems related to Boolean query such as term position. If the term position matters, you need to use another family of match queries, the phrase one.

The `match_phrase` type in match query builds long span queries from the query text.

The parameters that can be used to improve the quality of phrase query are the analyzer for text processing and the `slop`, which controls the distance between terms (refer to the *Using span queries* recipe).

If the last term is partially complete and you want to provide your users *query while writing* functionality, the phrase type can be set to `match_phrase_prefix`. This type builds a span near query in which the last clause is a span prefix term. This functionality is often used for `typehead` widgets such as the one shown in the following screenshot:

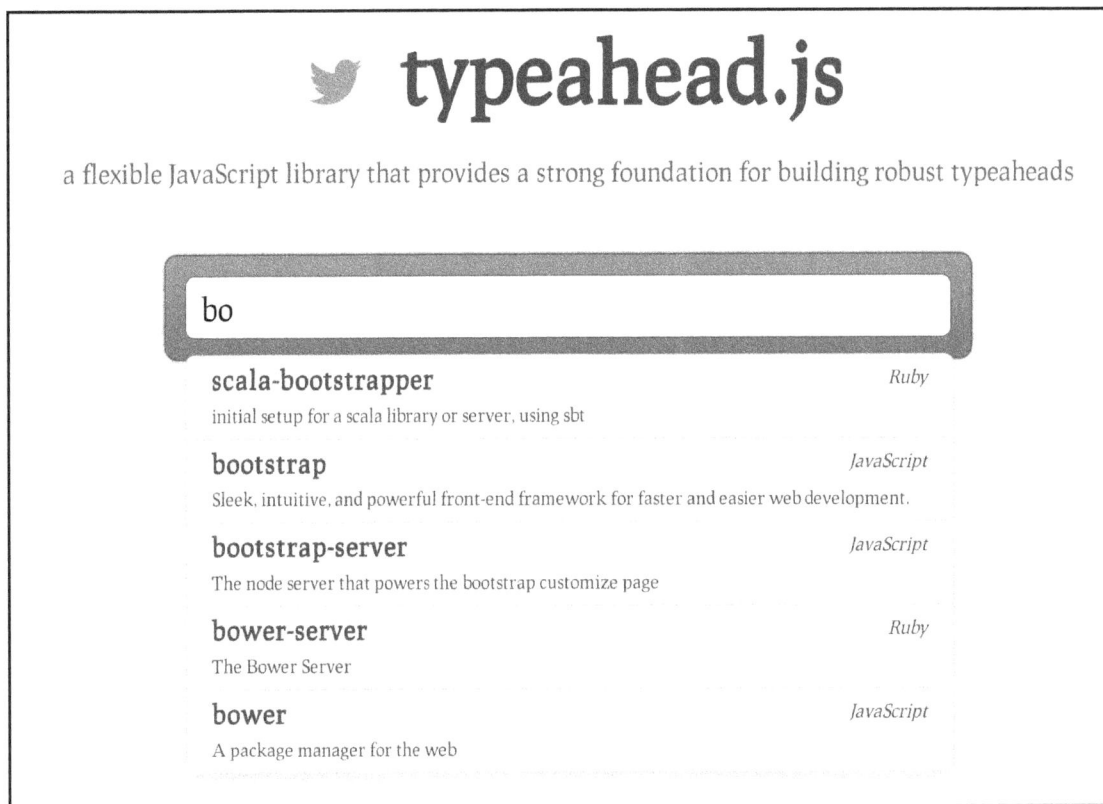

The match query is a very useful query type or, as I previously defined, it is a helper to build several common queries internally.

The `multi_match` parameter is similar to a `match` query that allows to define multiple fields to search on. For defining these fields, there are several helpers that can be used such as:

- **Wildcards field definition**: Using wildcards is a simple way to define multiple fields in one shot. For example, if you have fields for languages such as `name_en`, `name_es`, and `name_it`, you can define the search field as `name_*` to automatically search all the name fields.
- **Boosting some fields**: Not all the fields have the same importance. You can boost your fields using the ^ operator. For example, you have title and content fields and title is more important than content; you can define the fields in this way:

```
"fields":["title^3", "content"]
```

See also

- The *Using span queries* recipe
- The *Using prefix query* recipe

Using a query string query

In the previous recipes, we have seen several type of queries that use text to match the results. The query string query is a special type of query that allows defining complex queries by mixing the field rules.

It uses the Lucene query parser to parse text to complex queries.

Getting ready

You need an up-and-running Elasticsearch installation as we described in the *Downloading and installing Elasticsearch* recipe in `Chapter 2`, *Downloading and Setup*.

To execute `curl` via the command line, you need to install `curl` for your operative system.

To correctly execute the following commands, you need an index populated with the `chapter_05/populate_query.sh` script available in the online code.

How to do it...

For executing a `query_string` query, we will perform the following steps:

1. We want to search for text `nice guy`, but with a condition of discarding the term `not` and displaying a price lesser than 5. The query will be:

```
curl -XPOST 'http://127.0.0.1:9200/test-index/test-
type/_search?pretty=true' -d '{
  "query": {
    "query_string": {
      "query": ""nice guy" -parsedtext:not price:{ * TO 5 } ",
      "fields": [
        "parsedtext^5"
      ],
      "default_operator": "and"
    }
  }
}'
```

2. The result returned by Elasticsearch, if everything is alright, should be:

```
{
  "took" : 17,
  "timed_out" : false,
  "_shards" : {
    "total" : 5,
    "successful" : 5,
    "failed" : 0
  },
  "hits" : {
    "total" : 1,
    "max_score" : 3.8768208,
    "hits" : [
      {
        "_index" : "test-index",
        "_type" : "test-type",
        "_id" : "1",
        "_score" : 3.8768208,
        "_source" : {
```

```
        "position" : 1,
        "parsedtext" : "Joe Testere nice guy",
        "name" : "Joe Tester",
        "uuid" : "11111",
        "price" : 4.0
      }
    }
  ]
 }
}
```

How it works...

The `query_string` query is one of the most powerful types of queries. The only required field is `query` that contains the query that must be parsed with Lucene query parser (For more information, refer to the link:
`http://lucene.apache.org/core/6_2_0/queryparser/org/apache/lucene/queryparser/classic/package-summary.html`.

Lucene query parser is able to analyze a complex query syntax and convert it in many of the query types that we have seen in the previous recipes.

The optional parameters that can be passed to the query string query are:

- `default_field`: This defines the default field to be used to the query. It can also be set at index level defining the `index` property `index.query.default_field` (default `_all`).
- `fields`: This defines a list of fields to be used. It replaces the `default_field`. The `fields` parameter also allows using wildcards as values. (that is, `city.*`).
- `default_operator`: This is the default operator to be used for text in `query` parameter (the default `OR`; the available values are `AND` and `OR`).
- `analyzer` This is the analyzer that must be used for query string.
- `allow_leading_wildcard`: Here, the * and ? wildcards are allowed as first characters. Using similar wildcards gives performance penalties (default `true`).
- `lowercase_expanded_terms`: This controls if all expansion terms (generated by fuzzy, range, wildcard, and prefix) must be lowercased (default `true`).
- `enable_position_increments`: This enables the position increment in queries. For every query token, the positional value is incremented by 1 (default `true`).

- `fuzzy_max_expansions`: This controls the number of terms to be used in fuzzy term expansion (default `50`).
- `fuzziness`: This sets the fuzziness value for fuzzy queries (default `AUTO`).
- `fuzzy_prefix_length`: This sets the prefix length for fuzzy queries (default `0`).
- `phrase_slop`: This sets the default slop (number of optional terms that can be present in the middle of the given terms) for phrases. If it sets to zero, the query is an exact phrase match (default `0`).
- `boost`: This defines the boost value of the query (default `1.0`).
- `analyze_wildcard`: This enables the processing of wildcard terms in the query (default `false`).
- `auto_generate_phrase_queries`: This enables the autogeneration of phrase queries from the query string (default `false`).
- `minimum_should_match`: This controls how many `should` clauses should be verified to match the result. The value could be an integer value (that is, 3) or a percentage (that is, 40%) or a combination of both (default 1).
- `lenient`: If it's set to true, the parser will ignore all format-based failures (such as text to number of date conversion) (default `false`).
- `locale`: This is the locale used for string conversion (default `ROOT`).

There's more...

The query parser is very powerful to support a wide range of complex queries. The most common cases are:

- `field:text`: This is used to match a field that contains some text. It's mapped on a term query.
- `field:(term1 OR term2)`: This is used to match some terms in `OR`. It's mapped on a terms query.
- `field:"text"`: This is used to match the exact text. It's mapped on a match query.
- `_exists_:field`: This is used to match documents that have a field. It's mapped on an exists filter.
- `_missing_:field`: This is used to match documents that don't have a field. It's mapped on a missing filter.

- `field:[start TO end]`: This is used to match a range from the `start` value to the `end` value. The `start` and `end` values could be terms, numbers, or a valid datetime value. The `start` and `end` values are included in the range; if you want to exclude a range, you must replace the `[]` delimiters with `{}`.
- `field:/regex/`: This is used to match a regular express.

The query parser also supports text modifier, used to manipulate the text functionalities. The most used ones are:

- Fuzziness using the form `text~`. The default fuzziness value is 2, which allows a Damerau-Levenshtein edit-distance algorithm (http://en.wikipedia.org/wiki/Damerau%E2%80%93Levenshtein_distance) of 2.
- Wildcards with ? that replace a single character or * to replace zero or more characters. (that is, `b?ll` or `bi*` to match bill).
- Proximity search `"term1 term2"~3`, allows matching phrase terms with defined slop. (that is, `"my umbrella"~3` matches `"my green umbrella"`, `"my new umbrella"`, and so on).

See also

- Refer to the Lucene official query parser syntax at http://lucene.apache.org/core/6_2_0/queryparser/org/apache/lucene/queryparser/classic/package-summary.html that provides a complete description of all the syntax
- The official Elasticsearch documentation about query string query at https://www.elastic.co/guide/en/elasticsearch/reference/master/query-dsl-query-string-query.html

Using a simple query string query

Typically, the programmer has the control on building complex query using Boolean query and the other query types. Thus, Elasticsearch provides two kinds of queries that give the user the ability to create string queries with several operators in it.

These kinds of queries are very common on advanced search engine usage such as Google that allows to use + and – operators on terms.

Getting ready

You need an up-and-running Elasticsearch installation as we described in the *Downloading and installing Elasticsearch* recipe in `Chapter 2`, *Downloading and Setup*.

To execute `curl` via the command line, you need to install `curl` for your operative system.

To correctly execute the following commands, you need an index populated with the `chapter_05/populate_query.sh` script available in online code.

How to do it...

For executing a simple query string query, we will perform the following steps:

1. We want to search for text `nice guy`, but not excluding the term `not`. The query will be:

```
curl -XPOST 'http://127.0.0.1:9200/test-index/test-
type/_search?pretty=true' -d '{
  "query": {
    "simple_query_string": {
      "query": ""nice guy" -not",
      "fields": [
        "parsedtext^5",
        "_all"
      ],
      "default_operator": "and"
    }
  }
}'
```

2. The result returned by Elasticsearch, if everything is alright, should be:

```
{
    ...truncated...,
  "hits" : {
    "total" : 2,
    "max_score" : 4.90176,
    "hits" : [
      {
```

```
            "_index" : "test-index",
            "_type" : "test-type",
            "_id" : "2",
            "_score" : 4.90176,
            "_source" : {
              "parsedtext" : "Bill Testere nice guy",
              ...truncated...
            }
        },
        {
            "_index" : "test-index",
            "_type" : "test-type",
            "_id" : "1",
            "_score" : 4.90176,
            "_source" : {
              "parsedtext" : "Joe Testere nice guy",
              ...truncated...
            }
        }
      ]
    }
  }
```

How it works...

The simple query string query takes the query text, tokenizes it and builds a Boolean query applying the rules provided in your text query.

It's a good tool if given to the final user to express simple advanced queries. Its parser is very complex, so it's able to extract fragments for exact match to be interpreted as span queries.

The advantage of simple query string query is that the parser always gives you a valid query. The query string query will give you errors if it's malformed.

See also

- For a complete reference of these query type syntaxes, the official documentation is available at
  `https://www.elastic.co/guide/en/elasticsearch/reference/master/query-d sl-simple-query-string-query.html` for simple query string query

Using the range query

In every application, it's very common to search a range of values. The most common standard scenarios are:

- Filtering by numeric value range (that is, price, size, and age)
- Filtering by date (that is, events of 03/07/12 can be a range query from 03/07/12 00:00:00 to 03/07/12 24:59:59)
- Filtering by term range (that is, from A to D)

Getting ready

You need an up-and-running Elasticsearch installation as we described in the *Downloading and installing Elasticsearch* recipe in Chapter 2, *Downloading and Setup*.

To execute curl via the command line, you need to install curl for your operative system.

To correctly execute the following commands, you need an index populated with the chapter_05/populate_query.sh script available in the online code.

How to do it…

For executing a range query, we will perform the following steps:

1. Consider the sample data of the previous examples, which contains an integer field position; using it to execute a query for filtering positions between 3 and 5, we will have:

```
curl -XPOST 'http://127.0.0.1:9200/test-index/test-
type/_search?pretty=true' -d '{
    "query": {
        "range" : {
            "position" : {
                "from" : 3,
                "to" : 4,
                "include_lower" : true,
                "include_upper" : false
            }
        }
    }
}'
```

2. The result returned by Elasticsearch, if everything is alright, should be as follows:

```
{
  "took" : 5,
  "timed_out" : false,
  "_shards" : {
    "total" : 5,
    "successful" : 5,
    "failed" : 0
  },
  "hits" : {
    "total" : 1,
    "max_score" : 1.0,
    "hits" : [
      {
        "_index" : "test-index",
        "_type" : "test-type",
        "_id" : "3",
        "_score" : 1.0,
        "_source" : {
          "position" : 3,
          "parsedtext" : "Bill is not\n
           nice guy",
          "name" : "Bill Clinton",
          "uuid" : "33333",
          "price" : 6.0
        }
      }
    ]
  }
}
```

How it works...

The range query is used because scoring results can cover several interesting scenarios such as:

- Items with high availability in stocks should be presented first
- New items should be boosted
- Most bought items should be boosted.

The range query is very handy with numeric values, as the preceding example shows. The parameters that a range query accepts are:

- `from`: This is the starting value for the range (optional)
- `to`: This is the ending value for the range (optional)
- `include_in_lower`: This includes the starting value in the range (optional, default `true`)
- `include_in_upper`: This includes the ending value in the range (optional, default `true`).

In range query, other helper parameters are available to simplify search:

- `gt`: (greater than), this has the same functionality to set the `from` parameter and `include_in_lower` to `false`
- `gte`: (greater than or equal), this has the same functionality to set the `from` parameter and `include_in_lower` to `true`
- `lt`: (lesser than), this has the same functionality to set the `to` parameter and the `include_in_upper` to `false`
- `lte`: (lesser than or equal), this has the same functionality to set the `to` parameter and the `include_in_upper` to `true`

There's more...

In Elasticsearch, this kind of query covers several types of SQL range queries such as <, <=, >, >= on numeric values.

Because in Elasticsearch, date/time fields are managed internally as numeric fields, it's possible using the range queries/filters with date values. If the field is a `date` field, every value in the range query is automatically converted in a numeric value. For example, if you need to filter the documents of this year, the range fragment will be:

```
"range" : {
    "timestamp" : {
        "from" : "2014-01-01",
        "to" : "2015-01-01",
        "include_lower" : true,
        "include_upper" : false
    }
}
```

For date fields, it is also possible to specify a time_zone value to be used in order to correctly compute the matches.

The common terms query

When the user is searching some text with a query, not all the terms that the user uses have the same importance. The more common terms are generally removed for query execution, for reducing the noise generated by them: these terms are called stopwords and they are generally articles, conjunctions, and common language words (that is, the, a, so, and, or, and so on).

The list of stopwords depends on the language and is independent from your documents. Lucene provides ways to dynamically compute the stopwords list based on your indexed document a query time via the **common terms query**.

Getting ready

You need an up-and-running Elasticsearch installation as we described in the *Downloading and installing Elasticsearch* recipe in this Chapter 2, *Downloading and Setup*.

To execute curl via the command line, you need to install curl for your operative system.

To correctly execute the following commands, you need an index populated with the chapter_05/populate_query.sh script available in the online code.

How to do it...

For executing a common term query, we will perform the following steps:

1. We want to search for a nice guy, we will use the following code:

```
curl -XPOST 'http://127.0.0.1:9200/test-index/test-
type/_search?pretty=true' -d '{
  "query": {
    "common": {
      "parsedtext": {
        "query": "a nice guy",
        "cutoff_frequency": 0.001
      }
    }
  }
```

```
      }
    }'
```

2. The result returned by Elasticsearch, if everything is alright, should be as follows:

```
{
  ...truncated...
  "hits" : {
    "total" : 3,
     "max_score" : 0.5753642,
   "hits" : [
      {
         "_index" : "test-index",
         "_type" : "test-type",
         "_id" : "2",
         "_score" : 0.5753642,
           ...truncated...
      },
        ...truncated...
      }
    ]
  }
}
```

How it works...

Lucene, the core engine of Elasticsearch, provides a lot of statistics on your indexed terms that are required to compute the algorithms for the different score types.

These statistics use a query time, in common terms, query to differentiate the query terms in two categories:

- **Low frequency terms**: These are the less common terms in your index. They are generally the most important ones for your current query. For the preceding query, the terms could be `["nice", "guy"]`.
- **High frequency terms**: They are the most common ones and mainly defined as stopwords. For the preceding query, the terms could be `["a"]`.

The preceding query, based on term statistics, is internally converted in Elasticsearch into a similar query:

```
{
    "query": {
        "bool": {
            "must": [ // low frequency terms
            { "term": { "parsedtext": "nice"}},
            { "term": { "parsedtext": "guy"}}
            ],
            "should": [ // high frequency terms
            { "term": { "parsedtext": "a"}}
            ]
        }
    }
}
```

To control the common term query, the following options are available:

- `cutoff_frequency`: This value defines the cut frequency that allows to partitionate the low and high frequency term lists. Its better value depends on your data: some empirical tests are needed to evaluate the correct value.
- `minimum_should_match`. This can be defined in two ways:
  - As a single value, this defines the minimum terms that must be matched for low frequency terms, that is, `"minimum_should_match" : 2`
  - As an object containing the low and high values, that is:

```
"minimum_should_match" : {
    "low_freq":1,
    "high_freq":2
}
```

> Pay attention that the term's statistics depends on the data in your Lucene indices, so they are in Elasticsearch as shard level.

See also

- The *Using a term query* recipe
- The *Using a boolean query* recipe in Chapter 5, *Search*

Using IDs query

The ID's query and filter allows matching documents by their IDs.

Getting ready

You need an up-and-running Elasticsearch installation as we described in the *Downloading and installing Elasticsearch* recipe in Chapter 2, *Downloading and Setup*.

To execute curl via the command line, you need to install curl for your operative system.

To correctly execute the following commands, you need an index populated with the chapter_05/populate_query.sh script available in the online code.

How to do it...

For executing the ID's queries/filters, we will perform the step given as follows:

1. The IDs query for fetching IDs "1", "2", "3" of type test-type is in this form:

```
curl -XPOST 'http://127.0.0.1:9200/test-index/test-
type/_search?pretty=true' -d '{
    "query": {
            "ids" : {
                "type" : "test-type",
                "values" : ["1", "2", "3"]
            }
        }
    }
}'
```

2. The result returned by Elasticsearch, if everything is alright, should be as follows:

```
{
  "took" : 79,
  "timed_out" : false,
  "_shards" : {
    "total" : 5,
    "successful" : 5,
    "failed" : 0
  },
  "hits" : {
    "total" : 3,
    "max_score" : 1.0,
    "hits" : [
    {
      "_index" : "test-index",
      "_type" : "test-type",
      "_id" : "2",
      ... truncated...
    },
    {
      "_index" : "test-index",
      "_type" : "test-type",
      "_id" : "1",
      ... truncated...
    },
    {
      "_index" : "test-index",
      "_type" : "test-type",
      "_id" : "3",
      ... truncated...
    }
    ]
  }
}
```

In the results, the request ID order is not respected. So, in case you ask multitypes, you need to use the document metadata (_index, _type, _id) to better manage your results.

How it works...

Query by ID is a very fast operation because IDs are often cached in memory for fast lookup.

The parameters used in this query are:

- `ids`: This includes a list of IDs that must be matched (required)
- `type`: This is a string or a list of strings that defines the types in which we need to search. If not defined, they are taken from the URL of the call (optional).

> **TIP**
>
> Elasticsearch internally stores the ID of a document in a special field called `_uid` composed by `type#id`. A `_uid` is unique in an index.

Usually, the standard way of using ID's query is to select documents; this query allows fetching documents without knowing the shard that contains the documents.

The documents are stored in shards, that is chosen based on a modulo operation computed on the document ID. If a parent ID or a routing is defined, they are used to choose the shard: in this case, the only way to fetch the document knowing its ID is to use the IDS query.

If you need to fetch multi-IDs and there are no routing changes (due to `parent_id` or `routing` parameter at index time), it's better not to use this kind of query, but to use get/multi-get API calls to get documents as they are much more faster and also work in real-time.

See also

- The *Getting a document* recipe in `Chapter 4`, *Basic Operations*
- The *Speeding up GET operations (Multi GET)* recipe in `Chapter 4`, *Basic Operations*

Using the function score query

This kind of query is one of the most powerful queries available, because it allows extensive customization of scoring algorithm. The function score query allows defining a function that controls the score of the documents that are returned by a query.

Generally, these functions are CPU intensive and executing them on a large dataset requires a lot of memory, but computing them on a small subset can significantly improve the search quality.

The common scenarios used for this query are:

- Creating a custom score function (with decay function, for example)
- Creating a custom boost factor, for example, based on another field (that is, boosting a document by distance from a point)
- Creating a custom filter score function, for example, based on scripting Elasticsearch capabilities
- Ordering the documents randomly

Getting ready

You need an up-and-running Elasticsearch installation as we described in the *Downloading and installing Elasticsearch* recipe in `Chapter 2`, *Downloading and Setup*.

To execute `curl` via the command line, you need to install `curl` for your operative system.

To correctly execute the following commands, you need an index populated with the `chapter_05/populate_query.sh` script available in the online code.

How to do it...

For executing a function score query, we will perform the following steps:

1. We can execute a `function_score` query from the command line:

```
curl -XPOST 'localhost:9200/test-index/test-type/_search?
pretty' -d '{
    "query": {
        "function_score": {
            "query": {
                "query_string": {
```

```
                          "query": "bill"
                      }
                  },
                  "functions": [{
                      "linear": {
                          "position": {
                              "origin": "0",
                              "scale": "20"
                          }
                      }
                  }],
                  "score_mode": "multiply"
              }
          }
      }'
```

We execute a query searching for `bill` and we score the result with the `linear` function on the `position` field.

2. The result should be as follows:

```
{
  "took" : 2,
  "timed_out" : false,
  "_shards" : {
    "total" : 5,
    "successful" : 5,
    "failed" : 0
  },
  "hits" : {
    "total" : 2,
    "max_score" : 0.7287777,
    "hits" : [
      {
        "_index" : "test-index",
        "_type" : "test-type",
        "_id" : "2",
        "_score" : 0.7287777,
        "_source" : {
          "position" : 2,
          "parsedtext" : "Bill Testere nice guy",
          "name" : "Bill Baloney",
          "uuid" : "22222",
          "price" : 5.0
        }
      },
      {
        "_index" : "test-index",
```

```
                    "_type" : "test-type",
                    "_id" : "3",
                    "_score" : 0.36344242,
                    "_source" : {
                      "position" : 3,
                      "parsedtext" : "Bill is not\n
                      nice guy",
                      "name" : "Bill Clinton",
                      "uuid" : "33333",
                      "price" : 6.0
                    }
                  }
                ]
            }
        }
```

How it works...

The function score query is probably the most complex query type to master due to natural complexity of mathematical algorithm involved in the scoring.

The generic full form of the function score query is as follows:

```
"function_score": {
    "(query|filter)": {},
    "boost": "boost for the whole query",
    "functions": [
        {
            "filter": {},
            "FUNCTION": {}
        },
        {
            "FUNCTION": {}
        }
    ],
    "max_boost": number,
    "boost_mode": "(multiply|replace|...)",
    "score_mode": "(multiply|max|...)",
    "script_score": {},
    "random_score": {"seed ": number}
}
```

The parameters are as follows:

- query or filter: This is the query used to matched the required documents (optional, default a match all query).
- boost: This is the boost to apply to the whole query (default 1.0).
- functions: This is a list of functions used to score the queries. In a simple case, use only one function. In the function object, a filter can be provided to apply the function only to a subset of documents, because the filter is applied first.
- max_boost: This sets the maximum allowed value for the boost score (default java FLT_MAX).
- boost_mode: This parameter defines how the function score is combined with the query score (default "multiply"). The possible values are:
  - script_score: This allows you to define a script score function to be used to compute the score (optional). (Elasticsearch scripting will be discussed in Chapter 9, *Scripting*.) This parameter is very useful to implement simple script algorithms. The original score value is in the _score function scope. This allows defining similar algorithms:
  - multiply (default): Here, the query score and function score are multiplied
  - replace: Here, only the function score is used; the query score is ignored
  - sum: Here, the query score and function score are added
  - avg: Here, the average between query score and function score is taken
  - max: This is the max of query score and function score
  - min: This is the min of query score and function score
  - score_mode (default "multiply"): This parameter defines how the resulting function scores (when multiple functions are defined) are combined. The possible values are:
  - multiply: The scores are multiplied
  - sum: The scores are summed
  - avg: The scores are averaged

- `first`: The first function that has a matching filter is applied
- `max`: The maximum score is used
- `min`: The minimum score is used

```
"script_score": {
    "params": {
        "param1": 2,
        "param2": 3.1
    },
    "script": "_score * doc['my_numeric_field'].value /
    pow(param1, param2)"
}
```

- `random_score`: This allows to randomly score the documents. It is very useful to retrieve records randomly (optional).

Elasticsearch provides native support for the most common scoring decay distribution algorithms such as:

- **Linear**: This is used to linearly distribute the scores based on a distance from a value
- **Exponential (exp)**: This is used for exponential decay function
- **Gaussian (gauss)**: This is used for the Gaussian decay function

Choosing the correct function distribution depends on the context and data distribution.

See also

- Refer to the official Elasticsearch documentation at `https://www.elastic.co/guide/en/elasticsearch/reference/current/query-dsl-function-score-query.html` for a complete reference on all the function Score Query parameters
- Refer the blog posts at `http://jontai.me/blog/2013/01/advanced-scoring-in-elasticsearch/` and `https://www.elastic.co/blog/found-function-scoring` for several scenarios on using this kind of query

Using the exists query

One of the main characteristics of Elasticsearch is schema-less indexing capability. Records in Elasticsearch can have missing values. Due to its schema-less nature, two kinds of queries are required:

- **Exists field**: This is used to check if a field exists in a document
- **Missing field**: This is used to check if a field is missing

Getting ready

You need an up-and-running Elasticsearch installation as we described in the *Downloading and installing Elasticsearch* recipe in `Chapter 2`, *Downloading and Setup*.

To execute `curl` via the command line, you need to install `curl` for your operative system.

To correctly execute the following commands, you need an index populated with the `chapter_05/populate_query.sh` script available in the online code.

How to do it...

For executing existing and missing filters, we will perform the following steps:

1. To search all the test-type documents that have a field called `parsedtext`, the query will be:

   ```
   curl -XPOST 'http://127.0.0.1:9200/test-index/test-
   type/_search?pretty=true' -d '{
       "query": {
       "exists": {
                "field":"parsedtext"
           }
       }
   }'
   ```

2. To search all the test-type documents that do not have a field called `parsedtext`, the query will be as follows:

   ```
   curl -XPOST 'http://127.0.0.1:9200/test-index/test-
   type/_search?pretty=true' -d '{
     "query": {
       "bool": {
   ```

```
                    "must_not": {
                      "exists": {
                        "field": "parsedtext"
                      }
                    }
                  }
                }
              }'
```

How it works...

The exists and missing filters take only a `field` parameter, which contains the name of the field to be checked.

Using simple fields, there are no pitfalls; but if you are using a single embedded object or a list of them, you need to use a subobject field due to how Elasticsearch/Lucene works.

An example helps you to understand how Elasticsearch maps JSON objects to Lucene documents internally. If you are trying to index a JSON document:

```
{
    "name":"Paul",
    "address":{
        "city":"Sydney",
        "street":"Opera House Road",
        "number":"44"
    }
}
```

Elasticsearch will internally index it as follows:

```
name:paul
address.city:Sydney
address.street:Opera House Road
address.number:44
```

As we can see, there is no field `address` indexed, so exists filter on `address` fails. To match documents with an address, you must search for a subfield (that is, `address.city`).

Using the template query

Elasticsearch provides the capability of providing a template and some parameters to fill it. This functionality is very useful, because it allows managing query templates stored on the server filesystem or in the .scripts index and allows changing them without change in the application code.

Getting ready

You need a working Elasticsearch cluster and an index populated with the chapter_05/populate_query.sh geo script available in the online code.

How to do it...

The template query is composed of two components: the query and the parameters that must be filled in. We can execute a template query in several ways.

Using the new REST entrypoint _search/template is the best way to use the templates. To use it, perform the following steps:

1. We execute the query as follows:

```
curl -XPOST 'http://127.0.0.1:9200/_search/template?pretty' -d'
{
    "inline": {
        "query": {
            "term": {
                "uuid": "{{value}}"
            }
        }
    },
    "params": {
        "value": "22222"
    }
}'
```

2. The result returned by Elasticsearch, if everything is alright, should be:

```
{
  "took" : 1,
  "timed_out" : false,
  "_shards" : {
    "total" : 10,
    "successful" : 10,
    "failed" : 0
  },
  "hits" : {
    "total" : 1,
    "max_score" : 0.2876821,
    "hits" : [
      {
        "_index" : "test-index",
        "_type" : "test-type",
        "_id" : "2",
        "_score" : 0.2876821,
        "_source" : {
          "position" : 2,
          "parsedtext" : "Bill Testere nice guy",
          "name" : "Bill Baloney",
          "uuid" : "22222",
          "price" : 5.0
        }
      }
    ]
  }
}
```

If we want to use an indexed stored template, the steps are as follows:

1. We store the template in the .scripts index:

```
curl -XPOST 'http://127.0.0.1:9200/_search/template/
myTemplate' -d '
{
    "template": {
        "query": {
            "term": {
                "uuid": "{{value}}"
            }
        }
    }
}'
```

2. Now we can call the template with the following code:

```
curl -XPOST 'http://127.0.0.1:9200/test-index/test-
type/_search/template?pretty=true' -d '{
    "id": "myTemplate",
    "params": {
        "value": "22222"
    }
}'
```

If you have a stored template and you want to validate it, you can use the REST `render` entry-point.

For the preceding result, the following are the steps:

1. We render the template via the `_render/template` REST:

```
curl -XPOST 'http://127.0.0.1:9200/_render/template?
pretty' -d'{
    "id": "myTemplate",
    "params": {
        "value": "22222"
    }
}'
```

2. The result will be :

```
{
  "template_output" : {
    "query" : {
      "term" : {
        "uuid" : "22222"
      }
    }
  }
}
```

How it works...

A template query is composed of two components:

- A template is a query object that is supported by Elasticsearch. The template uses the `mustache` (`http://mustache.github.io/`) syntax, a very common syntax to express templates.
- An optional dictionary of parameters that is used to fill the template.

When the search query is called, the template is loaded, populated with the parameters data, and executed as a normal query. The template query is a shortcut to use the same query with different values.

Typically, the template is generated executing the query in the standard way and then adding parameters if required in the process of *templating* it; the template query allows also defining the template as a string, but the user must pay attention to escaping it (refer to the official documentation at `https://www.elastic.co/guide/en/elasticsearch/reference /current/query-dsl-template-query.html` for escaping templates).

It allows removing the query execution from application code and putting it on the filesystem or indices.

There's more...

The template query can retrieve a previous stored template from disk (it must be stored in the `config/scripts` directory with the `.mustache` extension) or in the special index `.scripts`.

The search template can be managed in Elasticsearch via the special end points `/_search/template`. They are used as follows:

- To store a template type the following command:

```
curl -XPOST
'http://127.0.0.1:9200/_search/template/<template_name>' -d
<template_body>
```

- To retrieve a template type the following command:

```
curl -XGET
'http://127.0.0.1:9200/_search/template/<template_name>'
```

- To delete a template type the following command:

```
curl -XDELETE
'http://127.0.0.1:9200/_search/template/<template_name>'
```

> The indexed templates and scripts are stored in the `.script` index. This is a normal index and it can be managed as a standard data index.

See also

- Check the official mustache documentation at `http://mustache.github.io/` to learn the template syntax.
- Check the official Elasticsearch documentation about search template at `https://www.elastic.co/guide/en/elasticsearch/reference/master/search-template.html` for more samples using the template syntax.
- Check the official Elasticsearch documentation about query template at `https://www.elastic.co/guide/en/elasticsearch/reference/master/query-dsl-template-query.html` with some samples of query usage.

7

Relationships and Geo Queries

In this chapter, we will cover the following recipes:

- Using the has_child query
- Using the has_parent query
- Using the nested query
- Using the geo_bounding_box query
- Using the geo_polygon query
- Using the geo_distance query
- Using the geo_distance_range query
- Using the geo_hash query

Introduction

In this chapter, we will explore special queries that work on the relationship between Elasticsearch documents and geolocation ones.

When we have a parent-child relation, we can use special queries to query for a similar relation. Elasticsearch doesn't provide the SQL join, but it lets you search child documents starting from a parent or getting a parent starting from the children.

In this chapter, we also see how to query nested objects via a nested query.

The last part of the chapter is related to geolocalization queries that provide queries based on the distance, box, and polygon for matching documents that meet this criterion.

Using the has_child query

Elasticsearch does not only support simple unrelated documents, it also lets you define a hierarchy based on our parent and children. The `has_child` query allows querying for parent documents of children matching other queries.

Getting ready

You need an up-and-running Elasticsearch installation as we described in the *Downloading and installing Elasticsearch* recipe in `Chapter 2`, *Downloading and Setup*.

To execute `curl` via the command line, you need to install `curl` for your operating system.

To correctly execute the following commands, you need an index populated with the `chapter_07/populate_relations.sh` script available in online code.

How to do it...

To execute the `has_child` queries, we will perform the following steps:

1. We want to search parents `test-type` of children `test-type2` , which has a term in the field value as `value1`. We can create this kind of query:

```
curl -XPOST 'http://127.0.0.1:9200/test-index/test-
type/_search?pretty' -d '{
    "query": {
        "has_child" : {
            "type" : "test-type2",
            "query" : {
                "term" : {
                    "value" : "value1"
                }
            }
        }
    }
}'
```

2. The result returned by Elasticsearch, if everything is alright, should be as follows:

```
{
  "took" : 69,
  "timed_out" : false,
  "_shards" : {
    "total" : 5,
    "successful" : 5,
    "failed" : 0
  },
  "hits" : {
    "total" : 1,
    "max_score" : 1.0,
    "hits" : [
      {
        "_index" : "test-index",
        "_type" : "test-type",
        "_id" : "1",
        "_score" : 1.0,
        "_source" : {
          "position" : 1,
          "parsedtext" : "Joe Testere nice guy",
          "name" : "Joe Tester",
          "uuid" : "11111",
          "price" : 4.0
        }
      }
    ]
  }
}
```

How it works...

This kind of query works by returning parent documents whose children match the query. The query executed on the children can be any type of query.

The prerequisite of this kind of query is that the children must be correctly indexed in the shard of their parent.

Internally, this kind of query is a query executed on the children and all the IDs of the children are used to filter the parent. A system must have enough memory to store the children IDs.

The parameters, that are used to control this process are as follows:

- The `type` parameter describes the type of children. This type is part of the same index of the parent.
- The `query` parameter can be executed for selection of the children. Any kind of query can be used.
- The `score_mode` parameter (the default is `none`; available values are `max`, `sum`, `avg`, and `none`) if defined, it allows aggregating the children scores with the parent ones.
- `min_children` and `max_children` are optional parameters. This is the minimum/maximum number of children required to match the parent document.
- `ignore_unmapped` (default `false`) when set to `true`, will ignore unmapped types. It is very useful when executing a query on multiple indices and some types are be missing. The default behavior is to throw an exception if there is a mapping error.

> In Elasticsearch, a document must have only one parent, because the parent ID is used to choose the shard to put the children in.
> When working with child documents, it is important to remember that they must be stored in the same shard as their parents. Special precautions must be taken in fetching, modifying, and deleting them if the parent ID is unknown. It's good practice to store the `parent_id` as a field of the child.

As the parent-child relation can be considered to be similar to a foreign key in standard SQL, there is some limitation due to the distributed nature of Elasticsearch, such as:

- There must be only one parent for each type
- The join part of child/parent is done in a shard and not distributed on all the clusters to reduce networking and increase performance

There's more...

Sometimes you need to sort the parents by their children field. In order to do this, you need to sort the parents with the max score of the child field. To execute this kind of query, you can use the `function_score` query in the following way:

```
curl -XPOST 'http://127.0.0.1:9200/test-index/test-type/_search?
pretty=true' -d '{
"query": {
        "has_child" : {
            "type" : "test-type2",
```

```
                    "score_mode" : "max",
                "query" : {
                    "function_score" : {
                        "script_score": {
                            "script": "doc["amount"].value"
                        }
                    }
                }
            }
        }
    }'
```

By executing this query for every child of a parent, the maximum score is taken and their maximum score (via the `function_score`) is the value of the field that we want to sort on.

In the above example, we have used scripting, which will be discussed in `Chapter 9`, *Scripting*, scripting needs to be active to be used.

See also

- The *Indexing a document* recipe in `Chapter 4`, *Basic Operations*
- The *Mapping child document* recipe in `Chapter 3`, *Managing Mapping*
- The *Using function score query* recipe in `Chapter 6`, *Text and Numeric Queries*

Using the has_parent query

In the previous recipes, we saw the `has_child` query; Elasticsearch provides a query to search child documents based on the parent query, `has_parent`.

Getting ready

You need an up-and-running Elasticsearch installation as we described in the *Downloading and installing Elasticsearch* recipe in `Chapter 2`, *Downloading and Setup*.

To execute `curl` via the command line, you need to install `curl` for your operating system.

To correctly execute the following commands, you need an index populated with the `chapter_07/populate_relations.sh` script available in the online code.

How to do it...

To execute the `has_parent` query, we will perform the following steps:

1. We want to search children `test-type2` of parents `test-type` that has a term `joe` in the `parsedtext` field. We can create this kind of query:

```
curl -XPOST 'http://127.0.0.1:9200/test-index/test-
type2/_search?pretty' -d '{
"query": {
        "has_parent" : {
            "type" : "test-type",
            "query" : {
                "term" : {
                    "parsedtext" : "joe"
                }
            }
        }
    }
}'
```

2. The result returned by Elasticsearch, if everything is alright, should be as follows:

```
{
  "took" : 4,
  "timed_out" : false,
  "_shards" : {
    "total" : 5,
    "successful" : 5,
    "failed" : 0
  },
  "hits" : {
    "total" : 1,
    "max_score" : 1.0,
    "hits" : [
      {
        "_index" : "test-index",
        "_type" : "test-type2",
        "_id" : "1",
```

```
            "_score" : 1.0,
            "_routing" : "1",
            "_parent" : "1",
            "_source" : {
              "name" : "data1",
              "value" : "value1",
              "amount" : 10
            }
          }
        }
      ]
    }
  }
}
```

How it works...

This kind of query works by returning child documents whose parent matches the query children that match a parent query.

Internally, this subquery is executed on the parents and all the IDs of the matching parents are used to filter the children. The system must have enough memory to store all the parent IDs.

The parameters that are used to control this processes are as follows:

- `parent_type`: This is the type of the parent.
- `query`: This is the query that can be executed to select the parents. Every kind of query can be used.
- `score`: The default value is `false`. Using the default configuration of `false`, Elasticsearch ignores the scores for parent documents, reducing memory and increasing performance. If it's set to `true`, the parent query score is aggregated into the children.

Using the score, you can sort based on a parent with the same approach shown in the previous recipe using `function_score`.

See also

- The *Indexing a document* recipe in Chapter 4, *Basic Operations*
- The *Mapping child document* recipe in Chapter 3, *Managing Mappings*

Using nested queries

For queries based on nested objects, there is a special nested query.

This kind of query is required because nested objects are indexed in a special way in Elasticsearch.

Getting ready

You need an up-and-running Elasticsearch installation as we described in the *Downloading and installing Elasticsearch* recipe in `Chapter 2`, *Downloading and Setup*.

To execute `curl` via the command line, you need to install `curl` for your operating system.

To correctly execute the following commands, you need an index populated with the `chapter_07/populate_relations.sh` script, available in the online code.

How to do it…

To execute the nested query, we will perform the following steps:

1. We want to search the document for nested objects that are `blue` and whose size is greater than `10`. The nested query will be as follows:

```
curl -XPOST 'http://127.0.0.1:9200/test-index/test-
type/_search?pretty=true' -d '{
"query": {
    "nested" : {
        "path" : "versions",
        "score_mode" : "avg",
        "query" : {
            "bool" : {
                "must" : [
                { "term" : {"versions.color" : "blue"} },
                { "range" : {"versions.size" : {"gt" : 10}} }
                ]
            }
        }
    }
}
}'
```

2. The result returned by Elasticsearch, if everything is alright, should be as follows:

```
{
  "took" : 5,
  "timed_out" : false,
  "_shards" : {
    "total" : 5,
    "successful" : 5,
    "failed" : 0
  },
  "hits" : {
    "total" : 1,
    "max_score" : 1.6931472,
    "hits" : [
      {
        "_index" : "test-index",
        "_type" : "test-type",
        "_id" : "1",
        "_score" : 1.6931472,
        "_source" : {
          "position" : 1,
          "parsedtext" : "Joe Testere nice guy",
          "name" : "Joe Tester",
          "uuid" : "11111",
          "price" : 4.0,
          "versions" : [
            {
              "color" : "yellow",
              "size" : 5
            },
            {
              "color" : "blue",
              "size" : 15
            }
          ]
        }
      }
    ]
  }
}
```

How it works...

Elasticsearch manages nested objects in a special way. During indexing, they are extracted from the main document and indexed as a separate document saved in the same Lucene chunk of the main document.

The nested query executes the first query on the nested documents and after gathering the result IDs they are used to filter the main document. The parameters that are used to control this process are:

- `path`: This is the path of the parent document that contains the nested objects.
- `query`: This is the query that can be executed to select the nested objects. Every kind of query can be used.
- `score_mode`: The default value is `avg`. The valid values are `avg`, `sum`, `min`, `max`, and `none`, which control how to use the score of the nested document matches to better improve the query.

Using `score_mode`, you can sort based on a nested object using the `function_score` query.

See also

- The *Managing nested objects* recipe in `Chapter 3`, *Managing Mappings*
- The *Using the has_child query* recipe

Using the geo_bounding_box query

One of most common operations in geolocalization is searching for a box (square).

Getting ready

You need an up-and-running Elasticsearch installation as we described in the *Downloading and installing Elasticsearch* recipe in `Chapter 2`, *Downloading and Setup*.

To execute `curl` via the command line, you need to install `curl` for your operating system.

To correctly execute the following commands, you need an index populated with the `chapter_07/populate_geo.sh` geoscript, available in the online code.

How to do it…

To execute a geobounding box query, we will perform the following steps:

1. A search to filter documents related to a bounding box 40.03, 72.0 and 40.717, 70.99 can be done with a similar query:

```
curl -XPOST http://127.0.0.1:9200/test-mindex/_search?pretty -d
'{
    "query": {
    "geo_bounding_box": {
            "pin.location": {
                "bottom_right": {
                    "lat": 40.03,
                    "lon": 72.0
                },
                "top_left": {
                    "lat": 40.717,
                    "lon": 70.99
                }
            }
        }
    }
}'
```

2. The result returned by Elasticsearch, if everything is alright, should be as follows:

```
{
  "took" : 103,
  "timed_out" : false,
  "_shards" : {
    "total" : 5,
    "successful" : 5,
    "failed" : 0
  },
  "hits" : {
    "total" : 1,
    "max_score" : 1.0,
    "hits" : [
      {
        "_index" : "test-mindex",
        "_type" : "test-type",
        "_id" : "2",
        "_score" : 1.0,
        "_source" : {
          "pin" : {
            "location" : {
```

```
                  "lat" : 40.12,
                  "lon" : 71.34
              }
          }
       }
      }
    ]
   }
  }
```

How it works...

Elasticsearch has a lot of optimizations to facilitate searching for a box shape. Latitude and longitude are indexed for fast range checks, so this kind of filter is executed very fast. In Elasticsearch 5.x, geoqueries are faster than previous in versions due to massive improvements on geodata indexing in Lucene 6.2.x.

The parameters required to execute a geobounding box filter are `top_left` (the top and left coordinates of the box) and `bottom_right` (the bottom and right coordinates of the box) geopoints.

It's possible to use several representations of geopoints as described in the *Mapping a GeoPoint field* recipe in `Chapter 3`, *Managing Mappings*.

See also

- The *Mapping a GeoPoint field* recipe in `Chapter 3`, *Managing Mappings*

Using the geo_polygon query

The *Using the geo_bounding_box query* recipe shows how to filter on the square section, which is the most common case; Elasticsearch provides a way to filter user-defined polygonal shapes via the `geo_polygon` filter. This query is useful if the polygon represents a country/region/district shape.

Getting ready

You need an up-and-running Elasticsearch installation as we described in the *Downloading and installing Elasticsearch* recipe in Chapter 2, *Downloading and Setup*.

To execute curl via the command line, you need to install curl for your operating system.

To correctly execute the following commands, you need an index populated with the chapter_07/populate_geo.sh geoscript available in the online code.

How to do it...

To execute a geopolygon query, we will perform the following steps:

1. Searching documents in which pin.location is part of a triangle (its shape is madeup of three geopoints) is done with a similar query:

```
curl -XGET "http://127.0.0.1:9200/test-mindex/_search?
pretty" -d '{
    "query": {
    "geo_polygon": {
            "pin.location": {
            "points": [
                {
                    "lat": 50,
                    "lon": -30
                },
                {
                    "lat": 30,
                    "lon": -80
                },
                {
                    "lat": 80,
                    "lon": -90
                }
            ]
        }
        }
    }
}'
```

2. The result returned by Elasticsearch, if everything is alright, should be as follows:

```
{
  "took" : 7,
  "timed_out" : false,
  "_shards" : {
    "total" : 5,
    "successful" : 5,
    "failed" : 0
  },
  "hits" : {
    "total" : 1,
    "max_score" : 1.0,
    "hits" : [
      {
        "_index" : "test-mindex",
        "_type" : "test-type",
        "_id" : "1",
        "_score" : 1.0,
        "_source" : {
          "pin" : {
            "location" : {
              "lat" : 40.12,
              "lon" : -71.34
            }
          }
        }
      }
    ]
  }
}
```

How it works...

The geopolygon query allows defining your own shape with a list of geopoints so that Elasticsearch can filter documents that are used in the polygon.

It can be considered as an extension of a geobounding box for generic polygonal forms.

The geopolygon query allows the usage of the `ignore_unmapped` parameter, which helps to safely execute a search in the case of multi-indices/types where the field is not defined (the geopoint field is not defined for some indices/shards, and thus fails silently without giving errors).

See also

- The *Mapping a GeoPoint field* recipe in Chapter 3, *Managing Mappings*
- The *Using the geo_bounding_box query* recipe

Using the geo_distance query

When you are working with geolocations, one common task is to filter results based on the distance from a location. This scenario covers very common site requirements such as:

- Finding the nearest restaurant within a distance of 20 km
- Finding my nearest friends within a range of 10 km

The geo_distance query is used to achieve this goal.

Getting ready

You need an up-and-running Elasticsearch installation as we described in the *Downloading and installing Elasticsearch* recipe in Chapter 2, *Downloading and Setup*.

To execute curl via the command line, you need to install curl for your operating system.

To correctly execute the following commands, you need an index populated with the chapter_07/populate_geo.sh geoscript available in the online code.

How to do it...

To execute a geo_distance query, we will perform the following steps:

1. Searching documents in which pin.location is 200km away from lat 40 and lon as 70 is done with a similar query:

    ```
    curl -XGET 'http://127.0.0.1:9200/test-mindex/_search?
    pretty' -d '{
        "query": {
        "geo_distance": {
                "pin.location": {
                    "lat": 40,
                    "lon": 70
    ```

```
            },
            "distance": "200km",
            "optimize_bbox": "memory"
        }
    }
}'
```

2. The result returned by Elasticsearch, if everything is alright, should be as follows:

```
{
  "took" : 5,
  "timed_out" : false,
  "_shards" : {
    "total" : 5,
    "successful" : 5,
    "failed" : 0
  },
  "hits" : {
    "total" : 1,
    "max_score" : 1.0,
    "hits" : [
      {
        "_index" : "test-mindex",
        "_type" : "test-type",
        "_id" : "2",
        "_score" : 1.0,
        "_source" : {
          "pin" : {
            "location" : {
              "lat" : 40.12,
              "lon" : 71.34
            }
          }
        }
      }
    ]
  }
}
```

How it works...

As we discussed in the *Mapping a GeoPoint field* recipe to, there are several ways to define a geopoint to internally save searched items in an optimized way.

The distance query executes a distance calculation between a given geopoint and the points in documents, returning hits that satisfy the distance requirement.

The parameters that control the distance query are:

- The field and the point of reference to be used to calculate the distance. In the preceding example, we have `pin.location` and `(40,70)`.
- `distance` defines the distance to be considered. It is usually expressed as a string by a number plus a unit
- `unit` (optional) can be the unit of the distance value, if distance is defined as a number. The valid values are:
    - `in` or `inch`
    - `yd` or `yards`
    - `m` or `miles`
    - `km` or `kilometers`
    - `m` or `meters`
    - `mm` or `millimeters`
    - `cm` or `centimeters`
- `distance_type` (default: `sloppy_arc`; valid choices are `arc/sloppy_arc/plane`) defines the type of algorithm to calculate the distance.
- `optimize_bbox` defines filtering first with a bounding box to improve performance. This kind of optimization removes a lot of document evaluations limiting the check to values that match a square. The valid values for this parameter are:
    - `memory` (default): This does a memory check
    - `indexed`: This checks using indexing values. It works only if lat and lon are indexed
    - `none`: This disables bounding box optimization
- `validation_method` (default `STRICT`) is used for validating the geopoint. The valid values are:
- `IGNORE_MALFORMED` is used to accept invalid values for latitude and longitude.
- `COERCE` is used to try to correct wrong values.
- `STRICT` is used to reject invalid values.
- `ignore_unmapped` is used to safely execute the query in the case of multi-indices/types that can have the GeoPoint field not defined

See also

- The *Mapping a GeoPoint field* recipe in Chapter 3, *Managing Mappings*
- The *Using range query* recipe in Chapter 6, *Text and Numeric Queries*

Using the geo_distance_range query

It's a common scenario to find documents distant from a single point (epicenter) in a range.

One example, is when you have indexed a list of points of interest (shops, monuments, airports, train stations, and so on) and you need to know how many of them are in the range between 100 and 200 kilometers.

Getting ready

You need an up-and-running Elasticsearch installation as we described in the *Downloading and installing Elasticsearch* recipe in Chapter 2, *Downloading and Setup*.

To execute curl via the command line, you need to install curl for your operating system.

To correct execute the following commands, you need an index populated with the chapter_07/populate_geo.sh geoscript available in the online code.

How to do it...

To execute a geo_distance_range query, we will perform the following steps:

1. Searching documents in which pin.location is 100km to 200km away from lat 40 and lon, is done with a similar query:

```
curl -XGET 'http://127.0.0.1:9200/test-mindex/_search?
pretty' -d '{
  "query": {
    "geo_distance_range": {
      "pin.location": {
        "lat": 40,
"lon": 70
  },
  "from": "100km",
  "to": "200km",
```

```
        "optimize_bbox": "memory"
    }
  }
}'
```

2. The result returned by Elasticsearch, if everything is alright, should be:

```
{
  "took" : 5,
  "timed_out" : false,
  "_shards" : {
    "total" : 5,
    "successful" : 5,
    "failed" : 0
  },
  "hits" : {
    "total" : 1,
    "max_score" : 1.0,
    "hits" : [
      {
        "_index" : "test-mindex",
        "_type" : "test-type",
        "_id" : "2",
        "_score" : 1.0,
        "_source" : {
          "pin" : {
            "location" : {
              "lat" : 40.12,
              "lon" : 71.34
            }
          }
        }
      }
    ]
  }
}
```

How it works...

The `distance_range` query executes a distance calculation between a given geopoint and points in documents, returning hits that satisfy the range distance requirement.

This kind of query accepts the same parameters as the *Using the geo_distance query* recipe plus all the standard parameters for a range query such as `from`, `to`, `gt`, `gte`, `lt`, and `lte`.

See also

- The *Mapping a GeoPoint field* recipe in Chapter 3, *Managing Mappings*
- The *Using range query* recipe in Chapter 6, *Text and Numeric Queries*

8
Aggregations

In this chapter, we will cover the following recipes:

- Executing an aggregation
- Executing stats aggregations
- Executing terms aggregations
- Executing significant terms aggregations
- Executing range aggregations
- Executing histogram aggregations
- Executing date histogram aggregations
- Executing filter aggregations
- Executing filters aggregations
- Executing global aggregations
- Executing geo distance aggregations
- Executing children aggregations
- Executing nested aggregations
- Executing top hit aggregations
- Executing a matrix stats aggregation
- Executing geo bounds aggregations
- Executing geo centroid aggregations

Introduction

In developing search solutions not only are results important, but they also help us to improve the quality and the search focus.

Elasticsearch provides a powerful tool to achieve these goals: the **aggregations**.

The main usage of aggregations is to provide additional data to the search results to improve their quality or to augment them with additional information.

For example, in a search for news articles, some facets that could be interesting to calculate, could be the authors who wrote the articles and the date histogram of the publishing date.

Thus aggregations are used not only to improve the results focus, but also to provide insight on stored data (analytics): this is the way that a lot of tools such as **Kibana** (`https ://www.elastic.co/products/kibana`) are born.

Generally, the aggregations are displayed to the end user with graphs or a group of filtering options (for example, a list of categories for the search results).

Because the Elasticsearch aggregation framework provides scripting functionalities, it is able to cover a wide spectrum of scenarios. In this chapter, some simple scripting functionalities are shown relating to aggregations, but we will cover in depth scripting in the next chapter.

The aggregation framework is also the base for advanced analytics, as shown in such software as Kibana. It's very important to understand how the various types of aggregations work and when to choose them.

Executing an aggregation

Elasticsearch provides several functionalities other than search; it allows executing statistics and real-time analytics on searches via the aggregations.

Getting ready

You need an up-and-running Elasticsearch installation, as we described in the *Downloading and installing Elasticsearch* recipe in `Chapter 2`, *Downloading and Setup*.

To execute `curl` via the command line, you need to install `curl` for your operative system.

To correctly execute the command, you need an index populated with the script (`chapter_08/populate_aggregations.sh`) available in the online code.

How to do it...

For executing an aggregation, we will perform the following steps:

1. We want to compute the top 10 tags by name. We can obtain this from the command line, executing a similar query with aggregations as follows:

```
curl -XGET 'http://127.0.0.1:9200/test-index/test-type/_search?
pretty&size=0' -d '{
    "query": {
        "match_all": {}
    },
    "aggregations": {
        "tag": {
            "terms": {
                "field": "tag",
                "size": 10
            }
        }
    }
}'
```

In this case, we have used a `match_all` query plus a term aggregation used to count terms.

2. The result returned by Elasticsearch, if everything is okay, should be:

```
{
  "took" : 3,
  "timed_out" : false,
  "_shards" : {... truncated ...},
  "hits" : {
   "total" : 1000,
    "max_score" : 0.0,
    "hits" : [ ]
  },
  "aggregations" : {
    "tag" : {
      "buckets" : [ {
        "key" : "laborum",
        "doc_count" : 25
      }, {
        "key" : "quidem",
        "doc_count" : 15
      }, {
        "key" : "maiores",
       "doc_count" : 14
```

```
      }, {
.... Truncated ....
      }, {
        "key" : "praesentium",
        "doc_count" : 9
      } ]
    }
  }
}
```

The results are not returned because we have fixed the result size to 0. The aggregation result is contained in the `aggregation` field. Each type of aggregation has its own result format (the explanation of this kind of result is given in the *Executing term aggregation* recipe in this chapter).

> **TIP**
>
> It's possible to execute only aggregation calculation, without returns search results, to reduce the bandwidth passing the search `size` parameter set to 0.

How it works...

Every search can return an aggregation calculation, computed on the query results: the aggregation phase is an additional step in query post-processing, as for example, the highlighting. To activate the aggregation phase, an aggregation must be defined using the `aggs` or `aggregations` keyword.

There are several types of aggregation that can be used in Elasticsearch.

In this chapter, we'll cover all the standard aggregations available; additional aggregation types can be provided with plugins and scripting.

The aggregations are the bases for real-time analytics. They allow us to execute the following:

- Counting
- Histogram
- Range aggregation
- Statistics
- Geo distance aggregation

There are the examples of graphs generated by histogram aggregations

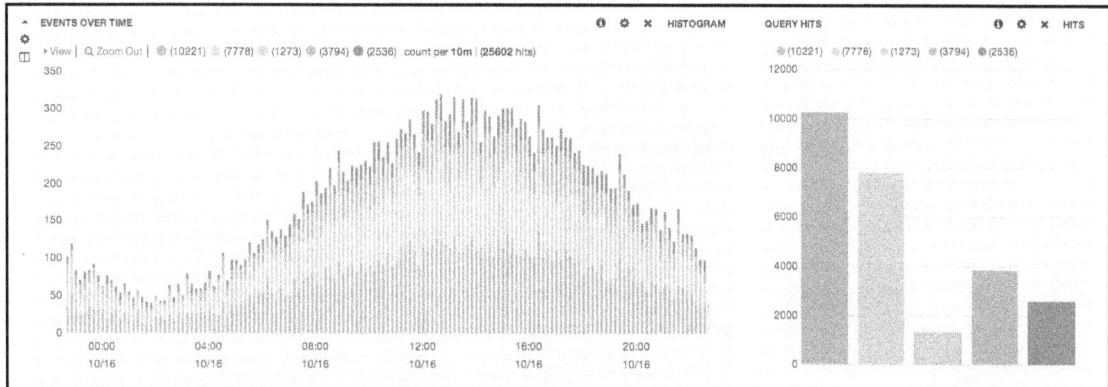

The aggregations are always executed on search hits; they are usually computed in a map/reduce way. The map step is distributed in shards, while the reduce step is done in the called node.

During aggregation computation a lot of data should be kept in memory, and it can therefore be very memory-intensive.

For example, when executing a term aggregation, it requires that all the unique terms in the field that are used for aggregating are kept in memory. Executing this operation on millions of documents requires perhaps storing a large number of values in memory.

The aggregation framework was introduced in Elasticsearch 1.x as an evolution of the facets feature. Its main difference from the old facet framework is the possibility to execute the analytics with several nesting levels of sub-aggregations. Aggregations keep information of which documents go into an aggregation bucket and an aggregation output can be the input of the next aggregation.

> Aggregations can be composed in a complex tree of sub-aggregations without depth limits.

The generic form for an aggregation is as follows:

```
"aggregations" : {
    "<aggregation_name>" : {
        "<aggregation_type>" : {
            <aggregation_body>
        }
        [,"aggregations" : { [<sub_aggregation>]+ } ]?
    }
    [,"<aggregation_name_2>" : { ... } ]*
}
```

The aggregation nesting allows for covering very advanced scenarios in executing analytics such as aggregating data by country, by region, and by persons' ages where age groups are ordered in descending order! There are no more limits in mastering analytics.

The following schema summarizes the main difference between the previous facet system and the aggregation framework

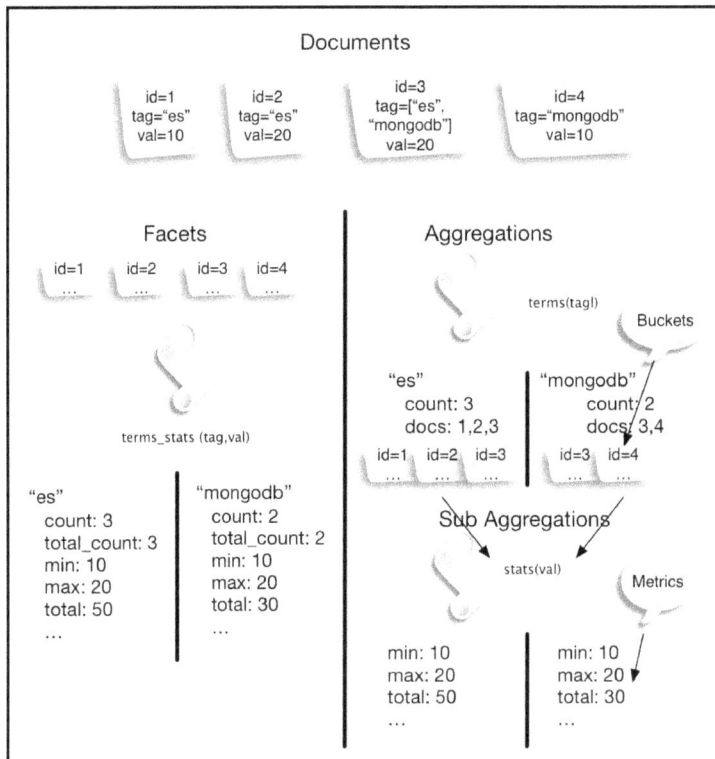

There are four kinds of aggregators that can be used in Elasticsearch 5.x:

- **Bucketing aggregators**: These produce buckets, where a bucket has an associated value and a set of documents (that is, the terms aggregator produces a bucket per term for the field it's aggregating on). A document can end up in multiple buckets if the document has multiple values for the field being aggregated on (in our example, the document with **id=3**). If a bucket aggregator has one or more *downstream* (that is, child) *aggregators,* these are run on each generated bucket.
- **Metric aggregators**: These receive a set of documents as input and produce statistical results computed for the specified field. The output of metric aggregators does not include any information linked to individual documents, just the statistical data.
- **Matrix aggregators**: These operate on multiple fields and produce a matrix result based on the values extracted from the requested document fields.
- **Pipeline aggregators**: These aggregate the output of other aggregations and their associated metrics. (This is an experimental feature and can change and be removed in the future.)

Generally, the order of buckets depends on the bucket aggregator used.

For example, using the terms aggregator the buckets are, by default, ordered by count. The aggregation framework allows to order by sub-aggregation metrics (that is, the preceding example can be ordered by `stats.avg` value).

> It's easy to create complex nested sub-aggregations that return huge numbers of results. Developers need to pay attention to the cardinality of returned aggregation results: it's very easy to returns thousands of values!

See also

- Refer to the *Executing a terms aggregation* recipe in this chapter for a more detailed explanation of aggregations used in the example. For pipeline aggregations, the official documentation can be found at `https://www.elastic.co/guide/en/ela sticsearch/reference/5.x/search-aggregations-pipeline.html`. Because, as the Official Elasticsearch Documentation says, it's not safe to use, this feature could be removed in the future, and it is therefore not described in detail in the book.

Executing stats aggregations

The most commonly used metric aggregations are stats aggregations. They are generally used as a terminal aggregation step to compute values to be used directly or for sorting.

Getting ready

You need an up-and-running Elasticsearch installation, as we described in the *Downloading and installing Elasticsearch* recipe in `Chapter 2`, *Downloading and Setup*.

To execute `curl` via the command line, you need to install `curl` for your operative system.

To correctly execute the following command, you need an index populated with the `chapter_08/populate_aggregations.sh` script available in the online code.

How to do it…

For executing a stat aggregation, we will perform the following steps:

1. We want to calculate all statistics values of a matched query on the `age` field. The `REST` call should be as follows:

```
curl -XPOST "http://127.0.0.1:9200/test-index/_search?
size=0" -d '
{
    "query": {
        "match_all": {}
    },
    "aggs": {
      "age_stats": {
        "extended_stats": {
          "field": "age"
        }
      }
    }
}'
```

2. The result, if everything is okay, should be as follows:

```
{
  "took" : 2,
  "timed_out" : false,
  "_shards" : { ...truncated...},
```

```
"hits" : {
  "total" : 1000,
  "max_score" : 0.0,
  "hits" : [ ]
},
"aggregations" : {
  "age_stats" : {
    "count" : 1000,
    "min" : 1.0,
    "max" : 100.0,
    "avg" : 53.243,
    "sum" : 53243.0,
    "sum_of_squares" : 3653701.0,
    "variance" : 818.8839509999999,
    "std_deviation" : 28.616148430562767
  }
}
}
```

In the answer, under the `aggregations` field, we have the statistical results of our aggregation under the defined field, `age_stats`.

How it works...

After the search phase, if any aggregations are defined they are computed.

In this case, we have request an `extended_stats` aggregation labeled `age_stats` which computes a lot of statistical indicators.

The available metric aggregators are as follows:

- `min`: which computes the minimum value for a group of buckets.
- `max`: which computes the maximum value for a group of buckets.
- `avg`: which computes the average value for a group of buckets.
- `sum`: which computes the sum of all the buckets.
- `value_count`: which computes the count of values in the bucket.
- `stats`: which computes all the base metrics such as the `min`, `max`, `avg`, `count`, and `sum`.
- `extended_stats`: which computes the `stats` metric plus `variance`, standard deviation (`std_deviation`), and sum of squares (`sum_of_squares`).

- `percentiles`: which computes the `percentiles` (the point at which a certain percentage of observed values occur) of some values. (See Wikipedia at `http://en.wikipedia.org/wiki/Percentile` for more information about percentiles.)
- `percentile_ranks`: which computes the rank of values that hit a percentile range.
- `cardinality`: which computes an approximate count of distinct values in a field.
- `geo_bounds`: which computes the maximum geo bounds in the document where GeoPoints are.
- `geo_centroid`: which computes the centroid in the document where GeoPoints are.

Every metric requires different computational needs, so it is good practice to limit the indicators only to required one, so as not to waste CPU, memory, and performance.

In the preceding listing, I cited only the most used natively metric aggregators available in Elasticsearch; other metrics can be provided via plugins.

The syntax of all the metric aggregations has the same pattern independently of the level of nesting in the aggregation DSL: they follow these patterns:

```
"aggs" : {
        "<name_of_aggregation>" : {
            "<metric_name>" : {
                "field" : "<field_name>"
            }
        }
    }
```

See also

- Official Elasticsearch documentation about stats ggregation at `https://www.elastic.co/guide/en/elasticsearch/reference/current/search-aggregations-metrics-stats-aggregation.html` and extended stats aggregation at `https://www.elastic.co/guide/en/elasticsearch/reference/current/search-aggregations-metrics-extendedstats-aggregation.html`

Executing terms aggregation

The most used bucket aggregation is the terms one. It groups the documents in buckets based on a single term value. This aggregation is often used to narrow down the search using the computed values as filters for the queries.

Getting ready

You need an up-and-running Elasticsearch installation, as we described in the *Downloading and installing Elasticsearch* recipe in Chapter 2, *Downloading and Setup*.

To execute curl via the command line, you need to install curl for your operative system.

To correctly execute the following command, you need an index populated with the chapter_08/populate_aggregations.sh script available in the online code.

How to do it...

For executing a term aggregation, we will perform the following steps:

1. We want to calculate the top 10 tags of all the documents: the REST call should be as follows:

```
curl -XGET 'http://127.0.0.1:9200/test-index/test-type/_search?
pretty&size=0' -d '{
    "query": {
        "match_all": {}
    },
    "aggs": {
        "tag": {
            "terms": {
                "field": "tag",
                "size": 10
            }
        }
    }
}'
```

In this example, we need to match all the items, so the match_all query is used.

2. The result returned by Elasticsearch, if everything is okay, should be as follows:

```
{
  "took" : 63,
  "timed_out" : false,
  "_shards" : { ...truncated...  },
  "hits" : {
    "total" : 1000,
    "max_score" : 0.0,
    "hits" : [ ]
  },
  "aggregations" : {
    "tag" : {
      "buckets" : [ {
        "key" : "laborum",
        "doc_count" : 25
      }, {
        "key" : "quidem",
        "doc_count" : 15
      }, {
        ....truncated ...
      }, {
        "key" : "praesentium",
        "doc_count" : 9
      } ]
    }
  }
}
```

The aggregation result is composed from several buckets with terms as follows:

- key: the term used to populate the bucket
- doc_count: the number of results with the key term

How it works...

During a search, there are a lot of *phases* that Elasticsearch executes. After the query execution, the aggregations are calculated and returned along with the results.

In this recipe, we will see the following parameters that the terms aggregation supports:

- field, which is the field to be used to extract the facets data. The field value can be a single string (as in the example *tag*) or a list of fields (that is, [field1, field2, ...).

- `size` (default 10), which controls the number of term values to be returned.
- `min_doc_count` (optional), which returns terms that have at least a minimum number of documents.
- `include` (optional), which defines the valid value to be aggregated via regular expression. This is evaluated before the `exclude` parameter. The regular expressions are controlled by the `flags` parameter. For example:

```
"include" : {
      "pattern" : ".*labor.*",
      "flags" : "CANON_EQ|CASE_INSENSITIVE"
},
```

- `exclude` (optional), which removes from the results the terms that are contained in the `exclude` list. The regular expressions are controlled by the `flags` parameter.
- `order` (optional, default `doc_count`), which controls how to calculate the top n bucket values to be returned. The `order` parameter can be one of these following types:
    - `_count` (default) returns the aggregation values ordered by `count`
    - `_term` returns the aggregation values ordered by term value; (that is, `"order" : { "_term" : "asc" })`
- A sub-aggregation name, for example:

```
{
    "aggs" : {
        "genders" : {
            "terms" : {
                "field" : "tag",
                "order" : { "avg_val" : "desc" }
            },
            "aggs" : {
                "avg_age" : { "avg" : { "field" : "age" } }
            }
        }
    }
}
```

Term aggregation is very useful to represent an overview of values used for further filtering.

In the following graph, they are often shown as a bar chart:

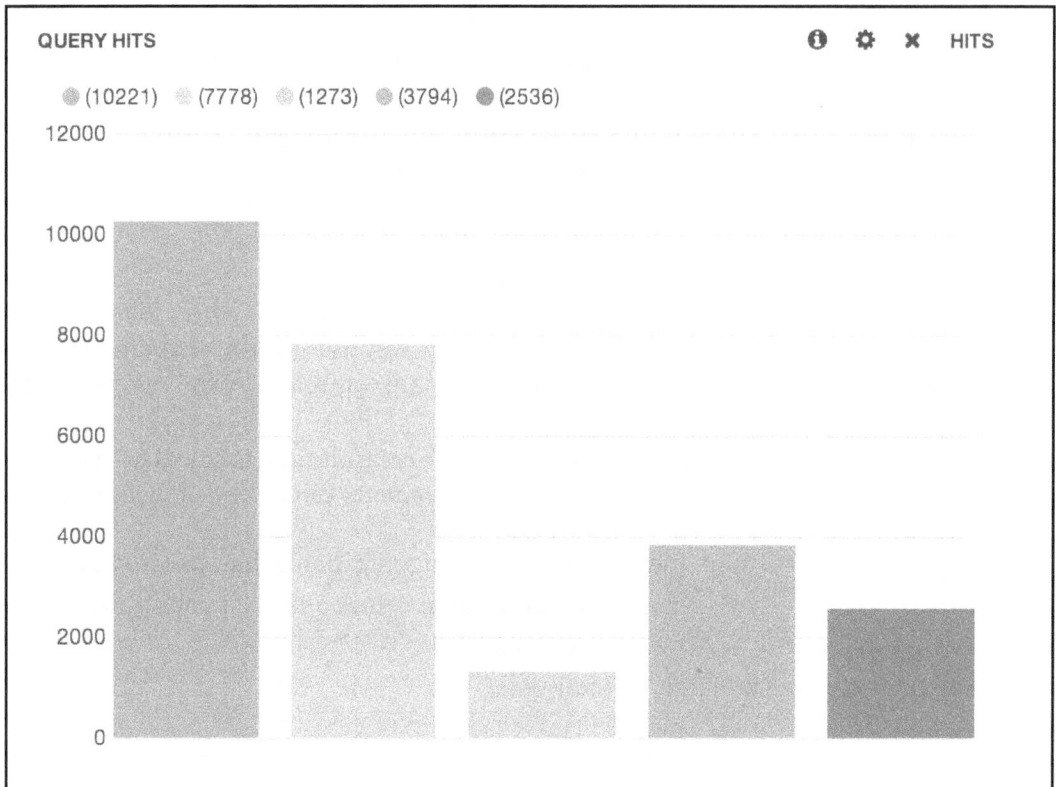

There's more...

Sometime we need to have much more control on terms aggregation: this can be achieved by adding an Elasticsearch script in the `script` field.

With scripting it is possible to modify the term used for the aggregation to generate a new value to be used. The following is a simple example, in which we append `123` to all terms:

```
{
    "query" : {
        "match_all" : {   }
    },
    "aggs" : {
        "tag" : {
            "terms" : {
```

```
                    "field" : "tag",
                    "script" : "_value + '123'"
                }
            }
        }
    }
```

Scripting can also be used to control the inclusion/exclusion of some terms. In this case, the return value from the script must be a Boolean (true/false). If we want an aggregation with terms that start with 'a', we can use a similar aggregation as follows:

```
{
    "query" : {
        "match_all" : {  }
    },
    "aggs" : {
        "tag" : {
            "terms" : {
                "field" : "tag",
                "script" : "_value.startsWith('a')"
            }
        }
    }
}
```

In the previous terms aggregation examples, we have provided the `field` or `fields` parameter to select the field to be used to compute the aggregation. It's also possible to pass a `script` parameter, which replaces `field` and `fields`, to define the field to be used to extract the data. The `script` can fetch from the `doc` variable in the context.

In the case of `doc`, the first example can be rewritten as:

```
...   "tag": {
            "terms": {
                "script": "doc['tag'].value",
                "size": 10
            }
        } ...
```

See also

- Refer to `Chapter 9`, *Scripting,*which will cover how to use scripting languages in Elasticsearch

Executing significant terms aggregation

This kind of aggregation is an evolution of the previous one in that it's able to cover several scenarios such as:

- Suggesting relevant terms related to current query text
- Discovering relations of terms
- Discover common patterns in text

In these scenarios cases, the result must not be as simple as the previous terms aggregations; it must be computed as a variance between a foreground set (generally the query) and a background one (a large bulk of data).

Getting ready

You need an up-and-running Elasticsearch installation, as we described in the *Downloading and installing Elasticsearch* recipe in `Chapter 2`, *Downloading and Setup*.

To execute `curl` via the command line, you need to install `curl` for your operative system.

To correctly execute the following command, you need an index populated with the script (`chapter_08/populate_aggregations.sh`) available in the online code.

How to do it…

For executing a significant term aggregation, we will perform the following steps:

1. We want to calculate the significant terms `tag` given some tags. The REST call should be as follows:

```
curl -XGET 'http://127.0.0.1:9200/test-index/test-type/_search?
pretty=true&size=0' -d '{
    "query" : {
        "terms" : {"tag" : [ "ullam", "in", "ex" ]}
    },
    "aggs": {
        "significant_tags": {
            "significant_terms": {
                "field": "tag"
            }
        }
    }
}
```

```
    }'
```

2. The result returned by Elasticsearch, if everything is okay, should be as follows:

```
{
  "took" : 6,
  "timed_out" : false,
  "_shards" : { ...truncated... },
  "hits" : { ...truncated... },
  "aggregations" : {
    "significant_tags" : {
      "doc_count" : 45,
      "buckets" : [
        {
          "key" : "ullam",
          "doc_count" : 17,
          "score" : 8.017283950617283,
          "bg_count" : 17
        },
        {
          "key" : "in",
          "doc_count" : 15,
          "score" : 7.0740740740740735,
          "bg_count" : 15
        },
        {
          "key" : "ex",
          "doc_count" : 14,
          "score" : 6.602469135802469,
          "bg_count" : 14
        },
        {
          "key" : "vitae",
          "doc_count" : 3,
          "score" : 0.674074074074074,
          "bg_count" : 6
        },
        {
          "key" : "necessitatibus",
          "doc_count" : 3,
          "score" : 0.3373737373737374,
          "bg_count" : 11
        }
      ]
    }
  }
}
```

The aggregation result is composed from several buckets with:

- `key`: the term used to populate the bucket
- `doc_count`: the number of results with the `key` term
- `score`: the score for this bucket
- `bg_count`: the number of background documents that contains the `key` term

How it works...

The execution of the aggregation is similar to the previous ones. Internally, two terms aggregations are computed: one related to the documents matched with the query or parent aggregation and one based on all the documents on the knowledge base. Then, the two results datasets are scored to compute the significant result.

Due to the large cardinality of terms queries and the cost of significant relevance computation, this kind of aggregation is very CPU intensive.

The significant aggregation returns terms that are evaluated as significant for the current query.

To compare the results of significant terms aggregation with the plain terms aggregation, we can execute the same aggregation with the `terms` one as follows:

```
curl -XGET
'http://127.0.0.1:9200/test-index/test-type/_search?pretty=true&size=0' -d
'{
"query" : {
        "terms" : {"tag" : [ "ullam", "in", "ex" ]}
    },
        "aggs": {
        "tags": {
            "terms": {
                "field": "tag"
            }
        }
    }
}'
```

The returned results will be as follows:

```
{
  ...truncated...
  "aggregations" : {
    "tags" : {
      "doc_count_error_upper_bound" : 2,
      "sum_other_doc_count" : 96,
      "buckets" : [
        {"key" : "ullam", "doc_count" : 17},
        {"key" : "in", "doc_count" : 15},
        {"key" : "ex", "doc_count" : 14},
        {"key" : "necessitatibus", "doc_count" : 3},
        {"key" : "vitae", "doc_count" : 3},
        {"key" : "architecto", "doc_count" : 2},
        {"key" : "debitis", "doc_count" : 2 },
        {"key" : "dicta", "doc_count" : 2},
        {"key" : "error", "doc_count" : 2},
        {"key" : "excepturi", "doc_count" : 2}
      ]
    }
  }
}
```

Executing range aggregations

The previous recipe describes an aggregation type that can be very useful if buckets must be computed on fixed terms or on a limited number of items. Otherwise, it's often required to return the buckets aggregated in ranges: the **range aggregations** meet this requirement. Commons scenarios are as follows:

- Price range (used in shops)
- Size range
- Alphabetical range

Getting ready

You need an up-and-running Elasticsearch installation, as we described in the *Downloading and installing Elasticsearch* recipe in Chapter 2, *Downloading and Setup*.

To execute `curl` via the command line, you need to install `curl` for your operative system.

To correctly execute the following command, you need an index populated with the `chapter_08/populate_aggregations.sh` script available in the online code.

How to do it...

For executing range aggregations, we will perform the following steps:

1. We want to provide three types of aggregation ranges:
    *   Price aggregation, which aggregates the price of items in ranges
    *   Age aggregation, which aggregates the age contained in a document in four ranges of 25 years
    *   Date aggregation, the ranges of 6 months of the previous year and all this year

2. To obtain this result, we need to execute a similar query as follows:

```
curl -XGET 'http://127.0.0.1:9200/test-index/test-type/_search?
pretty&size=0' -d ' {
  "query": {
    "match_all": {}
  },
  "aggs": {
    "prices": {
      "range": {
        "field": "price",
        "ranges": [
          {"to": 10},
          {"from": 10,"to": 20},
          {"from": 20,"to": 100},
          {"from": 100}
        ]
      }
    },
    "ages": {
      "range": {
        "field": "age",
        "ranges": [
          {"to": 25},
          {"from": 25,"to": 50},
          {"from": 50,"to": 75},
          {"from": 75}
        ]
      }
```

```
      },
      "range": {
        "range": {
          "field": "date",
          "ranges": [
            {"from": "2012-01-01","to": "2012-07-01"},
            {"from": "2012-07-01","to": "2012-12-31"},
            {"from": "2013-01-01","to": "2013-12-31"}
          ]
        }
      }
    }
  }
}'
```

3. The result returned by Elasticsearch, if everything is okay, should be:

```
{
  "took" : 7,
  "timed_out" : false,
  "_shards" : {...truncated...},
  "hits" : {...truncated...},
  "aggregations" : {
    "range" : {
      "buckets" : [ {
        "key" : "20120101-01-01T00:00:00.000Z-20120631-01-
          01T00:00:00.000Z",
        "from" : 6.348668943168E17,
        "from_as_string" : "20120101-01-01T00:00:00.000Z",
        "to" : 6.34883619456E17,
        "to_as_string" : "20120631-01-01T00:00:00.000Z",
        "doc_count" : 0
      }, ...truncated... ]
    },
    "prices" : {
      "buckets" : [ {
        "key" : "*-10.0",
        "to" : 10.0,
        "to_as_string" : "10.0",
        "doc_count" : 105
      }, ...truncated...]
    },
    "ages" : {
      "buckets" : [ {
        "key" : "*-25.0",
        "to" : 25.0,
        "to_as_string" : "25.0",
        "doc_count" : 210
      }, ...truncated...]
```

```
            }
          }
        }
```

All aggregation results have the following fields:

- `to`, `to_string`, `from`, and `from_string`: define the original range of the aggregation
- `doc_count`: the number of results in this range
- `key`: a string representation of the range

How it works...

This kind of aggregation is generally executed against numerical data types (`integer`, `float`, `long`, and `dates`). It can be considered as a list of range filters executed against the result of the query.

The `date/datetime` values, when used in a filter/query, must be expressed in string format: the valid string formats are `yyyy-MM-dd'T'HH:mm:ss` or `yyyy-MM-dd`.

Each range is computed independently, so in their definition they can overlap.

There's more...

There are two special range aggregations used for targeting date and IPv4 ranges.

They are similar to the preceding range aggregation, but they provide special functionalities to control the range on the date and IP address.

The date range aggregation (`date_range`) allows for defining `from` and `to` in date math expressions. For example, to execute an aggregation of hits in the previous 6 months and after, the aggregation will be as follows:

```
{
    "aggs": {
        "range": {
            "date_range": {
                "field": "date",
                "format": "MM-yyyy",
                "ranges": [
                    { "to": "now-6M/M" },
                    { "from": "now-6M/M" }
```

```
                            ]
                    }
                }
            }
        }
```

In this sample, the buckets will be formatted in the form month-year (MM-YYYY), in two
ranges. now means the actual datetime, -6M means minus 6 months, and /M is a shortcut for
dividing for months. (A complete reference of date math expressions and codes is available
at https://www.elastic.co/guide/en/elasticsearch/reference/current/search-agg
regations-bucket-daterange-aggregation.html.)

The IPv4 range aggregation (ip_range) allows for defining the ranges as follows:

- IP range form:

```
{
    "aggs" : {
        "ip_ranges" : {
            "ip_range" : {
                "field" : "ip",
                "ranges" : [
                    { "to" : "192.168.1.1" },
                    { "from" : "192.168.2.255" }
                ]
            }
        }
    }
}
```

- CIDR masks:

```
{
    "aggs" : {
        "ip_ranges" : {
            "ip_range" : {
                "field" : "ip",
                "ranges" : [
                    { "mask" : "192.168.1.0/25" },
                    { "mask" : "192.168.1.127/25" }
                ]
            }
        }
    }
}
```

See also

- Refer to the *Using range query* recipe in `Chapter 6`, *Text and Numeric Queries,*for details of using range queries, and the official documentation for IP aggregation at `https://www.elastic.co/guide/en/elasticsearch/reference/5.x/search-agg regations-bucket-iprange-aggregation.html`.

Executing histogram aggregations

Elasticsearch numerical values can be used to process histogram data. The histogram representation is a very powerful way to show data to end users, mainly via bar charts.

Getting ready

You need an up-and-running Elasticsearch installation, as we described in the *Downloading and installing Elasticsearch* recipe in `Chapter 2`, *Downloading and Setup*.

To execute `curl` via the command line, you need to install `curl` for your operative system.

To correctly execute the following command, you need an index populated with the `chapter_08/populate_aggregations.sh` script available in the online code.

How to do it...

For executing histogram aggregations, we will perform the following steps:

1. Using the items populated with the script, we want calculate the following aggregations:
    - age with an interval of 5 years
    - price with an interval of 10$
    - date with an interval of 6 months

2. The query will be as follows:

```
curl -XGET 'http://127.0.0.1:9200/test-index/test-type/_search?
pretty&size=0' -d '{
    "query": {
        "match_all": {}
    },
    "aggregations": {
        "age" : {
            "histogram" : {
                "field" : "age",
                "interval" : 5
            }
        },
        "price" : {
            "histogram" : {
                "field" : "price",
                "interval" : 10.0
            }
        }
    }
}'
```

3. The result returned by Elasticsearch, if everything is okay, should be as follows:

```
{
  "took" : 23,
  "timed_out" : false,
  "_shards" : {...truncated...},
  "hits" : {...truncated...},
  "aggregations" : {
    "price" : {
      "buckets" : [ {
        "key_as_string" : "0",
        "key" : 0,
        "doc_count" : 105
      }, {
        "key_as_string" : "10",
        "key" : 10,
        "doc_count" : 107
      ...truncated...        } ]
    },
    "age" : {
      "buckets" : [ {
        "key_as_string" : "0",
        "key" : 0,
        "doc_count" : 34
      }, {
```

```
            "key_as_string" : "5",
            "key" : 5,
            "doc_count" : 41
        }, {...truncated...        } ]
    }
  }
}
```

The aggregation result is composed by `buckets`: a list of aggregation results. These results are composed by:

- `key`: the value that is always on the *x* axis in the histogram graph
- `key_as_string`: a string representation of the `key` value
- `doc_count`: the document bucket size

How it works...

This kind of aggregation is calculated in a distributed manner in each shard with search results and then the aggregation results are aggregated in the search node server (arbiter) and returned to the user.

The histogram aggregation works only on numerical fields (`boolean`, `integer`, `long integer`, and `float`) and `date`/`datetime` fields (these are internally represented as `long`).

To control the histogram generation on a defined `field` the `interval` parameter is required, which is used to generate an interval to aggregate the hits.

For numerical fields, this value is a number (in the preceding example, we have done numerical calculus on age and price).

The general representation of a histogram could be a bar chart, similar to the following one:

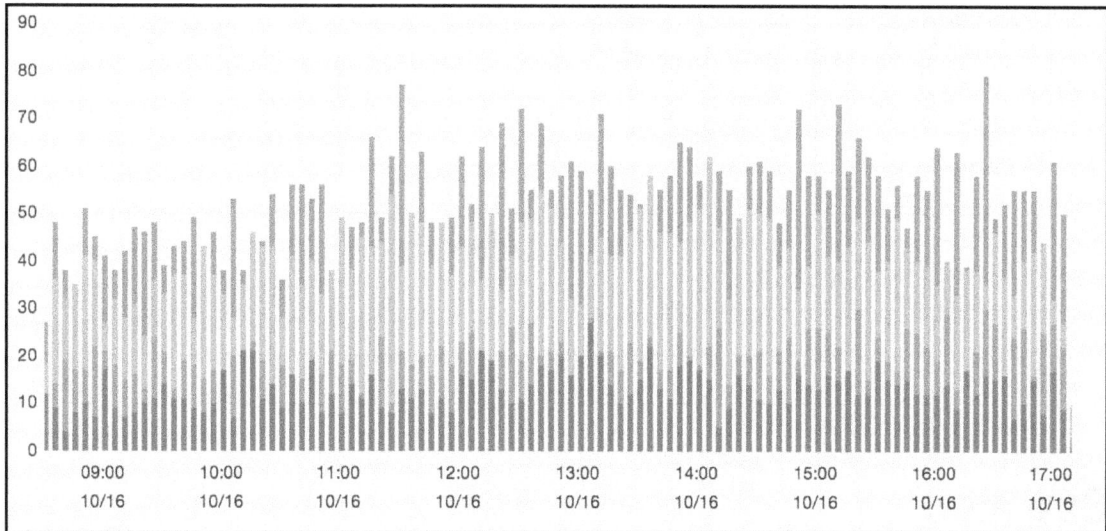

There's more...

The histogram aggregation can be also improved using Elasticsearch scripting functionalities. It is possible to script both using the _value if a field is stored or via the doc variable.

An example of scripted aggregation histogram, using _value, is the following:

```
curl -XGET
'http://127.0.0.1:9200/test-index/test-type/_search?pretty&size=0' -d '{
    "query": {
        "match_all": {}
    },
    "aggs": {
        "age" : {
            "histogram" : {
                "field" : "age",
                "script": "_value*3",
                "interval" : 5
            }
        }
    }
}'
```

An example of scripted aggregation histogram, using `_doc`, is the following:

```
curl -XGET
'http://127.0.0.1:9200/test-index/test-type/_search?pretty&size=0' -d '{
    "query": {
        "match_all": {}
    },
    "aggs": {
        "age" : {
            "histogram" : {
                "script": "doc['age'].value"*3,
                "interval" : 5
            }
        }
    }
}'
```

See also

- Refer to the *Executing date histogram aggregations* recipe in this chapter for histogram aggregations based on date/time values

Executing date histogram aggregations

The previous recipe used mainly numeric fields; Elasticsearch provides special functionalities to compute the date histogram aggregation which operates on `date`/`datetime` values.

This aggregation is required because date values need more customization to solve problems such as timezone conversion and special time intervals.

Getting ready

You need an up-and-running Elasticsearch installation, as we described in the *Downloading and installing Elasticsearch* recipe in `Chapter 2`, *Downloading and Setup*.

To execute `curl` via the command line, you need to install `curl` for your operative system.

To correctly execute the following command, you need an index populated with the `chapter_08/populate_aggregations.sh` script available in the online code.

How to do it...

For executing date histogram aggregations, we will perform the following steps:

1. We need two different date/time aggregations that are as follows:
   - An annual aggregation
   - A quarter aggregation, but with time zone +1:00

2. The query will be as follows:

```
curl -XGET 'http://127.0.0.1:9200/test-index/test-type/_search?
pretty&size=0' -d '
{
    "query": {
        "match_all": {}
    },
    "aggs": {
        "date_year": {
            "date_histogram": {
                "field": "date",
                "interval": "year"
            }
        },
        "date_quarter": {
            "date_histogram": {
                "field": "date",
                "interval": "quarter" ,
                "time_zone": "+01:00"
            }
        }
    }
}'
```

3. The result returned by Elasticsearch, if everything is okay, should be as follows:

```
{
  "took" : 29,
  "timed_out" : false,
  "_shards" : {...truncated...},
  "hits" : {...truncated...},
  "aggregations" : {
    "date_year" : {
      "buckets" : [ {
        "key_as_string" : "2010-01-01T00:00:00.000Z",
        "key" : 1262304000000,
        "doc_count" : 40
      }, {
```

```
              "key_as_string" : "2011-01-01T00:00:00.000Z",
              "key" : 1293840000000,
              "doc_count" : 182
            }, ...truncated...]
        },
        "date_quarter" : {
          "buckets" : [ {
                  "key_as_string" : "2010-10-01T00:00:00.000Z",
                  "key" : 1285891200000,
                  "doc_count" : 40
              }, {
                  "key_as_string" : "2011-01-01T00:00:00.000Z",
                  "key" : 1293840000000,
                  "doc_count" : 42
              }, ...truncated...]
          }
        }
      }
```

The aggregation result is composed by `buckets`: a list of aggregation results. These results are composed by the following:

- `key`: the value that is always on the *x* axis in the histogram graph
- `key_as_string`: a string representation of the `key` value
- `doc_count`: the document bucket size.

How it works...

The main difference from the previous recipe histogram is that the interval is not numerical, but generally date intervals are defined time constants. The `interval` parameter allows for using several values such as the following:

- `year`
- `quarter`
- `month`
- `week`
- `day`
- `hour`
- `minute`

When working with date values, it's important to use the correct timezone to prevent query errors.

By default, Elasticsearch uses the UTC milliseconds as the epoch to store datetime values. To better handle the correct timestamp, there are some parameters that can be used, such as the following:

- `time_zone` (or `pre_zone`) (optional), which allows for defining a timezone offset to be used in the value calculation. This value is used to preprocess the datetime value for the aggregation. The value can be expressed in numeric form (that is, -3) if specifying hours or if minutes must be defined in the timezone a string representation can be used (that is, +07:30).
- `post_zone` (optional), which takes the result and applies the timezone offset.
- `pre_zone_adjust_large_interval` (default: `false`) (optional), which applies the `hour` interval also for `day` or above intervals.

See also

- The official Elasticsearch documentation on date histogram aggregation at `https://www.elastic.co/guide/en/elasticsearch/reference/current/search-aggregations-bucket-datehistogram-aggregation.html` for more details on managing time zone issues.

Executing filter aggregations

Sometimes, we need to reduce the number of hits in our aggregation to satisfy a particular filter. To obtain this result, the filter aggregation is used.

Getting ready

You need an up-and-running Elasticsearch installation, as we described in the *Downloading and installing Elasticsearch* recipe in `Chapter 2`, *Downloading and Setup*.

To execute `curl` via the command line, you need to install `curl` for your operative system.

To correctly execute the following command, you need an index populated with the `chapter_08/populate_aggregations.sh` script available in the online code.

How to do it...

For executing filter aggregations, we will perform the following steps:

1. We need to compute two different filter aggregations that are as follows:
   - The count of documents that have `"ullam"` as a tag
   - The count of documents that have age equal to 37

2. The query to execute these aggregations is as follows:

```
curl -XGET 'http://127.0.0.1:9200/test-index/test-type/_search?
size=0&pretty' -d '
{
    "query": {
        "match_all": {}
    },
    "aggregations": {
        "ullam_docs": {
            "filter" : {
                "term" : { "tag" : "ullam" }
            }
        },
        "age37_docs": {
            "filter" : {
                "term" : { "age" : 37 }
            }
        }
    }
}'
```

In this case, we have used simple filters, but they can be more complex if needed.

3. The result returned by Elasticsearch, if everything is okay, should be as follows:

```
{
   "took" : 5,
   "timed_out" : false,
   "_shards" : {
      "total" : 5,
      "successful" : 5,
      "failed" : 0
   },
   "hits" : {
       "total" : 1000,
       "max_score" : 0.0,
       "hits" : [ ]
```

```
        },
              "aggregations" : {
                  "age37_docs" : {
                       "doc_count" : 6
        },
              "ullam_docs" : {
                  "doc_count" : 17
                }
              }
        }
```

How it works...

The filter aggregation is very trivial: it executes a count on a filter on a matched element. You can consider this aggregation as a count query on the results.

As we can see from the preceding result that the aggregation contains one value: doc_count, the count result.

It could be a very simple aggregation: generally users tend not to use it as they prefer the statistic one, which also provides a count, or in the worst cases, they execute another search generating more server workload.

The big advantage of this kind of aggregation is that the count, if possible, is executed via a filter: that is by far faster than iterating all the results.

Another important advantage is that the filter can be composed by every possible valid Query DSL element.

There's more...

It's often required to have the count of the document that doesn't match a filter or generally doesn't have a particular field (or is null). For this kind of scenario, there is a special aggregation type: the missing.

For example, to count the number of documents that are missing the code field, the query will be as follows:

```
curl -XGET
'http://127.0.0.1:9200/test-index/test-type/_search?size=0&pretty' -d '
{
    "query": {
        "match_all": {}
```

```
        },
        "aggs": {
            "missing_code": {
                "missing" : {
                    "field" : "code"
                }
            }
        }
    }'
```

The result will be as follows:

```
{
    ... truncated ...
    "aggregations" : {
        "missing_code" : {
            "doc_count" : 1000
        }
    }
}
```

See also

- Refer to the *Counting matched results* recipe in Chapter 5, *Search* for a standard count query

Executing filters aggregations

The filters aggregation answers the common requirement to split buckets documents using custom filters, which can be every kind of query supported by Elasticsearch.

Getting ready

You need an up-and-running Elasticsearch installation, as we described in the *Downloading and installing Elasticsearch* recipe in Chapter 2, *Downloading and Setup*.

To execute curl via the command line, you need to install curl for your operative system.

To correctly execute the following command, you need an index populated with the chapter_08/populate_aggregations.sh script available in the online code.

How to do it...

For executing filters aggregations, we will perform the following steps:

1. We need to compute a filters aggregation composed by the following queries:
   - Date greater than 2016/01/01 and price greater or equal to 50
   - Date lower than 2016/01/01 and price greater or equal to 50
   - All the documents that are not matched

2. The query to execute these aggregations is as follows:

```
curl -XGET 'http://127.0.0.1:9200/test-index/test-type/_search?
size=0&pretty' -d '
{
  "query": {
    "match_all": {}
  },
  "aggs": {
    "expensive_docs": {
      "filters": {
        "other_bucket": true,
        "other_bucket_key": "other_documents",
        "filters": {
          "2016_over_50": {
            "bool": {
              "must": [
                {
                  "range": {
                    "date": {
                      "gte": "2016-01-01"
                    }
                  }
                },
                {
                  "range": {
                    "price": {
                      "gte": 50
                    }
                  }
                }
              ]
            }
          },
          "previous_2016_over_50": {
            "bool": {
              "must": [
```

```
                                    {
                                      "range": {
                                        "date": {
                                          "lt": "2016-01-01"
                                        }
                                      }
                                    },
                                    {
                                      "range": {
                                        "price": {
                                          "gte": 50
                                        }
                                      }
                                    }
                                  ]
                                }
                              }
                            }
                          }
                        }
                      }
                    }
                  }'
```

3. The result returned by Elasticsearch, if everything is okay, should be as follows:

```
{
  "took" : 39,
  "timed_out" : false,
  "_shards" : {
    "total" : 5,
    "successful" : 5,
    "failed" : 0
  },
  "hits" : {
    "total" : 1000,
    "max_score" : 0.0,
    "hits" : [ ]
  },
  "aggregations" : {
    "expensive_docs" : {
      "buckets" : {
        "2016_over_50" : {
          "doc_count" : 24
        },
        "previous_2016_over_50" : {
          "doc_count" : 487
        },
        "other_documents" : {
```

```
                    "doc_count" : 489
                }
            }
        }
    }
}
```

How it works…

The filters aggregation is a very handy one, because it provides a convenient way to generate data buckets.

The filters, that compose the aggregation, can be every kind of query that Elasticsearch supports. For this reason, this aggregation can be used also to achieve complex relation management using children and nested queries.

Every query in the `filters` object generates a new bucket. Because the queries can be overlapped, the generated buckets can have overlapping documents.

To collect all the documents that are not matched in filters, it's possible use the `other_bucket` and `other_bucket_key` parameters.

The `other_bucket` is a `boolean` parameter: if it's `true`, it will return all the unmatched documents in a `_other_` bucket.

To control the name of the residual document bucket, the `other_bucket_key` is a string parameter that contains the label name of the other bucket.

If `other_bucket_key` is defined, it automatically implies that `other_bucket` is equal to `true`.

Executing global aggregations

The aggregations are generally executed on query search results; Elasticsearch provides a special aggregation `global` that is executed globally on all the documents without being influenced by the query.

Getting ready

You need an up-and-running Elasticsearch installation, as we described in the *Downloading and installing Elasticsearch* recipe in Chapter 2, *Downloading and Setup*.

To execute curl via the command line, you need to install curl for your operative system.

To correctly execute the following command, you need an index populated with the script (chapter_08/populate_aggregations.sh) available in the online code.

How to do it...

For executing global aggregations, we will perform the following steps:

1. We want compare a global average with a query one; the g:

```
curl -XGET 'http://127.0.0.1:9200/test-incall will be something
similar to the following:
curl -XGET 'http://127.0.0.1:9200/test-index/test-type/_search?
size=0&pretty' -d '
{
    "query": {
        "term" : { "tag" : "ullam" }
    },
    "aggregations": {
        "query_age_avg": {
            "avg" : {
                "field" :  "age"
            }
        },
        "all_persons":{
            "global": {},
            "aggs":{
                "age_global_avg": {
                    "avg" : {
                      "field" :  "age"
                    }
                }
            }
        }
    }
}'
```

2. The result returned by Elasticsearch, if everything is okay, should be as follows:

```
{
  "took" : 133,
  "timed_out" : false,
  "_shards" : {...truncated...},
   "hits" : {
    "total" : 17,
    "max_score" : 0.0,
     "hits" : [ ]
  },
   "aggregations" : {
   "all_persons" : {
      "doc_count" : 1000,
      "age_global_avg" : {
        "value" : 53.243
      }
    },
    "query_age_avg" : {
      "value" : 53.470588235294116
    }
  }
}
```

In the preceding example, the query_age_avg is computed on the query and the age_global_avg on all the documents.

How it works...

This kind of aggregation is mainly used as top aggregation as a start point for other sub-aggregations.

The JSON body of the global aggregations is empty: it doesn't have any optional parameter.

The most frequent use cases are comparing aggregations executed on filters with the ones without them, as done in the preceding example.

Executing geo distance aggregations

Among the other standard types that we have seen in the previous aggregations, Elasticsearch allows for executing aggregations against a GeoPoint: the geo distance aggregations. This is an evolution of the previous discussed range aggregations built to work on geo locations.

Getting ready

You need an up-and-running Elasticsearch installation, as we described in the *Downloading and installing Elasticsearch* recipe in Chapter 2, *Downloading and Setup*.

To execute curl via the command-line, you need to install curl for your operative system.

To correctly execute the following command, you need an index populated with the script (chapter_08/populate_aggregations.sh) available in the online code.

How to do it...

For executing geo distance aggregations, we will perform the following steps:

1. Using the position field available in the documents, we want to aggregate the other documents in five ranges:
   - Less than 10 kilometers
   - From 10 kilometers to 20
   - From 20 kilometers to 50
   - From 50 kilometers to 100
   - Above 100 kilometers

2. To achieve these goals, we create a geo distance aggregation with a code similar to following one:

```
curl -XGET 'http://127.0.0.1:9200/test-index/test-type/_search?
pretty&size=0' -d ' {
    "query" : {
        "match_all" : {}
    },
    "aggs" : {
        "position" : {
            "geo_distance" : {
                "field":"position",
                "origin" : {
                    "lat": 83.76,
                    "lon": -81.20
                },
                "ranges" : [
                    { "to" : 10 },
                    { "from" : 10, "to" : 20 },
                    { "from" : 20, "to" : 50 },
                    { "from" : 50, "to" : 100 },
```

```
                              { "from" : 100 }
                        ]
                  }
            }
      }
}'
```

3. The result returned by Elasticsearch, if everything is okay, should be as follows:

```
{
  "took" : 177,
  "timed_out" : false,
  "_shards" : {...truncated...},
  "hits" : {...truncated...},
  "aggregations" : {
    "position" : {
      "buckets" : [ {
        "key" : "*-10.0",
        "from" : 0.0,
        "to" : 10.0,
        "doc_count" : 0
      }, {
        "key" : "10.0-20.0",
        "from" : 10.0,
        "to" : 20.0,
        "doc_count" : 0
      }, {
        "key" : "20.0-50.0",
        "from" : 20.0,
        "to" : 50.0,
        "doc_count" : 0
      }, {
        "key" : "50.0-100.0",
        "from" : 50.0,
        "to" : 100.0,
        "doc_count" : 0
      }, {
        "key" : "100.0-*",
        "from" : 100.0,
        "doc_count" : 1000
      } ]
    }
  }
}
```

How it works...

The geo range aggregation is an extension of the range aggregations that works on geo localizations. It works only if a field is mapped as a `geo_point`.

The field can contain a single or a multi-values geo points.

The aggregation requires at least the following three parameters:

- `field`: the field of the geo point to work on
- `origin`: the geo point to be used for computing the distances
- `ranges`: a list of ranges to collect documents based on their distance from the target point

The GeoPoint can be defined in one of the following accepted formats:

- latitude and longitude as properties, that is: `{"lat": 83.76, "lon": -81.20 }`
- longitude and latitude as array, that is: `[-81.20, 83.76]`
- latitude and longitude as string, that is: `83.76, -81.20`
- geohash, that is: `fnyk80`

The ranges are defined as a couple of `from`/`to` values. If one of them is missing, they are considered unbound.

The values used for the range are by default set to kilometers, but using the property `unit` it's possible to set them as follows:

- `mi` or `miles`
- `in` or `inch`
- `yd` or `yard`
- `km` or `kilometers`
- `m` or `meters`
- `cm` or `centimeter`
- `mm` or `millimeters`

It's also possible to set how the distance is computed with the `distance_type` parameter. Valid values for this parameter are as follows:

- `arc`, which uses the Arc Length formula. It is the most precise. (See `http://en.wikipedia.org/wiki/Arc_length` for more details on the arc length algorithm.)
- `sloppy_arc` (default), which is a faster implementation of the arc length formula, but less precise.
- `plane`, which is used for the plane distance formula. It is the fastest and most CPU intensive, but it's also the least precise.

As for the range filter, the range values are treated independently, so the overlapping ranges are allowed.

When the results are returned, this aggregation provides a lot of information in its fields as follows:

- `from`/`to` defines the analyzed range
- `key` defines the string representation of the range
- `doc_count` defines the number of documents in the bucket that matches the range

See also

- Refer to the *Executing range aggregations* recipe in this chapter for common functionalities of range aggregations.
- Refer to the *Mapping a GeoPoint field* recipe in `Chapter 3`, *Managing Mappings*, to correctly define a GeoPoint field for executing geo aggregations.
- Refer to the *GeoHash grid Aggregation* recipe at `https://www.elastic.co/guide /en/elasticsearch/reference/current/search-aggregations-bucket-geoha shgrid-aggregation.html` for executing aggregations on geohash.

Executing children aggregations

This kind of aggregation allows for executing analytics, based on parent documents, on child documents. When working with complex structures, the nested objects are very common.

Getting ready

You need an up-and-running Elasticsearch installation, as we described in the *Downloading and installing Elasticsearch* recipe in Chapter 2, *Downloading and Setup*.

To execute curl via the command line, you need to install curl for your operative system.

To correctly execute the following command, you need an index populated with the chapter_08/populate_aggregations.sh script available in the online code.

How to do it...

For executing children aggregations, we will perform the following steps:

1. We must index documents with child/parent relations, as discussed in the *Managing a child document* recipe in Chapter 3, *Managing Mappings*. For the following example, we will use the same dataset of the child query.

2. We want execute a terms aggregation on the uuid of the parent and for every uUid collecting the terms of the children value, we create a children aggregation with a code similar to following one:

```
curl -XPOST "http://127.0.0.1:9200/myindex/test-type/_search?
size=0&pretty" -d '{
  "aggs": {
    "uuid": {
      "terms": {
        "field": "uuid",
        "size": 10
      },
      "aggs": {
        "to-children": {
          "children": {
            "type": "test-type2"
          },
          "aggs": {
            "top-values": {
```

```
            "terms": {
              "field": "value.keyword",
              "size": 10
            }
          }
        }
      }
    }
  }
}
}'
```

2. The result returned by Elasticsearch, if everything is okay, should be as follows:

```
{
  "took" : 7,
  "timed_out" : false,
  "_shards" : {...truncated...},
  "hits" : {...truncated...},
  "aggregations" : {
    "uuid" : {
      "doc_count_error_upper_bound" : 0,
      "sum_other_doc_count" : 0,
      "buckets" : [
        {
          "key" : "11111",
          "doc_count" : 1,
          "to-children" : {
            "doc_count" : 1,
            "top-values" : {
              "doc_count_error_upper_bound" : 0,
              "sum_other_doc_count" : 0,
              "buckets" : [
                {
                  "key" : "value1",
                  "doc_count" : 1
                }
              ]
            }
          }
        },
        {...truncated...},
        {
          "key" : "33333",
          "doc_count" : 1,
          "to-children" : {
            "doc_count" : 0,
            "top-values" : {
```

```
                "doc_count_error_upper_bound" : 0,
                "sum_other_doc_count" : 0,
                "buckets" : [ ]
              }
            }
          }
        ]
      }
    }
  }
```

How it works...

The children aggregation works by following these steps:

1. All the parent IDs are collected by the matched query or by previous bucket aggregations.
2. The parent IDs are used to filter the children and the matching document results are used to compute the children aggregation.

This type of aggregation, similar to the nested one, allows us to aggregate on different documents on searched ones.

Because children documents are stored in the same shard of the parents, they are very fast.

Executing nested aggregations

This kind of aggregation allows executing analytics on nested documents. When working with complex structures, the nested objects are very common.

Getting ready

You need an up-and-running Elasticsearch installation, as we described in the *Downloading and installing Elasticsearch* recipe in Chapter 2, *Downloading and Setup*.

To execute curl via the command line, you need to install curl for your operative system.

To correctly execute the following command, you need an index populated with the script (chapter_08/populate_aggregations.sh) available in the online code.

How to do it…

For executing nested aggregations, we will perform the following steps:

1. We must index documents with a nested type, as discussed in the *Managing nested objects* recipe in `Chapter 3`, *Managing Mappings*:

```
{
    "product" : {
        "properties" : {
            "resellers" : {
                "type" : "nested"
                "properties" : {
                    "username" : { "type" : "string", "index" :
                    "not_analyzed" },
                    "price" : { "type" : "double" }
                }
            },
            "tags" : { "type" : "string",
            "index":"not_analyzed"}
        }
    }
}
```

2. To return the minimum price products can be purchased at, we create a nested aggregation with a code similar to the following:

```
curl -XGET 'http://127.0.0.1:9200/test-index/product/_search?
pretty&size=0' -d ' {
    "query" : {
        "match" : { "name" : "my product" }
    },
    "aggs" : {
        "resellers" : {
            "nested" : {
                "path" : "resellers"
            },
            "aggs" : {
                "min_price" : { "min" : { "field" :
                "resellers.price" } }
            }
        }
    }
}'
```

3. The result returned by Elasticsearch, if everything is okay, should be as follows:

```
{
    "took" : 7,
    "timed_out" : false,
    "_shards" : {...truncated...},
    "hits" : {...truncated...},
    "aggregations": {
        "resellers": {
            "min_price": {
                "value" : 130
            }
        }
    }
}
```

In this case, the result aggregation is a simple min metric that we have already seen in the second recipe of this chapter.

How it works...

The nested aggregation requires only the `path` of the field, relative to the parent, which contains the nested documents.

After having defined the nested aggregation, all the other kinds of aggregations can be used in the sub-aggregations.

There's more...

Elasticsearch provides a way to aggregate values from nested documents to their parent: this aggregation is called `reverse_nested`.

In the preceding example, we can aggregate the top tags for the reseller with a similar query as follows:

```
curl -XGET 'http://127.0.0.1:9200/test-index/product/_search?pretty&size=0'
-d ' {
    "query" : {
        "match" : { "name" : "my product" }
    }
    "aggs" : {
        "resellers" : {
            "nested" : {
                "path" : "resellers"
```

```
                    },
                    "aggs" : {
                        "top_resellers" : {
                            "terms" : {
                                "field" : "resellers.username"
                            }
                        },
                        "aggs" : {
                            "resellers_to_product" : {
                                "reverse_nested" : {},
                                "aggs" : {
                                    "top_tags_per_reseller" : {
                                        "terms" : { "field" : "tags" }
                                    }
                                }
                            }
                        }
                    }
                }
            }
        }'
```

In this example, there are several steps:

1. We aggregate initially for nested `resellers`.
2. Having activated the nested resellers documents, we are able to term aggregate by the `username` field (`resellers.username`).
3. From the top resellers aggregation, we go back to aggregate on the parent via the `"reverse_nested"`.
4. Now we can aggregate the `tags` of the parent document.

The response is similar to this one:

```
{
    "took" : 93,
    "timed_out" : false,
    "_shards" : {...truncated...},
    "hits" : {...truncated...},
    "aggregations": {
        "resellers": {
            "top_usernames": {
                "buckets" : [
                    {
                        "key" : "username_1",
                        "doc_count" : 17,
                        "resellers_to_product" : {
```

```
                    "top_tags_per_reseller" : {
                        "buckets" : [
                            {
                                "key" : "tag1",
                                "doc_count" : 9
                            },...
                        ]
                    }
                },...
            }
        ]
    }
}
}
}
```

Executing top hit aggregations

The top hit aggregation is different from the other aggregation types: all the previous aggregations have metric (simple values) or bucket values; the top hit aggregation returns buckets of search hits.

Generally, the top hit aggregation is used as a sub-aggregation, so that the top matching documents can be aggregated in buckets.

Getting ready

You need an up-and-running Elasticsearch installation, as we described in the *Downloading and installing Elasticsearch* recipe in Chapter 2, *Downloading and Setup*.

To execute curl via the command line, you need to install curl for your operative system.

To correctly execute the following command, you need an index populated with the chapter_08/populate_aggregations.sh script available in the online code.

How to do it...

For executing a top hit aggregation, we will perform the following steps:

1. We want to aggregate the document hits by the tag (`tags`) and return only the name field of the document with the maximum age (`top_tag_hits`). We'll execute the search and aggregation with the following command:

```
curl -XGET 'http://127.0.0.1:9200/test-index/test-type/_search'
-d '{
    "query": {
      "match_all": {}
    },
    "size": 0,
    "aggs": {
      "tags": {
        "terms": {
          "field": "tag",
          "size": 2
        },
        "aggs": {
          "top_tag_hits": {
            "top_hits": {
              "sort": [
                {
                  "age": {
                    "order": "desc"
                  }
                }
              ],
              "_source": {
                "includes": [
                  "name"
                ]
              },
              "size": 1
            }
          }
        }
      }
    }
}'
```

2. The result returned by Elasticsearch, if everything is okay, should be as follows:

```
{
    "took" : 5,
    "timed_out" : false,
    "_shards" : ...truncated...,
    "hits" : ...truncated...,
    "aggregations" : {
     "tags" : {
       "buckets" : [ {
         "key" : "laborum",
         "doc_count" : 18,
         "top_tag_hits" : {
           "hits" : {
             "total" : 18,
             "max_score" : null,
             "hits" : [ {
               "_index" : "test-index",
               "_type" : "test-type",
               "_id" : "730",
               "_score" : null,
               "_source":{"name":"Gladiator"},
               "sort" : [ 90 ]
             } ]
           }
         }
       }, {
         "key" : "sit",
         "doc_count" : 10,
         "top_tag_hits" : {
           "hits" : {
             "total" : 10,
             "max_score" : null,
             "hits" : [ {
               "_index" : "test-index",
               "_type" : "test-type",
               "_id" : "732",
               "_score" : null,
               "_source":{"name":"Masked Marvel"},
               "sort" : [ 96 ]
             } ]
           }
         }
       } ]
      }
     }
}
```

How it works...

The top hit aggregation allows for collecting buckets of hits of another aggregation.

It provides optional parameters to control the results slicing. They are as follows:

- `from` (default: `0`): This is the starting position of the hits in the bucket.
- `size` (default: the parent bucket size): This is the hit bucket size.
- `sort` (default: `score`): This allows us to sort for different values. Its definition is similar to the search sort of `Chapter 5`, *Search*.

To control the returned hits, it's possible to use the same parameters used for the search, as follows:

- `_source`: This allows us to control the returned source. It can be disabled (`false`), partially returned (`obj.*`), or have multiple exclude/include rules. In the preceding example, we have returned only the name field:

```
"_source": {
  "include": [
    "name"
  ]
},
```

- `highlighting`: This allows us to define fields and settings to be used for calculating a query abstract.
- `fielddata_fields`: This allows us to return field data representation of our field.
- `explain`: This returns information on how the score is calculated for a particular document.
- `version` (default: `false`): This adds the version of a document in the results.

> **TIP**
>
> The top hit aggregation can be used for implementing a *field collapsing* feature: using first a `terms` aggregation on the field that we want collapsing, and when collecting the documents with a top hit aggregation.

See also

- Refer to the *Executing a search* recipe in `Chapter 5`, *Search*, for common parameters to be used in during search

Executing a matrix stats aggregation

Elasticsearch 5.x provided a special module called `aggs-matrix-stats` that automatically computes advanced statistics on several fields.

Getting ready

You need an up-and-running Elasticsearch installation, as we described in the *Downloading and installing Elasticsearch* recipe in `Chapter 2`, *Downloading and Setup*.

To execute `curl` via the command line, you need to install `curl` for your operative system.

To correctly execute the following command, you need an index populated with the `chapter_08/populate_aggregations.sh` script available in the online code.

How to do it…

For executing a top hot aggregation, we will perform the following steps:

1. We want to evaluate statistics related to price and age in our knowledge base. We'll execute the search and aggregation with the following command:

```
curl -XGET 'http://127.0.0.1:9200/test-index/test-type/_search?
size=0&pretty' -d '
{
    "query": {
        "match_all": {}
    },
    "aggs": {
        "matrixstats": {
            "matrix_stats": {
                "fields": ["age", "price"]
            }
        }
    }
}'
```

2. The result returned by Elasticsearch, if everything is okay, should be as follows:

```
{
  "took" : 114,
  "timed_out" : false,
  "_shards" : {
```

```
        "total" : 5,
        "successful" : 5,
        "failed" : 0
    },
    "hits" : {
        "total" : 1000,
        "max_score" : 0.0,
        "hits" : [ ]
    },
    "aggregations" : {
        "matrixstats" : {
            "fields" : [
                {
                    "name" : "price",
                    "count" : 1000,
                    "mean" : 50.295451175926246,
                    "variance" : 834.2714234338576,
                    "skewness" : -0.04757692114597178,
                    "kurtosis" : 1.8084832744827326,
                    "covariance" : {
                        "price" : 834.2714234338576,
                        "age" : 2.5236822082510146
                    },
                    "correlation" : {
                        "price" : 1.0,
                        "age" : 0.0030517752487823836
                    }
                },
                {
                    "name" : "age",
                    "count" : 1000,
                    "mean" : 53.243,
                    "variance" : 819.7036546546547,
                    "skewness" : -0.12618381352528785,
                    "kurtosis" : 1.8122869730963942,
                    "covariance" : {
                        "price" : 2.5236822082510146,
                        "age" : 819.7036546546547
                    },
                    "correlation" : {
                        "price" : 0.0030517752487823836,
                        "age" : 1.0
                    }
                }
            ]
        }
    }
}
```

How it works...

The Matrix Stats aggregation allows us to compute different metric on numeric fields, as follows:

- `count`: This is the number of per field samples included in the calculation.
- `mean`: This is the average value for each field.
- `variance`: This is per field measurement for how spread out the samples are from the mean.
- `skewness`: This is per field measurement quantifying the asymmetric distribution around the mean.
- `kurtosis`: This is per field measurement quantifying the shape of the distribution.
- `covariance`: This is a matrix that quantitatively describes how changes in one field are associated with another.
- `correlation`: This is the covariance matrix scaled to a range of -1 to 1, inclusive. It describes the relationship between field distributions. The higher the value of the correlation, the more the numeric fields are correlated.

> **TIP**
>
> The Matrix Stats aggregation is also a good code sample, for developing custom aggregation plugins to extend the power of the aggregation framework of Elasticsearch.

Executing geo bounds aggregations

It's a very common scenario having a set of documents that match a query and you need to know the box that contains them. The solution to this scenario is the metric aggregation geo bounds.

Getting ready

You need an up-and-running Elasticsearch installation, as we described in the *Downloading and installing Elasticsearch* recipe in `Chapter 2`, *Downloading and Setup*.

To execute `curl` via the command line, you need to install `curl` for your operative system.

To correctly execute the following command, you need an index populated with the `chapter_08/populate_aggregations.sh` script available in the online code.

How to do it...

1. For executing geo bounds aggregations, we will perform the following steps:We execute a query and we calculate the geo bounds on the results with a code similar to the following:

```
curl -XGET 'http://127.0.0.1:9200/test-index/test-type/_search?
pretty&size=0' -d ' {
    "query" : {
        "match_all" : {}
    },
    "aggs" : {
        "box" : {
            "geo_bounds" : {
                "field":"position",
                "wrap_longitude" : true
            }
        }
    }
}'
```

2. The result returned by Elasticsearch, if everything is okay, should be as follows:

```
{
    "took" : 68,
    "timed_out" : false,
    "_shards" : {...truncated...  },
    "hits" : { ...truncated... },
    "aggregations" : {
      "box" : {
        "bounds" : {
          "top_left" : {
            "lat" : 89.97587876860052,
            "lon" : 0.7563168089836836
          },
          "bottom_right" : {
            "lat" : -89.8060692474246,
            "lon" : -0.2987125888466835
          }
        }
      }
    }
}
```

```
            }
        }
    }
```

How it works...

The geo bounds aggregation is a metric aggregation that is able to compute the box of all the documents that are in a bucket.

It allows you to use the following parameters:

- `field`: This is the field that contains the geo point of the document
- `wrap_longitude` (default `true`): This is an optional parameter which specifies whether the bounding box should be allowed to overlap the International Date Line.

The returned box is given by two geo points: the top-left and the bottom-right.

See also

- Refer to the *Mapping a GeoPoint field* recipe in Chapter 3, *Managing Mappings*, to correctly define a GeoPoint field for executing geo aggregations

Executing geo centroid aggregations

If you have a lot of geo localized events and you need to know the center of these events, the geo centroid aggregation allows us to compute this geo point.

Getting ready

You need an up-and-running Elasticsearch installation, as we described in the *Downloading and installing Elasticsearch* recipe in Chapter 2, *Downloading and Setup*.

To execute `curl` via the command line, you need to install `curl` for your operative system.

To correctly execute the following command, you need an index populated with the `chapter_08/populate_aggregations.sh` script available in the online code.

How to do it...

For executing geo centroid aggregations, we will perform the following steps:

1. We execute a query and we calculate the geo centroid on the results with a code similar to the following:

```
curl -XGET 'http://127.0.0.1:9200/test-index/test-type/_search?
pretty&size=0' -d ' {
    "query" : {
        "match_all" : {}
    },
    "aggs" : {
        "centroid" : {
            "geo_centroid" : {
                "field":"position"
            }
        }
    }
}'
```

2. The result returned by Elasticsearch, if everything is okay, should be as follows:

```
{
  "took" : 16,
  "timed_out" : false,
  "_shards" : {
   "total" : 5,
   "successful" : 5,
    "failed" : 0
 },
  "hits" : {
    "total" : 1000,
    "max_score" : 0.0,
     "hits" : [ ]
  },
  "aggregations" : {
    "centroid" : {
      "location" : {
        "lat" : 3.094168079942465,
        "lon" : 0.5758688138611615
      }
    }
  }
}
```

How it works...

The geo centroid aggregation is a metric aggregation that is able to compute the geo point centroid of a bucket of documents.

It allows you to define only a single parameter in the `field` that contains the geo point of the document.

The returned result is a geo point that is the centroid of the document distribution.

For example, if your document contains earthquake events, using the geo centroid aggregation, you are able to compute the epicenter of the earthquake.

See also

- Refer to the *Mapping a GeoPoint field* recipe in `Chapter 3`, *Managing Mappings*, to correctly define a GeoPoint field for executing geo aggregations.

9
Scripting

In this chapter, we will cover the following recipes:

- Painless scripting
- Installing additional script plugins
- Managing scripts
- Sorting data using scripts
- Computing return fields with scripting
- Filtering a search via scripting
- Using scripting in aggregations
- Updating a document using scripts
- Reindexing with a script

Introduction

Elasticsearch has a powerful way to extend its capabilities with custom scripts that can be written in several programming languages. The most common ones are Painless, Groovy, JavaScript, and Python.

In this chapter, we will see how it's possible to create custom scoring algorithms, special processed return fields, custom sorting, and complex update operations on records.

The scripting concept of Elasticsearch is an advanced stored procedures system in the NoSQL world; so, for an advanced use of Elasticsearch, it is very important to master it.

Elasticsearch natively provides scripting in Java (a Java code compiled in JAR), Painless, Groovy, Express, and Mustache; but a lot of interesting languages are available as plugins, such as JavaScript and Python.

In older Elasticsearch releases, prior to version 5.0, the official scripting language was **Groovy**, but for better sandboxing and performance, the official language is now Painless, which is provided by default in Elasticsearch.

Painless scripting

Painless is a simple, secure scripting language available in Elasticsearch by default. It was designed by Elasticsearch guys specifically to be used with Elasticsearch and can safely be used with inline and stored scripting. Its syntax is similar to Groovy.

Getting ready

You need an up-and-running Elasticsearch installation as we described in the *Downloading and installing Elasticsearch* recipe in `Chapter 2`, *Downloading and Setup*.

To execute `curl` via the command line you need to install `curl` on your operating system.

To be able to use regular expressions in Painless scripting, you need to activate them in your `elasticsearch.yml` adding the following:

```
script.painless.regex.enabled: true
```

To correctly execute the following commands, you need an index populated with the `chapter_09/populate_for_scripting.sh` script available in the online code.

How to do it...

We'll use Painless scripting to compute the scoring with a script. A script code requires us to correctly escape special characters, and writing it in a single curl is quite complex and often difficult to read, so we'll save the script code in a separate file to avoid complex escaping and newline management:

1. We create the file containing the script `painless_script_score.json`:

```
{
  "query": {
    "function_score": {
      "script_score": {
        "script": {
          "lang": "painless",
```

```
                    "inline": "doc['price'].value * 1.2"
                }
            }
        }
    }
}
```

2. We can now execute the script via a `curl`:

```
curl -XPOST 'http://127.0.0.1:9200/test-index/test-type/_search?
pretty&size=2' -d @painless_script_score.json
```

3. The result will be as follows, if everything is all right:

```
{
  "took" : 26,
  "timed_out" : false,
  "_shards" : {...},
  "hits" : {
    "total" : 1000,
    "max_score" : 119.97963,
    "hits" : [
      {
        "_index" : "test-index",
        "_type" : "test-type",
        "_id" : "857",
        "_score" : 119.97963,
        "_source" : {
          ...
            "price" : 99.98302508488757,
          ...
        }
      },
      {
        "_index" : "test-index",
        "_type" : "test-type",
        "_id" : "136",
        "_score" : 119.90164,
        "_source" : {
          ...
            "price" : 99.91804048691392,
          ...
        }
      }
    ]
  }
}
```

How it works...

Painless is a scripting language developed for Elasticsearch for fast data processing and security (sandboxed to prevent malicious code injection).

The syntax is based on Groovy, and it's provided by default in every installation.

Painless is marked as "experimental" by the Elasticsearch team, because some features may change in the future, but it is the preferred language for scripting.

Elasticsearch processes the scripting language in two steps:

1. The script code is *compiled* in an object to be used in a script call. If the scripting code is invalid; then an exception is raised.
2. For every element, the script is called and the result is collected. If the script fails on some elements, the search/computation may fail.

> **TIP**
>
> Using scripting is a powerful Elasticsearch functionality, but it costs a lot in terms of memory and CPU cycles. The best practice, if it's possible, is to optimize the indexing of data to search or aggregate and avoid using scripting.

The way to define a script in Elasticsearch is always the same. The script is contained in an object `script` and it accepts several parameters:

- `inline/id/name`: This is the reference for the script that can be:
    - `inline` ,if it's provided with the call
    - `id` ,if it's stored in the cluster
    - `name` ,if it's stored on the filesystem
- `params` (an optional JSON object): This defines the parameters to be passed to, which are, in the context of scripting, variable `params`
- `lang` (default `painless`): This defines the scripting language to be used

There's more

Painless is the preferred choice if the script is not too complex; but otherwise, a native plugin provides a better environment to implement complex logic and data management.

For accessing document properties in Painless scripts, the same approach works as with other scripting languages:

- `doc._score`: This stores the document score. It's generally available in searching, sorting and aggregations.
- `doc._source`: This allows access to the source of the document. Use it wisely because it requires the entire source to be fetched and it's very CPU-and-memory-intensive.
- `_fields['field_name'].value`: This allows you to load the value from stored field (in mapping, the field has the `stored:true` parameter).
- `doc['field_name']`: This extracts the document field value from the doc values of the field. In Elasticsearch, doc values are automatically stored for every field that is not of type `text`.
- `doc['field_name'].value`: This extracts the value of the `field_name` field from the document. If the value is an array, or if you want to extract the value as an array, you can use `doc['field_name'].values`.
- `doc['field_name'].empty`: This returns `true` if the `field_name` field has no value in the document.
- `doc['field_name'].multivalue`: This returns `true` if the `field_name` field contains multiple values.

> For performance, the fastest access method for a field value is by doc value, then stored field, and finally, from the source.

If the field contains a GeoPoint value, additional methods are available, such as:

- `doc['field_name'].lat`: This returns the latitude of a GeoPoint. If you need the value as an array, you can use `doc['field_name'].lats`.
- `doc['field_name'].lon`: This returns the longitude of a GeoPoint. If you need the value as an array, you can use `doc['field_name'].lons`.
- `doc['field_name'].distance(lat,lon)`: This returns the plane distance in miles from a lat/lon point.
- `doc['field_name'].arcDistance(lat,lon)`: This returns the arc distance in miles given a lat/lon point.
- `doc['field_name'].geohashDistance(geohash)`: This returns the distance in miles given a GeoHash value.

By using these helper methods, it is possible to create advanced scripts to boost a document by a distance, which can be very handy for developing geospatial-centered applications.

See also

- The official announcement by Jack Conradson about the Painless development at `https://www.elastic.co/blog/painless-a-new-scripting-language`
- The Elasticsearch official page of Painless at `https://www.elastic.co/guide/en/elasticsearch/reference/master/modules-scripting-painless.html` to learn about its main functionalities
- The Painless syntax reference at `https://www.elastic.co/guide/en/elasticsearch/reference/master/modules-scripting-painless.html` to learn about Painless powerful syntax.

Installing additional script plugins

Elasticsearch provides native scripting (a Java code compiled in JAR) and Painless, but a lot of interesting languages are available, such as JavaScript and Python.

As previously stated, the official language is now Painless, and this is provided by default in Elasticsearch for better sandboxing and performance.

> Other scripting languages can be installed as plugins, thus they are now deprecated. We will present them in this recipe as they have a large user base.

Getting ready

You need an up-and-running Elasticsearch installation as we described in the *Downloading and installing Elasticsearch* recipe in `Chapter 2`, *Downloading and Setup*.

How to do it...

To install JavaScript language support for Elasticsearch, we will perform the following steps:

1. From the command line, simply call the following command:

   ```
   bin/elasticsearch-plugin install lang-javascript
   ```

2. It will print the following output:

   ```
   -> Downloading lang-javascript from elastic
   [=================================================] 100%??
   @@@@@@@@@@@@@@@@@@@@@@@@@@@@@@@@@@@@@@@@@@@@@@@@@@@@@@@@@@@@
   @     WARNING: plugin requires additional permissions     @
   @@@@@@@@@@@@@@@@@@@@@@@@@@@@@@@@@@@@@@@@@@@@@@@@@@@@@@@@@@@@
   * java.lang.RuntimePermission createClassLoader
   * org.elasticsearch.script.ClassPermission <<STANDARD>>
   * org.elasticsearch.script.ClassPermission
   org.mozilla.javascript.ContextFactory
   * org.elasticsearch.script.ClassPermission
   org.mozilla.javascript.Callable
   * org.elasticsearch.script.ClassPermission
   org.mozilla.javascript.NativeFunction
   * org.elasticsearch.script.ClassPermission
   org.mozilla.javascript.Script
   * org.elasticsearch.script.ClassPermission
   org.mozilla.javascript.ScriptRuntime
   * org.elasticsearch.script.ClassPermission
   org.mozilla.javascript.Undefined
   * org.elasticsearch.script.ClassPermission
   org.mozilla.javascript.optimizer.OptRuntime
    See http://docs.oracle.com/javase/8/docs/technotes/
    guides/security/permissions.html
    for descriptions of what these permissions allow and the
    associated risks.
    Continue with installation? [y/N]y
   -> Installed lang-javascript
   ```

If the installation is successful, the output will end with Installed; otherwise, an error is returned.

3. To install Python language support for Elasticsearch, just call the following command:

```
bin/elasticsearch-plugin install lang-python
```

4. It will print the following output:

```
-> Downloading lang-python from elastic
[================================================] 100%??
@@@@@@@@@@@@@@@@@@@@@@@@@@@@@@@@@@@@@@@@@@@@@@@@@@@@@@@@@@@@
@     WARNING: plugin requires additional permissions    @
@@@@@@@@@@@@@@@@@@@@@@@@@@@@@@@@@@@@@@@@@@@@@@@@@@@@@@@@@@@@
* java.lang.RuntimePermission createClassLoader
* java.lang.RuntimePermission getClassLoader
* org.elasticsearch.script.ClassPermission <<STANDARD>>
Continue with installation? [y/N]y
-> Installed lang-python
```

See http://docs.oracle.com/javase/8/docs/technotes/guides/secur ity/permissions.html for descriptions of what these permissions allow and the associated risks.

5. Restart your Elasticsearch server to check that the scripting plugins are loaded:

```
[...][INFO ][o.e.n.Node                ] [] initializing ...
[...][INFO ][o.e.e.NodeEnvironment     ] [R2Gp0ny] using [1]
data paths, mounts [[/ (/dev/disk1)]], net usable_space
[82.4gb], net total_space [930.7gb], spins? [unknown], types
[hfs]
[...][INFO ][o.e.e.NodeEnvironment     ] [R2Gp0ny] heap size
[1.9gb], compressed ordinary object pointers [true]
[...][INFO ][o.e.n.Node                ] [R2Gp0ny] node name
[R2Gp0ny] derived from node ID; set [node.name] to override
[...][INFO ][o.e.n.Node                ] [R2Gp0ny]
version[5.0.0-beta1], pid[58291], build[7eb6260/2016-09-
20T23:10:37.942Z], OS[Mac OS X/10.12/x86_64], JVM[Oracle
Corporation/Java HotSpot(TM) 64-Bit Server VM/1.8.0_101/25.101-
b13]
[...][INFO ][o.e.p.PluginsService      ] [R2Gp0ny] loaded module
[aggs-matrix-stats]
[...][INFO ][o.e.p.PluginsService      ] [R2Gp0ny] loaded module
[ingest-common]
[...][INFO ][o.e.p.PluginsService      ] [R2Gp0ny] loaded module
[lang-expression]
[...][INFO ][o.e.p.PluginsService      ] [R2Gp0ny] loaded module
[lang-groovy]
```

```
[...][INFO ][o.e.p.PluginsService      ] [R2Gp0ny] loaded module
[lang-mustache]
[...][INFO ][o.e.p.PluginsService      ] [R2Gp0ny] loaded module
[lang-painless]
[...][INFO ][o.e.p.PluginsService      ] [R2Gp0ny] loaded module
[percolator]
[...][INFO ][o.e.p.PluginsService      ] [R2Gp0ny] loaded module
[reindex]
[...][INFO ][o.e.p.PluginsService      ] [R2Gp0ny] loaded module
[transport-netty3]
[...][INFO ][o.e.p.PluginsService      ] [R2Gp0ny] loaded module
[transport-netty4]
[...][INFO ][o.e.p.PluginsService      ] [R2Gp0ny] loaded plugin
[lang-javascript]
[...][INFO ][o.e.p.PluginsService      ] [R2Gp0ny] loaded plugin
[lang-python]
[...][INFO ][o.e.n.Node                ] [R2Gp0ny] initialized
[...][INFO ][o.e.n.Node                ] [R2Gp0ny] starting ...
```

How it works...

Language plugins allow an extension of the number of supported languages to be used in scripting. During installation, they require special permissions to access classes and methods that are banned by the Elasticsearch security layer, such as access to ClassLoader or class permissions.

During the Elasticsearch start-up, an internal Elasticsearch service, PluginService, loads all the installed language plugins.

> Installing or upgrading a plugin requires a node restart.

From version 5.x, all the plugins have the same version of Elasticsearch.

The Elasticsearch community provides common scripting languages (a list is available on the Elasticsearch site plugin page at
`http://www.elastic.co/guide/en/elasticsearch/reference/current/modules-plugins.html`), others are available in GitHub repositories (a simple search on GitHub will help you find them).

The most used languages for scripting are as follows:

- **Groovy** (`http://www.groovy-lang.org/`): This language, embedded in Elasticsearch by default, is a simple language providing scripting functionalities. It's of the fastest available language extensions (except for Painless). Groovy is a dynamic object-oriented programming language with features similar to those of Python, Ruby, Perl, and Smalltalk. It also supports the writing of functional code.

- **JavaScript:** This is available as an external plugin. The JavaScript implementation is based on Java Rhino (`https://developer.mozilla.org/en-US/docs/Rhino`) and it's very fast.

- **Python**: This is available as an external plugin, based on Jython (`http://jython.org`). It allows Python to be used as a script engine. From several benchmarks, it's slower than other scripting languages.

> **TIP**
> The performance of every language is different; the fastest one is the native Java. In the case of dynamic scripting languages, Painless and Groovy are faster, as compared to JavaScript and Python.

There's more...

The PluginManager that we've used to install plugins also provides the following commands:

- `list`: To list all installed plugins.

    For example, executing:

    ```
    bin/elasticsearch-plugin list
    ```

    The following is the result:

    ```
    lang-javascript@5.0.0
    lang-python@5.0.0
    ```

- `remove`: to remove an installed plugin.

    For example, executing:

    ```
    bin/elasticsearch-plugin remove lang-javascript
    ```

Will result in the following:

```
-> Removing lang-javascript...
```

Managing scripts

Depending on your scripting usage, there are several ways to customize Elasticsearch to use your script extensions.

In this recipe, we will see how to provide scripts to Elasticsearch via files, index or inline.

Getting ready

You need an up-and-running Elasticsearch installation as we described in the *Downloading and installing Elasticsearch* recipe in `Chapter 2`, *Downloading and Setup*.

To execute `curl` via the command-line you need to install `curl` for your operative system.

To correctly execute the following commands, you need an index populated with the `chapter_09/populate_for_scripting.sh` script available in the online code.

How to do it...

To manage scripting, we will perform the following steps:

1. Dynamic scripting (except Painless) is disabled by default for security reasons. We need to activate it to use dynamic scripting languages such as JavaScript and Python. To do this, we need to enable scripting flags in the Elasticsearch config file (`config/elasticseach.yml`) and restart the cluster:

    ```
    script.inline: true
    script.stored: true
    ```

2. To increase security, Elasticsearch does not allow specifying scripts for non-sandboxed languages. Scripts can be placed in the `scripts` directory inside the configuration directory. To provide a script in a file we'll put a `my_script.groovy` in `config/scripts` with the following code content:

    ```
    doc["price"].value * factor
    ```

3. If the dynamic script is enabled (as done in the first step), Elasticsearch lets us store the scripts in a special part of the cluster state "_scripts". To put my_script in the cluster state execute the following code:

```
curl -XPOST localhost:9200/_scripts/groovy/my_script -d '
{
    "script":"doc["price"].value * factor"
}'
```

4. The script can be used by simply referencing it in the script/id field:

```
curl -XGET 'http://127.0.0.1:9200/test-index/test-type/_search?
&pretty &size=3' -d '
{
        "query":
        {
          "match_all": {}
        },
        "sort":
        {
          "_script":
          {
            "script":
            {
                "id": "my_script",
                "lang": "groovy",
                "params":
                {
                    "factor": 1.1
                }
            },
            "type": "number",
            "order": "asc"
          }
        }
}'
```

How it works...

Elasticsearch permits different ways to load your script, and each approach has pros and cons.

The most secure way to load or import scripts is to provide them as files in the `config/scripts` directory. This directory is continuously scanned for new files (by default every 60 seconds). The scripting language is automatically detected by the file extension and the script name depends on the filename.

If the file is put into subdirectories, the directory path becomes part of the filename: for example, if it is `config/scripts/mysub1/mysub2/my_script.groovy` the script name will be `mysub1_mysub2_my_script`.

If the script is provided via the filesystem, it can be referenced in the code via `"script":` `"script_name"` parameter.

The scripts can also be available in the special `_script` cluster state. The REST end points are:

```
GET http://<server>/_scripts/<language>/<id> (to retrieve a script)
PUT http://<server>/_scripts/<language>/<id> (to store a script)
DELETE http://<server>/_scripts/<language>/<id> (to delete a script)
```

The stored script can be referenced in the code via `"script":{"id":` `"id_of_the_script"}`.

The following recipes will use inline scripting because it's easier to use during the development and testing phases.

> Generally, a good workflow is to do the development using inline dynamic scripting in request, because it's faster to prototype. Once the script is ready and no more changes are required, it should be stored in the index to be simpler to call and manage in all the cluster nodes. In production, the best practice is to disable dynamic scripting and to store the script on disk (generally dumping the indexed script to disk) to improve security.

When you are storing files on disk, pay attention to the file extension. The following table summarizes the plugins status:

Language	Provided as	File extension	Status
Painless	Built-in/module	`painless`	default
Groovy	Built-in/module	`groovy`	deprecated
Expression	Built-in/module	`expression`	deprecated
Mustache	Built-in/module	`mustache`	default
JavaScript	External plugin	`js`	deprecated
Python	External plugin	`py`	deprecated

Other scripting parameters, that can be set in `config/elasticsearch.yml`, are as follows:

- `script.max_compilations_per_minute` (default `25`): The default scripting engine has a global limit for how many compilations can be done per minute. You can change this to a higher value:

  ```
  script.max_compilations_per_minute: 1000
  ```

- `script.cache.max_size` (default `100`): This defines how many scripts are cached. It depends on context, but generally it's better to increase this value.
- `script.max_size_in_bytes` (default `65535`): This defines the maximum text size for a script. For large scripts, the best practice is to develop native plugins.
- `script.cache.expire` (default disabled): This defines a time-based expiration for the cached scripts.

There's more...

In the above example, we activated Elasticsearch scripting for all the engines, but Elasticsearch provides fine-grained settings to control them.

In Elasticsearch, the scripting can be used in different contexts such as the following:

Context	Description
aggs	Aggregations
search	Search API, percolator API, and suggest API
update	Update API
plugin	Special scripts under the generic `plugin` category

Scripting can be selectively disabled for a single context. For example, to disable the update context, the following line must be added to `config/elasticsearch.yml`:

```
script.update: false
```

For more fine-grained control, scripting can be controlled at scripting engine level via these template entries:

```
script.engine.{lang}.{source}.{context}: true|false
script.engine.{lang}.{inline|file|stored}: true|false
```

A common configuration is to disable globally and activate functionality selectively in this way:

```
script.inline: false
script.stored: false
script.file:   false

script.engine.groovy.inline:           true
script.engine.groovy.stored.search:    true
script.engine.groovy.stored.aggs:      true
```

See also

- The scripting page on the Elasticsearch website at `https://www.elastic.co/gui de/en/elasticsearch/reference/current/modules-scripting.html`for general information about scripting
- The scripting security page at `https://www.elastic.co/guide/en/elasticsear ch/reference/current/modules-scripting-security.html`for other borderline cases security management

Sorting data using scripts

Elasticsearch provides scripting support for sorting functionality. In real-world applications, there is often a need to modify the default sort by match score using an algorithm that depends on the context and some external variables. Some common scenarios are as follows:

- Sorting places near a point
- Sorting by most read articles
- Sorting items by custom user logic
- Sorting items by revenue

> **TIP**
>
> Because the compute of scores on a large dataset is very CPU intensive, if you use scripting it's better execute it on a small dataset using standard score queries for detecting the top documents, and then execute a rescoring on the top subset.

Getting ready

You need an up-and-running Elasticsearch installation as we described in the *Downloading and installing Elasticsearch* recipe in `Chapter 2`, *Downloading and Setup*.

To execute `curl` via the command-line you need to install `curl` for your operating system.

To correctly execute the following commands, you need an index populated with the `chapter_09/populate_for_scripting.sh` script available in the online code.

How to do it…

For sorting using scripting, we will perform the following steps:

1. If we want to order our documents by the `price` field multiplied by a `factor` parameter (that is, sales tax), the search will be as shown in the following code:

   ```
   curl -XGET 'http://127.0.0.1:9200/test-index/test-type/_search?
   pretty&size=3' -d
   '{
       "query":
       {
         "match_all": {}
       },
   ```

```
    "sort":
    {
      "_script":
      {
        "script":
        {
          "inline": "Math.sqrt(doc["price"].value *
          params.factor)",
          "params":
          {
            "factor": 1.1
          }
        },
        "type": "number",
        "order": "asc"
      }
    }
}'
```

In this case, we have used a `match_all` query and a `sort` script. In real-world applications, the documents to be sorted must not be of a high cardinality.

2. If everything's correct, the result returned by Elasticsearch should be as shown in the following code:

```
{
  "took" : 7,
  "timed_out" : false,
  "_shards" : {
    "total" : 5,
    "successful" : 5,
    "failed" : 0
  },
  "hits" : {
    "total" : 1000,
    "max_score" : null,
    "hits" : [ {
      "_index" : "test-index",
      "_type" : "test-type",
      "_id" : "161",
      "_score" : null, "_source" : ... truncated ...,
      "sort" : [ 0.0278578661440021 ]
    }, {
      "_index" : "test-index",
      "_type" : "test-type",
      "_id" : "634",
```

```
      "_score" : null, "_source" : ... truncated ...,
      "sort" : [ 0.08131364254827411 ]
    }, {
      "_index" : "test-index",
      "_type" : "test-type",
      "_id" : "465",
      "_score" : null, "_source" : ... truncated ...,
      "sort" : [ 0.1094966959069832 ]
    } ]
  }
}
```

How it works...

The `sort` parameter, which we discussed in `Chapter 5`, *Search,* can be extended with the help of scripting.

The `sort` scripting allows defining several parameters, such as:

- `order (default "asc") ("asc" or "desc")`: This determines whether the order must be ascending or descending.
- `type`: This defines the type to convert the value.
- `script`: This contains the script object to be executed.

Extending the sort with scripting allows the use of a broader approach in scoring your hits.

> Elasticsearch scripting permits the use of any code that you want to use. You can create custom complex algorithms for scoring your documents.

There's more...

Painless and Groovy provides a lot of built-in functions (mainly taken from Java `Math` class) that can be used in scripts such as the following:

Function	Description
`time()`	The current time in milliseconds
`sin(a)`	Returns the trigonometric sine of an angle

`cos(a)`	Returns the trigonometric cosine of an angle
`tan(a)`	Returns the trigonometric tangent of an angle
`asin(a)`	Returns the arc sine of a value
`acos(a)`	Returns the arc cosine of a value
`atan(a)`	Returns the arc tangent of a value
`toRadians(angdeg)`	Converts an angle measured in degrees to an approximately equivalent angle measured in radians
`toDegrees(angrad)`	Converts an angle measured in radians to an approximately equivalent angle measured in degrees
`exp(a)`	Returns Euler's number raised to the power of a value
`log(a)`	Returns the natural logarithm (base e) of a value
`log10(a)`	Returns the base 10 logarithm of a value
`sqrt(a)`	Returns the correctly rounded positive square root of a value
`cbrt(a)`	Returns the cube root of a double value
`IEEEremainder(f1, f2)`	Computes the remainder operation on two arguments as prescribed by the IEEE 754 standard
`ceil(a)`	Returns the smallest (closest to negative infinity) value that is greater than or equal to the argument and is equal to a mathematical integer
`floor(a)`	Returns the largest (closest to positive infinity) value that is less than or equal to the argument and is equal to a mathematical integer
`rint(a)`	Returns the value that is closest in value to the argument and is equal to a mathematical integer
`atan2(y, x)`	Returns the angle, theta from the conversion of rectangular coordinates ($x,y\_$) to polar coordinates ($r,\_theta$)
`pow(a, b)`	Returns the value of the first argument raised to the power of the second argument
`round(a)`	Returns the closest integer to the argument
`random()`	Returns a random double value
`abs(a)`	Returns the absolute value of a value

`max(a, b)`	Returns the greater of two values
`min(a, b)`	Returns the smaller of two values
`ulp(d)`	Returns the size of the unit in the last place of the argument
`signum(d)`	Returns the signum function of the argument
`sinh(x)`	Returns the hyperbolic sine of a value
`cosh(x)`	Returns the hyperbolic cosine of a value
`tanh(x)`	Returns the hyperbolic tangent of a value
`hypot(x,y)`	Returns $sqrt(x^2+y^2)$ without intermediate overflow or underflow
`acos(a)`	Returns the arc cosine of a value
`atan(a)`	Returns the arc tangent of a value

If you want to retrieve records in a random order, you can use a script with a random method as shown in the following code:

```
curl -XGET 'http://127.0.0.1:9200/test-index/test-type/_search?
&pretty&size=3' -d '{
  "query": {
    "match_all": {}
  },
  "sort": {
    "_script": {
      "script": {
        "inline": "Math.random()"
      },
      "type": "number",
      "order": "asc"
    }
  }
}'
```

In this example, for every hit, the new sort value is computed executing the scripting function `Math.random()`.

Computing return fields with scripting

Elasticsearch allows us to define complex expressions that can be used to return a new calculated field value.

These special fields are called `script_fields`, and they can be expressed with a script in every available Elasticsearch scripting language.

Getting ready

You need an up-and-running Elasticsearch installation as we described the *Downloading and installing Elasticsearch* recipe in `Chapter 2`, *Downloading and Setup*.

To execute `curl` via the command-line you need to install `curl` for your operating system.

To correctly execute the following commands, you need an index populated with the script `chapter_09/populate_for_scripting.sh` script available in the online code.

How to do it...

For computing return fields with scripting, we will perform the following steps:

1. Return the following script fields:

   `"my_calc_field"`: This concatenates the texts of the `"name"` and `"description"` fields

   `"my_calc_field2"`: This multiplies the `"price"` value by the `"discount"` parameter

2. From the command line, we will execute the following code:

```
curl -XGET 'http://127.0.0.1:9200/test-index/test-type/_search?
pretty&size=3' -d '{
    "query": {
        "match_all": {}
    },
    "script_fields": {
        "my_calc_field": {
            "script": {
                "inline": "params._source.name + " -- " +
                    params._source.description"
            }
        },
        "my_calc_field2": {
            "script": {
                "inline": "doc["price"].value * params.discount",
                "params": {
```

```
                        "discount": 0.8
                    }
                }
            }
        }
    }'
```

3. If everything is all right, the result returned by Elasticsearch should be:

```
{
  "took": 95,
  "timed_out": false,
  "_shards": ... truncated ...,
  "hits": {
   "total": 1000,
    "max_score": 1,
     "hits": [
        {
          ... truncated ...
          "_id": "705",
          "fields": {
            "my_calc_field": [
              "Nimrod -- amet architecto ... truncated ..."
            ],
            "my_calc_field2": [
              18.594456481933594
            ]
          }
        },
        {
           ... truncated ...
          "_id": "708",
          "fields": {
            "my_calc_field": [
              "Sunstreak -- alias minus ... truncated ..."
            ],
            "my_calc_field2": [
              28.051638793945315
            ]
          }
        },
        {
          ... truncated ...
          "_id": "712",
          "fields": {
            "my_calc_field": [
               "Brant, Betty -- soluta praesentium ... truncated
                 ..."
```

```
        ],
        "my_calc_field2": [
          56.00410766601563
        ]
      }
    }
  ]
 }
}
```

How it works...

The script fields are similar to executing an SQL function on a field during a select.

In Elasticsearch, after a search phase is executed and hits to be returned are calculated, if some fields (standard or script) are defined, they are calculated and returned.

The script field, which can be defined with all supported languages, is processed by passing a value to the source of the document and, if some other parameters are defined in the script (in the example discount factor), they are passed to the script function.

The script function is a code snippet, so it can contain everything that the language allows to be written, but it must be evaluated to a value (or a list of values).

See also

- The *Installing additional script plugins* recipe in this chapter to install additional languages for scripting
- The *Sorting data using scripts* recipe in this chapter for a reference of extra built-in functions for Painless scripts

Filtering a search via scripting

In Chapter 5, *Search*, we've seen many filters. Elasticsearch scripting allows the extension of a traditional filter with custom scripts.

Using scripting to create a custom filter is a convenient way to write scripting rules not provided by Lucene or Elasticsearch, and to implement business logic not available in a DSL query.

Getting ready

You need an up-and-running Elasticsearch installation as we described in the *Downloading and installing Elasticsearch* recipe in `Chapter 2`, *Downloading and Setup*.

To execute `curl` via the command-line you need to install `curl` for your operating system.

To correctly execute the following commands, you need an index populated with the script (`chapter_09/populate_for_scripting.sh`) available in the online code and Javascript/Python Language scripting plugins installed.

How to do it…

For filtering a search using script, we will perform the following steps:

1. We'll write a search with a filter that filters out a document with an age value less than a parameter value:

```
curl -XGET 'http://127.0.0.1:9200/test-index/test-type/_search?
pretty&size=3' -d '{
  "query": {
    "bool": {
      "filter": {
        "script": {
          "script": {
            "inline": "doc["age"].value > params.param1",
            "params": {
              "param1": 80
            }
          }
        }
      }
    }
  }
}'
```

In this example, all documents, in which the age value is greater than param1, are taken as qualified for return.

This script filter is done for teaching reasons, in real-world applications it can be replaced with a range query which is much faster.

2. If everything is correct, the result returned by Elasticsearch should be as shown in the following code:

```
{
  "took" : 30,
  "timed_out" : false,
  "_shards" : {
    "total" : 5,
    "successful" : 5,
    "failed" : 0
  },
  "hits" : {
    "total" : 237,
    "max_score" : 1.0,
    "hits" : [ {
      "_index" : "test-index",
      "_type" : "test-type",
      "_id" : "9",
      "_score" : 1.0, "_source" :{ ... "age": 83, ... }
    }, {
      "_index" : "test-index",
      "_type" : "test-type",
      "_id" : "23",
      "_score" : 1.0, "_source" : { ... "age": 87, ... }
    }, {
      "_index" : "test-index",
      "_type" : "test-type",
      "_id" : "47",
      "_score" : 1.0, "_source" : {.... "age": 98, ...}
    } ]
  }
}
```

How it works...

The script filter is a language script that returns a boolean value (`true`/`false`). For every hit, the script is evaluated and if it returns `true`, the hit passes the filter. This type of scripting can only be used as Lucene filters, not as queries, because it doesn't affect the search.

The script code can be any code in your preferred supported scripting language that returns a boolean value.

There's more...

Using other languages is very similar to Painless/Groovy.

For the current example, I have chosen a standard comparison that works in several languages. To execute the same script using the JavaScript language, the code is:

```
curl -XGET
'http://127.0.0.1:9200/test-index/test-type/_search?pretty&size=3' -d '{
  "query": {
    "script": {
      "script": {
        "inline": "doc["age"].value > param1",
        "lang": "javascript",
        "params": {
          "param1": 80
        }
      }
    }
  }
}'
```

For Python, we have the following code:

```
curl -XGET
'http://127.0.0.1:9200/test-index/test-type/_search?pretty&size=3' -d '{
  "query": {
    "script": {
      "script": {
        "inline": "doc["age"].value > param1",
        "lang": "python",
        "params": {
          "param1": 80
        }
      }
```

```
      }
    }
  }'
```

See also

- *Installing additional script plugins* recipe in this chapter to install additional languages for scripting
- *Sorting data using script* recipe for a reference of extra built-in functions available for Painless scripts

Using scripting in aggregations

Scripting can be used in aggregations for extending its analytics capabilities both to change values used in metric aggregations or to define new rules to create buckets.

Getting ready

You need an up-and-running Elasticsearch installation as we described in the *Downloading and installing Elasticsearch* recipe in `Chapter 2`, *Downloading and Setup*.

To execute `curl` via the command-line you need to install `curl` for your operating system.

To correctly execute the following commands, you need an index populated with the `chapter_09/populate_for_scripting.sh` script available in the sonline code and Javascript/Python Language scripting plugins installed.

How to do it...

For using a scripting language in aggregation, we will perform the following steps:

1. We'll write a metric aggregation that selects the field via script:

    ```
    curl -XPOST 'http://127.0.0.1:9200/test-index/test-
    type/_search?pretty=true&size=0' -d ' {
      "aggs": {
        "my_value": {
          "sum": {
    ```

```
            "script": {
              "inline": "doc["price"].value * doc["price"].value"
            }
          }
        }
      }
    }
  }'
```

2. If everything is correct, the result returned by Elasticsearch should be as shown in the following code:

```
{
  "took": 5,
  "timed_out": false,
  "_shards": {...},
  "hits": {... },
  "aggregations": {
    "my_value": {
      "value": 3363069.561000402
    }
  }
}
```

3. We'll write a metric aggregation that uses the value field via script:

```
curl -XPOST 'http://127.0.0.1:9200/test-index/test-
type/_search?pretty=true&size=0' -d '{
  "aggs": {
    "my_value": {
      "sum": {
        "field":"price",
        "script": {
          "inline": "_value * _value"
        }
      }
    }
  }
}'
```

4. If everything is correct, the result returned by Elasticsearch should be as shown in the following code:

```
{
  "took": 5,
  "timed_out": false,
  "_shards": {...},
  "hits": {... },
  "aggregations": {
```

```
    "my_value": {
      "value": 3363069.561000402
    }
  }
}
```

5. We'll write a term bucket aggregation that changes the terms via script:

```
curl -XPOST 'http://127.0.0.1:9200/test-index/test-
type/_search?pretty=true&size=0' -d '{
  "aggs": {
    "my_value": {
      "terms": {
          "field":"tag",
  "size":5,
            "script": {
                "inline":
  "if(params.replace.containsKey(_value.toUpperCase())) {
  params.replace[_value.toUpperCase()] } else {
  _value.toUpperCase() }",
          "params":{"replace":{"PORRO":"Result1",
  "LABORUM":"Result2"}}
          }
        }
      }
    }
  }
}'
```

6. If everything is correct, the result returned by Elasticsearch should be as shown in the following code:

```
{
  "took": 4,
  "timed_out": false,
  "_shards": {...},
  "hits": {...   },
  "aggregations": {
    "my_value": {
      "doc_count_error_upper_bound": 29,
      "sum_other_doc_count": 2796,
      "buckets": [
        {
          "key": "Result1",
          "doc_count": 21
        },
        {
          "key": "Result2",
          "doc_count": 19
```

```
        },
        {
          "key": "IPSAM",
          "doc_count": 16
        },
        {
          "key": "MAIORES",
          "doc_count": 16
        },
        {
          "key": "SIT",
          "doc_count": 16
        }
      ]
    }
  }
}
```

How it works...

Elasticsearch provides two kinds of aggregation:

- Metrics that compute some values
- Buckets that aggregate documents in a bucket

In both cases, you can use script or value script (if you define the field to be used in the aggregation).

The object accepted in aggregation is the standard `script` object; the value returned by the script will be used for the aggregation.

If a `field` is defined in the aggregation, you can use the value script aggregation. In this case, in the context of the script there is a special `_value` variable available that contains the value of the field.

> Using scripting in aggregation is a very powerful feature, but using it on large cardinality aggregation could be very CPU intensive and slow down query times.

Updating a document using scripts

Elasticsearch allows the updating of a document in-place. Updating a document via scripting reduces network traffic (otherwise, you need to fetch the document, change the field/fields, and send them back) and improves performance when you need to process a huge amount of documents.

Getting ready

You need an up-and-running Elasticsearch installation as we described in the *Downloading and installing Elasticsearch* recipe in Chapter 2, *Downloading and Setup*.

To execute curl via the command-line you need to install curl for your operating system.

To correctly execute the following commands, you need an index populated with the chapter_09/populate_for_scripting.sh script available in the online code and Javascript/Python language scripting plugins installed.

How to do it...

For updating using scripting, we will perform the following steps:

1. We'll write an update action that adds a tag value to a list of tags available in the source of a document. It should look as shown in the following code:

```
curl -XPOST 'http://127.0.0.1:9200/test-index/test-type/9/_update?
    pretty' -d '{
        "script" : {
          "inline":"ctx._source.tag =
            ctx._source.tag.add(params.tag)",
          "params" : {
            "tag" : "cool"
          }
        }
      }'
```

2. If everything is correct, the result returned by Elasticsearch should be:

```
{
  "_index": "test-index",
  "_type": "test-type",
  "_id": "9",
```

```
      "_version": 8,
      "result": "updated",
      "_shards": {
        "total": 2,
        "successful": 1,
        "failed": 0
      }
    }
  }
```

3. If we now retrieve the document, we will have:

```
{
  "_index" : "test-index",
  "_type" : "test-type",
  "_id" : "9",
  "_version" : 2,
  "found" : true,
  "_source":{
    "in_stock": true,
    "tag": ["alias", "sit", "cool"],
    "name": "Frankie Raye", ...truncated...
    }
}
```

From the result, we can also see that the version number is increased by one.

How it works...

The REST HTTP method used to update a document is `POST`.

The URL contains only the index name, the type, the document ID, and the action:

```
http://<server>/<index_name>/<type>/<document_id>/_update
```

The update action is composed of three different steps:

1. **Get operation, very fast**: This operation works on real-time data (no need to refresh) and retrieves the record
2. **Script execution**: The script is executed on the document, and if required, it is updated
3. **Saving the document**: The document, if needed, is saved.

The script execution follows the workflow in the following manner:

- The script is compiled and the result is cached to improve re-execution. The compilation depends on the scripting language; it detects errors in the script such as typographical errors, syntax errors, and language-related errors. The compilation step can be CPU-bound, so Elasticsearch caches the compilation results for further execution.
- The document is executed in the script context. The document data is available in the ctx variable in the script.

The update script can set several parameters in the ctx variable. The most important parameters are:

- ctx._source: This contains the source of the document.
- ctx._timestamp: If it's defined, this value is set to the document timestamp.
- ctx.op: This defines the main operatih type to be executed. There are several available values, such as:
    - index: This is the default value, the record is re-indexed with the update values
    - delete: The document is deleted and not updated (that is, this can be used for updating a document or removing it if it exceeds a quota)
    - none: The document is skipped without re-indexing the document.

> If you need to execute a large number of update operations, it's better to perform them in bulk to improve your application's performance.

There's more...

In the following example, we'll execute an update that adds new tags and labels to an object, but we will mark for indexing the document only if the tags or labels values are changed:

```
curl -XPOST 'http://127.0.0.1:9200/test-index/test-type/9/_update?pretty' -
d ' {
  "script": {
    "inline": "ctx.op = "none";\n  if(ctx._source.containsValue("tags")){\n
```

```
for(def item : params.new_tags){\n
if(!ctx._source.tags.contains(item)){\n
ctx._source.tags.add(item);\n         ctx.op = "index";\n       }\n     }\n
}else{ ctx._source.tags=params.new_tags; ctx.op = "index"  }\n
if(ctx._source.containsValue("labels")){\n     for(def item :
params.new_labels){\n       if(!ctx._source.labels.contains(item)){\n
ctx._source.labels.add(item);\n         ctx.op = "index"\n       }\n     }\n
}else{\n     ctx._source.labels=params.new_labels;\n     ctx.op = "index"}",
      "params": {
        "new_tags": [
          "cool",
          "nice"
        ],
        "new_labels": [
          "red",
          "blue",
          "green"
        ]
      }
    }
  }
}'
```

The preceding code is quite complex to read because, when saving your script, the newline should be coded as \n character. Let me pretty print it:

```
ctx.op = "none";
if(ctx._source.containsValue("tags")){
    for(def item : params.new_tags){
        if(!ctx._source.tags.contains(item)){
            ctx._source.tags.add(item);
            ctx.op = "index";
        }
    }
} else {
    ctx._source.tags=params.new_tags;
    ctx.op = "index"
}
if(ctx._source.containsValue("labels")){
    for(def item : params.new_labels){
        if(!ctx._source.labels.contains(item)){
            ctx._source.labels.add(item);
            ctx.op = "index"
        }
    }
} else {
    ctx._source.labels=params.new_labels;
    ctx.op = "index"
}
```

The preceding script uses the following steps:

1. It marks the operation to `none` to prevent indexing if, in the following steps, the original source is not changed.
2. It checks if the `tags` field is available in the source object.
3. If the `tags` field is available in the source object, it iterates all the values of the `new_tags` list. If the value is not available in the current `tags` list, it adds it, and updates the operation to index.
4. It the `tags` field doesn't exist in the source object, it simply adds it to the source and marks the operation to index.
5. The steps from 2 to 4 are repeated for the `labels` value. The repetition is present in this example to show the Elasticsearch user how it is possible to update multiple values in a single update operation.

Use the approach to add sections in the script and change `ctx.op` if only the record is changed. It gives the ability to sum up different steps in a single script.

This script can be quite complex, but it shows the powerful capabilities of scripting in Elasticsearch.

Reindexing with a script

Reindex is a new functionality introduced in Elasticsearch 5.x for automatically reindexing your data in a new index. This action is often done for a variety of reasons, mainly mapping changes due to an improvement in mappings.

Getting ready

You need an up-and-running Elasticsearch installation as we described in the *Downloading and installing Elasticsearch* recipe in `Chapter 2`, *Downloading and Setup*.

To execute `curl` via the command-line you need to install `curl` for your operating system.

To correctly execute the following commands, you need an index populated with the `chapter_09/populate_for_scripting.sh` script available in the online code and Javascript/Python language scripting plugins installed.

How to do it...

For reindexing with a script, we will perform the following steps:

1. We create the destination index, because it's not created by `reindex` API:

```
curl -XPUT 'http://127.0.0.1:9200/reindex-test-index?
pretty=true' -d '{"mappings": {"test-type": {"properties":
{"name": {"index": "analyzed", "term_vector":
"with_positions_offsets", "boost": 1.0, "store": "yes",
"type": "text"}, "title": {"index": "analyzed",
"term_vector": "with_positions_offsets", "boost": 1.0,
"store": "yes", "type": "text"}, "parsedtext": {"index":
"analyzed", "term_vector": "with_positions_offsets",
"boost": 1.0, "store": "yes", "type": "text"}, "tag":
{"type": "keyword", "store": "yes"}, "processed": {"type":
"boolean"}, "date": {"type": "date", "store": "yes"},
"position": {"type": "geo_point", "store": "yes"}, "uuid":
{"index": "not_analyzed", "boost": 1.0, "store": "yes",
"type": "keyword"}}}}, "settings":
{"index.number_of_replicas": 1, "index.number_of_shards":
5}}'
```

2. We'll write a reindex action that adds a tag value to a list of tags available in the source of a document and a `processed` field (a Boolean field set to `true`). It should look as shown in the following code:

```
curl -XPOST 'http://127.0.0.1:9200/_reindex?pretty' -d '{
  "source": {
    "index": "test-index"
  },
  "dest": {
    "index": "reindex-test-index"
    },
  "script": {
    "inline": "ctx._source.tag.add(params.tag);if
    (!ctx._source.containsKey("processed"))
    {ctx._source.processed=true}",
    "params":{"tag":"nice"}
  }
}'
```

3. If everything is correct, the result returned by Elasticsearch should be:

```
{
  "took": 788,
  "timed_out": false,
```

```
      "total": 1000,
      "updated": 0,
      "created": 1000,
      "deleted": 0,
      "batches": 1,
      "version_conflicts": 0,
      "noops": 0,
      "retries": {
        "bulk": 0,
        "search": 0
        },
      "throttled_millis": 0,
      "requests_per_second": -1,
      "throttled_until_millis": 0,
      "failures": []
    }
```

4. If we now retrieve the same documents, we will have:

```
    {
      "_index": "reindex-test-index",
          "_type": "test-type",
          "_id": "14",
          "_score": 1,
          "_source": {
            "date": "2015-09-21T16:46:01.695734",
            "processed": true,
            ... truncated....,
            "tag": [
              "harum",
              "facilis",
              "laborum",
              "vero",
              "quia",
              "nice"
            ]...truncated...
          }
      }
```

From the result, we can also see that the script is applied.

How it works...

The scripting in `reindex` offers a very powerful functionality because it allows the execution of a lot of useful actions such as:

- Compute new fields
- Remove fields from a document
- Add new field with default values
- Modify field values

The scripting works as for update, but during reindexing you can also change document metadata fields such as:

- `_id`: This is the ID of the document
- `_type`: This is the type of the document
- `_index`: This is the destination index of the document
- `_version`: This is the version of the document
- `_routing`: This is the routing value to send the document in a specific shard
- `_parent`: This is the parent of the document

The possibility of changing these values provides a lot of options during the re-index; for example, splitting a type into two different types, or partitioning an index in several indices and changing the `_index` value.

10
Managing Clusters and Nodes

In this chapter, we will cover the following recipes:

- Controlling cluster health via API
- Controlling cluster state via API
- Getting cluster nodes information via API
- Getting node statistics via API
- Using the task management API
- Hot thread API
- Managing the shard allocation
- Monitoring segments with segment API
- Cleaning the cache

Introduction

In the **Elasticsearch** ecosystem, it's important to monitor nodes and clusters to manage and improve their performance and state. There are several issues that can arise at cluster level, such as:

- **Node overheads**: Some nodes can have too many shards allocated and become a bottleneck for the entire cluster
- **Node shutdown**: This can happen for many reasons, for example, full disks, hardware failures, and power problems
- **Shard relocation problems or corruptions**: Some shards cannot get an online status

- **Too large shards**: If a shard is too big, the index performance decreases due to massive Lucene segments merging
- **Empty indices and shards**: They waste memory and resources, but because every shard has a lot of active thread, if there are a huge number of unused indices and shards, the general cluster performance is degraded

Detecting malfunctioning or poor performance can be done via an API or through some frontends, as we will see in Chapter 12, *User Interfaces*. These allow the readers to have a working web dashboard on their Elasticsearch data, monitoring the cluster health, backing/restoring their data and allowing the testing of queries before implementing them in the code.

Controlling cluster health via an API

In the *Understanding cluster, replication and sharding* recipe in Chapter 1, *Getting Started*, we discussed the Elasticsearch clusters and how to manage them in a red and yellow state.

Elasticsearch provides a convenient way to manage the cluster state, which is one of the first things to check if any problems occur.

Getting ready

You need an up-and-running Elasticsearch installation as we described in the *Downloading and installing Elasticsearch* recipe in Chapter 2, *Downloading and Setup*.

To execute curl via command line you need to install curl for your operating system.

How to do it…

For controlling the cluster health, we will perform the following steps:

1. To view the cluster health, the HTTP method is GET and the curl command is as follows:

```
curl -XGET 'http://localhost:9200/_cluster/health?pretty'
```

2. The result will be as follows:

```
{
    "cluster_name" : "elasticsearch",
    "status" : "yellow",
    "timed_out" : false,
    "number_of_nodes" : 1,
    "number_of_data_nodes" : 1,
    "active_primary_shards" : 7,
    "active_shards" : 7,
    "relocating_shards" : 0,
    "initializing_shards" : 0,
    "unassigned_shards" : 7,
    "delayed_unassigned_shards" : 0,
    "number_of_pending_tasks" : 0,
    "number_of_in_flight_fetch" : 0,
    "task_max_waiting_in_queue_millis" : 0,
    "active_shards_percent_as_number" : 50.0
}
```

How it works...

Every Elasticsearch node keeps the cluster status. The `status` can be of three types as follows:

- `green`: This means that everything is okay.
- `yellow`: This means that some nodes or shards are missing, but they don't compromise the cluster functionality. Mainly some replicas are missing (a node is down or there are insufficient nodes for replicas), but there is a least one copy of each active shard; read and write are working. The yellow state is very common in the development stage, when users typically start a single Elasticsearch server.
- `red`: This indicates that some primary shards are missing and these indices are in red status. You cannot write to the indices that are in red status and results may not be complete or only partial results may be returned. Generally, you'll need to restart the node that is down and possibly create some replicas.

> The yellow/red states could be transient if some nodes are in recovery mode. In this case, just wait until recovery completes.

The cluster health contains a huge amount of information such as follows:

- `cluster_name`: This is the name of the cluster.
- `timeout`: This is a Boolean value indicating whether the REST API hits the timeout set in the call.
- `number_of_nodes`: This indicates the number of nodes that are in the cluster.
- `number_of_data_nodes`: This shows the number of nodes that can store data (see `Chapter 2`, *Downloading and Setup* to set up different node types for different types of nodes).
- `active_primary_shards`: This shows the number of active primary shards; the primary shards are the masters for writing operations.
- `active_shards`: This shows the number of active shards. These shards can be used for search.
- `relocating_shards`: This shows the number of shards that are relocating, migrating from a node to another one. This is due mainly to cluster node balancing.
- `initializing_shards`: This shows the number of shards that are in the initializing status. The initializing process is done at shard startup. It's a transient state before becoming active and it's composed of several steps, of which the most important are as follows:
  - Copy shard data copy if it's a replica of another one
  - Check Lucene indices
  - Process transaction log as needed
- `unassigned_shards`: This shows the number of shards that are not assigned to a node. This is usually due to having set a replica number larger than the number of nodes. During startup, shards not already initialized or initializing will be counted here.
- `delayed_unassigned_shards`: This shows the number of shards that will be assigned, but their nodes are configured for a delayed assignment. You can get more information on delayed shard assignment at `https://www.elastic.co/guide/en/elasticsearch/reference/5.0/delayed-allocation.html`.
- `number_of_pending_tasks`: This is the number of pending tasks at cluster level, such as updates to cluster state, creation indices, and shardsrelocations. It should rarely be anything other than 0.

- `number_of_in_flight_fetch`: Number of cluster updates that must be executed in shards. As the cluster updates are asynchronous, this number is tracking how many still have to be executed in shards.
- `task_max_waiting_in_queue_millis`: This is the maximum time that some cluster tasks have been waiting in the queue. It should rarely be anything other than 0. In case of value different from 0, it means that there are some cluster saturation of resource or similar problems.
- `active_shards_percent_as_number`: This is the percentage of active shards of the total required by the cluster. In a production environment, it should rarely differ from 100 percent, apart from some relocations and shard initializations.

Installed plugins can play an important role in shard initialization: if you use a mapping type provided by a native plugin and you remove the plugin (or the plugin cannot be initialized due to API changes), the shard initialization will fail. These issues are easily detected by reading the Elasticsearch log file.

> **TIP**
>
> When upgrading your cluster to a new Elasticsearch release, be sure to upgrade your mapping plugins or at least check that they can work with the new Elasticsearch release. If you don't do this, you risk your shards failing to initialize and giving a red status to your cluster.

There's more...

This API call is very useful; it's possible to execute it against one or more indices to obtain their health in the cluster. This approach allows the isolation of indices with problems. The API call to execute this is:

```
curl -XGET 'http://localhost:9200/_cluster/health/index1,index2,indexN'
```

The previous calls also have additional request parameters to control the health of the cluster. Additional parameters could be:

- `level`: This controls the level of the health information that is returned. This parameter accepts only `cluster`, `index` and `shards`.
- `timeout`: This is the wait time for a `wait_for_*` parameter (default `30s`).
- `wait_for_status`: This allows the server to wait for the provided status (`green`, `yellow` or `red`) until timeout.

- `wait_for_relocating_shards`: This allows the server to wait until the provided number of relocating shards has been reached, or until the timeout period has been reached (default 0).
- `wait_for_nodes`: This waits until the defined number of nodes is available in the cluster. The value for this parameter can also be an expression, such as: *>N, >=N, <N, <=N, ge(N), gt(N), le(N), lt(N)*.

If the number of pending tasks is different from zero, it's good practice to investigate which those pending tasks are. They can be shown using the following API URL:

```
curl -XGET 'http://localhost:9200/_cluster/pending_tasks'
```

The return value is a list of pending tasks. Beware that Elasticsearch applies cluster changes very fast, so it often faster to apply those that show themselves to you.

See also

- The *Understanding cluster, replication, and sharding* recipe in `Chapter 1`, *Getting Started* for a list of base concepts of cluster, indices and shards.
- The *Setting up different node types* recipe in `Chapter 2`, *Downloading and Setup* to set up some nodes as masters.
- The official documentation about pending cluster tasks at `https://www.elastic.co/guide/en/elasticsearch/reference/current/cluster-pending.html`, for example, the returned value from this call.

Controlling cluster state via an API

The previous recipe returns information only about the health of the cluster. If you need more details on your cluster, you need to query its state.

Getting ready

You need an up-and-running Elasticsearch installation as we described in the *Downloading and installing Elasticsearch* recipe in `Chapter 2`, *Downloading and Setup*.

To execute `curl` via the command-line, you need to install `curl` for your operating system.

How to do it...

To check the cluster state, we will perform the following steps:

1. To view the cluster state, the HTTP method is `GET`, and the `curl` command is as follows:

```
curl -XGET 'http://localhost:9200/_cluster/state'
```

2. The result will contain the following data sections:

   General cluster information:

```
{
  "cluster_name" : "es-cookbook",
  "version" : 13,
  "state_uuid" : "QANXXnzhS7aS5HxLlyNKsw",
  "master_node" : "7NwnFF1JTPOPhOYuP1AVNQ",
  "blocks" : { },
```

   Node address information:

```
"nodes" : {
"7NwnFF1JTPOPhOYuP1AVNQ" : {
  "name" : "7NwnFF1",
  "ephemeral_id" : "OL2uVn3BQ-qMAg32eq_ouQ",
  "transport_address" : "127.0.0.1:9300",
  "attributes" : { }
}
},
```

3. Cluster metadata information (templates, indices with mappings and alias):

```
"metadata" :
{
    "cluster_uuid" : "8SRm9IGDQcWU7-SoR6gWKg",
    "templates" : {
      ".monitoring-data-2" : {...}
    },
    "indices" : {
      "test-index" : {
        "state" : "open",
        "settings" : {
          "index" : {
            "creation_date" : "1477683993903",
            "number_of_shards" : "5",
            "number_of_replicas" : "1",
```

```
                    "uuid" : "KalW90nJSDCTMh42FH62iQ",
                    "version" : {
                        "created" : "5000099"
                     },
                    "provided_name" : "test-index"
                  }
              },
               "mappings" : {
                "test-type" : {...truncated...}
               },
               "aliases" : [ "my-cool-alias" ]
            }
          }
        },
```

4. Routing tables to find the shards:

```
    "routing_table" : {
        "indices" : {
        "test-index" : {
           "shards" : {
              "2" : [{
                  "state" : "STARTED",
                  "primary" : true,
                  "node" : "7NwnFF1JTPOPhOYuP1AVNQ",
                  "relocating_node" : null,
                  "shard" : 2,
                  "index" : "test-index",
                  "allocation_id" : {
                     "id" : "9I5Q8E0VTnCSq7qgpNjGGQ"
                  }
               },
             ... truncated...
            }
          }
        }
      },
```

5. Routing nodes:

```
    "routing_nodes" : {
       "unassigned" : [ ],
       "nodes" : {
         " 7NwnFF1JTPOPhOYuP1AVNQ" : [ {
           "state" : "STARTED",
            "primary" : true,
            "node" : "7NwnFF1JTPOPhOYuP1AVNQ",
             "relocating_node" : null,
```

```
            "shard" : 0,
            "index" : ".monitoring-es-2-2016.10.27",
            "allocation_id" : {
              "id" : "F-wl5nuwQqO6lkeV6k83iQ"
            }
      ...truncated... ]
        }
      },
    "allocations" : [ ]
  }
```

How it works...

The cluster state contains the information of the whole cluster; it's normal that its output is very large.

The call output contains common fields, which are as follows:

- cluster_name: This is the name of the cluster.
- master_node: This is the identifier of the master node. The master node is the primary node for cluster management, and several sections.
- blocks: This section shows the active blocks in a cluster.
- nodes: This shows the list of nodes of the cluster. For every node, we have:
  - id: This is the hash used to identify the node in Elasticsearch. (For example, 7NwnFF1JTPOPhOYuP1AVN)
  - name: This is the name of the node
  - transport_address: This is the IP and port used to connect to this node
  - attributes: These are additional node attributes
- metadata: This is the definition of indices (their settings and mappings), ingest pipelines, and stored_scripts.
- routing_table: These are the indices/shards routing tables, which are used to select primary and secondary shards and their nodes.
- routing_nodes: This is the routing for the nodes.

The metadata section is the most used one, because it contains all the information related to the indices and their mappings. This is a convenient way to gather all the indices mappings in one shot; otherwise you'll need to call the get mapping for every type.

The metadata section is composed of several sections, as follows:

- `templates`: These are templates that control the dynamic mapping for created indices
- `indices`: These are the indices that exist in the cluster
- `* ingest`: This stores all the ingest pipelines defined in the system
- `stored_scripts`: This stores the scripts, which are usually in the form of `language#script_name`

The indices subsection returns a full representation of all the metadata description for every index. It contains the following:

- `state` (open/closed): This describes if an index is open (it can be searched and can index data) or closed. (See the *Opening/Closing an Index* recipe in `Chapter 4`, *Basic Operations*)
- `settings`: These are the index settings. The most important ones are as follows:
    - `index.number_of_replicas`: This is the number of replicas of this index. If can be changed with an update index settings call.
    - `index.number_of_shards`: This is the number of shards in this index. This value cannot be changed in an index.
    - `index.codec`: This is the codec used to store index data. `default` is not shown, but the LZ4 algorithm is used. If you want a high compression rate use `best_compression` and the DEFLATE algorithm (this will slow down the writing performances slightly).
    - `index.version.created`: This is the index version.
- `mappings`: These are defined in the index. This section is similar to the get mapping response. (See the *How to Get a Mapping* recipe in `Chapter 4`, *Basic Operations*)
- `alias`: This is a list of index aliases, which allows the aggregation of indices in a single name or the definition of alternative names for an index.

The routing records for index and shards have similar fields and they are as follows:

- `state (UNASSIGNED, INITIALITING, STARTED, RELOCATING)`: This shows the state of the shard or index
- `primary (true/false)`: This shows whether the shard or node is primary
- `node`: This shows the ID of the node
- `relocating_node`: This field, if validated, shows the node `id` in which the shard is relocated
- `shard`: This shows the number of the shard
- `index`: This shows the name of the index in which the shard is contained

There's more...

The cluster state call returns a lot of information, and it's possible to filter out the different section parts via the URL.

The complete form URL of the cluster state API is:

```
http://{elasticsearch_server}/_cluster/state/{metrics}/{indices}
```

The `metrics` could be used to return only parts of the response. It's a comma separated list of the following values:

- `* version`: This is used to show the version part of the response
- `blocks`: This is used to show the blocks part of the response
- `master_node`: This is used to show the master node part of the response
- `nodes`: This is used to show the node part of the response
- `metadata`: This is used to show the metadata part of the response
- `routing_table`: This is used to show the routing_table part of the response

The `indices` value is a comma separated list of index names to include in the in metadata.

See also

- *Understanding cluster, replication and sharding* recipe in `Chapter 1`, *Getting Started* for a list of basic concepts of cluster, indices and shards.
- *Opening/closing an index* recipe in `Chapter 4`, *Basic Operations* for APIs on opening and closing indices. Remember that closed indices cannot be searched.
- *Getting a mapping* recipe in `Chapter 4`, *Basic Operations* for returning single mappings.

Getting nodes information via API

The previous recipes allow information to be reutrned to the cluster level; Elasticsearch provides calls to gather information at node level. In production clusters, it's very important to monitor nodes via this API to detect misconfiguration and problems relating to different plugins and modules.

Getting ready

You need an up-and-running Elasticsearch installation as we described in the *Downloading and installing Elasticsearch* recipe in `Chapter 2`, *Downloading and Setup*.

To execute `curl` via the commandline, you need to install `curl` for your operating system.

How to do it...

For getting nodes information, we will perform the following steps:

1. To retrieve the node information, the HTTP method is `GET` and the `curl` command is as follows:

   ```
   curl -XGET 'http://localhost:9200/_nodes'
   curl -XGET 'http://localhost:9200/_nodes/<nodeId1>,<nodeId2>'
   ```

2. The result will contain a lot of information about the node. It's huge, so the repetitive parts have been truncated below:

   ```
   {
     "_nodes" : {
       "total" : 1,
   ```

```
      "successful" : 1,
     "failed" : 0
  },
  "cluster_name" : "elasticsearch",
  "nodes" : {
     "7NwnFF1JTPOPhOYuP1AVNQ" : {
       "name" : "7NwnFF1",
       "transport_address" : "127.0.0.1:9300",
       "host" : "127.0.0.1",
       "ip" : "127.0.0.1",
       "version" : "5.0.0",
       "build_hash" : "253032b",
       "total_indexing_buffer" : 207775334,
       "roles" : [ "master", "data", "ingest" ],
       "settings" : {
          "cluster" : { "name" : "elasticsearch"},
          "node" : {"name" : "7NwnFF1"},
          "path" : {"logs" : ".../elasticsearch-5.0.0/logs",
            "home" : "...elasticsearch-5.0.0"
          },
          "client" : {"type" : "node"},
          "http" : {"type" : {"default" : "netty4"}},
          "transport" : {"type" : {"default" : "netty4"}},
          "script" : {"inline" : "true", "stored" : "true"}
       },
       "os" : {
          "refresh_interval_in_millis" : 1000,
          "name" : "Mac OS X",
          "arch" : "x86_64",
          "version" : "10.12.1",
          "available_processors" : 8,
          "allocated_processors" : 8
       },
       "process" : {
          "refresh_interval_in_millis" : 1000,
          "id" : 82228,
          "mlockall" : false
       },
       "jvm" : {
          "pid" : 82228,
          "version" : "1.8.0_101",
          "vm_name" : "Java HotSpot(TM) 64-Bit Server VM",
          "vm_version" : "25.101-b13",
          "vm_vendor" : "Oracle Corporation",
          "start_time_in_millis" : 1477840185555,
          "mem" : {
            "heap_init_in_bytes" : 2147483648,
            "heap_max_in_bytes" : 2077753344,
```

```
      "non_heap_init_in_bytes" : 2555904,
      "non_heap_max_in_bytes" : 0,
      "direct_max_in_bytes" : 2077753344
    },
    "gc_collectors" : [ "ParNew", "ConcurrentMarkSweep"],
    "memory_pools" : [ "Code Cache", "Metaspace",
    "Compressed Class Space", "Par Eden Space",
    "Par Survivor Space", "CMS Old Gen" ],
    "using_compressed_ordinary_object_pointers" : "true"
  },
  "thread_pool" : {
    "force_merge" : {
      "type" : "fixed",
      "min" : 1,
      "max" : 1,
      "queue_size" : -1
    }, ... truncated ...
  },
  "transport" : {
  "bound_address" : [ "[fe80::1]:9300", "
  [::1]:9300","127.0.0.1:9300"],
    "publish_address" : "127.0.0.1:9300",
    "profiles" : { }
  },
  "http" : {
    "bound_address" : [ "[fe80::1]:9200", "[::1]:9200",
    "127.0.0.1:9200"  ],
    "publish_address" : "127.0.0.1:9200",
    "max_content_length_in_bytes" : 104857600
  },
  "plugins" : [
    {
      "name" : "lang-javascript",
      "version" : "5.0.0",
      "description" : "The JavaScript language plugin
      allows to have javascript as the language of scripts
      to execute.", "classname" :
      "org.elasticsearch.plugin.javascript.JavaScriptPlugin"
    }... truncated ...
  ],
  "modules" : [
    {
      "name" : "aggs-matrix-stats",
      "version" : "5.0.0",
      "description" : "Adds aggregations whose input are a
      list of numeric fields and output includes a
      matrix.","classname" :
      "org.elasticsearch.search.aggregations.matrix
```

```
          .MatrixAggregationPlugin"
      }... truncated ...
  ],
  "ingest" : {
  "processors" : [
      {
         "type" : "append"
      }... truncated ...        ]
  }
}
}
}
```

How it works...

The nodes information call provides an overview of the node configuration. It covers a lot of information; the most important sections are as follows:

- `hostname`: This is the name of the host.
- `ip`: This is the IP of the host.
- `version`: This is the Elasticsearch version. It's best practice that all the nodes of a cluster have the same Elasticsearch version.
- `roles`: This is a list of roles that this node can cover. Developer nodes usually support the three kinds: `master`, `data` and `ingest`.
- `transport_address`: This is the address used by the node for cluster communication.
- `settings`: This section contains information about the current cluster and path of the Elasticsearch node. The most important fields are as follows:
    - `cluster_name`: This is the name of the cluster
    - `node.name`: This is the name of the node
    - `path.*`: This is configured path of this Elasticsearch instance
    - `script`: This section is useful to check the `script` configuration of the node
- `os`: This section provides operating system information about the node that is running Elasticsearch: processors available and allocated and the OS version.
- `process`: This section contains information about the currently running Elasticsearch process.

- `id`: This is the pid ID of the process.
- `mlockall`: This flag defines whether Elasticsearch can use direct memory access. In production, this must be set to active.
- `max_file_descriptors`: This is max file descriptor number.
- `jvm`: This section contains information about the node Java Virtual Machine: version, vendor, name, pid, memory (heap and non-heap).

> It's highly recommended to run all the nodes on the same JVM version and type.

- `thread_pool`: This section contains information about several types of thread pool running in a node.
- `transport`: This section contains information about the transport protocol. The transport protocol is used for intra-cluster communication or by the native client to communicate with a cluster. The response format is similar to the HTTP one, as follows:
    - `bound_address`: If a specific IP is not set in the configuration, Elasticsearch bounds all the interfaces
    - `publish_address`: This is the address used for publishing the native transport protocol
    - `http`: This section gives information about http configuration, such as:
    - `bound_address`: This is the address bound by Elasticsearch.
- `max_content_length_in_bytes` (default `104857600` 100 MB): This is the maximum size of HTTP content that Elasticsearch will allow to be received. HTTP payloads bigger than this size are rejected.

> The default 100 MB http limit, which can be changed in `elasticsearch.yml`, can result in a malfunction due to a large payload (often in conjunction with a mapper plugin attachment), so it's important to keep this limit in mind when doing bulk actions or working with attachment.

- `publish_address`: The address used to publish the Elasticsearch node.

- plugins: This section lists every plugin installed in the node, providing information about the following:
    - name: This is the plugin name
    - description: This is the plugin description
    - version: This is the plugin version
    - classname: This is the Java class used to load the plugin

> **TIP**
>
> All the nodes must have the same plugin version. Different plugin versions in a node bring unexpected failures.

- modules: This section lists every module installed in the node. The structure is the same as the plugin section.
- ingest: This section contains the list of active processors in the ingest node.

There's more...

The API call allows filtering of the section that must be returned. In the example, we've returned the wholesection. Alternatively, we could select one or more of the following sections:

- http
- thread_pool
- transport
- jvm
- os
- process
- plugins
- modules
- ingest
- settings

For example, if you need only the os and plugins information, the call will be as follows:

```
curl -XGET 'http://localhost:9200/_nodes/os,plugins'
```

See also

- *Using native protocol, Using HTTP protocol* recipes in `Chapter 1`, *Getting Started* about the different protocols used by Elasticseach.
- *Networking setup* recipe in `Chapter 2`, *Downloading and Setup* about how to configure networking for Elasticsearch.
- `Chapter 13`, *Ingest* for more information about Elasticsearch ingestion.

Getting node statistics via the API

The node statistics call API is used to collect real-time metrics of your node, such as memory usage, threads usage, number of indexes, search and so on.

Getting ready

You need an up-and-running Elasticsearch installation as we described in the *Downloading and installing Elasticsearch* recipe in `Chapter 2`, *Downloading and Setup*.

To execute curl via the command-line, you need to install curl for your operating system.

How to do it...

For getting nodes statistics, we will perform the following steps:

1. To retrieve the node statistic, the HTTP method is `GET`, and the `curl` command is as follows:

```
curl -XGET 'http://localhost:9200/_nodes/stats'curl -XGET
'http://localhost:9200/_nodes/<nodeId1>,<nodeId2>/stats'
```

2. The result will be a long list of all the node statistics. The most significant parts of the results are as follows:

A header describing the cluster name and the nodes section:

```
{
    "cluster_name" : "es-cookbook",
    "nodes" : {
        " 7NwnFF1JTPOPhOYuP1AVNQ" : {
            "timestamp" : 1477990951146,
            "name" : "7NwnFF1",
            "transport_address" : "127.0.0.1:9300",
            "host" : "127.0.0.1",
            "ip" : "127.0.0.1:9300",
            "roles" : [
                "master",
                "data",
                "ingest"
            ],
```

Statistics related to the indices:

```
"indices" : {
    "docs" : {
        "count" : 2030,
        "deleted" : 0
    },
    "store" : {
        "size_in_bytes" : 3290318,
        "throttle_time_in_millis" : 0
    },
    "indexing" : {
        "index_total" : 2000,
        "index_time_in_millis" : 3901,
        "index_current" : 0,
        "index_failed" : 0,
        "delete_total" : 0,
        "delete_time_in_millis" : 0,
        "delete_current" : 0,
        "noop_update_total" : 0,
        "is_throttled" : false,
        "throttle_time_in_millis" : 0
    },
    ... truncated ...
},
```

Statistics related to the operating system:

```
"os" : {
  "timestamp" : 1477990951181,
  "cpu" : {
    "percent" : 26,
    "load_average" : { "1m" : 3.34765625}
  },
  "mem" : {
    "total_in_bytes" : 17179869184,
    "free_in_bytes" : 1112723456,
    "used_in_bytes" : 16067145728,
    "free_percent" : 6,
    "used_percent" : 94
  }, ...truncated ...
},
```

Statistics related to the current Elasticsearch process:

```
"process" : {
  "timestamp" : 1477990951181,
  "open_file_descriptors" : 283,
  "max_file_descriptors" : 10240,
  "cpu" : {
    "percent" : 0,
    "total_in_millis" : 247287
  },
  "mem" : {
    "total_virtual_in_bytes" : 6683983872
  }
},
```

Statistics related to the current JVM

```
"jvm" : {
  "timestamp" : 1477990951182,
  "uptime_in_millis" : 61315659,
  "mem" : {
    "heap_used_in_bytes" : 364406464,
    "heap_used_percent" : 17,
    "heap_committed_in_bytes" : 2077753344,
    "heap_max_in_bytes" : 2077753344,
    "non_heap_used_in_bytes" : 115590776,
    "non_heap_committed_in_bytes" : 122032128,
... truncated ...
  }
},... truncated ...
},
```

Statistics related to thread pools:

```
"thread_pool" : {
  "bulk" : {
    "threads" : 8,
    "queue" : 0,
    "active" : 0,
    "rejected" : 0,
    "largest" : 8,
    "completed" : 10
  }, ...truncated....
},
```

Node filesystem statistics:

```
fs" : {
  "timestamp" : 1477990951182,
  "total" : {
    "total_in_bytes" : 999334871040,
    "free_in_bytes" : 75898884096,
    "available_in_bytes" : 75636740096
  },
  "data" : [
    {
      "path" : .../elasticsearch-5.0.0/data/nodes/0",
      "mount" : "/ (/dev/disk1)",
      "type" : "hfs",
      "total_in_bytes" : 999334871040,
      "free_in_bytes" : 75898884096,
      "available_in_bytes" : 75636740096
    }
  ]
}...truncated...]
},
```

Statistics related to communications between nodes:

```
"transport" : {
  "server_open" : 0,
  "rx_count" : 8,
  "rx_size_in_bytes" : 4264,
  "tx_count" : 8,
  "tx_size_in_bytes" : 4264
},
```

Statistics related to HTTP connections:

```
"http" : {
  "current_open" : 2,
  "total_opened" : 13
},
```

Statistics related to breaker caches:

```
breakers" : {
  "request" : {
    "limit_size_in_bytes" : 1246652006,
    "limit_size" : "1.1gb",
    "estimated_size_in_bytes" : 0,
    "estimated_size" : "0b",
    "overhead" : 1.0,
    "tripped" : 0
  },
  "fielddata" : {
    "limit_size_in_bytes" : 1246652006,
    "limit_size" : "1.1gb",
    "estimated_size_in_bytes" : 0,
    "estimated_size" : "0b",
    "overhead" : 1.03,
    "tripped" : 0
  } ... truncated ....
  }
 }
}
```

Script related to statistics:

```
"script" : {
      "compilations" : 2,
      "cache_evictions" : 0
    },
```

Cluster state queue:

```
"discovery" : {
      "cluster_state_queue" : {
        "total" : 0,
        "pending" : 0,
        "committed" : 0
      }
    }
```

Ingest statistics:

```
"ingest" : {
      "total" : {
        "count" : 0,
        "time_in_millis" : 0,
         "current" : 0,
         "failed" : 0
      },
      "pipelines" : {
        "xpack_monitoring_2" : {
          "count" : 0,
           "time_in_millis" : 0,
           "current" : 0,
           "failed" : 0
        }
      }
    }
```

How it works...

Every Elasticsearch node, during execution, collects statistics about several aspects of node management; these statistics are accessible via stats API call.

In the next recipes, we will see some example of monitoring applications that use this information to provide real-time status of a node or a cluster.

The main statistics collected by this API are as follows:

- fs: This section contains statistics about the filesystem; free space on devices, mount points, reads and writes. It can be used to remotely control disk usage for your nodes.
- http: This gives the number of current open sockets and their maximum number.
- indices: This section contains statistics of several indexing aspects:
    - Usage for fields and caches
    - Statistics about operations such as, get, indexing, flush, merges, refresh, warmer

- jvm: This section provides statistics about buffer, pools, garbage collector (creation/destruction of objects and their memory management), memory (used memory, heap, pools), threads and uptime. It should be checked to see if the node is running out of memory.

- network: This section provides statistics about TCP traffic, such as open connection, close connections, and data I/O.

- os: This sections collects statistics about the Operating System, such as:
    - CPU usage
    - Node load
    - Memory and swap
    - Uptime

- process: This section contains statistics about the CPU used by Elasticsearch, memory, and open file descriptors.

> It's very important to monitor the open file descriptors, because if you run out of them, the indices may be corrupted.

- thread_pool: This section monitors all the thread pools available in Elasticsearch. It's important, in the case of low performance, to control whether there are pools that have an excessive overhead. Some of them can be configured to a new maximum value.

- transport: This section contains statistics about the transport layer, mainly bytes read and transmitted.

- breakers: This section monitors the circuit breakers. It must be checked to see whether it's necessary to optimize resource or queries/aggregations to prevent them being called.

There's more...

The response is very large. It's possible to limit it requesting only required parts. To do this, you need to pass to the API call a query parameter specifying the following desired sections:

- fs
- http
- indices

- jvm
- network
- os
- process
- thread_pool
- transport
- breaker
- discovery
- script
- ingest

For example, to request only `os` and `http` statistics the call becomes:

```
curl -XGET 'http://localhost:9200/_nodes/stats/os,http'
```

Using the task management API

Elasicsearch 5.x allows the definition of actions that can take some time to complete. The most common ones are as follows:

- delete_by_query
- update_by_query
- reindex

When these actions are called, they create a server side task that executes the job. The task management API allows you to control these actions.

Getting ready

You need an up-and-running Elasticsearch installation as we described in the *Downloading and installing Elasticsearch* recipe in `Chapter 2`, *Downloading and Setup*.

To execute `curl` via the command-line, you need to install `curl` for your operating system.

How to do it...

For getting tasks information, we will perform the following steps:

1. To retrieve the node information, the HTTP method is GET and the curl command is as follows:

```
curl -XGET 'http://localhost:9200/_tasks'curl -XGET
'http://localhost:9200/_tasks?nodes=<nodeId1, nodeId2>'curl -
XGET 'http://localhost:9200/_tasks?nodes=<nodeId1,
nodeId2>&actions=cluster:'
```

2. The result will be something similar to the preceding one:

```
{
  "nodes" : {
    "7NwnFF1JTPOPhOYuP1AVNQ" : {
      "name" : "7NwnFF1",
      "transport_address" : "127.0.0.1:9300",
      "host" : "127.0.0.1",
      "ip" : "127.0.0.1:9300",
      "roles" : [
        "master",
        "data",
        "ingest"
      ],
      "tasks" : {
        "7NwnFF1JTPOPhOYuP1AVNQ:9822" : {
          "node" : "7NwnFF1JTPOPhOYuP1AVNQ",
          "id" : 9822,
          "type" : "transport",
          "action" : "cluster:monitor/tasks/lists",
          "start_time_in_millis" : 1477993984920,
          "running_time_in_nanos" : 102338,
          "cancellable" : false
        },
        "7NwnFF1JTPOPhOYuP1AVNQ:9823" : {
          "node" : "7NwnFF1JTPOPhOYuP1AVNQ",
          "id" : 9823,
          "type" : "direct",
          "action" : "cluster:monitor/tasks/lists[n]",
          "start_time_in_millis" : 1477993984920,
          "running_time_in_nanos" : 62786,
          "cancellable" : false,
          "parent_task_id" : "7NwnFF1JTPOPhOYuP1AVNQ:9822"
        }
      }
```

```
                }
            }
        }
```

How it works...

Every task that is executed in Elasticsearch is available in the task list.

The most important properties for the tasks are as follows:

- `node`: This defines the node that is executing the task.
- `id`: This define the unique ID of the task.
- `action`: This is the name of the action. It's generally composed by an action type, the : separator and the detailed action.
- `cancellable`: This defines if the task can be canceled. Some tasks such as `delete/update by query` or `reindex` can be canceled, other are mainly of management and cannot be canceled.
- `parent_task_id`: This defines the group of tasks. Some tasks can be split and executed in several sub-tasks. This value can be used to group these tasks by parent.

The `id` of the task can be used to filter the response via the `node_id` parameter in the API call:

```
curl -XGET 'http://localhost:9200/_tasks/7NwnFF1JTPOPhOYuP1AVNQ:9822'
```

If you need to monitor a group of tasks, you can filter by their `parent_task_id` with a similar API call:

```
curl -XGET 'http://localhost:9200/_tasks
?parent_task_id=7NwnFF1JTPOPhOYuP1AVNQ:9822'
```

There's more...

Generally, canceling a task could produce some data inconsistency in Elasticsearch due to partial updating or deleting of documents; but, when reindexing, it can make good sense. It's common, when you are reindexing a huge amount of data, that you need to change the mapping or reindex a script in the middle of it. So, in order to not waste time and CPU usage, canceling the reindexing is a sensible solution.

To cancel a task, the API URL is as follows:

```
curl -XPOST 'http://localhost:9200/_tasks/task_id:1/_cancel'
```

In the case of a group of tasks, they can be stopped with a single `cancel` call using query arguments to select them as follows:

```
curl -XPOST
'http://localhost:9200/_tasks/_cancel?nodes=nodeId1,nodeId2&actions=*reinde
x'
```

See also

- The official documentation about task management for some more borderline cases at https://www.elastic.co/guide/en/elasticsearch/reference/current/tasks.html

Hot thread API

Sometimes your cluster slows down due to massive CPU usage and you need to understand why.

Elasticsearch provides the ability to monitor hot threads to be able to understand where the problem is.

> In Java, hot threads are threads that are using a lot of CPU and take a long time to execute.

Getting ready

You need an up-and-running Elasticsearch installation as we described in the *Downloading and installing Elasticsearch* recipe in Chapter 2, *Downloading and Setup*.

To execute `curl` via the command-line, you need to install `curl` for your operating system.

How to do it...

For getting task information, we will perform the following steps:

1. To retrieve the node information, the HTTP method is GET and the curl command is as follows:

```
curl -XGET 'http://localhost:9200/_nodes/hot_threads'curl -XGET
'http://localhost:9200/_nodes/{nodesIds}/hot_threads'
```

2. The result will be something similar to the preceding one:

```
::: {7NwnFF1}{7NwnFF1JTPOPhOYuP1AVNQ}{OL2uVn3BQ-qMAg32eq_ouQ}
{127.0.0.1}{127.0.0.1:9300}   Hot threads at 2016-11-
01T10:53:39.796Z, interval=500ms, busiestThreads=3,
ignoreIdleThreads=true:    12.6% (63.1ms out of 500ms) cpu usage
by thread 'elasticsearch[7NwnFF1][refresh][T#3]'     4/10
snapshots sharing following 23 elements
org.apache.lucene.index.DocumentsWriterPerThread.flush
(DocumentsWriterPerThread.java:443)
org.apache.lucene.index.DocumentsWriter.doFlush
(DocumentsWriter.java:539)
org.apache.lucene.index.DocumentsWriter.flushAllThreads
(DocumentsWriter.java:653)
org.apache.lucene.index.IndexWriter.getReader
(IndexWriter.java:438)
org.apache.lucene.index.StandardDirectoryReader.
doOpenFromWriter
(StandardDirectoryReader.java:291)
org.apache.lucene.index.StandardDirectoryReader.
doOpenIfChanged(StandardDirectoryReader.java:266)
...truncated...
```

How it works...

The Hot threads API is quite particular. It returns a text representation of currently running hot threads, so that it's possible to check the causes of slowdown of every single thread by using the stack trace.

To control returned values, there are additional parameters that can be provided as query arguments such as follows:

- `threads` : This is the number of hot threads to provide (default `3`)
- `interval`: This is the interval for sampling of threads (default `500ms`)
- `type`: This allows the control of different types of hot threads, for example, to check wait and block states (default `cpu`, possible values are `cpu/wait/block`)
- `ignore_idle_threads`: This is used to filter out known idle threads (default `true`)

> **TIP**
>
> Hot threads are an advanced monitor feature provided by Elasticsearch, and it's very handy to debug slowness in a production cluster as it can be used as a *run-time debugger*.

Managing the shard allocation

During normal Elasticsearch usage, it is not necessary to change the shard allocation, because the default settings work very well with all standard scenarios. Sometimes, due to massive relocation, or due to nodes restarting, or some other cluster issues, it's necessary to monitor or define custom shard allocation.

Getting ready

You need an up-and-running Elasticsearch installation as we described in the *Downloading and installing Elasticsearch* recipe in `Chapter 2`, *Downloading and Setup*.

To execute `curl` via the command line, you need to install `curl` for your operating system.

How to do it…

For getting information about the current state of unassigned shard allocation, we will perform the following steps:

1. To retrieve the cluster allocation information, the HTTP method is `GET` and the `curl` command is as follows:

```
curl -XGET 'http://localhost:9200/_cluster/allocation/explain?
pretty'
```

2. The result will be something similar to the preceding one:

```
{
  "shard" : {
    "index" : ".monitoring-es-2-2016.10.27",
    "index_uuid" : "cD30b-qtQc2qw62yF-tirA",
    "id" : 0,
    "primary" : false
  },
  "assigned" : false,
  "shard_state_fetch_pending" : false,
  "unassigned_info" : {
    "reason" : "CLUSTER_RECOVERED",
    "at" : "2016-10-30T15:09:54.626Z",
    "delayed" : false,
    "allocation_status" : "no_attempt"
  },
  "allocation_delay_in_millis" : 60000,
  "remaining_delay_in_millis" : 0,
  "nodes" : {
    "7NwnFF1JTPOPhOYuP1AVNQ" : {
      "node_name" : "7NwnFF1",
      "node_attributes" : { },
      "store" : {
        "shard_copy" : "AVAILABLE"
      },
      "final_decision" : "NO",
      "final_explanation" : "the shard cannot be assigned
      because allocation deciders return a NO decision",
      "weight" : 8.15,
      "decisions" : [
        {
          "decider" : "same_shard",
          "decision" : "NO",
          "explanation" : "the shard cannot be allocated on the
          same node id [7NwnFF1JTPOPhOYuP1AVNQ] on which it
```

```
                          already exists"
                  }
              ]
          }
      }
    }
}
```

How it works...

Elasticsearch allows different shard allocator mechanisms. Sometimes your shards are not assigned to nodes, and it's useful to investigate why Elasticsearch has not allocated by querying the cluster allocation explanation API.

The call returns a lot of information about the unassigned shard, but the most important ones are the `decisions`. This is a list of objects that explain the reason that the shard cannot be allocated in the node. In the above example, the result was `the shard cannot be allocated on the same node id [7NwnFF1JTPOPhOYuP1AVNQ] on which it already exists"`, which is returned because the shard needs a replica, but the cluster is composed of only one node, so it's not possible to initialize the replicated shard in the cluster.

There's more...

The cluster allocation explains API provides capabilities to filter the result for searching particular shard: this is very handy if your cluster has a lot of shards. This can be done by adding parameters to be used as a filter in the get body; these parameters are as follows:

- `index`: This is the index that the shard belongs to.
- `shard`: This is the number of the shard. Shard numbers starts from 0.
- `primary`: `true`/`false`: Whether the shard to be checked is the primary one or not.

The preceding example shard can be filtered using a similar call such as:

```
curl -XGET 'http://localhost:9200/_cluster/allocation/explain' -d'{
  "index": ".monitoring-es-2-2016.10.27",
  "shard": 0,  "primary": false
}'
```

To manually relocate shards, Elasticsearch provides a Cluster Reroute API that allows the migration of shards between nodes. The following is an example of this API:

```
curl -XPOST 'localhost:9200/_cluster/reroute' -d '{
    "commands" : [ {
        "move" :
            {
"index" : "test-index", "shard" : 0,
            "from_node" : "node1", "to_node" : "node2"
            }
        }
    ]
}'
```

In this case, the shard 0 of the index `test-index` is migrated from `node1` to `node2`. If you force a shard migration, the cluster starts moving the other shard to rebalance itself.

See also

- The official documentation about the shard allocation and the settings that controls it at
  `https://www.elastic.co/guide/en/elasticsearch/reference/5.0/shards-all`
  `ocation.html`.
- The cluster reroute API official documentation at
  `https://www.elastic.co/guide/en/elasticsearch/reference/5.0/cluster-re`
  `route.html` that describes the complexity of manual relocation of shards in depth.

Monitoring segments with the segment API

Monitoring the index segments means monitoring the health of an index. It contains information about the number of segments and data stored in them.

Getting ready

You need an up-and-running Elasticsearch installation as we described in the *Downloading and installing Elasticsearch* recipe in `Chapter 2`, *Downloading and Setup*.

To execute `curl` via the command line, you need to install `curl` for your operating system.

How to do it...

For getting information about index segments, we will perform the following steps:

1. To retrieve the index segments, the HTTP method is `GET` and the `curl` command is as follows:

```
curl -XGET 'http://localhost:9200/test-index/_segments'
```

2. The result will be something similar to the preceding one:

```
{
  "_shards" : { ...truncated... },
  "indices" : {
   "test-index" : {
     "shards" : {
        "0" : [
          {
            "routing" : {
             "state" : "STARTED",
             "primary" : true,
             "node" : "7NwnFF1JTPOPhOYuP1AVNQ"
            },
            "num_committed_segments" : 9,
            "num_search_segments" : 9,
            "segments" : {
              "_0" : {
                "generation" : 0,
                "num_docs" : 15,
                "deleted_docs" : 0,
                "size_in_bytes" : 31497,
                "memory_in_bytes" : 6995,
                "committed" : true,
                "search" : true,
                "version" : "6.2.0",
                "compound" : true
              },
              "_1" : {
       ...truncated...
```

In Elasticsearch, there is the special `alias` _all that defines all the indices. This can be used in all the APIs that require a list of index names.

How it works...

The Indices Segments API returns statistics about the segments in an index. This is an important indicator about the health of an index. It returns the following information:

- `num_docs`: The number of documents stored in the index.
- `deleted_docs`: The number of deleted documents in the index. If this value is high, a lot of space is wasted to tombstone documents in the index.
- `size_in_bytes`: The size of the segments in bytes. If this value is too high, writing speed will be very low.
- `memory_in_bytes`: The memory taken up, in bytes, by the segment.
- `committed`: Whether the segment is committed to disk.
- `search`: Whether the segment is used for searching. During force merge / index optimization, the new segments are created and returned by the API, but they are not available for searching until the end of the optimization.
- `version`: The Lucene version used for creating the index.
- `compound`: Whether the index is a compound one.

The most important elements to monitor of the segments are `deleted_docs` and the `size_in_bytes` because they mean either a waste of disk space or that the shard is too large. If the shard is too large (above 10 GB), for improved performances in writing the best solution is to reindex the index with a large number of shards.

Having large shards also creates a problem in relocating, due to massive data moving between nodes.

> It's impossible to define the perfect size for a shard. In general, a good size for a shard that doesn't need to be frequently updated is between 10 GB to 25 GB.

See also

- *ForceMerge an index* recipe in `Chapter 4`, *Basic Operation* about how to optimize an index with a minor number of fragments to improve search performances
- *Shrink an index* recipe in `Chapter 4`, *Basic Operation* about how to reduce the number of shards if too large a number of shards are defined for an index

Cleaning the cache

During its execution, Elasticsearch caches data to speed up searching, such as cache results, items and filter results.

To free up memory, it's necessary to clean cache API.

Getting ready

You need an up-and-running Elasticsearch installation as we described in the *Downloading and installing Elasticsearch* recipe in `Chapter 2`, *Downloading and Setup*.

To execute `curl` via the command-line, you need to install `curl` for your operating system.

How to do it...

For cleaning the cache, we will perform the following steps:

1. We call the `cleancache` API on an index as follows:

   ```
   curl -XPOST 'http://localhost:9200/test-index/_cache/clear'
   ```

2. The result returned by Elasticsearch, if everything is okay, should be as follows:

   ```
   {
     "_shards" : {
       "total" : 10,
       "successful" : 5,
       "failed" : 0
     }
   }
   ```

How it works...

The cache clean API frees the memory used to cache values in Elasticsearch.

Generally, it's not a good idea to clean the cache because Elasticsearch manages the cache internally itself and cleans obsolete values, but it can be very handy if your node is running out of memory or you want to force a complete cache clean-up.

11
Backup and Restore

In this chapter, we will cover the following recipes:

- Managing repositories
- Executing a snapshot
- Restoring a snapshot
- Setting up an NFS share for backup
- Reindexing from a remote cluster

Introduction

Elasticsearch is very commonly used as a datastore for logs and other kind of data, so if you store valuable data you also need tools to back up and restore this data to support disaster recovery.

In the first versions of Elasticsearch the only viable solution was to dump your data with a complete scan and then reindex it. As Elasticsearch matured as a complete product, it supported native functionalities to back up the data and to restore it.

In this chapter, we'll see how to configure a shared storage via NFS for storing your backups, and how to execute and restore a backup.

In the last recipe of the chapter we will see how to use the reindex functionality to clone data between different Elasticsearch clusters. This approach is very useful if you are not able to use standard backup/restore functionalities due to moving from an old Elasticsearch version to the new one.

Managing repositories

Elasticsearch provides a built-in system to rapidly ot and restore your data. When working with live data, keeping a backup is complex, due to the large number of concurrency problems.

An Elasticsearch snapshot allows for the creation of snapshots of individual indices (or aliases), or an entire cluster, into a remote repository.

Before starting to execute a snapshot, a repository must be created–this is where your backups/snapshots will be stored.

Getting ready

You need an up-and-running Elasticsearch installation as we described in the *Downloading and installing Elasticsearch* recipe in `Chapter 2`, *Downloading and Setup*.

To execute `curl` via the command line you need to install `curl` for your operating system.

We need to edit `config/elasticsearch.yml` and add the directory of your backup repository:

```
path.repo: /tmp/
```

For our examples, we'll be using the `/tmp` directory available in every Unix system. Generally, in a production cluster, this directory should be a shared repository.

How to do it...

To manage a repository, we will perform the following steps:

1. To create a repository called `my_repository`, the HTTP method is `PUT` and the `curl` command is:

```
curl -XPUT 'http://localhost:9200/_snapshot/my_repository' -d
'{
    "type": "fs",
    "settings": {
        "location": "/tmp/my_repository",
        "compress": true
    }
}'
```

The result will be:

```
{"acknowledged":true}
```

If you check on your filesystem, the /tmp/my_repository directory is created.

2. To retrieve repository information, the HTTP method is GET and the curl command is:

```
curl -XGET 'http://localhost:9200/_snapshot/my_repository'
```

The result will be:

```
{
  "my_repository" : {
    "type" : "fs",
    "settings" : {
      "compress" : "true",
      "location" : "/tmp/my_repository"
    }
  }
}
```

3. To delete a repository, the HTTP method is DELETE and the curl command is:

```
curl -XDELETE 'http://localhost:9200/_snapshot/my_repository'
```

The result will be as follows:

```
{"acknowledged":true}
```

How it works...

Before starting to take a snapshot of our data, we must create a repository: a place where we store our backup data. The parameters that can be used to create a repository are:

- type: Used to define the type of shared filesystem repository (generally fs)
- settings: The options to set up the shared filesystem repository

In the case of `fs` type usage, the settings are as follows:

- `location`: This is the location on the filesystem to store snapshots.
- `compress`: This turns on compression for the snapshot files. Compression is applied only to metadata files (index mapping and settings); data files are not compressed (default `true`).
- `chunk_size`: This defines the size for chunks of files during snapshotting. The chunk size can be specified in bytes or by using size value notation (that is, 1g, 10m, 5k) (the default is disabled).
- `max_restore_bytes_per_sec`: This controls the throttle per node restore rate (default `20mb`).
- `max_snapshot_bytes_per_sec`: This controls of the throttle per node snapshot rate (default `20mb`).

- `readonly`: This flag defines the repository as read-only (default `false`).

  It is possible to return all the defined repositories by executing GET without giving the repository name:

  ```
  curl -XGET 'http://localhost:9200/_snapshot'
  ```

There's more...

The most common type for a repository backend is **filesystem** (**fs**), but there are other official repository backends, such as:

- **S3 repository**:
  https://www.elastic.co/guide/en/elasticsearch/plugins/5.0/repository-s3.html
- **HDFS**:
  https://www.elastic.co/guide/en/elasticsearch/plugins/5.0/repository-hdfs.html for Hadoop environments
- **Azure Cloud**:
  https://www.elastic.co/guide/en/elasticsearch/plugins/5.0/repository-azure.html for Azure storage repositories
- **Google Cloud**:
  https://www.elastic.co/guide/en/elasticsearch/plugins/5.0/repository-gcs.html for Google Cloud storage repositories

When a repository is created, it's immediately verified on all data nodes to be sure that it's functional.

Elasticsearch also provides a manual way to verify the node status repository, which is very useful in order to check the status of the cloud repository storage. The command to manually verify a repository is the following:

```
curl -XPOST 'http://localhost:9200/_snapshot/my_repository/_verify'
```

See also

- The official Elasticsearch documentation at `https://www.elastic.co/guide/en/elasticsearch/reference/5.0/modules-sn apshots.html` provides a lot of information about borderline cases for repository usage

Executing a snapshot

In the previous recipe, we defined a repository: the place where we will store the backups. Now we can create snapshots of indices, a full backup of an index, in the exact instant that the command is called.

For every repository it's possible to define multiple snapshots.

Getting ready

You need an up-and-running Elasticsearch installation as we described in the *Downloading and installing Elasticsearch* recipe in `Chapter 2`, *Downloading and Setup*.

To execute `curl` via the command line you need to install `curl` for your operating system.

To correctly execute the following command, the repository created in the previous recipe is required.

How to do it…

To manage a snapshot, we will perform the following steps:

1. To create a snapshot called snap_1 for the test and test1 indices, the HTTP method is PUT and the curl command is as follows:

```
curl -XPUT
"http://localhost:9200/_snapshot/my_repository/snap_1?
wait_for_completion=true" -d '{
"indices": " test-index,test-2",
"ignore_unavailable": "true",
"include_global_state": false
}'
```

The result will be as follows:

```
{
 "snapshot" : {
   "snapshot" : "snap_1",
   "uuid" : "h01mw-HATOiDMVp2k1xaLg",
   "version_id" : 5000099,
   "version" : "5.0.0",
   "indices" : [ "test-index" ],
   "state" : "SUCCESS",
   "start_time" : "2016-11-06T10:43:56.064Z",
   "start_time_in_millis" : 1478429036064,
   "end_time" : "2016-11-06T10:43:56.066Z",
   "end_time_in_millis" : 1478429036066,
   "duration_in_millis" : 2,
   "failures" : [ ],
   "shards" : {
   "total" : 5,
     "failed" : 0,
     "successful" : 5
    }
  }
}
```

If you check your filesystem, the /tmp/my_repository directory is populated with some files such as: index (a directory that contains our data), metadata-snap_1, snapshot-snap_1.

2. To retrieve snapshot information, the HTTP method is GET and the curl command is:

```
curl -XGET
'http://localhost:9200/_snapshot/my_repository/snap_1?pretty'
```

The result will be the same of previous step.

3. To delete a snapshot, the HTTP method is DELETE and the curl command is:

```
curl -XDELETE
'http://localhost:9200/_snapshot/my_repository/snap_1'
```

The result will be:

```
{"acknowledged":true}
```

How it works...

The minimum configuration required to create a snapshot is the name of the repository and the name of the snapshot (that is snap_1).

If no other parameters are set, the snapshot command will dump all the cluster data. To control the snapshot process, some parameters are available:

- indices (a comma delimited list of indices, wildcards are accepted), this controls the indices that must be dumped.
- ignore_unavailable (default false), this prevents the snapshot from failing if some indices are missing.
- include_global_state (defaults to true, available values are true/false/partial), this controls storing the global state in the snapshot. If a primary shard is not available, the snapshot fails.

The query argument wait_for_completion, used also in the example, allows you to wait for the snapshot to end before returning the call. It's very useful if you want to automate your snapshot script to sequentially back up indices.

If the wait_for_completion is not set, in order to check the snapshot status, a user must monitor it via the snapshot GET call.

The snapshots are incremental, so only changed files are copied between two snapshots of the same index. This approach reduces both the time and disk usage during snapshots.

The snapshot process is designed to be as fast as possible, so it implemented a direct copy of Lucene index segments in the repository. To prevent changes and index corruption during the copy, all the segments needed to be copied are blocked from changing until the end of the snapshot.

> Lucene's segment copy is at the shard level, so if you have a cluster of several nodes, and you have a local repository, the snapshot is spread through all the nodes. For this reason, in a production cluster the repository must be shared in order to easily collect all the backup fragments.

Elasticsearch takes care of everything during a snapshot, including preventing writing data to files that are in the snapshot process, and managing cluster events (shard relocating, failures, and so on).

To retrieve all the available snapshots for a repository the command is:

```
curl -XGET 'http://localhost:9200/_snapshot/my_repository/_all'
```

There's more...

The snapshot process can be monitored via the _status endpoint, which provides a complete overview of the snapshot status.

For the current example, the snapshot _status API call will be:

```
curl -XGET
"http://localhost:9200/_snapshot/my_repository/snap_1/_status?pretty"
```

The result is very long and consists of the following sections:

- Information about the snapshot:

```
{
  "snapshots" : [ {
    "snapshot" : "snap_1",
    "uuid" : "BZQRYMPTRAyGr6b8k0h9jQ",
    "repository" : "my_repository",
    "state" : "SUCCESS",
```

- Global shards statistics:

```
"shards_stats" : {
  "initializing" : 0,
  "started" : 0,
  "finalizing" : 0,
  "done" : 5,
  "failed" : 0,
  "total" : 5
},
```

- Snapshot's global statistics:

```
"stats" : {
  "number_of_files" : 125,
  "processed_files" : 125,
  "total_size_in_bytes" : 1497330,
  "processed_size_in_bytes" : 1497330,
  "start_time_in_millis" : 1415914845427,
  "time_in_millis" : 1254
},
```

- Drill-down of snapshot index statistics:

```
"indices" : {
  "test-index" : {
    "shards_stats" : {
      "initializing" : 0,
      "started" : 0,
      "finalizing" : 0,
      "done" : 5,
      "failed" : 0,
      "total" : 5
    },
    "stats" : {
      "number_of_files" : 125,
      "processed_files" : 125,
      "total_size_in_bytes" : 1497330,
      "processed_size_in_bytes" : 1497330,
      "start_time_in_millis" : 1415914845427,
      "time_in_millis" : 1254
    },
```

- Statistics for each index and shard:

```
"shards" : {
  "0" : {
    "stage" : "DONE",
    "stats" : {
      "number_of_files" : 25,
      "processed_files" : 25,
      "total_size_in_bytes" : 304773,
      "processed_size_in_bytes" : 304773,
      "start_time_in_millis" : 1415914845427,
      "time_in_millis" : 813
    }
  },... truncated...
```

The status response is very rich, and it can also be used to estimate the performance of the snapshot and the size required in time for the incremental backups.

Restoring a snapshot

Once you have snapshots of your data, it can be restored. The restore process is very fast: the indexed shard data is simply copied on the nodes and activated.

Getting ready

You need an up-and-running Elasticsearch installation as we described in the *Downloading and installing Elasticsearch* recipe in Chapter 2, *Downloading and Setup*.

To execute curl via the command line, you need to install curl for your operative system.

To correctly execute the following command, the backup created in the previous recipe is required.

How to do it...

To restore a snapshot, we will perform the following steps:

1. To restore a snapshot called `snap_1` for the `test` and `test1` indices, the HTTP method is `PUT` and the `curl` command is:

```
curl -XPOST
"http://localhost:9200/_snapshot/my_repository/snap_1/_restore?
pretty" -d '{
    "indices": "test-index,test-2",
    "ignore_unavailable": "true",
    "include_global_state": false,
    "rename_pattern": "test-(.+)",
    "rename_replacement": "copy_$1"
}'
```

The result will be:

```
{
   "accepted" : true
}
```

2. The restore is finished when the cluster state changes from `red` to `yellow` or `green`.

How it works...

The restore process is very fast. The process comprises the following steps:

1. The data is copied on the primary shard of the restored index (during this step the cluster is in `red` state).
2. The primary shards are recovered (during this step the cluster turns from red to yellow/green).
3. If a replica is set, the primary shards are copied onto other nodes.

It's possible to control the restore process via some parameters, including:

- `indices`: This controls the indices that must be restored. If not defined, all indices in the snapshot are restored (a comma delimited list of indices; wildcards are accepted).
- `ignore_unavailable`: This stops the restore from failing if some indices are missing (default `false`).
- `include_global_state`: This allows the restoration of the global state from the snapshot (defaults to `true`, available values are `true`/`false`).
- `rename_pattern` and `rename_replacement`: The first one is a pattern that must be matched, and the second one uses regular expression replacement to define a new index name.
- `partial`: If it set to `true`, it is allows the restoration of indices with missing shards (default `false`).

Setting up a NFS share for backup

Managing the repository is the most import issue in Elasticsearch backup management. Due to its native distributed architecture, the snapshot and the restore are designed in a cluster style.

During a snapshot, the shards are copied to the defined repository. If this repository is local to the nodes, the backup data is spread across all the nodes. For this reason, it's necessary to have shared repository storage if you have a multimode cluster.

A common approach is to use a **Network File System** (**NFS**), as it's very easy to set up and it's a very fast solution (also, standard Windows Samba shares can be used.)

Getting ready

We have a network with the following nodes:

- **Host server**: `192.168.1.30` (where we will store the backup data)
- **Elasticsearch master node 1**: `192.168.1.40`
- **Elasticsearch data node 1**: `192.168.1.50`
- **Elasticsearch data node 2**: `192.168.1.51`

You need an up-and-running Elasticsearch installation as we described in the *Downloading and installing Elasticsearch* recipe in `Chapter 2`, *Downloading and Setup*.

The following instructions are for standard Debian or Ubuntu distributions: they can be easily changed for other Linux distribution.

How to do it...

To create an NFS shared repository, we need to execute the following steps on the NFS server:

1. We need to install the NFS server (generally the `nfs-kernel-server` package) on the host server. On the host server `192.168.1.30` we will execute:

   ```
   sudo apt-get update
   sudo apt-get install nfs-kernel-server
   ```

2. Once the package is installed, we can create a directory to be shared among all the clients. Let's create a directory:

   ```
   sudo mkdir /mnt/shared-directory
   ```

3. Give the access permission of this directory to user `nobody` and group `nogroup`. These are a special reserved user/group in Linux operating systems that do not need any special permission to run things:

   ```
   sudo chown -R nobody:nogroup /mnt/shared-directory
   ```

4. Then, we need to configure the NFS exports, where we can specify that this directory will be shared with certain machines. Edit the `/etc/exports` file (`sudo nano /etc/exports`) and add the following line containing the directory to be shared and space-separated client IP lists:

   ```
   /mnt/shared-directory   192.168.1.40(rw,sync,no_subtree_check)
   192.168.1.50(rw,sync,no_subtree_check)
   192.168.1.51(rw,sync,no_subtree_check)
   ```

5. To refresh the NFS table that holds the export of the share, the following command must be executed:

   ```
   sudo exportfs -a
   ```

6. Finally, we can start the NFS service by running the following command:

```
sudo service nfs-kernel-server start
```

After the NFS server is up-and-running, we need to configure the clients. We'll repeat the following steps on every Elasticsearch node:

1. We need to install the NFS client on our Elasticsearch node:

```
sudo apt-get update
sudo apt-get install nfs-common
```

2. Now, create a directory on the client machine and we'll try to mount the remote shared directory:

```
sudo mkdir /mnt/nfs
sudo mount 192.168.1.30:/mnt/shared-directory /mnt/nfs
```

3. If everything is fine, we can add the mount directory in our node /etc/fstab file, so that it will be mounted at the next boot:

```
sudo nano /etc/fstab
```

4. And add following lines into this file:

```
192.168.1.30:/mnt/shared-directory    /mnt/nfs/    nfs
auto,noatime,nolock,bg,nfsvers=4,sec=krb5p,intr,tcp,actimeo
=1800 0 0
```

5. We update our Elasticsearch node configuration (config/elasticsearch.yml) path.repo in this way:

```
path.repo: /mnt/nfs/
```

6. After having restarted all Elasticsearch nodes, we can create our share repository on the cluster via a single standard repository creation call:

```
curl -XPUT 'http://192.168.1.40:9200/_snapshot/my_repository' -
d '{
    "type": "fs",
    "settings": {
        "location": "/ mnt/nfs/my_repository",
        "compress": true
    }
}'
```

How it works...

NFS is a distributed filesystem protocol that is very common in the Unix world, and which allows you to mount remote directories on your server. The mounted directories look like the local directory of the server, and therefore, by using NFS, multiple servers can write to same directory.

This is very handy if you need to do a shared backup: all the nodes will write/read from the same shared directory.

> If you need to snapshot an index that will be rarely updated, such as an old time-based index, the best practice is to optimize it before backing it up, cleaning up deleted documents, and reducing the Lucene fragments.

Reindexing from a remote cluster

The snapshot and restore APIs are very fast and the preferred way to back up data, but they have some limitations, such as:

- The backup is a safe Lucene index copy, so it depends on the Elasticsearch version used. If you are switching from a version of Elastisearch that is prior to version 5.x, it's not possible to restore old indices.
- It's not possible to restore backups of a newer Elasticsearch version in an older version. The restore is only forward-compatible.
- It's not possible to restore partial data from a backup.

To be able to copy data in this scenario, the solution is to use the reindex API using a remote server.

Getting ready

You need an up-and-running Elasticsearch installation as we described in the *Downloading and installing Elasticsearch* recipe in `Chapter 2`, *Downloading and Setup*.

To execute `curl` via command line, you need to install `curl` for your operative system.

How to do it...

To copy an index from a remote server, we need to execute the following steps:

1. We need to add the remote server address in the `config/elasticsearch.yml` section `reindex.remote.whitelist` in a similar line:

   ```
   reindex.remote.whitelist: ["192.168.1.227:9200"]
   ```

2. After having restarted the Elasticsearch node to take the new configuration, we can call the reindex API to copy a `test-source` index data in a `test-dest` via the remote REST endpoint in this way:

   ```
   curl -XPOST "http://localhost:9200/_reindex" -d'
   {
     "source": {
       "remote": {
         "host": "http://192.168.1.227:9200"
       },
       "index": "test-source"
     },
     "dest": {
       "index": "test-dest"
     }
   }'
   ```

The result will be similar to a local reindex that we have already seen in the *Reindex an index* recipe in `Chapter 4`, *Basic Operations*.

How it works...

The reindex API allows you to call a remote cluster. Every version of the Elasticsearch server is supported (mainly 1.x or above).

The reindex API executes a scan query on the remote index cluster and puts the data in the current cluster. This process can take a lot of time, depending on the amount of data that needs to be copied and the time required to index that data.

The source section contains important parameters to control the fetched data, such as:

- `remote`: This is a section that contains information on the remote cluster connection.
- `index`: This is the remote index that must be used to fetch the data. It can also be an alias or multiple indices via globs.
- `query`: This parameter is optional: it's a standard query that can be used to select the document that must be copied.
- `size`: This parameter is optional and the buffer is up to 200MB, the number of the documents to be used for the bulk read/write.

The `remote` section of the configuration is composed of the following parameters:

- `host`: The remote REST endpoint of the cluster
- `username`: The username to be used for copying the data (an optional parameter)
- `password`: The password for the user to access the remote cluster (optional)

There are a lot advantages to using this approach on standard snapshot and restore, including:

- Ability to copy data from older clusters (from version 1.x or above).
- Ability to use a query to copy on a selection of documents. This is very handy for copying data from a production cluster to a dev/test one.

See also

- The *Reindex an index* recipe in `Chapter 4`, *Basic Operations,* and the official Elasticsearch documentation at
  `https://www.elastic.co/guide/en/elasticsearch/reference/5.0/docs-reind ex.html`, which provides more detailed information about the reindex API and some borderline cases in using this API

12
User Interfaces

In this chapter we will cover the following recipes:

- Installing and using Cerebro
- Installing Kibana and X-Pack
- Managing Kibana dashboards
- Monitoring with Kibana
- Using Kibana console
- Visualizing data with Kibana
- Installing Kibana plugins
- Generating Graph with Kibana

Introduction

In Elasticsearch ecosystem, it can be immensely useful to monitor nodes and cluster to manage and improve their performance and state. There are several issues that can arise at cluster level, such as:

- Node overheads, where some nodes can have too many shards allocated and can become a bottleneck for the entire cluster
- Node shutdown can happen due to many reasons, for example, full disks, hardware failures, and power problems
- Shard relocation problems or corruptions, in which some shards are unable to get an online status

- Too large shards happens when a shard is too big; the index performance decreases due to Lucene massive segments merging
- Empty indices and shards waste memory and resources, but because every shard has a lot of active threads if there is a huge number of unused indices and shards, the general cluster performance is degraded
- Node problems such as high CPU usage or disk full

Detecting malfunction or bad performances can be done via API or via some frontends that are designed to be used in Elasticsearch.

Some of the frontends introduced in this chapter allow the readers to have a working web dashboard on their Elasticsearch data, monitoring the cluster health, backuping/restoring your data and allow testing queries before implementing them in the code. In this chapter, we will have an overview of these frontends due to their complexity and the large number of features that will require a book to themselves. For an in-depth description I suggest the reader to have a look at the official documentation of Kibana at `https://www.elastic.co/guide/en/kibana/current/index.html` or dedicated books.

> In this chapter, we will see an Elasticsearch commercial product called X-Pack. Generally, I prefer to use open source solutions and applications, but for functionalities that are present in X-Pack there are no opensource alternatives at the moment.

Installing and using Cerebro

Cerebro is the evolution of the previous Elasticsearch plugin Elasticsearch kopf (`https://github.com/lmenezes/elasticsearch-kopf`) that doesn't work in Elasticsearch 5.x or above due to removing of site plugins.

Cerebro is a partial rewrite of the previous plugin available as a self-working application server.

Getting ready

You need an up-and-running Elasticsearch installation as we described in the *Downloading and installing Elasticsearch* recipe in `Chapter 2`, *Downloading and Setup*.

Java JVM version 8.x or above must be installed to run Cerebro.

How to do it...

For installing Cerebro, you need to download it and manually install its plugin. We will now perform the following steps:

1. You can download a binary distro of Cerebro at
   `https://github.com/lmenezes/cerebro/releases`. For Linux/MacOSX, we can use the following command:

   ```
   wget
   https://github.com/lmenezes/cerebro/releases/download
   /v0.4.2/cerebro-0.4.2.tgz
   ```

2. Now you can extract it, via the following command:

   ```
   tar xfvz cerebro-0.4.2.tgz
   ```

3. Now you can execute it via following command:

   ```
   cerebro-0.4.2/bin/cerebro
   ```

4. Alternatively, for Windows, use the following command:

   ```
   cerebro-0.4.2\bin\cerebro.bat
   ```

5. In the console, you should see the following output:

   ```
   [warn] application - Logger configuration in conf files is
   deprecated and has no effect. Use a logback configuration file
   instead.
   [info] play.api.Play - Application started (Prod)
   [info] p.c.s.NettyServer - Listening for HTTP on
   /0:0:0:0:0:0:0:0:9000
   ```

6. To access the web interface, you need to navigate with your browser at the address:

   ```
   http://0.0.0.0:9000/
   ```

How it works...

Cerebro is a modern reactive application written in Scala via the Play Framework for the backend REST and Elasticsearch communication and a **Single Page Application** (**SPA**) frontend written in Javascript with AngularJS.

By default, Cerebro binds on port 9000. You can navigate with a browser at the address `http://0.0.0.0:9000` to view the following start page:

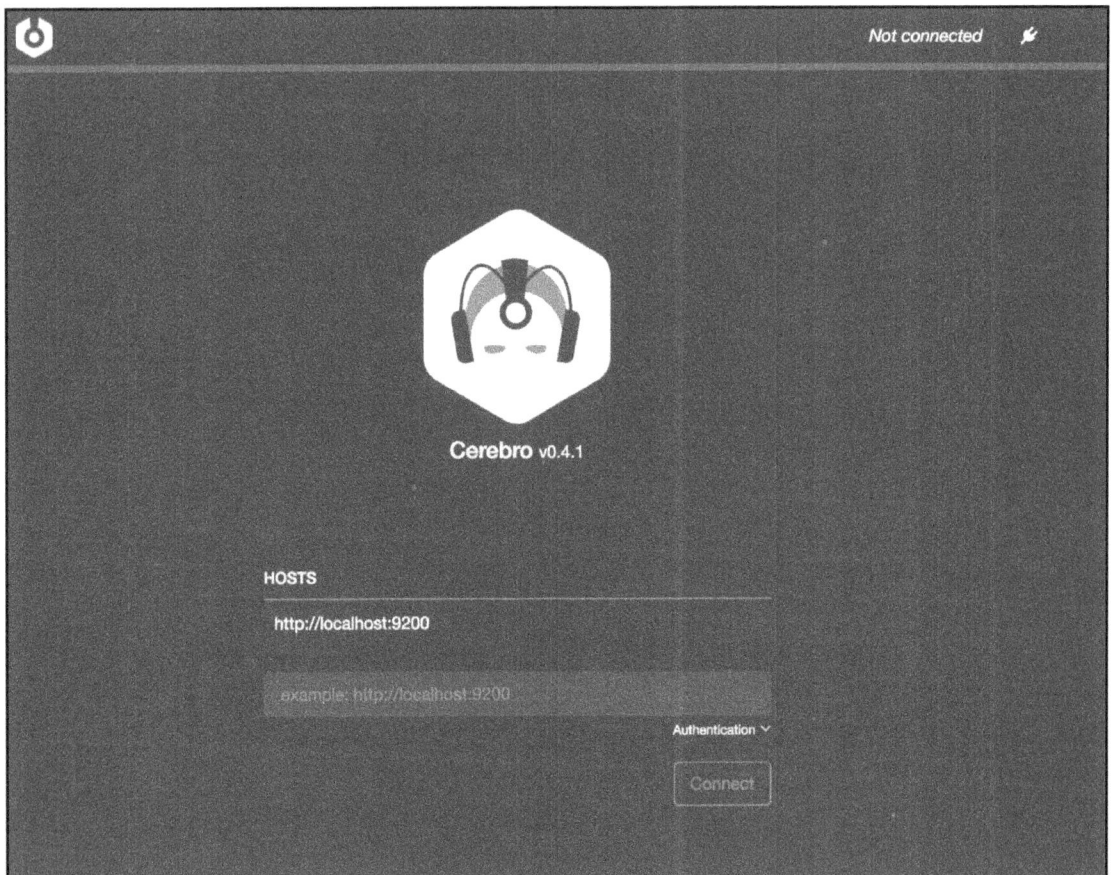

In the start page, you can select a predefined host or you can manually insert the address of your Elasticsearch server. If you need, you can provide credentials for accessing your Elasticsearch cluster.

After having pressed connect, if everything is okay, you can access the Cerebro main page with your nodes view as shown in the following screenshot:

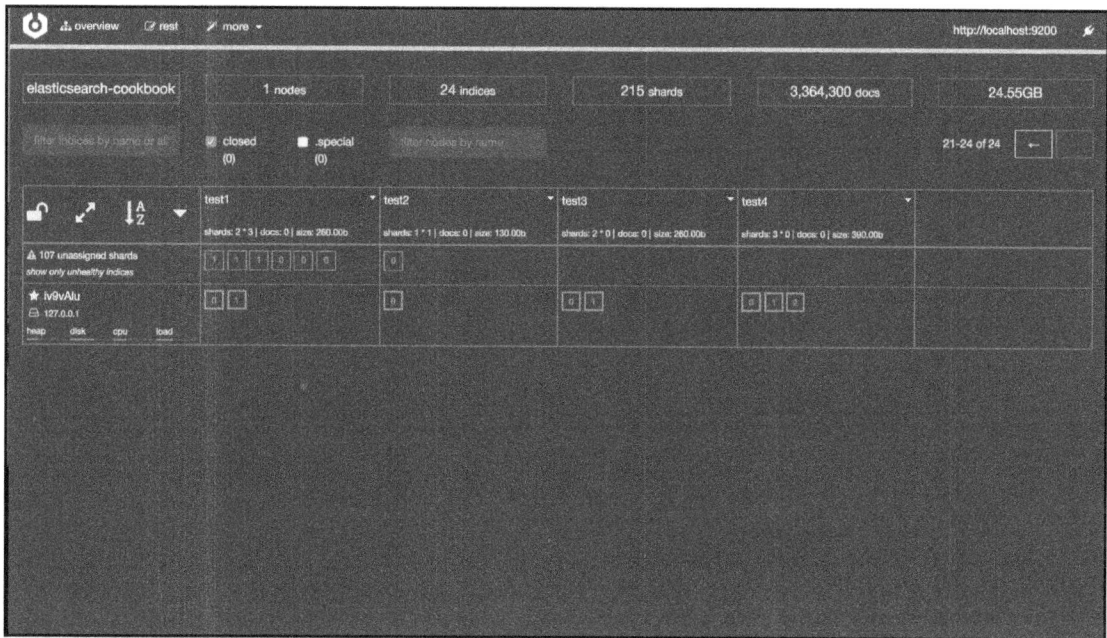

The Cerebro main page provides a very large overview of your cluster and data; from top to bottom we have as follows:

- The menu, where **overview** is a link to homepage, **rest** allows to send generic REST calls, and clicking on **more** we have additional admin functionalities as shown in the following screenshot:

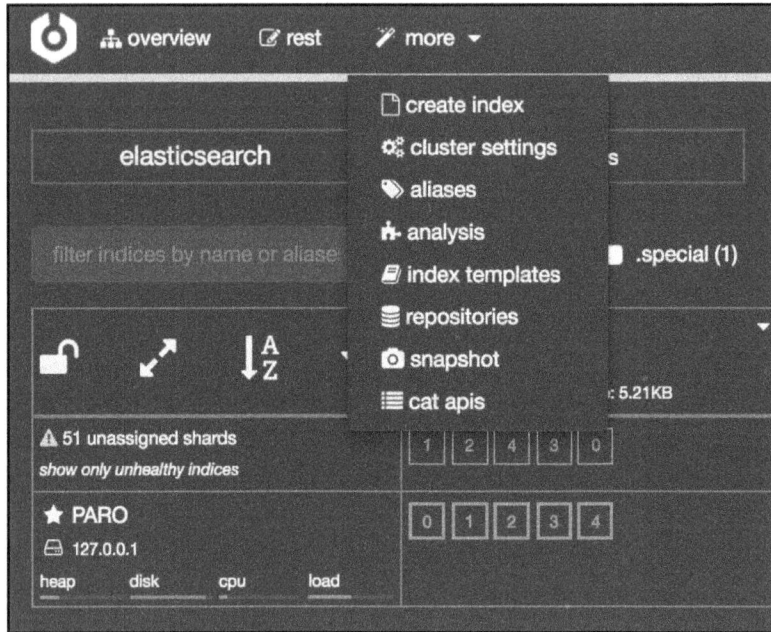

- The status line (green, yellow, or red: in this case, it is yellow because my cluster needs more nodes).
- The line with cluster global stats, that includes the name of the cluster, number of nodes, number of indices, number of shards, number of documents, and size of your data.
- The filter indices line where you can do as follows:
  - Filter the indices by name
  - Show/hide closed indices
  - Show/hide special indices (dot starting ones)
  - Filter by node names
  - Control the indices pagination

- The main grid block that contains node and indices information. In the first column, we have as follows:

    - The general cluster control functionalities. The lock symbol allows you to lock the shard relocation at cluster level (useful for cluster restart management). The second symbol allows you to show extra node information such as JVM version and Elasticsearch version. The sorting simply allows you to sort nodes by name. The arrow symbol allows you to execute actions to all the selected indices such as close/open/refresh and cache clear.

    - The unassigned shards line allows you to check the unassigned shard for index.

    - The node information, where in a single cell we have node name, node ip, and heap/disk/cpu/load on the node. If these values are too high, they are showed in red.

- In the other columns, we have indices information as follows:

    - Index name, number of shards, number of documents, and the total size. From the arrow, you can access action that can be executed against the index:

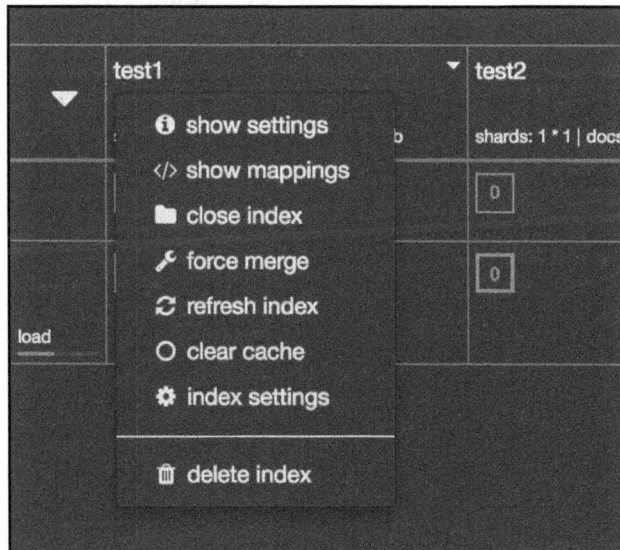

- The **shards** are represented as a box with its number. Clicking on it, you can see additional shard info.

The main page or **overview** view is very rich of useful data. With a single look, you can scope nodes with high loads or full disk, how the shards are distributed in your cluster, and if there are problems with some indices.

Clicking on a particular **index settings** a form is open to change all the index options that can be changed as shown in the following screenshot:

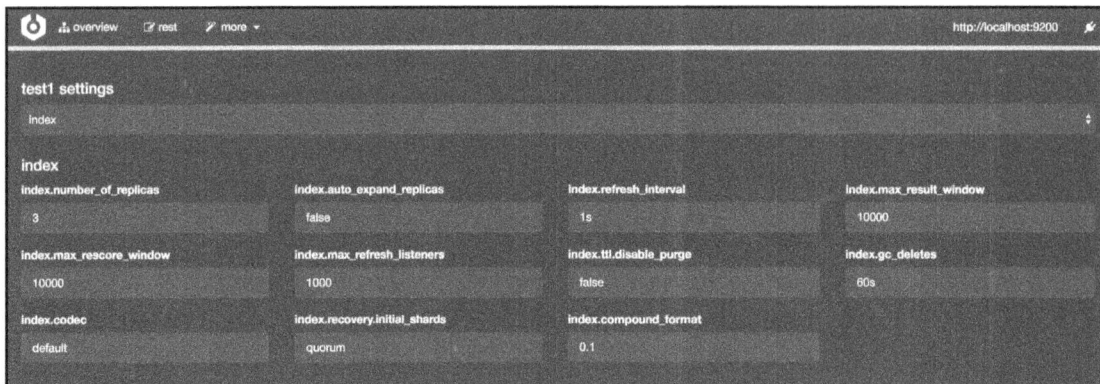

The **create index** page allows easy creating an index defining shards, replicas, or templates as shown in the following screenshot:

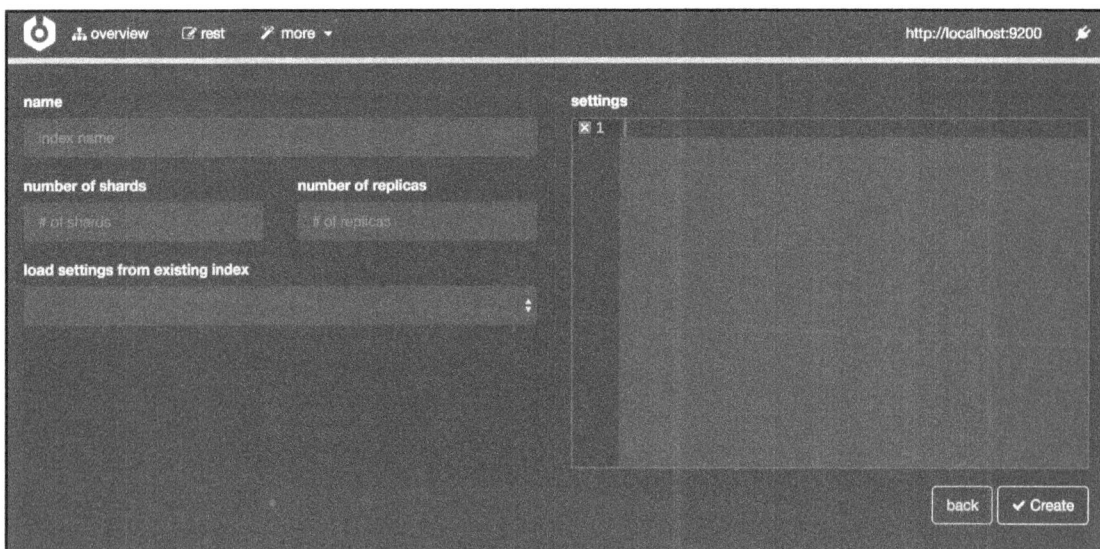

The **cluster settings** page allows changing cluster mutable parameters from a simple interface. This is advanced usage, but the simplicity of the form speeds up cluster settings management as shown in the following screenshot:

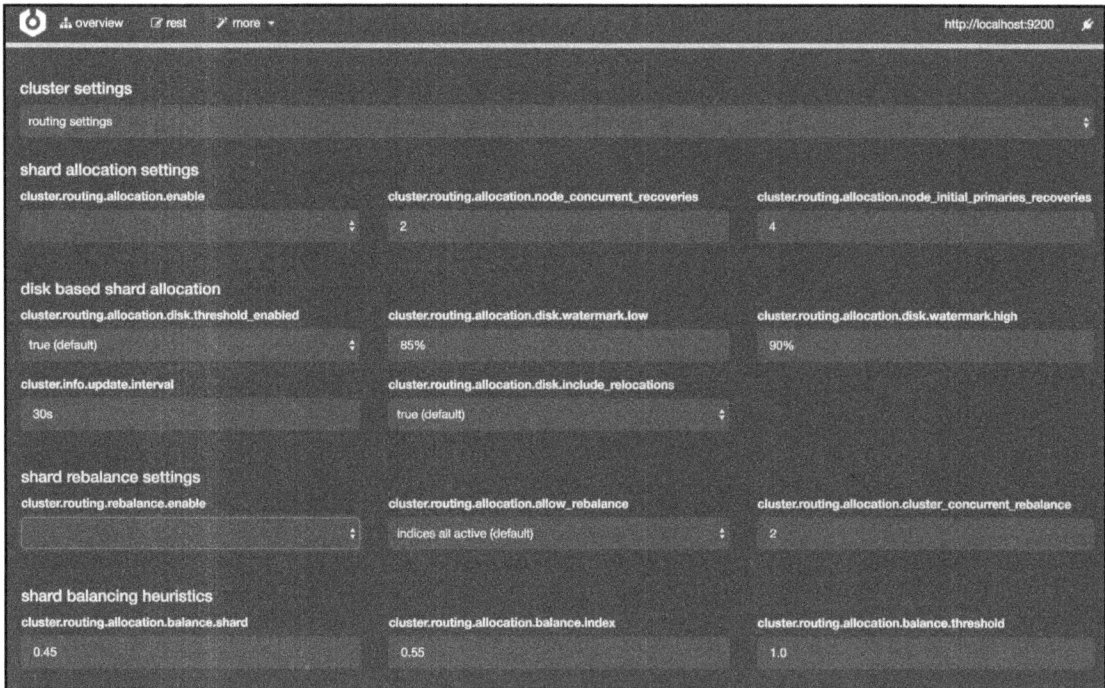

Managing repository can be achieved by using the **repositories** menu. The page allows you to define the name and the type of the repository to be used for future backup/restore actions as shown in the following screenshot:

If a repository is created via interfaces or API, it can be used to execute backup and restore actions. Clicking on **shapshot** menu, you can access a page where:

- On the right, you can create a snapshot selecting the repository, giving it a name, and selecting the indices that need to be backed up.
- On the left, there is a list of available snaphots that can be restored as shown in the following screenshot:

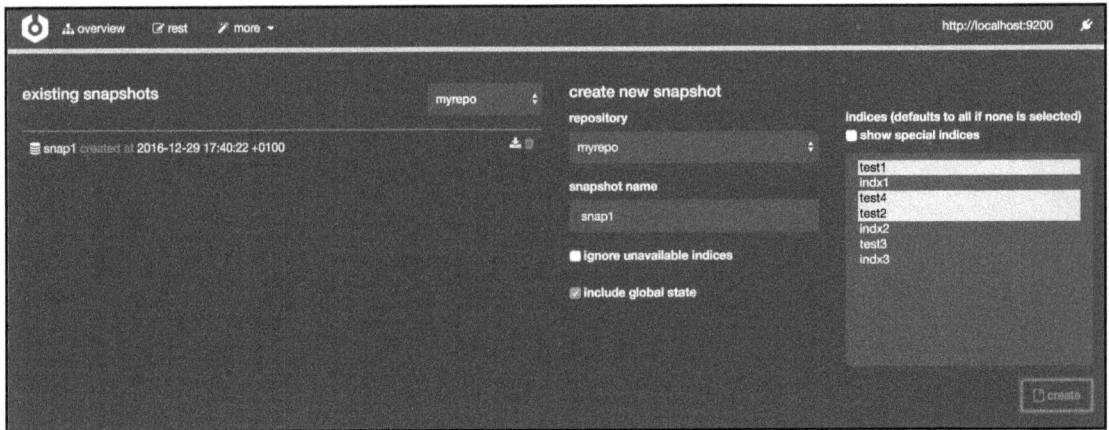

There's more...

The preceding part of Cerebro allows you to cover special aspects of Elasticsearch management; in the rest menu, you can access a page where you can execute raw REST calls against Elasticsearch as shown in the following screenshot:

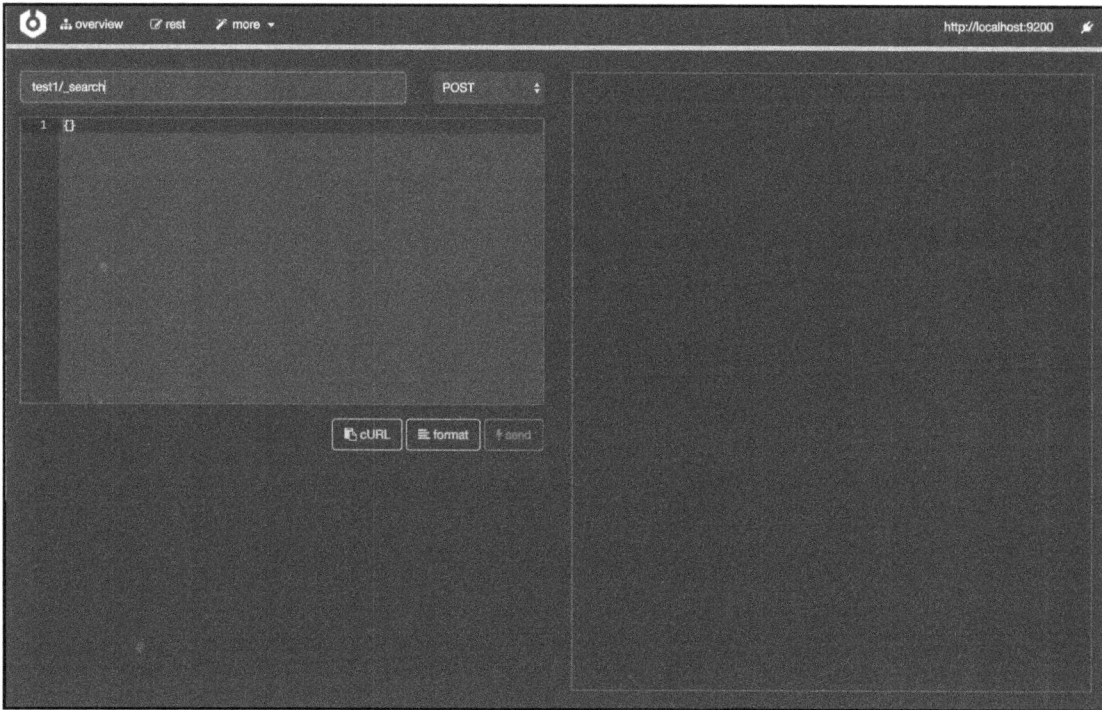

Cerebro doesn't provide data visualization or discovery as Kibana, but it can execute raw REST against an Elasticsearch endpoint. With this functionality, queries can be tested against an Elasticsearch server. This is very handy to work a low level with Elasticsearch.

The rest interface also allows you to export the call as a curl command.

The Cerebro interface is quite new. The new features are in development and will be released in the near future.

Installing Kibana and X-Pack

The most famous Elasticsearch interface is Kibana, which from Elasticsearch 5.x version has the same version of Elasticsearch. Kibana is an opensource pluggable interface, free to change to be used for Elasticsearch. It provides data visualization and data discovery and with commercial products such as X-Pack, and also supports security, graph, and cluster monitoring.

Getting ready

You need an up-and-running Elasticsearch installation as we described in the *Downloading and installing Elasticsearch* recipe in `Chapter 2`, *Downloading and Setup*.

How to do it...

For installing Kibana, we will perform the following steps:

1. Download a binary version for Elasticsearch website and unpack it. For Linux, the commands are as follows:

```
wget https://artifacts.elastic.co/downloads/kibana/kibana-
5.1.1-linux-x86_64.tar.gz
tar -xzf kibana-5.1.1-linux-x86_64.tar.gz
```

2. On MacOsX, you can install Kibana via the following command:

```
brew install kibana
```

3. If we want to install Xpack, we first need to install it in Elasticsearch via following command:

```
bin/elasticsearch-plugin install x-pack
```

4. The result will be similar to the following output:

```
[=================================================] 100%
@@@@@@@@@@@@@@@@@@@@@@@@@@@@@@@@@@@@@@@@@@@@@@@@@@@@@@@@@@@@@@
@     WARNING: plugin requires additional permissions     @
@@@@@@@@@@@@@@@@@@@@@@@@@@@@@@@@@@@@@@@@@@@@@@@@@@@@@@@@@@@@@@
* java.lang.RuntimePermission
accessClassInPackage.com.sun.activation.registries
* java.lang.RuntimePermission getClassLoader
* java.lang.RuntimePermission setContextClassLoader
* java.lang.RuntimePermission setFactory
* java.security.SecurityPermission createPolicy.JavaPolicy
* java.security.SecurityPermission getPolicy
* java.security.SecurityPermission putProviderProperty.BC
* java.security.SecurityPermission setPolicy
* java.util.PropertyPermission * read,write
* java.util.PropertyPermission sun.nio.ch.bugLevel write
* javax.net.ssl.SSLPermission setHostnameVerifier
See http://docs.oracle.com/javase/8/docs/technotes/guides
/security/permissions.html
```

```
for descriptions of what these permissions allow and the
associated risks.
Continue with installation? [y/n]y
-> Installed x-pack
```

5. After having started Elasticsearch, a similar log line should appear as follows:

```
... loaded plugin [x-pack]
```

6. And then, install it in Kibana using the `kibana-plugin` command line via following command:

```
bin/kibana-plugin install x-pack
```

7. The output will be as follows:

```
Transferring 123275957 bytes...................
Transfer complete
Retrieving metadata from plugin archive
Extracting plugin archive
Extraction complete
Optimizing and caching browser bundles...
DeprecationWarning: os.tmpDir() is deprecated. Use os.tmpdir()
instead.
Plugin installation complete
```

> Maybe Kibana/X-Pack could be hard to be get ready for using it, there is a Docker image which simplify a lot this jump start at `http://elk-docker.readthedocs.io/#installation`, with two commands on Linux you have the stack up and running.

How it works...

Kibana is the official Elasticsearch frontend. It's an open source analytics and visualization platform to work with Elasticsearch based on AngularJS. It's served by a Node.js backend webserver. The development of Kibana is highly tight to Elasticsearch ones and the best practice is to use a Kibana version aligned to Elasticsearch ones.

Kibana allows us to navigate data in Elasticsearch and organize it in dashboards that are created, shared, and updated in real-time.

After having setup Elasticsearch and Kibana and started both, you can navigate Kibana at `http://localhost:5601`. If everything is alright, you can now login via the **Username** `Kibana` and **Password** `changeme` as shown in the following screenshot:

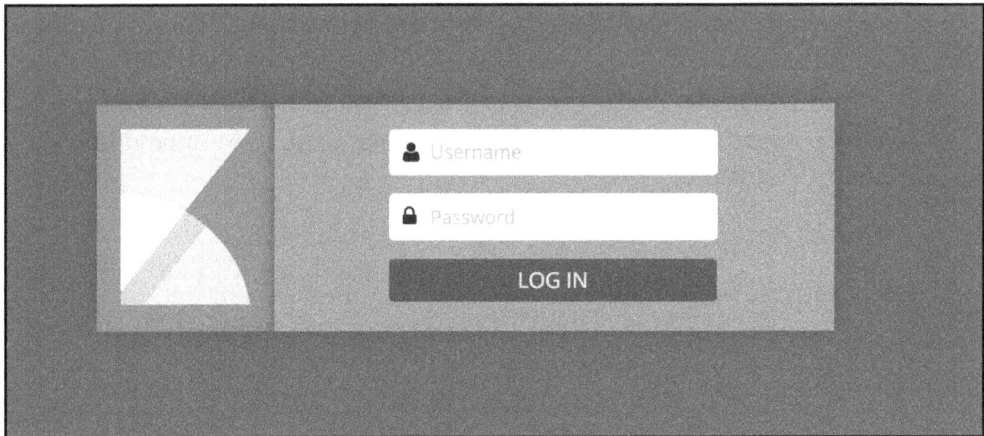

After having logged in Kibana, you must define the index patterns that must be used by default. Generally they are the `logstash-*` indices or `.monitor-*` indices (if the X-Pack monitor is installed) as shown in the following screenshot:

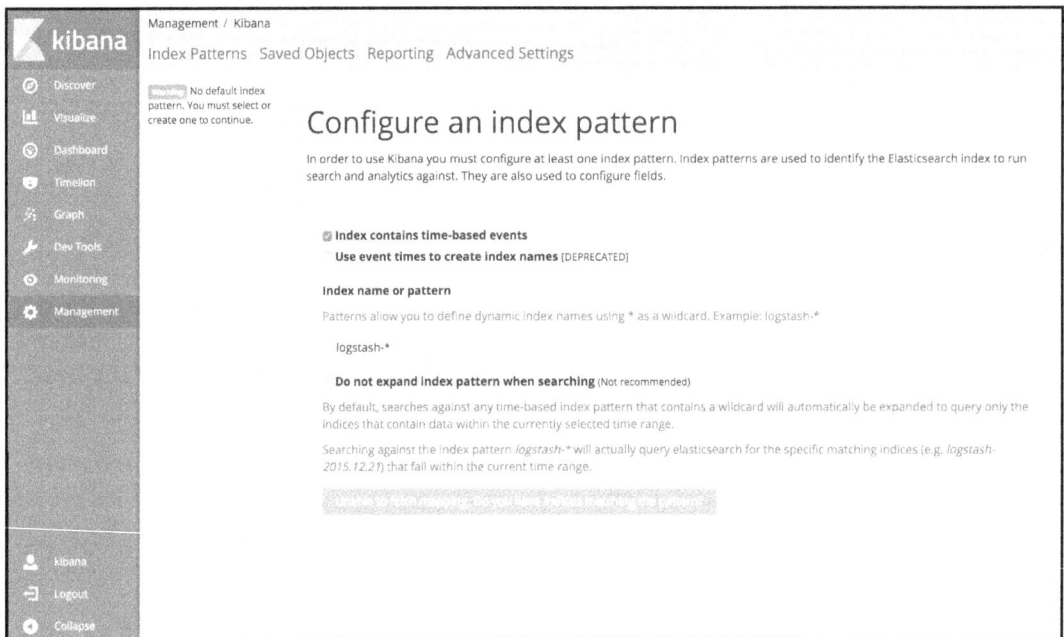

Kibana does mappings analysis on indices of index pattern to discover the format of your data and provide facilities for building queries and filters as shown in the following screenshot:

Kibana and Elasticsearch can be extended via X-Pack; it is composed of five special extensions in a single package that are as follows:

- **Security**: This is used to secure your cluster via authentication and SSL data encryption
- **Monitor**: This is used to monitor your node functionalities and the cluster overall
- **Graph**: This provides graph API for Elasticsearch–a graph-based approach for data discovery
- **Watcher**: This is a system that provided registered queries that allows us to monitor and keep an alert on your data
- **Reporting**: This is a module that is able to create reports from your dashboards

X-Pack is released as a single package for both Elasticsearch and Kibana. It extends the Elasticsearch server functionalities with monitoring, graph, and security. In Kibana, the X-pack provides new interface dashboards for its extended functionalities.

Managing Kibana dashboards

The core of Kibana are the dashboards–an aggregation of widgets that are results of queries and aggregations.

Getting ready

You need an up-and-running Elasticsearch installation as we described in the *Downloading and installing Elasticsearch* recipe in `Chapter 2`, *Downloading and Setup*.

You also need a functional Kibana installation as described in the *Installing Kibana and X-Pack* recipe.

How to do it...

For managing Kibana dashboards, we will perform the following steps:

1. We access the **Discovery** section of Kibana as shown in the following screenshot:

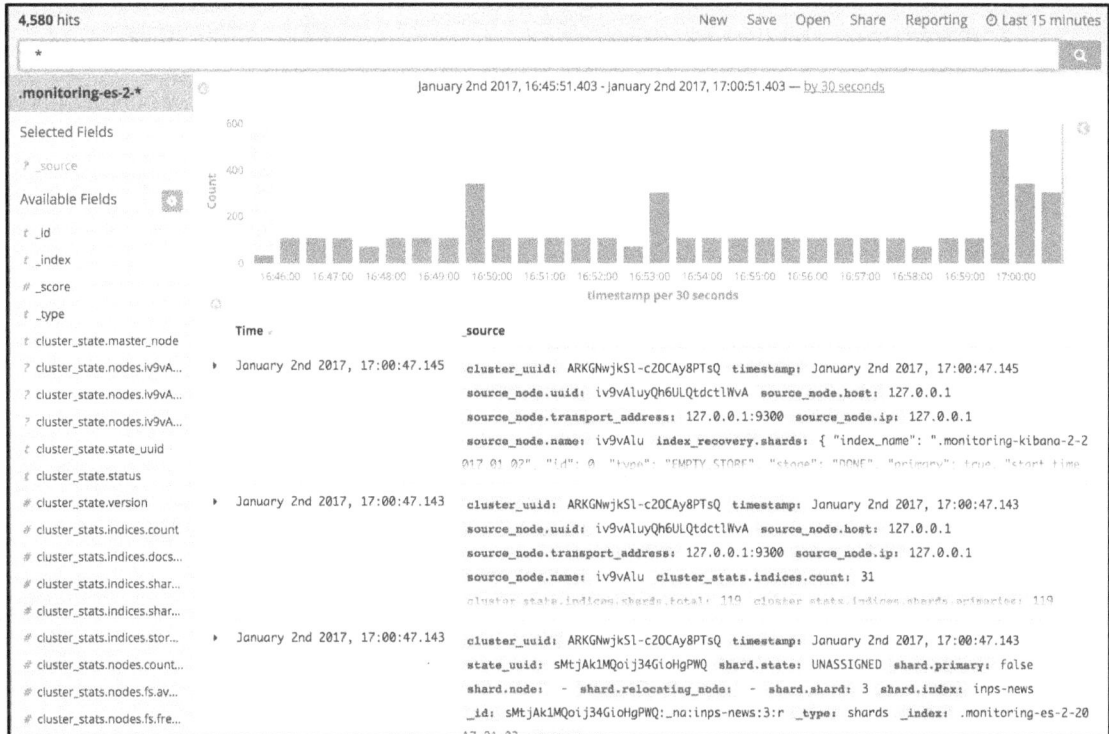

2. After a few seconds, the default search frontend should appear. The default query is *, which is executed against the _all field.

How it works...

The Kibana interface is divided into sections: **Discovery**, **Visualize**, **Dashboards**, **Dev Tools**, and **Management** are available in the opensource version of Kibana. The X-Pack adds **Graph** and **Monitoring** ones.

The dashboard top menu allows us to do as follows:

- Create a new dashboard starting from scratch via the **New** menu entry.
- **Save** the current dashboard / query giving it a name.
- Open the dashboards that you have already saved.
- **Share** a dashboard or a dashboard snapshot (with date/time value fixed) via a link.
- Generate a PDF from the current dashboard via the **Reporting** menu entry. To generate a report, your dashboard must be saved. The reporting entry is available only if X-Pack is installed.
- If you are using autorefresh dashboards, you can pause autorefresh via the pause icon. By clicking on the refresh interval, you can change it as shown in the following screenshot:

- Change/define the time interval range by clicking on the time range value.

Internally, the Kibana dashboards are stored in an Elasticsearch special index `.kibana` and in case of some asynchronous task the data is read from this index.

Monitoring with Kibana

X-Pack provides cluster functionalities that allows to control and monitor your nodes and cluster. This is a very useful component of X-Pack as it is the lifesaver on large installations.

Getting ready

You need an up-and-running Elasticsearch installation as we described in the *Downloading and installing Elasticsearch* recipe in `Chapter 2`, *Downloading and Setup*.

You also need a functional Kibana installation as described in the *Installing Kibana and X-Pack* recipe.

> Monitor plugin (X-Pack) must be installed in every Elasticsearch node of the cluster, to be able to correctly collect the data metrics.

How to do it...

To use X-Pack Elasticsearch monitor, we will perform the following steps:

1. We access the **Monitoring** section of Kibana as shown in the following screenshot:

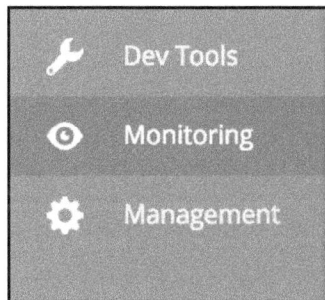

2. In the main page, you can access the different sections on monitoring applications as shown in the following screenshot:

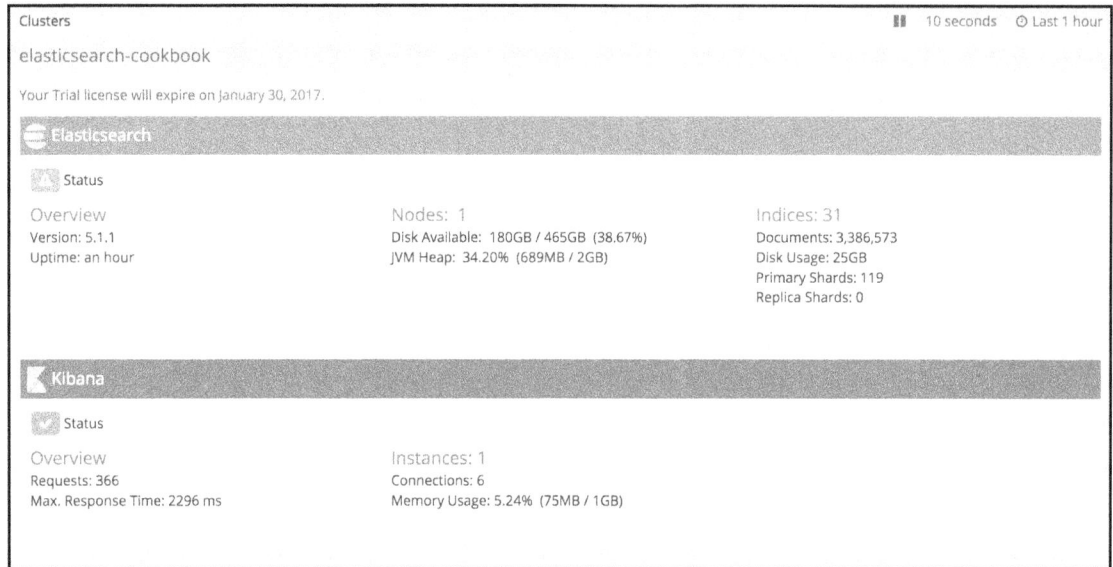

Clusters			‖ 10 seconds ⊘ Last 1 hour
elasticsearch-cookbook			

Your Trial license will expire on January 30, 2017.

Elasticsearch

🔲 Status

Overview	Nodes: 1	Indices: 31
Version: 5.1.1	Disk Available: 180GB / 465GB (38.67%)	Documents: 3,386,573
Uptime: an hour	JVM Heap: 34.20% (689MB / 2GB)	Disk Usage: 25GB
		Primary Shards: 119
		Replica Shards: 0

Kibana

🔲 Status

Overview	Instances: 1
Requests: 366	Connections: 6
Max. Response Time: 2296 ms	Memory Usage: 5.24% (75MB / 1GB)

3. If you click on the **Overview** cluster, you are able to see global cluster status and statistics as shown in the following screenshot:

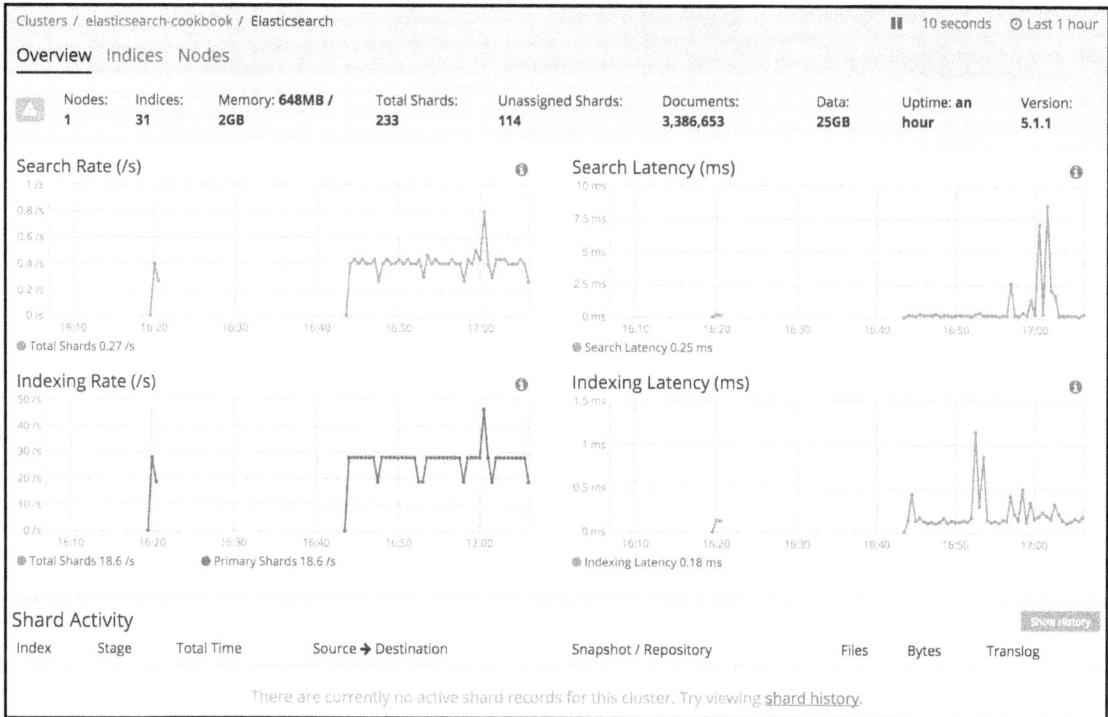

4. If you click on the **Nodes** cluster, you are able to see the node's status and statistics as shown in the following screenshot:

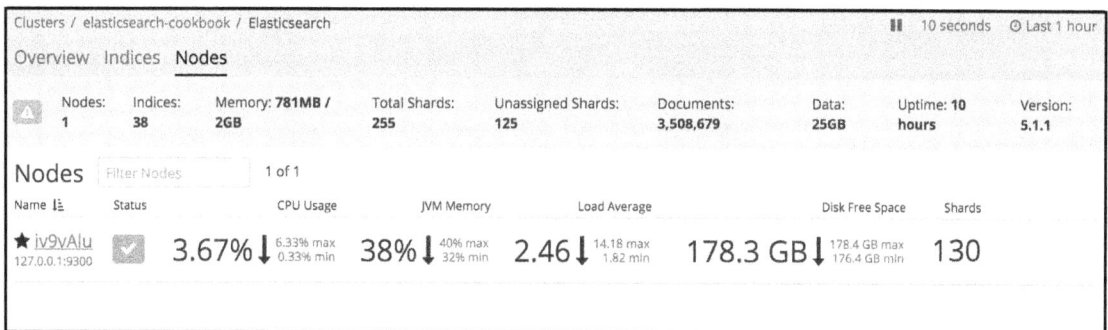

5. If you click on the **Indices** cluster, you are able to see the node's status and statistics as shown in the following screenshot:

Clusters / elasticsearch-cookbook / Elasticsearch									⏸ 10 seconds ⏱ Last 1 hour
Overview **Indices** Nodes									

	Nodes: 1	Indices: 38	Memory: **577MB /** 2GB	Total Shards: 255	Unassigned Shards: 125	Documents: 3,509,185	Data: 25GB	Uptime: **10** hours	Version: 5.1.1

Indices Filter indices   20 of 25   Show system indices

Name	Status ↓	Document Count	Data	Index Rate	Search Rate	Unassigned Shards
test3		0	318.0 B	0 /s	0 /s	0
test4		0	477.0 B	0 /s	0 /s	0
indx2		0	795.0 B	0 /s	0 /s	5

How it works...

The monitoring application is composed of two components: a part that is installed in Elasticsearch server and another one that is installed in Kibana.

The part that is installed in Elasticsearch does active cluster monitoring, sending on-time interval statistics to Elasticsearch monitor server/cluster.

In this case, we have used the same cluster both for data and logs, but it can be configured to use an external cluster for monitoring.

The configurations for this part of the plugin are, as usual, in the `elasticsearch.yml` file. The most important properties are as follows:

- `monitor.agent.exporter.es.hosts`: This is a list of hosts in hostname:port format to which statistics and events will be sent (default `["localhost:9200"]`)
- `monitor.agent.enabled`: This can be set to `false` to disable all exporting of data (default `true`)
- `monitor.agent.indices`: This allows us to control which indices to export data for. It's a comma-separated list of names that can be wildcards as well, for example, `+test*,-test1` (default `*`)
- `monitor.agent.interval`: This controls the interval between data samples; set it to `-1` to temporarily disable exporting (detault `10s`)

The insight part is in the frontend as the monitoring app in Kibana, which allows a powerful customization of the interface to provide advanced analytics.

The interface is very simple to understand and common issues are marked with red to give attention to the user.

Probably, Elasticsearch monitoring is the most complete available solution to monitoring an Elasticsearch cluster, easy to use, and fully customizable.

See also

- `https://www.elastic.co/products/x-pack/monitoring` for Monitor licensing and overview
- `https://www.elastic.co/guide/en/x-pack/current/xpack-monitoring.html` for Monitor documentation
- `https://www.elastic.co/products/kibana` for Kibana overview

Using Kibana dev-console

X-Pack provides cluster functionalities that allow you to control and monitor your nodes and cluster. This is a very useful component of X-Pack as it is the lifesaver on large installations.

Getting ready

You need an up-and-running Elasticsearch installation as we described in the *Downloading and installing Elasticsearch* recipe in chapter 2, *Downloading and Setup*.

You also need a functional Kibana installation as described in the *Installing Kibana and X-Pack* recipe. The X-Pack is not needed.

How to do it...

To use X-Pack Elasticsearch monitor, we will perform the following steps:

1. We access the **Dev Tools** section of Kibana as shown in the following screenshot:

2. Now we can use the dev console to create/execute/test queries and other Elasticsearch HTTP API via it as shown in the following screenshot:

How it works...

The Kibana console is very similar to the Cerebro interface that we have previously seen.

It allows us to execute every kind of REST API call via the http interface to Elasticsearch. It can be used for several purposes such as follows:

- Creating complex queries and aggregations. The console interface helps the user by providing code completion and syntax checking during editing.
- Analyzing the returned results. It is very useful to check particular aggregation responses or the structure of the API answers.
- Testing/Debugging queries before embedding them in your application code.
- Executing REST services that are now wrapped in Elasticsearch interfaces, such as repository/snapshot/restore ones.

There's more...

The Kibana**Dev Tools** also provides support to drill down the times needed to execute a particular query via the **Profiler** section. As the execution of a query with some aggregation can be very complex and can take a lot of time to profile the query, this is the most advanced interface available in Elasticsearch to profile query execution. It's available in the open source part of Kibana as shown in the following screenshot:

Visualizing data with Kibana

Kibana allows you to create reusable data representations called Visualizations. They are representations of aggregations and can be used to power up the dashboard with custom graphs.

Getting ready

You need an up-and-running Elasticsearch installation as we described in the *Downloading and installing Elasticsearch* recipe in `Chapter 2`, *Downloading and Setup*.

You also need a functional Kibana installation as described in *Installing Kibana and X-Pack* recipe. The X-Pack is not needed.

How to do it...

To use Kibana to create custom widgets, we will perform the following steps:

1. We access the **Visualize** section of Kibana as shown in the following screenshot:

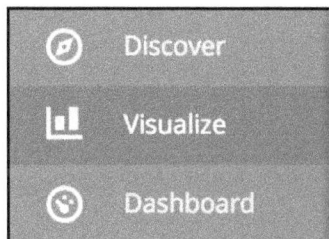

2. Now we can choose the visualization that we want to create as shown in the following screenshot:

Visualize / Step / 1

Create New Visualization

Area chart

Great for stacked timelines in which the total of all series is more important than comparing any two or more series. Less useful for assessing the relative change of unrelated data points as changes in a series lower down the stack will have a difficult to gauge effect on the series above it.

Data table

The data table provides a detailed breakdown, in tabular format, of the results of a composed aggregation. Tip, a data table is available from many other charts by clicking the grey bar at the bottom of the chart.

Line chart

Often the best chart for high density time series. Great for comparing one series to another. Be careful with sparse sets as the connection between points can be misleading.

</> Markdown widget

Useful for displaying explanations or instructions for dashboards.

Metric

One big number for all of your one big number needs. Perfect for showing a count of hits, or the exact average of a numeric field.

Pie chart

Pie charts are ideal for displaying the parts of some whole. For example,

Or, Open a Saved Visualization

Q Visualizations Filter...

0 of 0 Manage Visualizations

Name ▲

No matching visualizations found.

3. If we want to create a **Tag cloud** visualization, we select it and populate the required fields as shown in the following screenshot:

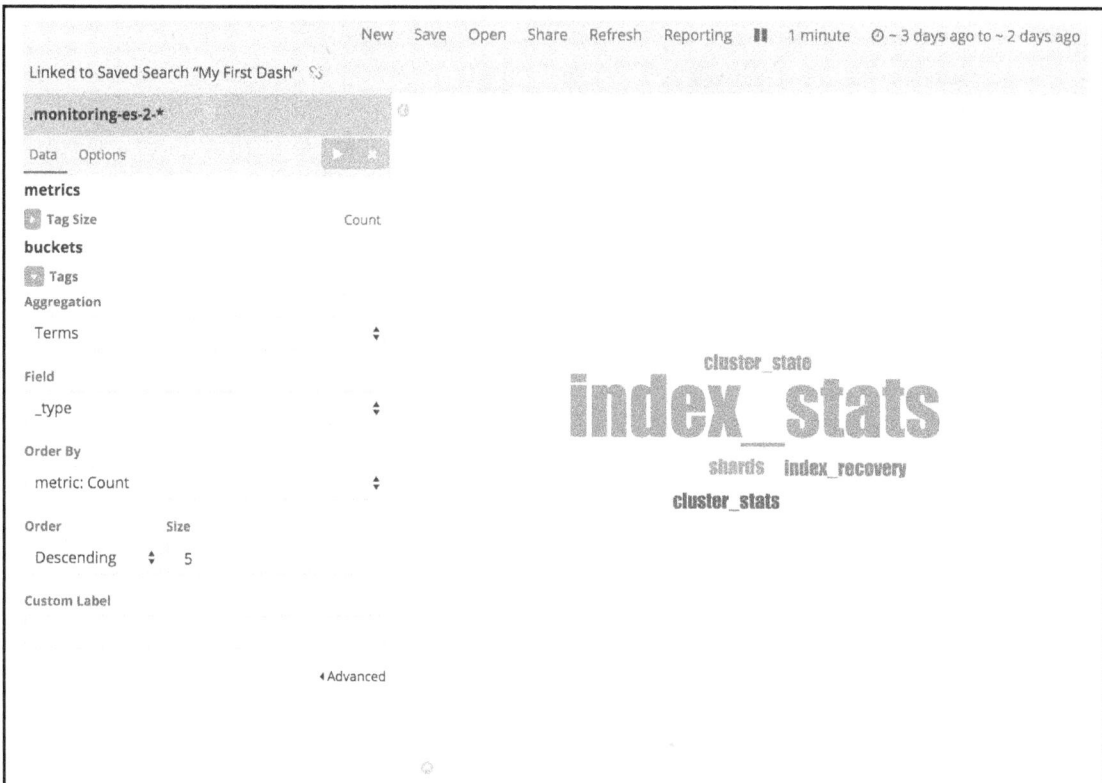

How it works...

Aggregations and searches can be grouped in the visualization widgets that can be used as building blocks for creating custom interfaces.

The built-in visualizations are as follows:

- **Area chart**: This is useful to represent stacked timelines
- **Data table**: This allows you to create a data table using aggregation results
- **Line chart**: This is useful to represent time-based hits and compare them
- **Markdown widget**: This is useful for displaying explanations or instructions for dashboards

- **Metric**: This represents a numeric metric value
- **Pie chart**: This is useful to represent low cardinality values
- **Tag cloud**: This is useful to represent term values such as tags and labels
- **Tile map**: This is useful to represent GeoPoint values
- **Time series**: This allows you to use Timelion expression language to create time series charts
- **Vertical bar chart**: This is the general purpose bar representation for histogram

After having selected a visualization, a custom form is presented on the left for allowing to populate all the required values. On the right, we have the widget representation updated in near-realtime with the result of the queries/aggregations.

After the configuration of the visualization is completed, it must be saved to be used as a widget in dashboards.

Installing Kibana plugins

As Elasticsearch, Kibana allows to be extended with plugins that can be installed to increment its functionalities.

In this recipe, we will install 3D pie chart, bars chart, and bubbles chart visualizations available at `https://github.com/aparo/3D_kibana_charts_vis`.

Getting ready

You need an up-and-running Elasticsearch installation as we described in the *Downloading and installing Elasticsearch* recipe in `Chapter 2`, *Downloading and Setup*.

You also need a functional Kibana installation as described in the *Installing Kibana and X-Pack* recipe. The X-Pack is not needed.

As the plugins that we are installing is very new, they are not packaged as binary zip, we need to install via source code using `git` and `npm` of Node.js.

How to do it…

To install a source Kibana plugin, we will perform the following steps:

1. We need to be in a shell in the `kibana/plugins` directory.
2. We fetch the source from github via following command:

   ```
   git clone https://github.com/aparo/3D_kibana_charts_vis.git
   3D_kibana_charts_vis
   ```

3. We can now build the plugin via following command:

   ```
   cd 3D_kibana_charts_vis
   npm install
   ```

4. Now, we can restart Kibana and use the new visualization widgets, which should appear in the **Visualize** section as shown in the following screenshot:

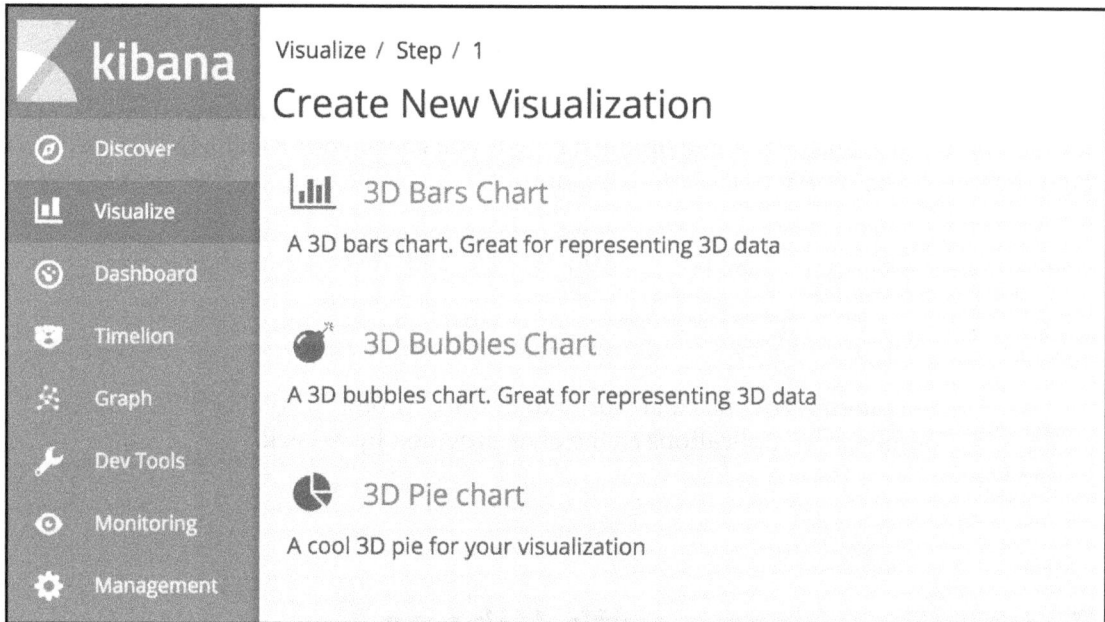

How it works...

Kibana is extendable via plugin: due to fast release of Elasticsearch 5.x and Kibana 5.x, developers are moving their plugins for Kibana 4.x to Kibana 5.x.

If there is a plugin zip package, the standard way of installing a plugin is to use the `bin/kibana-plugin install <url>` command.

In case of plugins in development, it is common to fetch the source and compile it on Kibana node or build a package zip in a development machine and then deploy it on other installations.

Like Elasticsearch, a Kibana plugin must have the same version of Kibana: in this case 5.1.1.

If you fetch a Kibana plugins code, the first step is to download all the required resources. Because Kibana is built on node.js and the plugins are mini apps, standard `npm` commands are used to execute the tasks.

`npm install` reads the `package.json` file that contains the dependencies and downloads all the required files. If needed, it compiles the code to be used.

For activating the plugin, you need to restart Kibana. The first restart can take several minutes, because Kibana does some optimization. If you check your Kibana logs at restart, you'll see something similar to the following output:

```
log   [...] [info][optimize] Optimizing and caching bundles for graph,
monitoring, kibana, timelion, login, logout and status_page. This may take
a few minutes
log   [...] [info][optimize] Optimization of bundles for graph, monitoring,
kibana, timelion, login, logout and status_page complete in 147.24 seconds
```

> Via plugins, Kibana can be used to develop/prototype platform for custom dashboards/applications as the ones provided by X-Pack.

Generating graph with Kibana

X-Pack for Elasticsearch and Kibana 5.x or above provides a graph API to discover relations in your data. The Elasticsearch graph is built in real-time, extracting relations from the indexed data.

Getting ready

You need an up-and-running Elasticsearch installation as we described in the *Downloading and installing Elasticsearch* recipe in `Chapter 2`, *Downloading and Setup*.

You also need a functional Kibana installation as described in the *Installing Kibana and X-Pack* recipe.

How to do it...

To create a custom graph view, we will perform the following steps:

1. We access the **Graph** section of Kibana as shown in the following screenshot:

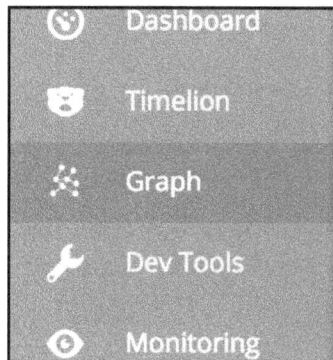

2. A graph works on an index pattern, so we need to select the one that is available to start creating our graph as shown in the following screenshot:

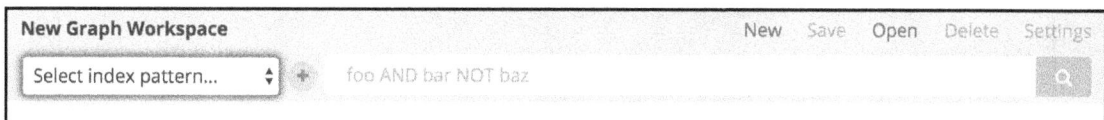

3. In an Elasticsearch graph, values in a field are our vertices: we need to select the field that contains our vertices. The field list is extracted from the index pattern as shown in the following screenshot:

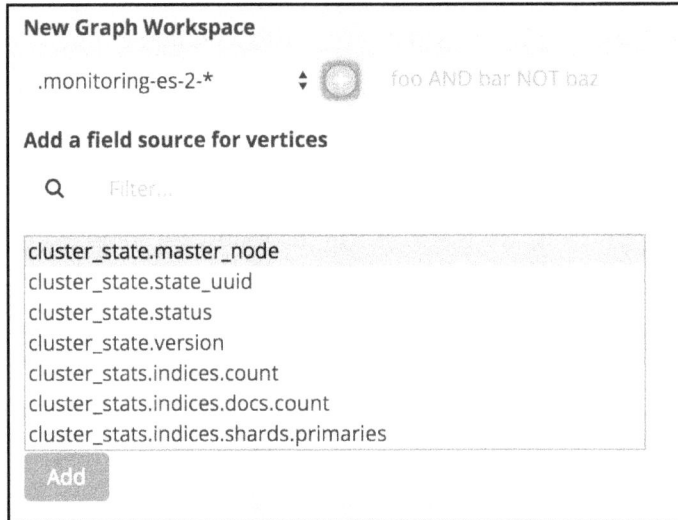

4. After having selected the field, we need to define the vertices **color/icon** and max number of terms for hop as shown in the following screenshot:

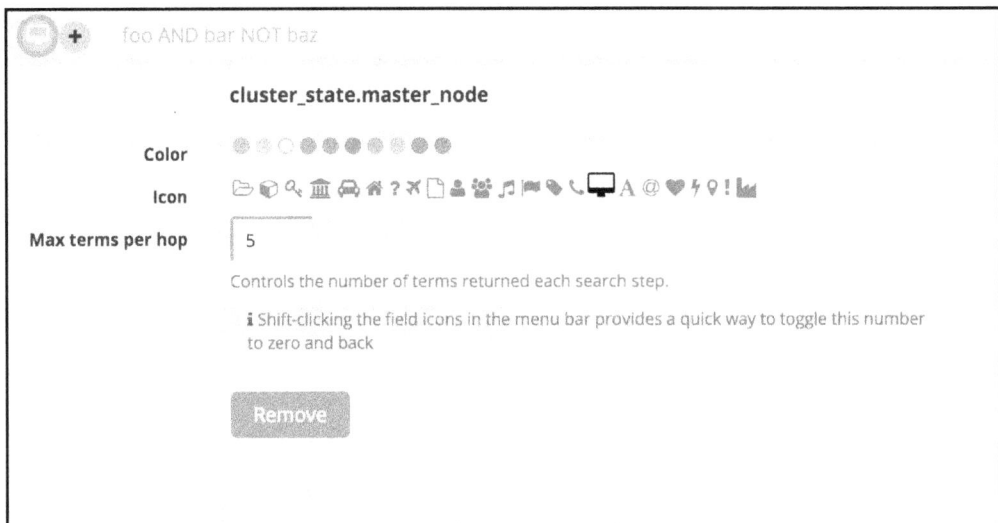

5. For showing a graph, a query must be executed. You can use * to match all the documents and press the search icon to execute it. If there are results, they are shown in the middle of the page. Clicking on a vertex menu will appear on the right providing other navigation options as shown in the following screenshot:

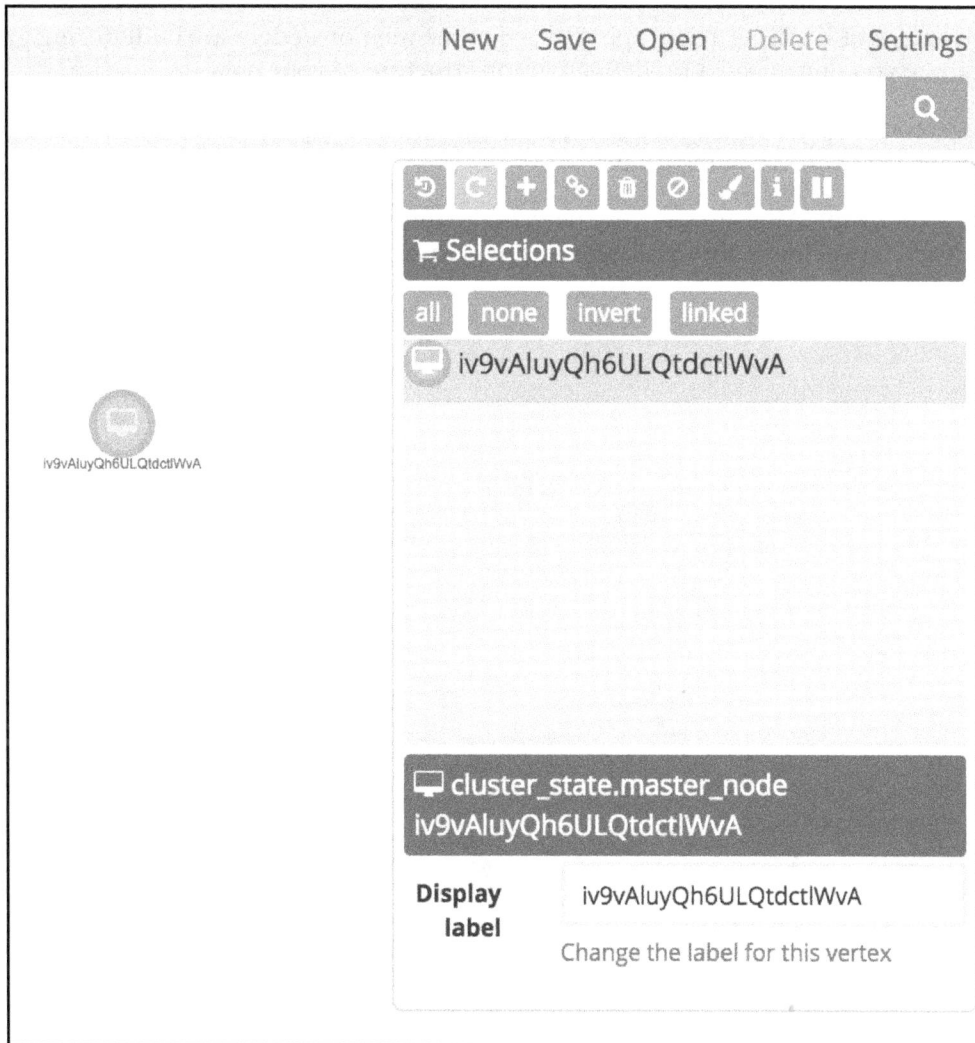

How it works...

Elasticsearch graph APIs are provided by X-Pack. The graph API allows exploring your data in a graph way. Elasticsearch is not a GraphDB datastore: it doesn't provide graph algorithms such as the shortest path or similar.

The advantage of Elasticsearch graph API is that the relations/edges are built during graph exploration: you don't need a predefined graph structure of your data.

For every node expansion, a query is executed and special aggregated values are collected to build the new vertices of the graph.

Probably, the graph APIs are still very new; in the future, they will be expanded by the Elastic team to provide more significant business cases.

13
Ingest

In this chapter, we will cover the following recipes:

- Pipeline definition
- Put an ingest pipeline
- Get an ingest pipeline
- Delete an ingest pipeline
- Simulate a pipeline
- Built-in processors
- The grok processor
- Using the ingest attachment plugin
- Using the ingest GeoIP plugin

Introduction

Elasticsearch 5.x introduces a set of powerful functionalities, targeting the problems that arise during ingestion of documents via the ingest node.

An Elasticsearch node can be master, data, or ingest.

The idea to split the ingest component from the others, is to create a more stable cluster due to problems that can arise during pre-processing documents.

To create a more stable cluster, the ingest nodes should be isolated by the master or data nodes, in the event that some problems may occur, such as a crash due to an attachment plugin and high loads due to complex type manipulation.

> The ingestion node can replace a Logstash installation in simple scenarios.

Pipeline definition

The job of ingest nodes is to pre-process the documents before sending them to the data nodes. This process is called a pipeline definition and every single step of this pipeline is a processor definition.

Getting ready

You need an up-and-running Elasticsearch installation as we described in the *Downloading and installing Elasticsearch* recipe in `Chapter 2`, *Downloading and Setup*.

How to do it…

To define an ingestion pipeline, you need to provide a description and some processors, as follows:

1. We will define a pipeline that adds a field `user` with the value, `john`:

```
{
  "description" : "Add user john field",
  "processors" : [
    {
      "set" : {
        "field": "user",
        "value": "john"
      }
    }
  ]
}
```

How it works...

The generic template representation is the following one:

```
{
  "description" : "...",
  "processors" : [ ... ],
  "version": 1,
  "on_failure" : [ ... ],

}
```

The description contains a definition of the activities done by this pipeline. It's very useful if you store a lot of pipelines in your cluster.

The processors field contains a list of processor actions. They will be executed in order.

In the preceding example, we have used a simple processor action set that allows us to set a field with a value.

The version field is optional, but it is very useful in keeping track of your pipeline versions.

The optional on_failure field allows us to define a list of processors to be applied if there are failures during normal pipeline execution.

There's more...

To prevent failure in case of missing fields or similar constrains, some processors provide the ignore_failure property.

For example, a pipeline with a `rename` field that handles the missing field should be defined in this way:

```
{
  "description" : "my pipeline with handled exceptions",
  "processors" : [
    {
      "rename" : {
        "field" : "foo",
        "target_field" : "bar",
        "ignore_failure" : true
      }
    }
  ]
}
```

Put an ingest pipeline

The power of the pipeline definition is the ability for to be updated and created without a node restart (compared to Logstash). The definition is stored in a cluster state via the put pipeline API.

After having defined a pipeline, we need to provide it to the Elasticsearch cluster.

Getting ready

You need an up-and-running Elasticsearch installation, as we described in the *Downloading and installing Elasticsearch* recipe in `Chapter 2`, *Downloading and Setup*.

To execute `curl` via the command line, you need to install `curl` for your operative system.

How to do it…

To store or update an ingestion pipeline in Elasticsearch, we will perform the following steps:

1. We can store the ingest pipeline via a `PUT` call:

```
curl -XPUT 'http://127.0.0.1:9200/_ingest/pipeline/add-user-
john' -d '{
  "description" : "Add user john field",
```

```
      "processors" : [
        {
          "set" : {
            "field": "user",
            "value": "john"
          }
        }
      ] ,
      "version":1
    }'
```

2. The result returned by Elasticsearch, if everything is okay, should be as follows:

```
{"acknowledged":true}
```

How it works...

The PUT pipeline method works both for creating a pipeline as well as updating an existing one.

The pipelines are stored in a cluster state, and they are immediately propagated to all ingest nodes. When the ingest nodes receive the new pipeline, they will update their node in-memory pipeline representation: the pipeline changes take effect immediately.

When you store a pipeline in the cluster, pay attention to provide a meaningful name to it (in the example, add-user-john) so as to easily understand what the pipeline does.

The name of the pipeline used in the put call will be the ID of the pipeline in other pipeline flows.

After having stored your pipeline in Elasticsearch, you can index a document providing the pipeline name as query argument.

For example:

```
curl -XPUT
http://localhost:9200/my_index/my_type/my_id?pipeline=add-user-john -d '{}'
```

The document will be enriched by the pipeline before being indexed.

Get an ingest pipeline

After having stored your pipeline, it is common to retrieve its content, for checking its definition. This action can be done via the get pipeline API.

Getting ready

You need an up-and-running Elasticsearch installation, as we described in the *Downloading and installing Elasticsearch* recipe in `Chapter 2`, *Downloading and Setup*.

To execute `curl` via the command line, you need to install `curl` for your operative system.

How to do it...

To retrieve an ingestion pipeline in Elasticsearch, we will perform the following steps:

1. We can retrieve the ingest pipeline via a `GET` call:

   ```
   curl -XGET 'http://127.0.0.1:9200/_ingest/pipeline/add-user-
   john'
   ```

2. The result returned by Elasticsearch, if everything is okay, should be as follows:

   ```
   {
     "add-user-john" : {
       "description" : "Add user john field",
       "processors" : [
         {
           "set" : {
             "field" : "user",
             "value" : "john"
           }
         }
       ],
       "version" : 1
     }
   }
   ```

How it works...

To retrieve an ingestion pipeline, you need its name/ID.

For each returned pipeline, all the data is returned: the source and the version if it are defined.

The GET pipeline allows us to use a wildcard in names, so you can:

- Retrieve all pipelines via *:

```
curl -XGET 'http://127.0.0.1:9200/_ingest/pipeline/*'
```

- Retrieve partial pipeline:

```
curl -XGET 'http://127.0.0.1:9200/_ingest/pipeline/add-*'
```

> In case you have a lot of pipelines, using a good name convention helps a lot in their management.

There's more...

If you need only a part of the pipeline, such as the version, you can use the filter_path to filter the pipeline only for the parts needed.

For example, using:

```
curl -XGET 'http://127.0.0.1:9200/_ingest/pipeline/add-user-john?
filter_path=*.version'
```

It will return, only the version part of the pipeline:

```
{
  "add-user-john" : {
    "version" : 1
  }
}
```

Delete an ingest pipeline

To clean up our Elasticsearch cluster for obsolete or unwanted pipelines, we need to call the delete pipeline API with the ID of the pipeline.

Getting ready

You need an up-and-running Elasticsearch installation, as we described in the *Downloading and installing Elasticsearch* recipe in `Chapter 2`, *Downloading and Setup*.

To execute `curl` via the command line, you need to install `curl` for your operative system.

How to do it...

To delete an ingestion pipeline in Elasticsearch, we will perform the following steps:

1. We can delete the ingest pipeline via a `DELETE` call:

   ```
   curl -XDELETE 'http://127.0.0.1:9200/_ingest/pipeline/add-user-
   john'
   ```

2. The result returned by Elasticsearch, if everything is okay, should be:

   ```
   {"acknowledged":true}
   ```

How it works...

The delete pipeline API removes the named pipeline from Elasticsearch.

As the pipelines are kept in memory in every node due to their cluster level storage and the pipelines are always up and running in the ingest node; it's best practice to keep only the needed pipelines in the cluster.

> The delete pipeline API does not allow using wildcards in pipeline names/IDs.

Simulate an ingest pipeline

The ingest part of every architecture is very sensitive, so the Elasticsearch team has created the possibility of simulating your pipelines without the need to store them in Elasticsearch.

The simulate pipeline API allows a user to test/improve and check functionalities of your pipeline without *deployment* in the Elasticsearch cluster.

Getting ready

You need an up-and-running Elasticsearch installation, as we described in the *Downloading and installing Elasticsearch* recipe in `Chapter 2`, *Downloading and Setup*.

To execute `curl` via the command-line, you need to install `curl` for your operative system.

How to do it...

To simulate an ingestion pipeline in Elasticsearch, we will perform the following steps:

1. We can need to execute a call passing both the pipeline and a sample subset of a document to test the pipeline against:

```
curl -XPOST 'http://127.0.0.1:9200/_ingest/pipeline/_simulate'
-d '{
  "pipeline": {
    "description": "Add user john field",
    "processors": [
      {
        "set": {
          "field": "user",
          "value": "john"
        }
      },
      {
        "set": {
          "field": "job",
          "value": 10
        }
      }
    ],
    "version": 1
  },
  "docs": [
```

```
            {
              "_index": "index",
              "_type": "type",
              "_id": "1",
              "_source": {
                "name": "docs1"
              }
            },
            {
              "_index": "index",
              "_type": "type",
              "_id": "2",
              "_source": {
                "name": "docs2"
              }
            }
          ]
        }'
```

2. The result returned by Elasticsearch, if everything okay, should be a list of documents with the pipeline processed:

```
{
  "docs" : [
    {
      "doc" : {
        "_index" : "index",
        "_id" : "1",
        "_type" : "type",
        "_source" : {
          "name" : "docs1",
          "job" : 10,
          "user" : "john"
        },
        "_ingest" : {
          "timestamp" : "2016-12-10T13:33:24.375+0000"
        }
      }
    },
    {
      "doc" : {
        "_index" : "index",
        "_id" : "2",
        "_type" : "type",
        "_source" : {
          "name" : "docs2",
          "job" : 10,
          "user" : "john"
```

```
        },
        "_ingest" : {
          "timestamp" : "2016-12-10T13:33:24.375+0000"
        }
      }
    }
  ]
}
```

How it works...

In a single call, the simulated pipeline API is able to test a pipeline on a subset of documents. It internally executes the following steps:

1. It parses the provided pipeline definition, creating an in-memory representation of the pipeline.
2. It reads the provided documents applying the pipeline.
3. It returns the processed results.

The only required sections are pipeline one and docs containing a list of documents. The documents (provided in docs) must be formatted with metadata fields and the source field, similar to a query result.

There are processors that are able to modify the metadata fields; for example, they are able to change _index or _type based on some contents. The metadata fields are _index, _type, _id, _routing, and _parent.

For debugging purposes, it is possible to add the URL query argument verbosely to return all the intermediate steps of the pipeline. For example, if we change the call of the previous simulation in:

```
curl -XPOST 'http://127.0.0.1:9200/_ingest/pipeline/_simulate?
verbose' -d '...truncated...'
```

The result will be expanded for every pipeline step:

```
{
  "docs" : [
    {
      "processor_results" : [
        {
          "doc" : {
            "_index" : "index",
            "_id" : "1",
```

```
        "_type" : "type",
        "_source" : {
          "name" : "docs1",
          "user" : "john"
        },
        "_ingest" : {
          "timestamp" : "2016-12-10T13:53:29.771+0000"
        }
      }
    },
    {
      "doc" : {
        "_index" : "index",
        "_id" : "1",
        "_type" : "type",
        "_source" : {
          "name" : "docs1",
          "job" : 10,
          "user" : "john"
        },
        "_ingest" : {
          "timestamp" : "2016-12-10T13:53:29.771+0000"
        }
      }
    }
  ]
}, ...truncated...
```

There's more...

The simulate pipeline API is very handy when a user needs to check a complex pipeline that uses special fields access, such as:

- **Ingest metadata fields**: These are special metadata fields, such as `_ingest.timestamp`, that are available during ingestion. This kind of field provides values to be added in the document; for example:

```
{
  "set": {
    "field": "received"
    "value": "{{_ingest.timestamp}}"
  }
}
```

- **Field replace templating**: Using the templating with `{{}}`, it's possible to inject other fields or join their values:

```
{
  "set": {
    "field": "full_name"
    "value": "{{name}} {{surname}}"
  }
}
```

The ingest metadata fields (accessible via `_ingest`) are as follows:

- `timestamp`: This contains the current pipeline timestamp.
- `on_failure_message`: This is available only in the `on_failure` block in case of failure. It contains the failure message.
- `on_failure_processor_type`: This is available only in the `on_failure` block in case of failure. It contains the failure processor type that has generated the failure.
- `on_failure_processor_tag`: This is available only in the `on_failure` block in case of failure. It contains the failure tag that has generated the failure.

Built-in processors

Elasticsearch provides by default a large set of ingest processors. Their number and functionalities can also change from minor versions to extended versions for new scenarios.

In this recipe, we will see the most commonly used ones.

Getting ready

You need an up-and-running Elasticsearch installation, as we described in the *Downloading and installing Elasticsearch* recipe in Chapter 2, *Downloading and Setup*.

To execute `curl` via the command-line, you need to install `curl` for your operative system.

How to do it...

To use several processors in an ingestion pipeline in Elasticsearch, we will perform the following steps:

1. We execute a simulate pipeline API call using several processors with a sample subset of a document to test the pipeline against:

```
curl -XPOST 'http://127.0.0.1:9200/_ingest/pipeline/_simulate?
pretty' -d '{
  "pipeline": {
    "description": "Testing some build-processors",
    "processors": [
      {
        "dot_expander": {
          "field": "extfield.innerfield"
        }
      },
      {
        "remove": {
          "field": "unwanted"
        }
      },
      {
        "trim": {
          "field": "message"
        }
      },
      {
        "set": {
          "field": "tokens",
          "value": "{{message}}"
        }
      },
      {
        "split": {
          "field": "tokens",
          "separator": "\\s+"
        }
      },
      {
        "sort": {
          "field": "tokens",
          "order": "desc"
        }
      },
      {
```

```
        "convert": {
          "field": "mynumbertext",
          "target_field": "mynumber",
          "type": "integer"
        }
      }
    ]
  },
  "docs": [
    {
      "_index": "index",
      "_type": "type",
      "_id": "1",
      "_source": {
        "extfield.innerfield": "booo",
        "unwanted": 32243,
        "message": "    155.2.124.3 GET /index.html 15442
        0.038   ",
        "mynumbertext": "3123"
      }
    }
  ]
}'
```

2. The result will be as follows:

```
{
  "docs" : [
    {
      "doc" : {
        "_index" : "index",
        "_type" : "type",
        "_id" : "1",
        "_source" : {
          "mynumbertext" : "3123",
          "extfield" : {
            "innerfield" : "booo"
          },
          "tokens" : [
            "GET",
            "155.2.124.3",
            "15442",
            "0.038",
            "/index.html"
          ],
          "message" : "155.2.124.3 GET /index.html 15442
          0.038",
          "mynumber" : 3123
```

```
      },
      "_ingest" : {
        "timestamp" : "2016-12-10T16:49:40.875+0000"
      }
    }
  }
 ]
}
```

How it works...

The preceding example shows how to build a complex pipeline to pre-process a document. There are a lot of built-in processors to cover the most common scenarios in log and text processing.

More complex ones can be done via scripting.

At the time of writing, Elasticsearch provides built-in pipelines the following processors:

Name	Description
Append	Appends values to a field. If required, it converts them in an array.
Convert	Converts a field value to a different type.
Date	Parses a date and uses it as a timestamp for the document.
Date Index Name	Allows us to set the _index name based on date field.
Fail	Raises a failure.
Foreach	Processes the element of an array with the provided processor.
Grok	Applies grok pattern extraction.
Gsub	Executes a regular expression replace on a field.
Join	Joins an array of values using a separator.
JSON	Convert a JSON string to a JSON object.
Lowercase	Lowercases a field.
Remove	Removes a field.
Rename	Renames a field.
Script	Allows us to execute a script.
Set	Sets the value of a field.

Split	Splits a field in an array using regular expression.
Sort	Sorts the values of an array field.
Trim	Trims whitespaces from a field.
Uppercase	Uppercases a field.
Dot expander	Expands a field with a dot in the objects.

See also

- In Chapter 17, *Plugin Development*, we will cover how to write a custom processor in Java to extend the capabilities of Elasticsearch

Grok processor

Elasticsearch provides a large number of built-in processors that increases with every release. In the preceding examples, we have seen the set and the replace ones. In this recipe, we will cover one of the most used for log analysis: the grok processor, which is well known to Logstash users.

Getting ready

You need an up-and-running Elasticsearch installation, as we described in the *Downloading and installing Elasticsearch* recipe in Chapter 2, *Downloading and Setup*.

To execute curl via the command line, you need to install curl for your operative system.

How to do it...

To test a grok pattern against some log lines, we will perform the following steps:

1. We will execute a call passing both the pipeline with our grok processor and a sample subset of a document to test the pipeline against:

```
curl -XPOST 'http://127.0.0.1:9200/_ingest/pipeline/_simulate?
pretty' -d '{
  "pipeline": {
    "description": "Testing grok pattern",
    "processors": [
      {
        "grok": {
          "field": "message",
          "patterns": [
            "%{IP:client} %{WORD:method} %
            {URIPATHPARAM:request} %{NUMBER:bytes} %
            {NUMBER:duration}"
          ]
        }
      }
    ]
  },
  "docs": [
    {
      "_index": "index",
      "_type": "type",
      "_id": "1",
      "_source": {
        "message": "155.2.124.3 GET /index.html 15442 0.038"
      }
    }
  ]
}'
```

2. The result returned by Elasticsearch, if everything is okay, should be a list of documents with the pipeline processed:

```
{
  "docs" : [
    {
      "doc" : {
        "_index" : "index",
        "_id" : "1",
        "_type" : "type",
        "_source" : {
```

```
          "duration" : "0.038",
          "request" : "/index.html",
          "method" : "GET",
          "bytes" : "15442",
          "client" : "155.2.124.3",
          "message" : "155.2.124.3 GET /index.html 15442 0.038"
        },
        "_ingest" : {
          "timestamp" : "2016-12-10T14:42:30.368+0000"
        }
      }
    }
  ]
}
```

How it works...

The grok processor allows you to extract structure fields out of a single text field in a document. A grok pattern is like a regular expression that supports aliased expressions that can be reused. It was used mainly in another Elastic software Logstash for its powerful syntax for log data extraction.

Elastisearch has a built-in of about 120 grok expressions (you can analyse them at `https://github.com/elastic/elasticsearch/tree/master/modules/ingest-common/src/main/resources/patterns`).

Defining a grok expression is quite simple, as the syntax is human readable. If we want to extract colors from an expression (pattern) and check if their value is in a subset of RED, YELLOW, and BLUE via pattern_definitions, we can define a similar processor:

```
curl -XPOST 'http://127.0.0.1:9200/_ingest/pipeline/_simulate?
pretty' -d '{
  "pipeline": {
  "description" : "custom grok pattern",
  "processors": [
    {
      "grok": {
        "field": "message",
        "patterns": ["my favorite color is %{COLOR:color}"],
        "pattern_definitions" : {
          "COLOR" : "RED|GREEN|BLUE"
        }
      }
    }
  ]
```

```
        },
      "docs":[
        {
          "_source": {
            "message": "my favorite color is RED"
          }
        },
        {
          "_source": {
            "message": "happy fail!!"
          }
        }
      ]
    }'
```

The result will be as follows:

```
{
  "docs" : [
    {
      "doc" : {
        "_index" : "_index",
        "_id" : "_id",
        "_type" : "_type",
        "_source" : {
          "message" : "my favorite color is RED",
          "color" : "RED"
        },
        "_ingest" : {
          "timestamp" : "2016-12-10T15:06:21.823+0000"
        }
      }
    },
    {
      "error" : {
        "root_cause" : [
          {
            "type" : "exception",
            "reason" : "java.lang.IllegalArgumentException:
            java.lang.IllegalArgumentException: Provided Grok
            expressions do not match field value: [happy fail!!]",
            "header" : {
              "processor_type" : "grok"
            }
          }
        ],
        "type" : "exception",
        "reason" : "java.lang.IllegalArgumentException:
```

```
        java.lang.IllegalArgumentException: Provided Grok expressions
        do not match field value: [happy fail!!]",
        "caused_by" : {
          "type" : "illegal_argument_exception",
          "reason" : "java.lang.IllegalArgumentException: Provided Grok
          expressions do not match field value: [happy fail!!]",
          "caused_by" : {
            "type" : "illegal_argument_exception",
            "reason" : "Provided Grok expressions do not match field
            value: [happy fail!!]"
          }
        },
        "header" : {
          "processor_type" : "grok"
        }
      }
    }
  ]
}
```

In real applications, the failing grok processor exceptions will prevent your document from being indexed for this reason. When you design your grok pattern be sure to test it on a large subset.

See also

- There are online sites where you can test your grok expressions, such as `http://g rokdebug.herokuapp.com` and `http://grokconstructor.appspot.com`.

Using the ingest attachment plugin

It's easy to make a cluster irresponsive in Elasticsearch prior to 5.x, using the attachment mapper. The metadata extraction from a document requires a very high CPU operation and if you are ingesting a lot of documents, your cluster is under load.

To prevent this scenario, Elasticsearch introduces the ingest node. An ingest node can be held under very high pressure without causing problems to the rest of the Elasticsearch cluster.

The attachment processor allows us to use the document extraction capabilities of Tika in an ingest node.

Getting ready

You need an up-and-running Elasticsearch installation, as we described in the *Downloading and installing Elasticsearch* recipe in `Chapter 2`, *Downloading and Setup*.

To execute `curl` via the command line, you need to install `curl` for your operative system.

How to do it...

To be able to use the ingest attachment processor, perform the following steps:

1. You need to install it as a plugin via:

   ```
   bin/elasticsearch-plugin install ingest-attachment
   ```

2. The output will be something similar to the following one:

   ```
   -> Downloading ingest-attachment from elastic
   [=================================================] 100%??
   @@@@@@@@@@@@@@@@@@@@@@@@@@@@@@@@@@@@@@@@@@@@@@@@@@@@@@@@@@@@@@@@@
   @     WARNING: plugin requires additional permissions     @
   @@@@@@@@@@@@@@@@@@@@@@@@@@@@@@@@@@@@@@@@@@@@@@@@@@@@@@@@@@@@@@@@@
   * java.lang.RuntimePermission getClassLoader
   * java.lang.reflect.ReflectPermission suppressAccessChecks
   * java.security.SecurityPermission createAccessControlContext
   * java.security.SecurityPermission insertProvider
   * java.security.SecurityPermission putProviderProperty.BC
   Continue with the installation? [y/n] y
   -> Installed ingest-attachment
   ```

   You must accept the security permissions to complete successfully the installation.

   See
   `http://docs.oracle.com/javase/8/docs/technotes/guides/security/permissions.html` for more details on the allowed permissions and the associated risks.

3. After having installed a new plugin, your node must be restarted to be able to load it. Now you can create a pipeline ingest with the attachment processor:

   ```
   curl -XPUT 'http://127.0.0.1:9200/_ingest/pipeline/attachment'
   -d '{
     "description" : "Extract data from an attachment via Tika",
     "processors" : [
   ```

```
        {
          "attachment" : {
            "field" : "data"
          }
        }
      ],
      "version":1
    }'
```

4. If everything is okay, you should receive the acknowledged:

```
{"acknowledged":true}
```

5. Now we can index a document via a pipeline:

```
curl -XPUT 'http://127.0.0.1:9200/my_index/my_type/my_id?
pipeline=attachment' -d '{
  "data":
  "e1xydGYxXGFuc2kNCkxvcmVtIGlwc3VtIGRvbG9yIHNpdCBhbW
  V0DQpccGFyIH0="
  }'
```

6. And we can recall it:

```
curl -XGET 'http://127.0.0.1:9200/my_index/my_type/my_id?
pretty'
```

7. The result will be as follows:

```
{
  "_index" : "my_index",
  "_type" : "my_type",
  "_id" : "my_id",
  "_version" : 2,
  "found" : true,
  "_source" : {
    "data" :
  "e1xydGYxXGFuc2kNCkxvcmVtIGlwc3VtIGRvbG9yIHNpdCBhbWV0DQp
  ccGFyIH0=",
    "attachment" : {
      "content_type" : "application/rtf",
      "language" : "ro",
      "content" : "Lorem ipsum dolor sit amet",
      "content_length" : 28
    }
  }
}
```

How it works...

The attachment ingest processor is provided by a separate plugin that must be installed.

After having installed it, it works like every other processor. The properties that control it are as follows:

- `field`: This is the field that will contain the base 64 representation of the binary data.
- `target_field`: This will hold the attachment information (default `attachment`).
- `indexed_char`: The number of characters to be extracted to prevent very huge fields. If it set to `-1`, all the characters are extracted (default `100000`).
- `properties`: Other metadata fields of the document that need to be extracted. They can be `content`, `title`, `name`, `author`, `keywords`, `date`, `content_type`, `content_length`, and `language` (default `all`).

Using the ingest GeoIP plugin

Another interesting processor is the GeoIP one that allows us to map an IP address to a GeoPoint and other location data.

Getting ready

You need an up-and-running Elasticsearch installation, as we described in the *Downloading and installing Elasticsearch* recipe in `Chapter 2`, *Downloading and Setup*.

To execute `curl` via the command line, you need to install `curl` for your operative system.

How to do it...

To be able to use the ingest GeoIP processor, perform the following steps:

1. You need to install it as a plugin via:

```
bin/elasticsearch-plugin install ingest-geoip
```

2. The output will be something like the following one:

```
-> Downloading ingest-geoip from elastic
[=================================================] 100%??
@@@@@@@@@@@@@@@@@@@@@@@@@@@@@@@@@@@@@@@@@@@@@@@@@@
@       WARNING: plugin requires additional permissions       @
@@@@@@@@@@@@@@@@@@@@@@@@@@@@@@@@@@@@@@@@@@@@@@@@@@
* java.lang.RuntimePermission accessDeclaredMembers
See
http://docs.oracle.com/javase/8/docs/technotes/guides/
security/permissions.html
for descriptions of what these permissions allow and the
associated risks.
Continue with the installation? [y/n] y.
-> Installed ingest-geoip
```

You must accept the security permissions to complete successfully the installation.

3. After having installed a new plugin, your node must be restarted to be able to load it.

4. Now you can create a pipeline ingest with the attachment processor:

```
curl -XPUT 'http://127.0.0.1:9200/_ingest/pipeline/geoip' -d '{
  "description" : "Extract geopoint from an IP",
  "processors" : [
     {
       "geoip" : {
         "field" : "ip"
       }
     }
  ],
  "version":1
}'
```

5. If everything is okay, you should receive the acknowledged:

```
{"acknowledged":true}
```

6. Now we can index a document via a pipeline:

```
curl -XPUT 'http://127.0.0.1:9200/my_index/my_type/my_id?
pipeline=geoip' -d '{
  "ip": "8.8.8.8"
}'
```

7. And we can recall it:

```
curl -XGET 'http://127.0.0.1:9200/my_index/my_type/my_id?
pretty'
```

8. The result will be as follows:

```
{
  "_index" : "my_index",
  "_type" : "my_type",
  "_id" : "my_id",
  "_version" : 3,
  "found" : true,
  "_source" : {
    "geoip" : {
      "continent_name" : "North America",
      "city_name" : "Mountain View",
      "country_iso_code" : "US",
      "region_name" : "California",
      "location" : {
        "lon" : -122.0838,
        "lat" : 37.386
      }
    },
    "ip" : "8.8.8.8"
  }
}
```

How it works...

The GeoIP ingest processor is provided by a separate plugin that must be installed.

It uses data from the MaxMind databases to extract information about the geographical location of IP addresses. This processor adds this information by default under the `geoip` field. The GeoIP processor can resolve both IPv4 and IPv6 addresses.

After having installed it, it works like every other processor. The properties that control it are as follows:

- `field`: This is the field that will contain the IP from which the geo data is extracted.
- `target_field`: This will hold the `geoip` information (default `geoip`).
- `database_file`: This is the database file that contains maps from `ip` to geolocations. The default one is installed during the plugin installation (default `GeoLite2-City.mmdb`).
- `properties`: The properties values depends on the database. You should refer to the database description to have details on the extracted fields (default `all`).

See also

- The official documentation about the GeoIP processor plugin and how to use it with other GeoIP2 databases can be found at `https://www.elastic.co/guide/en/elasticsearch/plugins/master/ingest-geoip.html`.

14
Java Integration

In this chapter, we will cover the following recipes:

- Creating a standard Java HTTP client
- Creating an HTTP Elasticsearch client
- Creating a native client
- Managing indices with the native client
- Managing mappings
- Managing documents
- Managing bulk actions
- Building a query
- Executing a standard search
- Executing a search with aggregations
- Executing a scroll search

Introduction

Elasticsearch functionalities can be easily integrated in any Java application in several ways, both via a REST API and native ones.

In Java it's easy to call a REST HTTP interface with one of the many of libraries available, such as the Apache HttpComponents client `http://hc.apache.org/`. In this field there's no such thing as the most used library; typically, developers choose the library that best suits their preferences or that they know very well.

Each JVM language can also use the native protocol (discussed in C) to integrate Elasticsearch with their applications.

`Chapter 1`, *Getting Started* is one of the faster protocols available to communicate with Elasticsearch due to many factors such as its binary nature, its fast native serializer or deserializer of the data, its asynchronous approach to communicating, and the hop reduction (native client nodes are able to communicate directly with the node that contains the data without executing the double hop needed in REST calls).

The main disadvantage of using native protocol is that it evolves during the development stage of the Elasticsearch life cycle and there is no guarantee of compatibility between versions.

For example, if a field of a request or a response changes, its binary serialization changes, generating incompatibilities between the client and server with different versions.

The Elasticsearch community tries not to make changes often, but in every version, some parts of Elasticsearch are improved and these changes often modify the native API call signature, thus breaking the applications.

It is recommended to use the REST API when integrating with Elasticsearch as it is much more stable across versions.

In Elasticsearch 5.x a new special REST client was delivered by the Elasticsearch team to use REST on Java. This client is managed by them and will receive more improvements in future.

In this chapter, we will see how to initialize different clients and how to execute the commands that we have seen in the previous chapters. We will not cover every call in depth, as we have already described for the REST API ones.

Elasticsearch uses the native protocol and API internally, so these are the most tested ones compared to REST calls due to unit and integration tests available in the Elasticsearch code base.

The official documentation for the native Java API is available at
`http://www.elasticsearch.org/guide/en/elasticsearch/client/java-api/current/`
but it doesn't cover all the API calls.

In many of the recipes in this chapter, the same code is executed mainly with the native client because the REST one is too-low level, and its use is like plain CURL calls as there are no helpers for now (apart from the connection management). It's up to the user to choose the best solution that covers their need.

If you want a complete suite of examples, they are available in the `src/test` directory of the source code base of Elasticsearch.

As we have already discussed in `Chapter 1`, *Getting Started*, the Elasticsearch community recommends using the REST APIs when integrating as they are more stable between releases and well-documented.

All the code presented in these recipes is available in the book code repository and can be built with Maven.

Creating a standard Java HTTP client

An HTTP client is one of the easiest clients to create. It's very handy because it allows for the calling, not only of the internal methods as the native protocol does, but also of third-party calls implemented in plugins that can be only called via HTTP.

Getting ready

You need an up-and-running Elasticsearch installation as we described in the *Downloading and installing Elasticsearch* recipe in `Chapter 2`, *Downloading and Setup*.

A Maven tool, or an IDE that natively supports it for Java programming such as Eclipse or IntelliJ IDEA, must be installed.

The code for this recipe is in the `chapter_14/http_java_client` directory.

How to do it...

For creating a HTTP client, we will perform the following steps:

1. For these examples, we have chosen the Apache HttpComponents that is one of the most widely used libraries for executing HTTP calls. This library is available in the main Maven repository `search.maven.org`. To enable the compilation in your Maven `pom.xml` project just add the following code:

```xml
<dependency>
    <groupId>org.apache.httpcomponents</groupId>
    <artifactId>httpclient</artifactId>
    <version>4.5.2</version>
</dependency>
```

2. If we want to instantiate a client and fetch a document with a `get` method the code will look like the following:

```java
import org.apache.http.*;
import org.apache.http.client.methods.CloseableHttpResponse;
import org.apache.http.client.methods.HttpGet;
import org.apache.http.impl.client.CloseableHttpClient;
import org.apache.http.impl.client.HttpClients;
import org.apache.http.util.EntityUtils;

import java.io.*;

public class App {

    private static String wsUrl = "http://127.0.0.1:9200";

    public static void main(String[] args) {
        CloseableHttpClient client = HttpClients.custom()
                .setRetryHandler(new
                MyRequestRetryHandler()).build();

        HttpGet method = new HttpGet(wsUrl+"/test-index/test-
        type/1");
        // Execute the method.

        try {
            CloseableHttpResponse response =
            client.execute(method);

            if (response.getStatusLine().getStatusCode() !=
            HttpStatus.SC_OK) {
                System.err.println("Method failed: " +
```

```
                  response.getStatusLine());
         }else{
         HttpEntity entity = response.getEntity();
         String responseBody = EntityUtils.toString(entity);
         System.out.println(responseBody);
    }

    } catch (IOException e) {
         System.err.println("Fatal transport error: " +
         e.getMessage());
         e.printStackTrace();
         } finally {
         // Release the connection.
         method.releaseConnection();
    }
  }
}
```

3. The result, if the document will be:

```
{"_index":"test-index","_type":"test-
type","_id":"1","_version":1,"exists":true, "_source" : {...}}
```

How it works...

We perform the previous steps to create and use an HTTP client:

1. The first step is to initialize the HTTP client object. In the previous code this is done via the following code:

```
CloseableHttpClient client = HttpClients.custom()
        .setRetryHandler(new MyRequestRetryHandler()).build();
```

2. Before using the client, it is a good practice to customize it; in general the client can be modified to provide extra functionalities such as retry support. Retry support is very important for designing robust applications; the IP network protocol is never 100% reliable, so it automatically retries an action if something goes bad (HTTP connection closed, server overhead, and so on).

3. In the previous code, we defined an HttpRequestRetryHandler, which monitors the execution and repeats it three times before raising an error.

4. After having set up the client we can define the method call.

3. In the previous example we want to execute the GET REST call. The used method will be for `HttpGet` and the URL will be item `index/type/id` (similar to the CURL example in the *Getting a document* recipe in `Chapter 4`, *Basic Operations*). To initialize the method, the code is:

```
HttpGet method = new HttpGet(wsUrl+"/test-index/test-type/1");
```

6. To improve the quality of our REST call it's a good practice to add extra controls to the method, such as authentication and custom headers.

7. The Elasticsearch server by default doesn't require authentication, so we need to provide some security layer at the top of our architecture.

8. A typical scenario is using your HTTP client with the search guard plugin (`https://github.com/floragunncom/search-guard`) or the shield plugin, which is part of X-Pack (`https://www.elastic.co/products/x-pack`) which allows the Elasticsearch REST to be extended with authentication and SSL. After one of these plugins is installed and configured on the server, the following code adds a host entry that allows the credentials to be provided only if context calls are targeting that host.

9. The authentication is simply `basicAuth`, but works very well for non-complex deployments:

```
HttpHost targetHost = new HttpHost("localhost", 9200, "http");
CredentialsProvider credsProvider = new
BasicCredentialsProvider();
credsProvider.setCredentials(
new AuthScope(targetHost.getHostName(), targetHost.getPort()),
new UsernamePasswordCredentials("username", "password"));

// Create AuthCache instance
AuthCache authCache = new BasicAuthCache();
// Generate BASIC scheme object and add it to local auth cache
BasicScheme basicAuth = new BasicScheme();
authCache.put(targetHost, basicAuth);

// Add AuthCache to the execution context
HttpClientContext context = HttpClientContext.create();
context.setCredentialsProvider(credsProvider);
```

9. The create `context` must be used in executing the call:

```
response = client.execute(method, context);
```

10. Custom headers allow for passing extra information to the server for executing a call. Some examples could be API keys, or hints about supported formats.

11. A typical example is using `gzip` data compression over HTTP to reduce bandwidth usage. To do that, we can add a custom header to the call informing the server that our client accepts encoding: `Accept-Encoding, gzip`:

```
request.addHeader("Accept-Encoding", "gzip");
```

12. After configuring the call with all the parameters, we can fire up the request:

```
response = client.execute(method, context);
```

13. Every response object must be validated on its return status: if the call is OK, the return status should be 200. In the previous code the check is done in the `if` statement:

```
if (response.getStatusLine().getStatusCode() !=
HttpStatus.SC_OK)
```

14. If the call was OK and the status code of the response is 200, we can read the answer:

```
HttpEntity entity = response.getEntity();
        String responseBody = EntityUtils.toString(entity);
```

The response is wrapped in `HttpEntity`, which is a stream.

The HTTP client library provides a helper method `EntityUtils.toString` that reads all the content of `HttpEntity` as a string. Otherwise we'd need to create some code to read from the string and build the string.

Obviously, all the read parts of the call are wrapped in a `try-catch` block to collect all possible errors due to networking errors.

See also

- The Apache HttpComponents at `http://hc.apache.org/` for a complete reference and more examples about this library

- The search guard plugin to provide authenticated Elasticsearch access at `https://github.com/floragunncom/search-guard` or the Elasticsearch official shield plugin at `https://www.elastic.co/products/x-pack`
- The *Using HTTP protocol* recipe in `Chapter 1`, *Getting Started* describes the advantages of the HTTP protocol for communicating with Elasticsearch
- The *Getting a document* recipe in `Chapter 4`, *Basic Operations* covers the API call used in these examples

Creating an HTTP Elasticsearch client

With Elasticsearch 5.x, the Elasticsearch team has provided a custom low-level HTTP client to communicate with Elasticsearch. Its main features are as follows:

- Minimal dependencies
- Load balancing across all available nodes
- Failover in the case of node failures and upon specific response codes
- Failed connection penalization (whether a failed node is retried depends on how many consecutive times it failed; the more failed attempts, the longer the client will wait before trying that same node again)
- Persistent connections
- Trace logging of requests and responses
- Optional automatic discovery of cluster nodes

Getting ready

You need an up-and-running Elasticsearch installation as we described in the *Downloading and installing Elasticsearch* recipe in `Chapter 2`, *Downloading and Setup*.

A Maven tool, or an IDE that natively supports it for Java programming such as Eclipse or IntelliJ IDEA, must be installed.

The code for this recipe is in the `chapter_14/http_es_client` directory.

How to do it...

For creating `RestClient`, we will perform the following steps:

1. For these examples, we need to add the Elasticsearch HTTP client library used to execute HTTP calls. This library is available in the main Maven repository `search.maven.org`. To enable compilation in your `Maven pom.xml` project just add the following code:

   ```
   <dependency>
       <groupId>org.elasticsearch.client</groupId>
       <artifactId>rest</artifactId>
       <version>5.0.0</version>
   </dependency>
   ```

2. If we want to instantiate a client and fetch a document with a `get` method, the code will look like the following:

   ```
   package com.packtpub;

   import org.apache.http.HttpEntity;
   import org.apache.http.HttpHost;
   import org.apache.http.HttpStatus;
   import org.apache.http.util.EntityUtils;
   import org.elasticsearch.client.Response;
   import org.elasticsearch.client.RestClient;

   import java.io.IOException;

   public class App {

       public static void main(String[] args) {
           RestClient client = RestClient.builder(
               new HttpHost("localhost", 9200, "http")).build();

           try {
               Response response = client.performRequest("GET",
               "/test-index/test-type/1");

               if (response.getStatusLine().getStatusCode() !=
               HttpStatus.SC_OK) {
                   System.err.println("Method failed: " +
                   response.getStatusLine());
               } else {
               HttpEntity entity = response.getEntity();
               String responseBody = EntityUtils.toString(entity);
               System.out.println(responseBody);
   ```

```
            }

        } catch (IOException e) {
            System.err.println("Fatal transport error: " +
            e.getMessage());
            e.printStackTrace();
        } finally {
            // Release the connection.
            try {
                client.close();
            } catch (IOException e) {
                e.printStackTrace();
            }
        }
    }
}
```

3. The result, if the document will be:

```
{"_index":"test-index","_type":"test-
type","_id":"1","_version":1,"exists":true, "_source" : {...}}
```

How it works...

Internally the Elasticseach `RestClient` uses Apache HttpComponents and wraps it with more convenient methods.

We perform the previous steps to create and use a `RestClient`:

1. The first step is to initialize the `RestClient` object.
2. In the previous code this is done via the following code:

```
RestClient client = RestClient.builder(
        new HttpHost("localhost", 9200, "http")).build();
```

3. The `builder` method accepts a multi-value `HttpHost` (in this way you can pass a list of HTTP addresses) and returns `RestClientBuilder` under the hood.
4. `RestClientBuilder` allows client communication to be customized by several methods such as:
   - `setDefaultHeaders(Header[] defaultHeaders)`: This allows the custom headers that must be sent for every request to be provided.

- `setMaxRetryTimeoutMillis(int maxRetryTimeoutMillis)`: This allows the max retry timeout to be defined if there are multiple attempts for the same request.
- `setPathPrefix(String pathPrefix)`: This allows a custom path prefix to be defined for every request.
- `setFailureListener(FailureListener failureListener)`: This allows a custom failure listener to be provided, which is called in an instance of node failure. This can be used to provide user defined behavior in the case of node failure.
- `setHttpClientConfigCallback(RestClientBuilder.HttpClientConfigCallback httpClientConfigCallback)`: This allows modification to the HTTP client communication, such as adding compression or an encryption layer.
- `setRequestConfigCallback(RestClientBuilder.RequestConfigCallback requestConfigCallback)`: This allows the configuration of request authentications, timeout, and other properties that can be set a request level.

4. After having created the `RestClient`, we can execute some requests against it via the several `performRequest` for synchronous calls and `performRequestAsync` methods for asynchronous ones.

5. These methods allow the setting of parameters such as:

    - `String method`: This is theHTTP method or verb to be used in the call (required)
    - `String endpoint`: This is the API endpoint (required). In the previous example, it is `/test-index/test-type/1`
    - `Map<String, String> params`: This is a map of values to be passed as query parameters
    - `HttpEntity entity`: This is the body of the request. It's a `org/apache/http/HttpEntity` (http://hc.apache.org/httpcomponents-core-ga/httpcore/apidocs/org/apache/http/HttpEntity.html?is-external=true)
    - `HttpAsyncResponseConsumer<HttpResponse> responseConsumer`: This is used to manage responses in an asynchronous request (http://hc.apache.org/httpcomponents-core-ga/httpcore-nio/apidocs/org/apache/http/nio/protocol/HttpAsyncResponseConsumer.html). By default, it's used to keep all the responses in heap memory (the top memory limit is 100Mb)

- ResponseListener responseListener: This is used to register callbacks during asynchronous calls
- Header... headers: They are additional headers passed during the call

4. In the previous example, we have executed the GET REST call with the following code:

```
Response response = client.performRequest("GET", "/test-
index/test-type/1");
```

8. The response object is an org.elasticsearch.client.Response that wraps the Apache HttpComponents response one: for this reason, the code to manage the response is the same as the previous recipe.

> The RestClient is a low level one; it has no helpers on build queries or actions. For now, using it consists of building the JSON string of the request and then parsing the JSON response string.

See also

- The official documentation about the RestClient at https://www.elastic.co/guide/en/elasticsearch/client/java-rest/current/index.html for more usage examples and more about the Sniffer extension at https://www.elastic.co/guide/en/elasticsearch/client/java-rest/current/sniffer.html to support node discovery
- The Apache HttpComponents at http://hc.apache.org/ for a complete reference and more examples about this library
- The *Using HTTP protocol recipe* in Chapter 1, *Getting Started* that describes the advantages of HTTP protocol for communicating with Elasticsearch
- The *Getting a document recipe* in Chapter 4, *Basic Operations* that covers the API call used in these examples

Creating a native client

There are two ways to create a native client to communicate with an Elasticsearch server:

- Creating a transport client: This is a standard client that requires the address and port of nodes to connect to.
- Creating a client or coordinating only one node (it's a node that is not a data, master, or ingest node) and get the client from it. This node will appear in the cluster state nodes and can use the discovery capabilities of Elasticsearch to join the cluster (so no node address is required to connect to a cluster). This kind of client can reduce node routing due to knowledge of cluster topology. It can also load Elasticsearch plugins.

In this recipe, we will see how to create these clients.

Getting ready

You need an up-and-running Elasticsearch installation as we described in the *Downloading and installing Elasticsearch* recipe in `Chapter 2`, *Downloading and Setup*

A Maven tool, or an IDE that natively supports it for Java programming such as Eclipse or IntelliJ IDEA, must be installed

The code for this recipe is in the `chapter_14/nativeclient` directory.

How to do it...

To create a native client, we will perform the following steps:

1. Before starting, we must be sure that Maven loads the Elasticsearch JAR and the `log4j` required dependencies, by adding the following lines to the `pom.xml`:

```
<dependency>
    <groupId>org.elasticsearch.client</groupId>
    <artifactId>transport</artifactId>
    <version>5.0.0</version>
</dependency>
<dependency>
    <groupId>org.apache.logging.log4j</groupId>
    <artifactId>log4j-api</artifactId>
    <version>2.6.2</version>
</dependency>
```

```
<dependency>
    <groupId>org.apache.logging.log4j</groupId>
    <artifactId>log4j-core</artifactId>
    <version>2.6.2</version>
</dependency>
```

I always suggest using the latest available release of Elasticsearch or, in the case of a connection to a specific cluster, using the same version of Elasticsearch as the cluster is using.
Native clients only work well if the client and the server have the same Elasticsearch version.

2. We need to configure the logging by adding (as a resource) the `log4j2.properties` file with a similar content:

```
appender.console.type = Console
appender.console.name = console
appender.console.layout.type = PatternLayout

rootLogger.level = info
rootLogger.appenderRef.console.ref = console
```

3. Now, to create a client, we have two ways:

Getting the client from the transport protocol, which is the simplest way to get an Elasticsearch client:

```
import org.elasticsearch.client.Client;
import org.elasticsearch.client.transport.TransportClient;
import org.elasticsearch.common.settings.Settings;
import
org.elasticsearch.common.transport.InetSocketTransportAddress;
import
org.elasticsearch.transport.client.PreBuiltTransportClient;

// on startup
final Settings settings = Settings.builder()
    .put("client.transport.sniff", true)
    .put("cluster.name", "elasticsearch").build();
TransportClient client = new PreBuiltTransportClient(settings)
    .addTransportAddress(new
InetSocketTransportAddress(InetAddress.getByName("127.0.0.1"),
9300));

// on shutdown
client.close();
```

Getting the client from a node, which is quite tricky, because we need to define a `PluginNode` that loads the transport plugin and retrieve a connection from it:

```
import org.elasticsearch.client.Client;
import org.elasticsearch.common.settings.Settings;
import org.elasticsearch.node.Node;

// on startup
private final Node node;
private final Client client;

private static class PluginNode extends Node {
    public PluginNode(Settings preparedSettings, List<Class<?
    extends Plugin>> plugins) {
super(InternalSettingsPreparer.prepareEnvironment
(preparedSettings, null), plugins);
    }
}

public NativeClient() throws NodeValidationException {
    final Settings settings = Settings.builder()
            .put("path.home", "/tmp")
            .put("client.transport.sniff", true)
            .put("cluster.name", "elasticsearch")
            .put("node.data", false)
            .put("node.master", false)
            .put("node.ingest", false).build();

    node = new PluginNode(settings, Collections.<Class<?
    extends Plugin>>singletonList(Netty4Plugin.class));
    node.start();
    client = node.client();
}

// on shutdown
client.close();
node.close();
```

How it works...

The steps to create a `TransportClient` are as follows:

1. Create the settings required to configure the client. Typically, they hold the cluster name and some other options that we'll discuss later:

```
final Settings settings = Settings.settingsBuilder()
                .put("client.transport.sniff", true)
                .put("cluster.name", "elasticsearch").build();
```

2. Now we can create the client by passing it the settings, addresses, and port of our cluster:

```
TransportClient client = new PreBuiltTransportClient(settings)
    .addTransportAddress(new
InetSocketTransportAddress(InetAddress.getByName("127.0.0.1"),
9300));
;
```

3. The `addTransportAddress` method can be called several times until all the required addresses and ports are set.

> The `TransportClient` method is the simplest way to create a native connection to an Elasticsearch server.

4. Creating a node client is more complex as the new node becomes part of the cluster and we need to perform some tricks to load the transport plugin required for communication.

5. In your Maven `pom.xml` the transport plugin must be defined as follows:

```
<dependency>
  <groupId>org.elasticsearch.plugin</groupId>
  <artifactId>transport-netty4-client</artifactId>
  <version>5.0.0</version>
</dependency>
```

6. The standard node class doesn't have helpers for creating an Elasticsearch node with plugins, so we need a class helper `PluginNode`, which allows the transport plugin to be loaded:

```
private static class PluginNode extends Node {
    public PluginNode(Settings preparedSettings, List<Class<?
```

```
        extends Plugin>> plugins) {
        super(InternalSettingsPreparer.prepareEnvironment
        (preparedSettings, null), plugins);
        }
    }
```

7. Now we can define the settings needed to initialize `node`. We need to disable the master, data, and ingest functionalities:

```
final Settings settings = Settings.builder()
        .put("path.home", "/tmp")
        .put("client.transport.sniff", true)
        .put("cluster.name", "elasticsearch")
        .put("node.data", false)
        .put("node.master", false)
        .put("node.ingest", false).build();
```

8. After having defined the settings, we can build (by passing the transport plugin) and start our `node`:

```
node = new PluginNode(settings, Collections.<Class<? extends
Plugin>>singletonList(Netty4Plugin.class));
node.start();
```

9. From the `node` object, `client` can be easily obtained:

```
client = node.client();
```

10. If `client` is retrieved from an embedded node, before closing the application, we need to free the resource needed by the node; this can be done by calling the `close()` method on the `client` and `node`:

```
client.close();
node.close();
```

The result is the same with both approaches to creating a native client–a working client allows the execution of native calls on an Elasticsearch server.

In both approaches, it is important to correctly define the name of the cluster, otherwise there are problems in node-joining or the transport client gives you a warning about invalid names.

There's more...

There are several settings that can be passed when creating a transport client. They are as follows:

- `client.transport.ignore_cluster_name`: If you set it to `true`, the cluster name validation of connected nodes is ignored. This prevents a warning being printed if the client cluster name is different from the connected cluster name (default: `false`).
- `client.transport.ping_timeout`: Every client pings the node to check its state. This value defines how much time it waits before a timeout (default: `5s`).
- `client.transport.nodes_sampler_interval`: This interval defines how often to sample/ping the nodes listed and connected. These pings reduce the failures if a node is down and allows the requests to be balanced with the available node (default: `5s`).

See also

- The *Using the native protocol* recipe in `Chapter 1`, *Getting Started* for information on the native protocol
- The official Elasticsearch documentation about `TransportClient` at `https://www.elastic.co/guide/en/elasticsearch/client/java-api/current/transport-client.html` for more details about it

Managing indices with the native client

In the previous recipe, we saw how to initialize a client to send calls to an Elasticsearch cluster. In this recipe, we will see how to manage indices via client calls.

Getting ready

You need an up-and-running Elasticsearch installation as we described in the *Downloading and installing Elasticsearch* recipe in `Chapter 2`, *Downloading and Setup*.

A Maven tool, or an IDE that natively supports it for Java programming such as Eclipse or IntelliJ IDEA, must be installed.

The code for this recipe is in the `chapter_14/nativeclient` directory and the referred class is `IndicesOperations`.

How to do it...

An Elasticsearch client maps all index operations under the `admin.indices` object of the client. All the indices operation are here (`create`, `delete`, `exists`, `open`, `close`, `optimize`, and so on).

The following code retrieves a client and executes the main operations on indices:

1. We import the required classes:

```
import
org.elasticsearch.action.admin.indices.exists.indices
.IndicesExistsResponse;
import org.elasticsearch.client.Client;
```

2. We define an `IndicesOperations` class that manages the index operations:

```
public class IndicesOperations {
    private final Client client;

    public IndicesOperations(Client client) {
        this.client = client;
    }
```

3. We define a function used to check the index's existence:

```
public boolean checkIndexExists(String name){
    IndicesExistsResponse
response=client.admin().indices().prepareExists(name).execute()
.actionGet();
    return response.isExists();
}
```

4. We define a function used to create an index:

```
public void createIndex(String name){
  client.admin().indices().prepareCreate(name).execute()
.actionGet();
}
```

5. We define a function used to delete an index:

```
public void deleteIndex(String name){
client.admin().indices().prepareDelete(name).execute()
.actionGet();
}
```

6. We define a function used to close an index:

```
public void closeIndex(String name){
client.admin().indices().prepareClose(name).execute()
.actionGet();
}
```

7. We define a function used to open an index:

```
public void openIndex(String name){
client.admin().indices().prepareOpen(name).execute()
.actionGet();
}
```

8. We test all the previously defined functions:

```
public static void main( String[] args ) throws
InterruptedException, IOException, NodeValidationException {
NativeClient nativeClient=new NativeClient();
Client client =nativeClient.getClient();
IndicesOperations io=new IndicesOperations(client);
String myIndex = "test";
if(io.checkIndexExists(myIndex))
    io.deleteIndex(myIndex);
io.createIndex(myIndex);
Thread.sleep(1000);
io.closeIndex(myIndex);
io.openIndex(myIndex);
io.deleteIndex(myIndex);

//we need to close the client to free resources
nativeClient.close();
}
```

How it works...

Before executing every index operation, a client must be available (we saw how to create one in the previous recipe).

The client has a lot of methods grouped by functionalities:

- In the root `client.*` we have record operations such as index, deletion of records, search, and update
- Under `admin.indices.*` we have index related methods, such as create index, delete index, and so on
- Under `admin.cluster.*`, we have cluster-related methods, such as state and health

Client methods usually follow some conventions:

- Methods starting with `prepare*` (that is `prepareCreate`) returns a request builder that can be executed with the `execute` method
- Methods that starts with a verb (that is `create`) require a build request and optional some action listener

After building the request, it can be executed with an `actionGet` that can receive an optional timeout, and a response is returned.

In the previous example, we have several index calls:

- Checking the existence, the method call is `prepareExists` and returns an `IndicesExistsResponse` object, which contains information about whether the index exists or not:

```
IndicesExistsResponse
response=client.admin().indices().prepareExists(name).execute()
.actionGet();
        return response.isExists();
```

- Creating an index, with the `prepareCreate` call:

```
client.admin().indices().prepareCreate(name).execute()
.actionGet();
```

- Closing an index, with the `prepareClose` call:

```
client.admin().indices().prepareClose(name).execute()
.actionGet();
```

- Opening an index, with the `prepareOpen` call:

```
client.admin().indices().prepareOpen(name).execute()
.actionGet();
```

- Deleting an index with the `prepareDelete` call:

```
client.admin().indices().prepareDelete(name).execute()
.actionGet();
```

> We have put a delay of 1 second (`Thread.wait(1000)`) in the code to prevent fast actions on indices, because their shard allocations are asynchronous and they require some milliseconds to be ready. The best practice is not to use a similar hack, but to poll an index's state before perform further operations, and only performing those operations when it goes green.

See also

- The *Creating an index* recipe in `Chapter 4`, *Basic Operations* for details on index creation
- The *Deleting an index* recipe in `Chapter 4`, *Basic Operations* for details on index deletion
- The *Opening/closing an index* recipe in `Chapter 4`, *Basic Operations* for the description of opening/closing index APIs

Managing mappings

After creating an index the next step is to add some mappings to it. We have already seen how to put a mapping via the REST API in `Chapter 4`, *Basic Operations*. In this recipe, we will see how to manage mappings via a native client.

Getting ready

You need an up-and-running Elasticsearch installation as we described in the *Downloading and installing Elasticsearch* recipe in `Chapter 2`, *Downloading and Setup*.

A Maven tool, or an IDE that natively supports it for Java programming such as Eclipse or IntelliJ IDEA, must be installed.

The code for this recipe is in the `chapter_14/nativeclient` directory and the referred class is `MappingOperations`.

How to do it...

In the following code, we add a `mytype` mapping to a `myindex` index via the native client:

1. We import the required classes:

    ```
    import org.elasticsearch.action.admin.indices.mapping.put
    .PutMappingResponse;
    import org.elasticsearch.client.Client;
    import org.elasticsearch.common.xcontent.XContentBuilder;

    import java.io.IOException;

    import static org.elasticsearch.common.xcontent.XContentFactory
    .jsonBuilder;
    ```

2. We define a class to contain our code and to initialize `client` and `index`:

    ```
    public class MappingOperations {

        public static void main( String[] args ) throws
        UnknownHostException
        {
            String index="mytest";
            String type="mytype";
            Client client =NativeClient.createTransportClient();
            IndicesOperations io=new IndicesOperations(client);
            if(io.checkIndexExists(index))
                io.deleteIndex(index);
            io.createIndex(index);
    ```

3. We prepare the JSON mapping to put in index:

    ```
    XContentBuilder builder = null; try { builder = jsonBuilder().
    startObject(). field("type1"). startObject().
    field("properties"). startObject(). field("nested1").
    startObject(). field("type"). value("nested").
    endObject().endObject().endObject(). endObject();
    ```

3. We put the mapping in `index`:

    ```
    PutMappingResponse
        response=client.admin().indices().preparePutMapping(index)
        .setType(type).setSource(builder).execute().actionGet();
                if(!response.isAcknowledged()){
                    System.out.println("Something strange happens");
                }
    ```

```
                    } catch (IOException e) {
                        ex.printStackTrace();
                        System.out.println("Unable to create mapping");
                    }
```

6. We remove `index` as follows:

```
        io.deleteIndex(index);
```

7. Now we can close the client to free up resources:

```
    //we need to close the client to free resources
    client.close();
    } }
```

How it works...

Before executing a mapping operation, a client must be available and the index must be created.

In the previous example, if the index exists, it's deleted and a new one is recreated, so we are sure to start from scratch:

```
Client client =NativeClient.createTransportClient();
IndicesOperations io=new IndicesOperations(client);
if(io.checkIndexExists(index)) io.deleteIndex(index);
io.createIndex(index);
```

Now we have a fresh `index` to put the mapping we need to create it. The mapping, as with every standard object in Elasticsearch, is a JSON object. Elasticsearch provides a convenient way to create JSON programmatically via `XContentBuilder.jsonBuilder`.

To use this, you need to add these imports to your Java file:

```
import org.elasticsearch.common.xcontent.XContentBuilder;
import static
org.elasticsearch.common.xcontent.XContentFactory.jsonBuilder;
```

The `XContentBuilder.jsonBuilder` method allows JSON to be built programmatically, as it's the Swiss Army Knife of JSON generation in Elasticsearch, due to its ability to being chained, and it has a lot of methods. These methods always return a builder so they can be easily chained. The most important ones are as follows:

- `startObject()` and `startObject(name)`, where the name is the name of the JSON object. It starts the definition of a JSON object. The object must be closed with an `endObject()`.
- `field(name)` or `field(name, value)`: The name must always be a string, and the value must be a valid value that can be converted to JSON. It's used to define a field in a JSON object.
- `value(value)`: The value must be a valid value that can be converted to JSON. It defines a single value in a field.
- `startArray ()` and `startArray(name)`, where name is the name of the JSON array. It starts the definition of a JSON array and must be ended with an `endArray()`.

Generally, in Elasticsearch every method that accepts a JSON object as parameter also accepts a JSON builder.

Now that we have the mapping in the builder we need to call the `Put` mapping API. This API is in the `client.admin().indices()` namespace and you need to define the index, the type and the mapping to execute this call:

```
PutMappingResponse
response=client.admin().indices().preparePutMapping(index).setType(type).se
tSource(builder).execute().actionGet();
```

If everything is okay, you can check the status in the `response.isAcknowledged()` that must be `true` (Boolean). Otherwise an error is raised.

If you need to update a mapping, you need to execute the same call, but in the mapping put only the fields that you need to add.

There's more...

There is another important call used to manage the mapping–the `Get` Mapping API. The call is like delete and returns a `GetMappingResponse`:

```
GetMappingResponse
response=client.admin().indices().prepareGetMapping(index).setType(type).ex
ecute().actionGet();
```

The `response` contains the mapping information. The data returned is structured as in an index map; it contains mapping mapped as name and `MappingMetaData`.

`MappingMetaData` is an object that contains all the mapping information and all the sections that we discussed in `Chapter 4`, *Basic Operations*.

See also

- The *Putting a mapping in an index* recipe in `Chapter 4`, *Basic Operations* for more details about the `Put` mapping API.
- The *Getting a mapping* recipe in `Chapter 4`, *Basic Operations* for more details about the `Get` mapping API.

Managing documents

The native APIs for managing documents (index, delete, and update) are the most important after the search APIs. In this recipe, we will see how to use them. In the next recipe, we will proceed to bulk actions to improve performances.

Getting ready

You need an up-and-running Elasticsearch installation as we described in the *Downloading and installing Elasticsearch* recipe in `Chapter 2`, *Downloading and Setup*.

A Maven tool, or an IDE that natively supports it for Java programming such as Eclipse or IntelliJ IDEA, must be installed.

The code for this recipe is in the `chapter_14/nativeclient` directory and the referred class is `DocumentOperations`.

How to do it…

For managing documents, we will perform the following steps:

1. We'll need to import the required classes to execute all the document CRUD operations via the native client:

```
import org.elasticsearch.action.delete.DeleteResponse;
import org.elasticsearch.action.get.GetResponse;
import org.elasticsearch.action.index.IndexResponse;
import org.elasticsearch.action.update.UpdateResponse;
import org.elasticsearch.client.Client;
import org.elasticsearch.common.xcontent.XContentFactory;
import org.elasticsearch.script.Script;

import java.io.IOException;
import java.net.UnknownHostException;
```

2. We create the client and will remove the index that contains our data if it exists:

```
public class DocumentOperations {

    public static void main(String[] args) throws
    UnknownHostException {
        String index = "mytest";
        String type = "mytype";
        Client client = NativeClient.createTransportClient();
        IndicesOperations io = new IndicesOperations(client);
        if (io.checkIndexExists(index))
            io.deleteIndex(index);
```

3. We will call the create `index` by providing the required mapping:

```
try {
    client.admin().indices().prepareCreate(index)
        .addMapping(type, XContentFactory.jsonBuilder()
            .startObject()
            .startObject(type)
            .startObject("properties")
            .startObject("text").field("type",
            "text").field("store", "yes").endObject()
            .endObject()
            .endObject()
            .endObject())
        .execute().actionGet();
} catch (IOException e) {
 System.out.println("Unable to create mapping");
}
```

4. Now, we can store a document in Elasticsearch via the `prepareIndex` call:

```
IndexResponse ir = client.prepareIndex(index, type,
"2").setSource("text", "unicorn").execute().actionGet();
System.out.println("Version: " + ir.getVersion());
```

5. We can retrieve the stored document via the `prepareGet` call:

```
GetResponse gr = client.prepareGet(index, type,
"2").execute().actionGet();
System.out.println("Version: " + gr.getVersion());
```

6. We can update the stored document via the `prepareUpdate` call using a script in
   `painless`:

```
UpdateResponse ur = client.prepareUpdate(index, type,
"2").setScript(new Script("ctx._source.text =
'v2'")).execute().actionGet();
System.out.println("Version: " + ur.getVersion());
```

7. We can delete the stored document via the `prepareDelete` call:

```
DeleteResponse dr = client.prepareDelete(index, type,
"2").execute().actionGet();
```

8. We can now free up the resources used:

```
io.deleteIndex(index);
//we need to close the client to free resources
client.close();
 }
}
```

9. The console output result will be:

```
no modules loaded
loaded plugin [org.elasticsearch.index.reindex.ReindexPlugin]
loaded plugin [org.elasticsearch.percolator.PercolatorPlugin]
loaded plugin
[org.elasticsearch.script.mustache.MustachePlugin]
loaded plugin [org.elasticsearch.transport.Netty3Plugin]
loaded plugin [org.elasticsearch.transport.Netty4Plugin]
Version: 1
Version: 1
Version: 2
```

10. The document version, after an update action and if the document is re-indexed with new changes, is always incremented by 1.

How it works...

Before executing a document action, a client and the index must be available and document mapping should be created (the mapping is optional, because it can be inferred from the indexed document).

To index a document via the native client, the `prepareIndex` method is created. It requires the index and the type as arguments. If an ID is provided, it will be used; otherwise a new one will be created.

In the previous example, we put the source in the form of a key, value, but many forms are available to pass as source. They are:

- A JSON string `{"field": "value"}`
- A string and a value (from 1 up to 4 couples): `field1, value1, field2, value2, field3, value3, field4, value4`
- A builder `jsonBuilder().startObject().field(field,value).endObject()`
- A byte arrays

Obviously, it's possible to add all the parameters that we looked at in the *Indexing a Document* recipe in `Chapter 4`, *Basic Operations*, such as parent, routing, and so on. In the previous example, the call was:

```
IndexResponse ir=client.prepareIndex(index, type, "2").setSource("text",
"unicorn").execute().actionGet();
```

The `IndexReponse` return value can be used in several ways:

- Checking if the index was successfully
- Getting the ID of the indexed document, if it was not provided during index action
- Retrieving the document version

To retrieve a document, you need to know the index/type/ID; the client method is
`prepareGet`. It requires the usual triplet (`index`, `type`, `id`), but a lot of other methods are
available to control the routing (such as souring, parent) or fields as we have seen in
the *Getting a Document* recipe in `Chapter 4`, *Basic Operations*. In the previous example, the
call is as follows:

```
GetResponse gr=client.prepareGet(index, type, "2").execute().actionGet();
```

The `GetResponse` return type contains all the requests (if the document exists) and
document information (`source`, `version`, `index`, `type`, `id`).

To update a document, it's necessary to know the index/type/ID and provide a script or a
document to be used for the update. The client method is `prepareUpdate`.

In the previous example, there is:

```
UpdateResponse ur = client.prepareUpdate(index, type, "2").setScript(new
Script("ctx._source.text = 'v2'")).execute().actionGet();
```

The script code must be a string. If the script language is not defined, the default `painless`
method is used.

The returned response contains information about the execution and the new version value
to manage concurrency.

To delete a document (without the need to execute a query), we need to know the
index/type/ID triple and we can use the `prepareDelete` client method to create a delete
request. In the previous code, we used:

```
DeleteResponse dr = client.prepareDelete("test", "type",
"2").execute().actionGet();
```

The delete request allows all the parameters to be passed to it that we saw in the *Deleting a
document* recipe in `Chapter 4`, *Basic Operations*, to control the routing and version.

See also

In our recipes we have used all the CRUD operations on a document. For more details about these actions refers to:

- The *Indexing a document* recipe in Chapter 4, *Basic Operations* on indexing a document
- The *Getting a document* recipe in Chapter 4, *Basic Operations* on retrieving a stored document
- The *Deleting a document* recipe in Chapter 4, *Basic Operations* about deleting a document
- The *Updating a document* recipe in Chapter 4, *Basic Operations* on updating a document

Managing bulk actions

Executing automatic operations on items via a single call is often the cause of a bottleneck if you need to index or delete thousands/millions of records: the best practice in this case is to execute a bulk action.

We have discussed bulk actions via the REST API in the *Speeding up atomic operations (bulk)* recipe in Chapter 4, *Basic Operations*.

Getting ready

You need an up-and-running Elasticsearch installation as we described in the *Downloading and installing Elasticsearch* recipe in Chapter 2, *Downloading and Setup*.

A Maven tool, or an IDE that natively supports it for Java programming such as Eclipse or IntelliJ IDEA, must be installed.

The code of this recipe is in the chapter_14/nativeclient directory and the referred class is the BulkOperations.

How to do it...

For managing a bulk action, we will perform these steps:

1. We'll need to import the required classes to execute bulks via the native `client`:

```
import org.elasticsearch.action.bulk.BulkRequestBuilder;
import org.elasticsearch.client.Client;
import org.elasticsearch.common.xcontent.XContentFactory;
import org.elasticsearch.script.Script;

import java.io.IOException;
import java.net.UnknownHostException;
```

2. We'll create the `client`, remove the old index if it exists, and create a new one:

```
public class BulkOperations {
public static void main(String[] args) throws
UnknownHostException {
String index = "mytest";
String type = "mytype";
Client client = NativeClient.createTransportClient();
IndicesOperations io = new IndicesOperations(client);
if (io.checkIndexExists(index))
    io.deleteIndex(index);

try {
    client.admin().indices().prepareCreate(index)
            .addMapping(type, XContentFactory.jsonBuilder()
                    .startObject()
                    .startObject(type)
                    .startObject("properties")
                    .startObject("position").field("type",
                    "integer").field("store", "yes").endObject()
                    .endObject()
                    .endObject()
                    .endObject())
            .execute().actionGet();
} catch (IOException e) {
    System.out.println("Unable to create mapping");
}
```

3. Now we can bulk-index `1000` documents, adding the bulk `index` actions to the `bulker`:

```
BulkRequestBuilder bulker = client.prepareBulk();
for (Integer i = 1; i <= 1000; i++) {
```

```
        bulker.add(client.prepareIndex(index, type,
            i.toString()).setSource("position", i.toString())));
    }
    System.out.println("Number of actions for index: " +
    bulker.numberOfActions());
    bulker.execute().actionGet();
```

4. We can bulk-update the previously created 1000 documents via a script, adding the bulk update action to the bulker:

```
    bulker = client.prepareBulk();
    for (Integer i = 1; i <= 1000; i++) {
        bulker.add(client.prepareUpdate(index, type,
            i.toString()).setScript(new Script("ctx._source.position +=
            2")));
    }
    System.out.println("Number of actions for update: " +
    bulker.numberOfActions());
    bulker.execute().actionGet();
```

5. We can bulk-delete 1000 documents, adding the bulk delete actions to the bulker:

```
    bulker = client.prepareBulk();
    for (Integer i = 1; i <= 1000; i++) {
        bulker.add(client.prepareDelete(index, type,
            i.toString())));
    }
    System.out.println("Number of actions for delete: " +
    bulker.numberOfActions());
    bulker.execute().actionGet();
```

6. We can now free up the resources used:

```
    io.deleteIndex(index);
    //we need to close the client to free resources
    client.close();
        }
    }
```

7. The result will be as follows:

```
    Number of actions for index: 1000
    Number of actions for update: 1000
    Number of actions for delete: 1000
```

How it works...

Before executing these bulk actions, a client must be available, an index must be created, and document mapping can optionally be created.

We can consider `bulkBuilder` as a collector of different actions:

```
IndexRequest or IndexRequestBuilder
UpdateRequest or UpdateRequestBuilder
DeleteRequest or DeleteRequestBuilder
a bulk formatted array of bytes.
```

Generally, when used in code, we can consider it as a `List` in which we add actions of the supported types:

1. To initialize `bulkBuilder` we use the following code:

   ```
   BulkRequestBuilder bulker=client.prepareBulk();
   ```

2. In the previous example we added 1,000 index actions (`IndexBuilder` is similar to the previous recipe one):

   ```
   for (Integer i=1; i<=1000; i++){
       bulker.add(client.prepareIndex(index, type,
   i.toString()).setSource("position", i.toString()));
   }
   ```

3. After adding all the actions, we can print (for example) the number of actions and then execute them:

   ```
   System.out.println("Number of action: " +
   bulker.numberOfActions());
   bulker.execute().actionGet();
   ```

4. After executing `bulkBuilder`, the bulker is empty.

5. We have populated the bulk with 1,000 update actions:

   ```
   bulker = client.prepareBulk();
   for (Integer i = 1; i <= 1000; i++) {
       bulker.add(client.prepareUpdate(index, type,
   i.toString()).setScript(new Script("ctx._source.position +=
   2")));
     }
   ```

6. After adding all the update actions, we can execute them in bulk:

```
bulker.execute().actionGet();
```

7. Next, the same step is done with the delete action:

```
for (Integer i=1; i<=1000; i++){
        bulker.add(client.prepareDelete(index, type,
        i.toString())));
}
```

8. To commit the delete, we need to execute the bulk.

> In this example, to simplify it, I have created bulk actions with the same type of actions, but, as described previously, you can put any supported type of action into the same bulk operation.

Building a query

Before search, a query must be built, Elasticsearch provides several ways to build these queries. In this recipe, will see how to create a query object via `QueryBuilder` and via simple strings.

Getting ready

You need an up-and-running Elasticsearch installation as we described in the *Downloading and installing Elasticsearch* recipe in `Chapter 2`, *Downloading and Setup*.

A Maven tool, or an IDE that natively supports it for Java programming such as Eclipse or IntelliJ IDEA, must be installed.

The code for this recipe is in the `chapter_14/nativeclient` directory and the referred class is `QueryCreation`.

How to do it...

To create a query, we will perform the following steps:

1. We need to import the `QueryBuilders`:

```
import org.elasticsearch.index.query.BoolQueryBuilder;
import org.elasticsearch.index.query.RangeQueryBuilder;
import org.elasticsearch.index.query.TermQueryBuilder;
```

2. We'll create a query using `QueryBuilder`:

```
TermQueryBuilder filter = termQuery("number2", 1);
RangeQueryBuilder range = rangeQuery("number1").gt(500);
BoolQueryBuilder query = boolQuery().must(range).filter(filter)
```

3. Now we can execute a search (the searching via native API will be discussed in the next recipes):

```
SearchResponse response =
client.prepareSearch(index).setTypes(type).setQuery(query)
.execute().actionGet();
System.out.println("Matched records of elements: " +
response.getHits().getTotalHits());
```

4. I've removed the redundant parts that are similar to the example of the previous recipe. The result will be as follows:

```
Matched records of elements: 250
```

How it works...

There are several ways to define a query in Elasticsearch; they are interchangeable.

Generally, a query can be defined as a:

- `QueryBuilder`: A helper to build a query.
- `XContentBuilder`: A helper to create JSON code. We discussed this in the *Managing mapping* recipe in this chapter. The JSON code to be generated is similar to the previous REST, but converted in programmatic code.
- `Array of Bytes` or `String`: In this case, it's usually the JSON to be executed as we have seen in REST calls.
- `Map`, which contains the query and the value of the query.

In the previous example, we created a query via `QueryBuilders`. The first step is to import the `QueryBuilder` from the namespace:

```
import static org.elasticsearch.index.query.QueryBuilders.*;
```

The query of the example is a Boolean query with a `termQuery` as filter. The goal of the example is to show how to mix several query types to create a complex query.

We need to define a filter.

In this case we have used a term query, which is one of the most used:

```
TermQueryBuilder filter = termQuery("number2", 1);
```

The `termQuery` accepts a field and a value, which must be a valid Elasticsearch type.

The previous code is similar to the JSON REST `{"term": {"number2":1}`.

The Boolean query contains a `must` clause with a `range` query. We start to create the range query:

```
RangeQueryBuilder range = rangeQuery("number1").gte(500);
```

This range query matches, in the `number1` field, all the values that are greater than or equal to (`gte`) `500`.

After creating the range query, we can add it to a Boolean query in the `must` block and the `filter` query in the `filter` block:

```
BoolQueryBuilder bool = boolQuery().must(range).filter(filter);
```

In real-world complex queries, you can have a lot of nested queries in a Boolean query or filter.

> Before executing a query and to be sure not to miss any results, the index must be refreshed.

In the example it's done with the following code:

```
client.admin().indices().prepareRefresh(index).execute().actionGet();
```

There's more...

The possible native queries/filters are the same as REST ones and have the same parameters: the only difference is that they are accessible via builder methods.

The most common query builders are:

- `matchAllQuery`: This allows matching all the documents to be matched
- `matchQuery`, `matchPhraseQuery`: These are used to match against text strings
- `termQuery`, `termsQuery`: These are used to match a term value(s) against a specific field
- `boolQuery`: This is used to aggregate other queries with Boolean logic
- `idsQuery`: This is used to match a list of IDs
- `fieldQuery`: This is used to match a field with text
- `wildcardQuery`: This is used to match terms with wildcards (*?.)
- `regexpQuery`: This is used to match terms via a regular expression
- Span query family (`spanTermsQuery`, `spanTermQuery`, `spanORQuery`, `spanNotQuery`, `spanFirstQuery`, and so on): These are a few examples of the span query family, which are used in building span queries
- `hasChildQuery`, `hasParentQuery`, `nestedQuery`: These are used to manage related documents

The previous list is not complete, because it constantly evolves throughout the life of Elasticsearch. New query types are added to cover new search cases or they are occasionally renamed, such as text query in match query.

Executing a standard search

In the previous recipe, we have seen how to build queries; in this recipe we can execute a query to retrieve some documents.

Getting ready

You need an up-and-running Elasticsearch installation as we described in the *Downloading and installing Elasticsearch* recipe in the `Chapter 2`, *Downloading and Setup*.

A Maven tool, or an IDE that natively supports it for Java programming such as Eclipse or IntelliJ IDEA, must be installed.

The code for this recipe is in the `chapter_14/nativeclient` directory and the referred class is the `QueryExample`.

How to do it...

To execute a standard query, we will perform the following steps:

1. We need to import `QueryBuilders` to create the query:

   ```
   import static org.elasticsearch.index.query.QueryBuilders.*;
   ```

2. We can create an `index` and populate it with some data:

   ```
   String index = "mytest";
   String type = "mytype";
   QueryHelper qh = new QueryHelper();
   qh.populateData(index, type);
   Client client = qh.getClient();
   ```

3. Now we build a query with the `number1` field greater than or equal to `500` and filter it for `number2` equal to `1`:

   ```
   QueryBuilder query =
   boolQuery().must(rangeQuery("number1").gte(500))
   .filter(termQuery("number2", 1));
   ```

4. After creating a query, it is enough to execute it using the following code:

   ```
   prepareQuery call and pass to it your query object:
   SearchResponse response =
   client.prepareSearch(index).setTypes(type)
           .setQuery(query).highlighter(new
   HighlightBuilder().field("name"))
           .execute().actionGet();
   ```

5. When we have `SearchResponse`, we need to check it's status and we can iterate it on `SearchHit`:

   ```
   if (response.status().getStatus() == 200) {
       System.out.println("Matched number of documents: " +
       response.getHits().totalHits());
       System.out.println("Maximum score: " +
   ```

```
      response.getHits().maxScore());
      for (SearchHit hit : response.getHits().getHits()) {
      System.out.println("hit: " + hit.getIndex() + ":" +
      hit.getType() + ":" + hit.getId());
      }
   }
```

6. The result should be similar to this:

```
Matched number of documents: 251
Maximum score: 1.0
hit: mytest:mytype:505
hit: mytest:mytype:517
hit: mytest:mytype:529
hit: mytest:mytype:531
hit: mytest:mytype:543
hit: mytest:mytype:555
hit: mytest:mytype:567
hit: mytest:mytype:579
hit: mytest:mytype:581
hit: mytest:mytype:593
```

How it works...

The call to execute a `search` is the `prepareSearch`, which returns a `SearchResponse`.

```
import org.elasticsearch.action.search.SearchResponse;
....
SearchResponse response =
client.prepareSearch(index).setTypes(type).setQuery(query).execute().action
Get();
```

The `Search` call has a lot of methods to allow setting of all the parameters that we have already seen in the recipe *Executing a Search* in Chapter 5, *Search*. The most used are:

- * `setIndices`: This allows the indices to be defined.
- * `setTypes`: This allows the document types to be defined.
- * `setQuery`: This allows the query to be executed to be set.
- * `addStoredField`: This allows setting fields to be returned (used to reduce the bandwidth by returning only needed fields).
- * `addAggregation`: This allows adding aggregations to be computed.
- * `addHighlighting`: This allows adding highlighting to be returned.

- `addScriptField`: This allows a scripted field to be returned. A scripted field is a field computed by server-side scripting, using one of the available scripting languages. For example, it can be:

```
Map<String, Object> params = MapBuilder.<String,
Object>newMapBuilder().put("factor", 2.0).map();
.addScriptField("sNum1", new Script("_doc.num1.value * factor", params))
```

After executing, a search a response object is returned.

It's good practice to check if the search has been successful by checking the returned status and optionally the number of hits. If the search was executed correctly, the return status is `200`.

```
if(response.status().getStatus()==200){
```

The response object contains a lot of sections that we analyzed in the *Executing a search* recipe in `Chapter 5`, *Search*. The most important one is the `hits` section that contains our results. The main accessor methods of this section are:

- `totalHits`: This allows the total number of results to be obtained

    ```
    System.out.println("Matched number of documents: " +
    response.getHits().totalHits());
    ```

- `maxScore`: This gives the maximum score for the documents. It is the same score value of the first `SearchHit`.

    ```
    System.out.println("Maximum score: " +
    response.getHits().maxScore());
    ```

- `hits`: This is an array of `SearchHit`, which contains the results, if available.

The `SearchHit` is the result object. It has a lot of methods, of which the most important ones are:

- `index()`: This is the index that contains the document
- `type()`: This is the type of the document
- `id()`: This is the ID of the document
- `score()`: This is, if available, the query score of the document
- `version()`: This is, if available, the version of the document
- `source()`, `sourceAsString()`, `sourceAsMap()`, and so on: These return the source of the document in different forms, if available

- explanation(): If available (required in the search), it contains the query explanation
- fields, field(String name): These returns the fields requested if passed fields to search object
- sortValues(): This is the value/values used to sort this record. It's only available if sort is specified during thr search phase
- shard(): This is the shard of the search hit, this value is very important for custom routing

In the example, we have printed only the index, type and ID of each hit:

```
for(SearchHit hit: response.getHits().getHits()){
System.out.println("hit:
"+hit.getIndex()+":"+hit.getType()+":"+hit.getId());
}
```

> The number of returned hits, if not defined, is limited to 10. To retrieve more hits you need or to define a larger value in the size method or paginate using from method

See also

- The *Executing a search* recipe in Chapter 5, *Search* for more detailed information about executing a query

Executing a search with aggregations

The previous recipe can be extended to support aggregations, to retrieve analytics on indexed data.

Getting ready

You need an up-and-running Elasticsearch installation as we described in the *Downloading and installing Elasticsearch* recipe in Chapter 2, *Downloading and Setup*.

A Maven tool, or an IDE that natively supports it for Java programming such as Eclipse or IntelliJ IDEA, must be installed.

The code for this recipe is in the `chapter_14/nativeclient` directory and the referred class is `AggregationExample`

How to do it...

For executing a search with aggregations, we will perform the steps given as follows:

1. We need to import the classes needed for the aggregations:

```
import org.elasticsearch.search.aggregations.AggregationBuilder;
import org.elasticsearch.search.aggregations.bucket.terms.Terms;
import org.elasticsearch.search.aggregations.metrics.stats.
extended.ExtendedStats;
import org.elasticsearch.search.aggregations.metrics.stats.
extended.ExtendedStatsAggregationBuilder;
import static org.elasticsearch.index.query.QueryBuilders.
matchAllQuery;
import static org.elasticsearch.search.aggregations.
AggregationBuilders.extendedStats;
import static org.elasticsearch.search.aggregations.
AggregationBuilders.terms;
```

2. We can create an index and populate it with some data that we will use for the aggregations:

```
String index = "mytest";
String type = "mytype";
QueryHelper qh = new QueryHelper();
qh.populateData(index, type);
Client client = qh.getClient();
```

3. We calculate two different aggregations (terms and extended statistics):

```
AggregationBuilder aggsBuilder = terms("tag").field("tag");
ExtendedStatsAggregationBuilder aggsBuilder2 =
extendedStats("number1").field("number1");
```

4. Now we can execute a search passing the aggregations. We use `setSize(0)` because we don't need the hits:

```
SearchResponse response =
client.prepareSearch(index).setTypes(type).setSize(0)
.setQuery(matchAllQuery()).addAggregation(aggsBuilder).
        addAggregation(aggsBuilder2)
.execute().actionGet();
```

5. We need to check the response validity and wrap the aggregation results:

```
if (response.status().getStatus() == 200) {
System.out.println("Matched number of documents: " +
response.getHits().totalHits());
Terms termsAggs = response.getAggregations().get("tag");
System.out.println("Aggregation name: " + termsAggs.getName());
System.out.println("Aggregation total: " +
termsAggs.getBuckets().size());
for (Terms.Bucket entry : termsAggs.getBuckets()) {
System.out.println(" - " + entry.getKey() + " " +
entry.getDocCount());
}
ExtendedStats extStats =
response.getAggregations().get("number1");
System.out.println("Aggregation name: " + extStats.getName());
System.out.println("Count: " + extStats.getCount());
System.out.println("Min: " + extStats.getMin());
System.out.println("Max: " + extStats.getMax());
System.out.println("Standard Deviation: " +
extStats.getStdDeviation());
System.out.println("Sum of Squares: " +
extStats.getSumOfSquares());
System.out.println("Variance: " + extStats.getVariance());
}
```

6. The result should be as follows:

```
Matched number of documents: 1000
Aggregation name: tag
Aggregation total: 4
 - bad 264
 - amazing 246
 - cool 245
 - nice 245
Aggregation name: number1
Count: 1000
Min: 2.0
Max: 1001.0
Standard Deviation: 288.6749902572095
Sum of Squares: 3.348355E8
Variance: 83333.25
```

How it works...

The search part is similar to the previous example. In this case, we have used a `matchAllQuery`, which matches all the documents.

To execute an aggregation, first you need to create it. There are three ways to do so:

- Using a string, that maps a JSON object
- Using a `XContentBuilder`, which will be used to produce a JSON object
- Using a `AggregationBuilder`

The first two ways are trivial; the third one needs the builders to be imported:

```
import static org.elasticsearch.search.aggregations.AggregationBuilders.*;
```

There are several types of aggregation, as we have already seen in `Chapter 6`, *Text and Numeric Queries*.

The first one, which we created with `AggregationBuilder`, is a `Terms` one, which collects and counts all `terms` occurrences in buckets.

```
AggregationBuilder aggsBuilder = terms("tag").field("tag");
```

The required value for every aggregation is the name, passed in the builder constructor. In the case of a terms aggregation, the field is required to be able to process the request. (There are a lot of other parameters; see the *Executing terms aggregations* recipe in `Chapter 8`, *Aggregations* for full details).

The second `aggregationBuilder` that we created, is an extended statistical one based on the `number1` numeric field:

```
ExtendedStatsBuilder aggsBuilder2 =
extendedStats("number1").field("number1");
```

Now that we have created `aggregationBuilders`, we can add them on a search method via the `addAggregation` method:

```
SearchResponse response =
client.prepareSearch(index).setTypes(type).setSize(0)
.setQuery(matchAllQuery()).addAggregation(aggsBuilder).
addAggregation(aggsBuilder2).execute().actionGet();
```

Now the response holds information about our aggregations. To access them we need to use the `getAggregations` method of the response.

The aggregation's results are contained in a hash-like structure and you can retrieve them with the names that you have previously defined in the request.

To retrieve the first aggregation results we need to get them:

```
Terms termsAggs = response.getAggregations().get("tag");
```

Now that we have an aggregation result of type `Terms` (see the recipe *Executing terms aggregations* in `Chapter 8`, *Aggregations*) we can get the aggregation properties and iterate in buckets:

```
System.out.println("Aggregation name: " + termsAggs.getName());
System.out.println("Aggregation total: " + termsAggs.getBuckets().size());
for (Terms.Bucket entry : termsAggs.getBuckets()) {
    System.out.println(" - " + entry.getKey() + " " + entry.getDocCount());
}
```

To retrieve the second aggregation result, because the result is of type ExtendedStats, you need to cast to it:

```
ExtendedStats extStats = response.getAggregations().get("number1");
```

Now you can access the result properties of this kind of aggregation:

```
System.out.println("Aggregation name: " + extStats.getName());
System.out.println("Count: " + extStats.getCount());
System.out.println("Min: " + extStats.getMin());
System.out.println("Max: " + extStats.getMax());
System.out.println("Standard Deviation: " + extStats.getStdDeviation());
System.out.println("Sum of Squares: " + extStats.getSumOfSquares());
System.out.println("Variance: " + extStats.getVariance());
```

> Using aggregations with a native client is quite easy, and you need only pay attention to the returned aggregation type to execute the correct type cast to access your results.

See also

- The *Executing terms aggregations* recipe in `Chapter 8`, *Aggregations*, which describes the terms aggregation in depth
- The *Executing statistical aggregations* recipe in `Chapter 8`, *Aggregations* for more details about statistical aggregations

Executing a scroll search

Pagination with a standard query works very well if you are matching documents with the documents that do not change too often; otherwise, doing pagination with live data returns unpredictable results. To bypass this problem, Elasticsearch provides an extra parameter in the query: scroll.

Getting ready

You need an up-and-running Elasticsearch installation as we described in the *Downloading and installing Elasticsearch* recipe in `Chapter 2`, *Downloading and Setup*.

A Maven tool, or an IDE that natively supports it for Java programming such as Eclipse or IntelliJ IDEA, installed.

The code for this recipe is in the `chapter_14/nativeclient` directory and the referred class is `ScrollQueryExample`.

How to do it...

The search is done as in the *Execute a standard search* recipe. The main difference is a `setScroll` timeout, which allows the resulting IDs to be stored in memory for a query for a defined timeout. The steps are like those for a standard search apart from:

1. We import the `TimeValue` object to define time in a more human way:

   ```
   import org.elasticsearch.common.unit.TimeValue;
   ```

2. We execute the search by setting the `setScroll` value. We can change the code of the *Execute a standard search* recipe to use scroll in this way:

   ```
   SearchResponse response =
   client.prepareSearch(index).setTypes(type).setSize(30)
   .setQuery(query).setScroll(TimeValue.timeValueMinutes(2))
   .execute().actionGet();
   ```

3. To manage the scrolling we need to create a loop until the results are returned:

   ```
   do {
       for (SearchHit hit : response.getHits().getHits()) {
           System.out.println("hit: " + hit.getIndex() + ":" +
           hit.getType() + ":" + hit.getId());
   ```

```
      }
      response = client.prepareSearchScroll
      (response.getScrollId()).setScroll
      (TimeValue.timeValueMinutes(2)).execute(
} while (response.getHits().getHits().length != 0);
```

4. The loop will iterate on all the results until records are available. The output will be similar to this one:

```
hit: mytest:mytype:499
hit: mytest:mytype:531
hit: mytest:mytype:533
hit: mytest:mytype:535
hit: mytest:mytype:555
hit: mytest:mytype:559
hit: mytest:mytype:571
hit: mytest:mytype:575
...truncated...
```

How it works...

To use the scrolling result, it's enough to add `setScroll` with a timeout to the method call.

When using scrolling, some behaviors must be considered:

*   The timeout defines the time slice that an Elasticsearch server keeps the results for. If you ask for a scroll after the timeout, the server returns an error. So, the user must be careful with short timeouts.
*   The scroll consumes memory until it ends or a timeout is raised. Setting too large a timeout without consuming the data, results in a big memory overhead. Using a large number of open scrollers consumes a lot of memory proportional to the number of IDs and their related data (score, order, and so on) in the results.
*   With scrolling it's not possible to paginate the documents, as there is no start. Scrolling is designed to fetch consecutives results.

A standard search is changed in a scroll in this way:

```
SearchResponse response =
client.prepareSearch(index).setTypes(type).setSize(30)
    .setQuery(query).setScroll(TimeValue.timeValueMinutes(2))
    .execute().actionGet();
```

The response contains the results as the standard search, plus a scroll ID, which is required to fetch the next results.

To execute the scroll, you need to call the `prepareSearchScroll` client method with a scroll ID and a new timeout. In the example, we process all the result documents:

```
do {
    for (SearchHit hit : response.getHits().getHits()) {
        //process your hit
    }
    response =
client.prepareSearchScroll(response.getScrollId()).setScroll(TimeValue.time
ValueMinutes(2)).execute(
    } while (response.getHits().getHits().length != 0);
```

To understand that we are at the end of the scroll, we can check that no results are returned.

There are a lot of scenarios in which scroll is very important; but when working on big data solutions, when the results number of results is very large, it's easy to hit the timeout. In these scenarios, it is important to have good architecture in which you fetch the results as fast as possible, and don't process the results iteratively in the loop, but defer the manipulation result in a distributed way.

In this case the best solution is to use the `search_after` functionality of Elasticsearch sorting by `_uid` as described in *Using search_after functionality* recipe in `Chapter 5`, *Search*.

See also

- Refer to the *Executing a scroll Query* recipe in `Chapter 5`, *Search*, which describes scroll queries in depth, and the *Using search_after functionality* recipe in `Chapter 5`, *Search* for scrolling on very large datasets

15
Scala Integration

In this chapter, we will cover the following recipes:

- Creating a client in Scala
- Managing indices
- Managing mappings
- Managing documents
- Executing a standard search
- Executing a search with aggregations

Introduction

Scala is becoming one of the most used languages in big data scenarios. This language provides a lot of facilities for managing data, such as immutability and functional programming.

In Scala, you can simply use the libraries seen in the previous chapter for Java, but they are not *scalastic* as they don't provide type safety (because many of these libraries take a JSON as a string) and it is easy to use asynchronous programming.

In this chapter, will see how to use elastic4s, a mature library, to use Elasticsearch in Scala. Its main features are:

- Type safe concise DSL
- Integrates with standard Scala futures
- Uses the Scala collections library over Java collections
- Returns option where the Java methods would return `null`
- Uses Scala durations instead of strings/longs for time values
- Uses typeclass for marshalling and unmarshalling classes to/from Elasticsearch documents, backed by Jackson, Circe, Json4s, and PlayJson implementations
- Leverages the built-in Java client
- Provides reactive-streams implementation
- Provides embedded node and testkit sub-projects, ideal for your tests

In this chapter, we will see mainly examples about standard elastic4s DSL usage and some helpers such as the `circe` extension for the easy marshalling/unmarshalling of documents in classes.

Creating a client in Scala

The first step for working with elastic4s is to create a connection client to call ElasticSearch. Similar to Java, the connection client is native and can be a node or a transport one.

Getting ready

You will need an up-and-running Elasticsearch installation, as we described in the *Downloading and installing Elasticsearch* recipe in `Chapter 2`, *Downloading and Setup*.

A Maven tool or an IDE that supports Scala programming, such as Eclipse (ScalaIDE) or IntelliJ IDEA, with the Scala plugin should be installed globally.

The code for this recipe can be found in the `chapter_15/elastic4s_sample` directory and the reference file is `ClientSample.scala`.

How to do it...

To create an Elasticsearch client and for create/search a document, we will perform the following steps:

1. The first step is to add the `elastic4s` library to the `build.sbt` configuration via:

    ```
    libraryDependencies += "com.sksamuel.elastic4s" %% "elastic4s-
    core" % "5.0.0"
    ```

2. If you are using Maven, to enable the compilation in your `pom.xml` project, just add the following code:

    ```
    <dependency>
        <groupId>com.sksamuel.elastic4s</groupId>
        <artifactId>elastic4s-core_2.11</artifactId>
        <version>5.0.0</version>
    </dependency>
    ```

3. To use the library, we need to import client classes and implicits:

    ```
    import com.sksamuel.elastic4s.{ElasticClient,
    ElasticsearchClientUri}
    import com.sksamuel.elastic4s.ElasticDsl._
    ```

4. Now we can initialize the client, providing an Elasticsearch URI:

    ```
    object ClientSample extends App {
      val uri =
      ElasticsearchClientUri("elasticsearch://127.0.0.1:9300?
      cluster.name=elasticsearch")
      val client = ElasticClient.transport(uri)
    ```

5. To index a document, we execute `indexInto` with the document in the following way:

    ```
    client.execute { indexInto("bands" / "artists") fields "name"-
    >"coldplay" }.await
    Thread.sleep(2000) //to be sure that the record is indexed
    ```

6. Now we can search for the document we indexed earlier:

```
val resp = client.execute { search("bands" / "artists") query
"coldplay" }.await
  println(resp)
}
```

The result, if the document is available, will be as follows:

```
RichSearchResponse({"took":2,"timed_out":false,"_shards":
{"total":5,"successful":5,"failed":0},"hits":
{"total":1,"max_score":0.2876821,"hits":
[{"_index":"bands","_type":"artists","_id":"AViBXXEWXe9IuvJzw-
HT","_score":0.2876821,"_source":{"name":"coldplay"}}]}})
```

How it works...

Elastic4s hides a lot of the boilerplate required for initializing an Elasticsearch client.

The simpler way to define a connection to Elasticsearch is via `ElasticsearchClientUri` and this allows you to provide the following:

- Multiple server endpoints, separated by commas (that is, `elasticsearch://localhost:9300,boo:9876`)
- The other settings to be provided to the transporter with query arguments (that is, `?cluster.name=elasticsearch`)

After having defined `ElasticsearchClientUri`, you can create `ElasticClient`, which is used for every Elasticsearch call.

You can initialize `ElasticClient` in several ways:

- Via `ElasticsearchClientUri`, similar to a JDBC connection, which is very handy because you can store it as a simple string in your application configuration file:

```
val client = ElasticClient.transport(uri)
```

- By providing a simple host and port:

```
val client = ElasticClient.transport("127.0.0.1", 9300)
```

- By providing custom settings, `ElasticsearchClientUri`, and a list of plugin classes to the advanced customization:

```
val client = ElasticClient.transport(settings, uri,
classOf[ReindexPlugin], classOf[ReindexPlugin])
```

- Via an already defined Elasticsearch node:

```
val node=...
val client = ElasticClient.fromNode(node)
```

- Via an already defined Elasticsearch client:

```
val client = ElasticClient.fromClient(elasticSearchJavaClient)
```

See also

- The *Using the native protocol* recipe in `Chapter 1`, *Getting Started*, for information on the native protocol
- The official Elasticsearch documentation about the `TransportClient` at `https://www.elastic.co/guide/en/elasticsearch/client/java-api/current/transport-client.html`.
- The official documentation of elastic4s at `https://github.com/sksamuel/elastic4s` for more examples of client initialization

Managing indices

After having a client, the first action to do is to create a custom index with an optimized mapping for it. Elastic4s provides a powerful DSL to do this kind of operation.

Getting ready

You need an up-and-running Elasticsearch installation, as we described in the *Downloading and installing Elasticsearch* recipe in `Chapter 2`, *Downloading and Setup*.

A Maven tool or an IDE that supports Scala programming, such as Eclipse (ScalaIDE) or IntelliJ IDEA, should be installed with the Scala plugin should be installed.

The code for this recipe can be found in the `chapter_15/elastic4s_sample` directory and the reference file is `IndicesExample`.

How to do it…

The Elasticsearch client maps all index operations under the `admin.indices` object of the client.

Here you will find all the index operations (`create`, `delete`, `exists`, `open`, `close`, `optimize`, and so on).

The following code retrieves a client and executes the main operations on indices:

1. We import the required classes:

```
import com.sksamuel.elastic4s.ElasticDsl._
 object IndicesExample extends App with
 ElasticSearchClientTrait{
 val indexName="test"
   if(client.execute{ indexExists(indexName) }.await.isExists){
     client.execute{ deleteIndex(indexName) }.await
   }
 }
```

2. We define an `IndicesExample` class that manages the index operations:

```
object IndicesExample extends App with
ElasticSearchClientTrait{
```

3. We check if the index exists. If `true`, we delete it:

```
val indexName="test"
if(client.execute{ indexExists(indexName)}.await.isExists){
   client.execute{ deleteIndex(indexName)}.await
}
```

4. We create an index including a mapping:

```
client.execute{
    createIndex(indexName) shards 1 replicas 0 mappings (
      mapping("mytype")as (textField("name").termVector
      ("with_positions_offsets").stored(true),
      keywordField("tag"),
      )
   )
}.await

Thread.sleep(2000)
```

5. We close an index as follows:

```
client.execute(closeIndex(indexName)).await
```

6. We open an index as follows:

```
client.execute(openIndex(indexName)).await
```

7. We delete an index as follows:

```
client.execute(deleteIndex(indexName)).await
```

8. We close the client to clean up the resources as follows:

```
client.close()
```

How it works...

The Elasticsearch **Domain Script Language** (**DSL**) that uses elastic4s is very simple and easy to use. It models the standard Elasticsearch functionalities in a more natural way to work on. It is also strong-typed so it prevents common errors such as typographic errors or value type changes.

To simply the code in the samples, we have created a trait that contains the code to initialize the `ElasticSearchClientTrait` client.

All the API calls in elastic4s are asynchronous, so they return `Future`. To materialize the result we need to add `.wait` to the end of the call.

Under the hood, elastic4s uses the Java standard Elasticsearch client, but wraps it in the DSL so the methods and the parameters have the same meaning as the standard Elasticsearch documentation.

> **TIP**
>
> In the code, we have put a delay of 1 second (`Thread.sleep(2000)`) to prevent fast actions on indices, because their shard allocations are asynchronous and they require some milliseconds to be ready. The best practice is not to have a similar hack, but to poll an index's state before performing further operations, and to only performing those operations when it goes green.

See also

* In Chapter 4, *Basic Operations*, refer to the *Creating an index* recipe for details on index creation, the *Deleting an index* recipe for details on index deletion, and the *Opening/closing an index* recipe for a description of open/close index APIs

Managing mappings

After creating an index, the next step is to add some mappings to it. We have already seen how to include a mapping via the REST API in Chapter 4, *Basic Operations*. In this recipe, we will see how to manage mappings via a native client.

Getting ready

You need an up-and-running Elasticsearch installation, as we described in the *Downloading and installing Elasticsearch* recipe in `Chapter 2`, *Downloading and Setup*.

A Maven tool or an IDE that supports Scala programming, such as Eclipse (ScalaIDE) or IntelliJ IDEA, with the Scala plugin should be installed.

The code of this recipe can be found in the `chapter_15/elastic4s_sample` file and the referred class is `MappingExample`.

How to do it...

In the following code, we add a `mytype` mapping to a `myindex` index via the native client:

1. We import the required classes:

   ```
   package com.packtpub
       import com.sksamuel.elastic4s.ElasticDsl._
   ```

2. We define a class to contain our code and to initialize the client and the index:

   ```
   object MappingExample extends App with
   ElasticSearchClientTrait{
     val indexName="myindex"
     if(client.execute{ indexExists(indexName) }.await.isExists){
       client.execute{ deleteIndex(indexName) }.await
     }
   ```

3. We create the index providing the `mytype` mapping:

   ```
   client.execute{
     createIndex(indexName) shards 1 replicas 0 mappings (
       mapping("mytype")as (textField("name").termVector
       ("with_positions_offsets").stored(true)
       )
       )
   }.await
   Thread.sleep(2000)
   ```

4. We add another field in the mapping via a `putMapping` call:

```
client.execute{
  putMapping(indexName / "mytype").as(
    keywordField("tag")
  )
}.await
```

5. We can now retrieve our mapping to test it:

```
val myMapping=client.execute{
  getMapping(indexName / "mytype")
}.await
```

6. From the mapping, we extract the `tag` field:

```
val tagMapping=myMapping.fieldFor(indexName / "mytype",
"tag")
println(tagMapping)
```

7. We remove the index by the following command:

```
client.execute(deleteIndex(indexName)).await
```

8. Now we can close the client to free up resources:

```
//we need to close the client to free resources
client.close();
    }
}
```

How it works...

Before executing a mapping operation, a client must be available.

We can include the mapping during index creation via the `mappings` method in the `createIndex` builder:

```
createIndex(indexName) shards 1 replicas 0 mappings (
    mapping("mytype")as (
      textField("name").termVector("with_positions_offsets").stored(true)
    )
    )
```

The elastic4s DSL provides strong typed definition for mapping fields.

If we forgot to put a field in the mapping, or during our application life we need to add a new field, `putMapping` can be called with the new field or a new complete type mapping.

```
putMapping(indexName / "mytype").as(
    keywordField("tag")
  )
```

In this way, if the type exists it is updated; otherwise, it is created.

In the admin console, or to check our index types stored in mappings, we need to retrieve them from the cluster state. The method that we have already seen is the `getMapping` method:

```
val myMapping=client.execute{
    getMapping(indexName / "mytype")
  }.await
```

The returned mapping object also has some help methods to check the mappings for a single field via the `fieldFor` call:

```
val tagMapping=myMapping.fieldFor(indexName / "mytype", "tag")
  println(tagMapping)
```

The returned value is a `Map[String, Any]`.

See also

- The *Putting a mapping in an index* recipe in `Chapter 4`, *Basic Operations*, for more details about the `put` mapping API
- The *Getting a mapping* recipe in `Chapter 4`, *Basic Operations*, for more details about the `get` mapping API

Managing documents

The APIs for managing documents (`index`, `delete`, and `update`) are the most important after the search ones. In this recipe, we will see how to use them.

Getting ready

You need an up-and-running Elasticsearch installation, as we described in the *Downloading and installing Elasticsearch* recipe in `Chapter 2`, *Downloading and Setup*.

A Maven tool, or an IDE that supports Scala programming, such as Eclipse (ScalaIDE) or IntelliJ IDEA, with the Scala plugin should be installed.

The code of this recipe can be found in the `chapter_15/elastic4s_sample` file and the referred class is `DocumentExample`.

How to do it...

For managing documents, we will perform the following steps:

1. We'll need to import the required classes to execute all the document CRUD operations:

   ```
   import com.sksamuel.elastic4s.ElasticDsl._
   ```

2. We create the client and ensure that the index and mapping exists:

   ```
   object DocumentExample extends App with
   ElasticSearchClientTrait{
   val indexName="myindex"
   val typeName="mytype"

   ensureIndexMapping(indexName, typeName)
   ```

3. Now, we can store a document in Elasticsearch via the `indexInto` call:

   ```
   client.execute {
   indexInto(indexName / typeName) id "0" fields (
       "name" -> "brown",
     "tag" -> List("nice", "simple")
     )
   }.await
   ```

4. We can retrieve the stored document via the `get` call:

```
val bwn=client.execute {
get("0") from indexName / typeName
}.await
println(bwn.sourceAsString)
```

5. We can update the stored document via the `update` call using a script in Painless:

```
client.execute {
    update("0").in(indexName /
    typeName).script("ctx._source.name = 'red'")
    }.await
```

6. We can check if our update was applied:

```
val red=client.execute {
    get("0") from indexName / typeName
    }.await

    println(red.sourceAsString)
```

7. The console output result will be:

```
no modules loaded
loaded plugin [org.elasticsearch.index.reindex.ReindexPlugin]
loaded plugin [org.elasticsearch.percolator.PercolatorPlugin]
loaded plugin
[org.elasticsearch.script.mustache.MustachePlugin]
loaded plugin [org.elasticsearch.transport.Netty3Plugin]
loaded plugin [org.elasticsearch.transport.Netty4Plugin]
{"name":"brown","tag":["nice","simple"]}
{"name":"red","tag":["nice","simple"]}
```

The document version, following an update action and if the document is re-indexed with new changes, is always incremented by 1.

How it works...

Before executing a document action, a client and the index must be available and document mapping should be created (the mapping is optional, because it can be inferred from the indexed document).

To index a document, elastic4s allows us to provide the document content in several ways, such as via:

- `fields`:
    - A sequence of tuples `(String, Any)` as in the preceding example
    - A `Map[String, Any]`
    - An `Iterable[(String, Any)]`
- `doc/source`:
    - A string
    - A typeclass that derives `Indexable[T]`

Obviously, it's possible to add all the parameters that we saw in the *Indexing a document* recipe in `Chapter 4`, *Basic Operations*, such as parent, routing, and so on.

The return value, `IndexReponse`, is the same retuned object from the Java call.

To retrieve a document, we need to know the index/type/id; the method is `get`. It requires the id and the index, type provided in the `from` method. A lot of other methods are available to control the routing (such as souring, parent) or fields as we have seen in the *Getting a document* recipe in `Chapter 4`, *Basic Operations*. In the preceding example, the call is:

```
val bwn=client.execute {
    get("0") from indexName / typeName
}.await
```

The return type, `GetResponse`, contains all the requests (if the document exists) and the document information (`source`, `version`, `index`, `type`, and `id`).

To update a document, it's required to know the index/type/id and provide a script or a document to be used for the update. The client method is `update`. In the preceding example, we have used a script:

```
client.execute {
    update("0").in(indexName / typeName).script("ctx._source.name = 'red'")
}.await
```

The script code must be a string. If the script language is not defined, the default Painless is used.

The returned response contains information about the execution and the new version value to manage concurrency.

To delete a document (without the need to execute a query), we must know the index/type/id and we can use the client method, delete, to create a delete request. In the preceding code, we have used:

```
client.execute {
    delete("0") from indexName / typeName
}.await
```

The delete request allows all the parameters we saw in the *Deleting a document* recipe in Chapter 4, *Basic Operations*, to control routing and versions, to be passed to it.

There's more...

Scala programmers love typeclass, automatic marshalling/unmarshalling from case classes, and a strong type management of the data. For this, elastics4 provides additional support for the common JSON serialization library, such as:

- Circe (https://circe.github.io/circe/). To use this library, you need to add the dependency of:

    ```
    "com.sksamuel.elastic4s" %% "elastic4s-circe" % elastic4sV
    ```

- Jackson (http://wiki.fasterxml.com/JacksonHome). To use this library, you need to add the dependency of:

    ```
    "com.sksamuel.elastic4s" %% "elastic4s-jackson" % elastic4sV
    ```

- Json4s (http://json4s.org/). To use this library, you need to add the dependency of:

    ```
    "com.sksamuel.elastic4s" %% "elastic4s-json4s" % elastic4sV
    ```

For example, if you want to use Circe, perform the following steps:

1. You need to import the `circe` implicits:

```
import com.sksamuel.elastic4s.circe._
import io.circe.generic.auto._
import com.sksamuel.elastic4s.Indexable
```

2. You need to define the `case` class that needs to be deserialized:

```
case class Place(id: Int, name: String)
```

3. You need to force the implicit serializer:

```
implicitly[Indexable[Cafe]]
```

4. Now you can index the case classes directly:

```
val cafe=Cafe("nespresso", Place(20,"Milan"))

client.execute {
  indexInto(indexName / typeName).id(cafe.name).source(cafe)
}.await
```

See also

In the recipes, we have used all CRUD operations on a document. For more details about these actions, refers to:

- The *Indexing a document* recipe in Chapter 4, *Basic Operations*
- The *Getting a document* recipe in Chapter 4, *Basic Operations*, on retrieving a stored document
- The *Deleting a document* recipe in Chapter 4, *Basic Operations*
- The *Updating a document* recipe in Chapter 4, *Basic Operations*

Executing a standard search

Obviously, the most common action in Elasticsearch is searching. Elastic4s leverages the query DSL, bringing to Scala a type-safe definition for the queries. One of the most common advantages of this functionality is that, as Elasticsearch evolves, in Scala code via elastic4s, you can have deprecation or your compilation breaks, requiring you to update your code.

Getting ready

You need an up-and-running Elasticsearch installation, as we described in the *Downloading and installing Elasticsearch* recipe in `Chapter 2`, *Downloading and Setup*.

A Maven tool or an IDE that supports Scala programming, such as Eclipse (ScalaIDE) or IntelliJ IDEA, with the Scala plugin should be installed.

The code for this recipe can be found in the `chapter_15/elastic4s_sample` file and the referred class is `QueryExample`.

How to do it...

To execute a standard query, we will perform the following steps:

1. We import the classes and implicits required to index and search the data:

```
import com.sksamuel.elastic4s.ElasticDsl._
import com.sksamuel.elastic4s.circe._
import com.sksamuel.elastic4s.Indexable
import io.circe.generic.auto._
```

2. We create an index and populate it with some data. We use bulk calls for speed up:

```
object QueryExample extends App with ElasticSearchClientTrait {
  val indexName = "myindex"
  val typeName = "mytype"

  case class Place(id: Int, name: String)
  case class Cafe(name: String, place: Place)

  implicitly[Indexable[Cafe]]

  ensureIndexMapping(indexName, typeName)
```

```
client.execute {
  bulk(
    indexInto(indexName /
    typeName).id("0").source(Cafe("nespresso", Place(20,
    "Milan"))),
    ...truncated...
    indexInto(indexName /
    typeName).id("8").source(Cafe("nespresso", Place(23,
    "Chicago"))),
    indexInto(indexName /
    typeName).id("9").source(Cafe("java", Place(89,
    "London")))
  )
}.await
Thread.sleep(2000)
```

3. We can use a `bool` filter for search documents with the `name` equal to `java` and `place.id` greater than or equal to `80`:

```
val resp = client.execute {
  search(indexName / typeName).bool(must(termQuery("name",
  "java"), rangeQuery("place.id").gte(80)))
}.await
```

4. When we have the `response` parameter, we need to check its count and we can convert it back to a list of classes:

```
println(resp.size)
println(resp.to[Cafe].toList)
```

5. The result should be similar to this one:

```
2
List(Cafe(java,Place(80,Chicago)), Cafe(java,Place(89,London)))
```

How it works...

The Elastic4s query DSL wraps the Elasticsearch one in a more human-readable way.

The `search` method allows us to define, via DSL, a complex query. The result is a wrapper of the original Java result that provides some helpers to be more productive.

The common methods of the Java result are available at a top level, but they also provide two interesting methods: `to` and `safeTo`.

They are able to convert the results in case classes via the implicit conversions available in the scope. In the case of the `to[T]` method, the result is an iterator of `T` (in the preceding example, we have the conversion back to a `List` of `Cafe`). In the case of `safeTo[T]`, the result is an `Either[Throwable, T]`; in this way, it's possible to collect the conversion errors/exceptions.

> **TIP**
>
> Using the typeclass in Scala allows you to write a cleaner and eas- t0-understand code and also reduces the errors due to string management in Elasticsearch.

See also

- The *Executing a search* recipe in `Chapter 5`, *Search*, for more detailed information about executing a query

Executing a search with aggregations

The next step after searching in Elasticsearch is to execute the aggregations. The elastic4s DSL also provides support for aggregation so it can be built in a safer typed way.

Getting ready

You need an up-and-running Elasticsearch installation, as we described in the *Downloading and installing Elasticsearch* recipe in `Chapter 2`, *Downloading and Setup*.

A Maven tool or an IDE that supports Scala programming, such as Eclipse (ScalaIDE) or IntelliJ IDEA, with the Scala plugin should be installed.

The code for this recipe can be found in the `chapter_15/elastic4s_sample` file and the referred class is `AggregationExample`.

How to do it...

For executing a search with aggregations, we will perform the following steps:

1. We need to import the classes needed for the aggregations:

```
import com.sksamuel.elastic4s.ElasticDsl._
import
 org.elasticsearch.search.aggregations.metrics.geocentroid
 .InternalGeoCentroid
import org.elasticsearch.search.aggregations.metrics.stats
.extended.InternalExtendedStats
import scala.collection.JavaConversions._
```

2. We create an index and populate it with some data that will be used for the aggregations:

```
object AggregationExample extends App with
ElasticSearchClientTrait {
  val indexName = "myindex"
  val typeName = "mytype"
  ensureIndexMapping(indexName, typeName)
  populateSampleData(indexName, typeName, 1000)
```

3. We know how to execute a search with aggregation using terms Aggregation with several sub-aggregations (extended statistics, geocentroid):

```
val resp = client.execute {
  search(indexName / typeName) size 0 aggregations (
    termsAggregation("tag") size 100 subAggregations(
      extendedStatsAggregation("price") field "price",
      extendedStatsAggregation("size") field "size",
      geoBoundsAggregation("centroid") field "location"
    ))
}.await
```

4. Now we can process the response. We extract the aggregation results and show some values:

```
val tagsAgg = resp.aggregations.stringTermsResult("tag")
println(s"Result Hits: ${resp.size}")
println(s"number of tags: ${tagsAgg.getBuckets.size()}")
println(s"max price of first tag
${tagsAgg.getBuckets.head.getKey}:
${tagsAgg.getBuckets.head.getAggregations.get
[InternalExtendedStats]("price").value("max")}")
println(s"min size of first tag
${tagsAgg.getBuckets.head.getKey}:
${tagsAgg.getBuckets.head.getAggregations.get
[InternalExtendedStats]("size").value("min")}")
```

5. At the end, we clean up the used resources:

```
client.execute(deleteIndex(indexName)).await
client.close()
}
```

6. The result should be like this one:

```
number of tags: 5
max price of first tag awesome: 10.799999999999999
min size of first tag awesome: 0.0
```

How it works...

Elastic4s provides a powerful DSL for more type-safe aggregations.

In the preceding example, we used `termsAggregation` to initially aggregate the buckets by tag settings to collect at least 100 buckets (`termsAggregation("tag") size 100`), then we have two types of sub-aggregations:

- `extendedStatsAggregation`: This is used to collect extended statistics on the price and size fields
- `geocentroidAggregation`: This is used to compute the center of documents results

The elastic4s DSL provides all the official Elasticsearch aggregations.

Also the aggregation result contains helpers for managing aggregations, such as automatic casing for some types:

- `stringTermsResult`: This wraps a string terms Aggregation result
- `termsResult`: This wraps a generic terms Aggregation result
- `missingResult`: This wraps a missing aggregation result
- `cardinalityResult`: This wraps a cardinality aggregation result
- `avgResult`: This wraps an average metric aggregation result
- `maxResult`: This wraps a max metric aggregation result
- `sumResult`: This wraps a sum metric aggregation result
- `minResult`: This wraps a min metric aggregation result
- `histogramResult`: This wraps a histogram aggregation result
- `valueCountResult`: This wraps a count aggregation result

If the aggregation result is not part of these aggregations results, an helper method, `get[T]:T`, allows you to retrieve a casted aggregation result.

See also

- The *Executing term Aggregations* recipe in `Chapter 8`, *Aggregations*, which describes term Aggregation
- The *Executing statistical aggregations* recipe in `Chapter 8`, *Aggregations*, for more detail about statistical aggregations

16
Python Integration

In this chapter, we will cover the following recipes:

- Creating a client
- Managing indices
- Managing mappings
- Managing documents
- Executing a standard search
- Executing a search with aggregations

Introduction

In the previous chapter, we saw how it is possible to use a native client to access the Elasticsearch server via Java. This chapter is dedicated to the Python language and how to manage common tasks via its clients.

Apart from Java, the Elasticsearch team supports official clients for Perl, PHP, Python, .NET, and, Ruby. (See the announcement post on the Elasticsearch blog at `http://www.elasticsearch.org/blog/unleash-the-clients-ruby-python-php-perl/`.) These clients have a lot of advantages over other implementations. A few of them are mentioned as follows:

- They are strongly tied to the Elasticsearch API:

    "These clients are direct translations of the native Elasticsearch REST interface"
    — The Elasticsearch team

- They handle dynamic node detection and failover: they are built with a strong networking base for communicating with the cluster.
- They have full coverage of the REST API. They share the same application approach for every language in which they are available, so switching from one language to another is fast.
- They are easily extensible.

The Python client plays very well with other Python frameworks such as Django, web2py, and Pyramid. It allows very fast access to documents, indices, and clusters.

In this chapter, I'll try to describe the most important functionalities of the Elasticsearch official Python client; for additional examples, I suggest you to take a look at the online GitHub repository and documentation at the following URL:
`https://github.com/elastic/elasticsearch-py`.

Creating a client

The official Elasticsearch clients are designed to manage a lot of issues that typically are required to create solid REST clients, such as `retry` if there are network issues, autodiscovery of other nodes of the cluster, and data conversions for communicating on the HTTP layer.

In this recipe, we'll see how to instantiate a client with varying options.

Getting ready

You need an up-and-running Elasticsearch installation, as we described in the *Downloading and installing Elasticsearch* recipe in `Chapter 2`, *Downloading and Setup*.

A Python 2.x or 3.x distribution should be installed. In Linux and the MacOsX system, it's already provided by the standard installation. To manage Python, `pip` packages (`https://pypi.python.org/pypi/pip/`) must be also installed.

The full code of this recipe is in the `chapter_16/client_creation.py` file.

How to do it...

For creating a client, we will perform the following steps:

1. Before using the Python client, we need to install it (possibly in a Python virtual environment). The client is officially hosted on PyPi (http://pypi.python.org/) and it's easy to install with the `pip` command:

   ```
   pip install elasticsearch
   ```

   This standard installation only provides the HTTP protocol.

2. If you need to use the requests library for HTTP communication, you need to install it:

   ```
   pip install requests
   ```

3. After having installed the package, we can instantiate the client. It resides in the Python `elasticsearch` package and it must be imported to instantiate the client:

   ```
   import elasticsearch
   ```

4. If you don't pass arguments to the `Elasticsearch` class, it instantiates a client that connects to the localhost and port `9200` (the default Elasticsearch HTTP one):

   ```
   es = elasticsearch.Elasticsearch()
   ```

5. If your cluster is composed of more than one node, you can pass the list of nodes as a round-robin connection between them and distribute the HTTP load:

   ```
   es = elasticsearch.Elasticsearch(["search1:9200",
   "search2:9200"])
   ```

6. Often, the complete topology of the cluster is unknown; if you know a least one node IP, you can use the `sniff_on_start=True` option. This option activates the client's ability to detect other nodes in the cluster:

   ```
   es = elasticsearch.Elasticsearch(["search1:9200"],
   sniff_on_start=True)
   ```

7. The default transport is `Urllib3HttpConnection`, but if you want to use the HTTP requests transport, you need to override the `connection_class` passing `RequestsHttpConnection`:

```
from elasticsearch.connection import RequestsHttpConnection
es = elasticsearch.Elasticsearch( sniff_on_start=True,
connection_class= RequestsHttpConnection)
```

How it works...

To communicate with an Elasticsearch cluster, a client is required.

The client manages all communication layers from your application to an Elasticsearch server, using the HTTP REST calls.

The Elasticsearch Python client allows using one of the following library implementations:

- **urllib3**: This is the default implementation provided by the Elasticserch Python driver (https://pypi.python.org/pypi/urllib3)
- **requests**: The requests library is one of the most used libraries to perform HTTP requests in Python (https://pypi.python.org/pypi/requests)

The Elasticsearch Python client requires a server to connect to. If not defined, it tries to use one on the local machine (localhost). If you have more than one node, you can pass a list of servers to connect to.

> The client automatically tries to balance operations on all cluster nodes. This is a very powerful functionality provided by the Elasticsearch client.

To improve the list of available nodes, it is possible to set the client to auto-discover new nodes. I suggest using this feature because it is common to have a cluster with a lot of nodes and you need to shut down some of them for maintenance. The options that can be passed to the client to control discovery are as follows:

- `sniff_on_start`: The default value is `False`, which allows obtaining the list of nodes from the cluser at startup time
- `sniffer_timeout`: The default value is `None`; it is the number of seconds between automatic sniffing of the cluster nodes
- `sniff_on_connection_fail`: The default value is `False`, which controls if a connection failure triggers a sniff of cluster nodes

The default client configuration uses the HTTP protocol via the `urllib3` library. If you want to use other transport protocols, you need to pass the type of the transport class to the `transport_class` variable. The current implemented classes are as follows:

- `Transport`: This is a default value, that is, a wrapper around `Urllib3HttpConnection` that uses HTTP (usually on port `9200`)
- `RequestsHttpConnection`: This is an alternative to `Urllib3HttpConnection` based on requests library

See also

- The official documentation about the Python Elasticsearch client, available at `https://elasticsearch-py.readthedocs.io/en/master/index.html`, provides a more detailed explanation of the several options available to initialize the client

Managing indices

In the previous recipe, we saw how to initialize a client to send calls to an Elasticsearch cluster. In this recipe, we will look at how to manage indices via client calls.

Getting ready

You need an up-and-running Elasticsearch installation, as we described in the *Downloading and installing Elasticsearch* recipe in `Chapter 2`, *Downloading and Setup*.

You also need the Python-installed packages from the *Creating a client* recipe in this chapter.

The full code for this recipe can be found in the `chapter_16/indices_management.py` file.

How to do it...

In Python, managing the life cycle of your indices is very easy. We will perform the following steps:

1. We initialize a client:

```
import elasticsearch
es = elasticsearch.Elasticsearch()
index_name = "my_index"
```

2. We need to check if the index exists, and, if so, we need to delete it:

```
if es.indices.exists(index_name):
    es.indices.delete(index_name)
```

3. All the `indices` methods are available in the `client.indices` namespace. We can create and wait for the creation of an index:

```
es.indices.create(index_name)
es.cluster.health(wait_for_status="yellow")
```

4. We can close/open an index:

```
es.indices.close(index_name)
es.indices.open(index_name)
es.cluster.health(wait_for_status="yellow")
```

5. We can optimize an index:

```
es.indices.forcemerge(index_name)
```

6. We can delete an index:

```
es.indices.delete(index_name)
```

How it works...

The Elasticsearch Python client has two special managers: one for indices (`<client>.indices`) and one for the cluster (`<client>.cluster`).

For every operation that needs to work with indices, the first value is generally the name of the index. If you need to execute an action on several indices in one go, the indices must be concatenated with a comma , (that is, `index1,index2,indexN`). It's possible to also use glob patterns to define multi-indexes, such as `index*`.

To create an index, the call requires `index_name` and other optional parameters such as index settings and mapping. We'll see this advanced feature in the next recipe.

```
es.indices.create(index_name)
```

Index creation can take some time (from a few milliseconds to seconds); it is an asynchronous operation and it depends on the complexity of the cluster, the speed of the disk, the network congestion, and so on. To be sure that this action is completed, we need to check that the cluster's health becomes `yellow` or `green`, as follows:

```
es.cluster.health(wait_for_status="yellow")
```

> It's good practice to wait till the cluster status is `yellow` (at least) after operations that involve index creation and opening, because these actions are asynchronous.

To close an index, the method is `<client>.indices.close`, giving the name of the index to close:

```
es.indices.close(index_name)
```

To open an index, the method is `<client>.indices.open`, giving the name of the index to open:

```
es.indices.open(index_name)
es.cluster.health(wait_for_status="yellow")
```

Similar to index creation, after an index is opened, it is a good practice to wait till the index is fully opened before executing an operation on the index. This action is done by checking the cluster's health.

To improve the performance of an index, Elasticsearch allows optimizing it by removing deleted documents (documents are marked deleted, but not purged from the segment's index for performance reasons) and reducing the number of segments. To optimize an index, `<client>.indices.forcemerge` must be called on the index:

```
es.indices.forcemerge(index_name)
```

Finally, if we want to delete the index, we can call `<client>.indices.delete`, giving the name of the index to remove.

> Remember that deleting an index removes everything related to it including all the data, and this action cannot be reversed.

There's more...

The Python client wraps the Elasticsearch API in groups such as:

- `<client>.indices`: This wraps all the REST APIs related to index management
- `<client>.ingest`: This wraps all the REST APIs related to ingest calls
- `<client>.cluster`: This wraps all the REST APIs related to cluster management
- `<client>.cat`: This wraps the CAT API, a subset of the API that returns a textual representation of traditional JSON calls
- `<client>.nodes`: This wraps all the REST API related to nodes management
- `<client>.snapshot`: This allows us to execute a snapshot and restore data from Elasticsearch
- `<client>.tasks`: This wraps all the REST API related to task management

Standard document operations (CRUD) and search are available at the top level of the client.

See also

- The *Creating an index* recipe in Chapter 4, *Basic Operations*, for more details on index creation and index name limits; the *Deleting an index* recipe in Chapter 4, *Basic Operations*, for more details about index deletion: and the *Opening/closing an index* recipe in Chapter 4, *Basic Operations*, for more details about the actions that are used to save cluster/node memory

Managing mappings include the mapping

After creating an index, the next step is to add some type mappings to it. We have already seen how to include a mapping via the REST API in `Chapter 4`, *Basic Operations*.

Getting ready

You need an up-and-running Elasticsearch installation, as we described in the *Downloading and installing Elasticsearch* recipe in `Chapter 2`, *Downloading and Setup*.

You also need the Python installed packages of *Creating a client* recipe of this chapter.

The code for this recipe is in the `chapter_16/mapping_management.py` file.

How to do it...

After having initialized a client and created an index, the steps for managing the indices are as follows:

1. Create a mapping.
2. Retrieve a mapping.

These steps are easily managed with the following code:

1. We initialize the client:

```
import elasticsearch
es = elasticsearch.Elasticsearch()
```

2. We create an index:

```
index_name = "my_index"
type_name = "my_type"
if es.indices.exists(index_name):
    es.indices.delete(index_name)
es.indices.create(index_name)
es.cluster.health(wait_for_status="yellow")
```

3. We include the mapping:

```
es.indices.put_mapping(index=index_name, doc_type=type_name,
body={type_name:{"properties": {
"uuid": {"type": "keyword", "store": "true"},
"title": {"type": "text", "store": "true", "term_vector":
"with_positions_offsets"},
"parsedtext": { "type": "text", "store": "true", "term_vector":
"with_positions_offsets"},
"nested": {"type": "nested", "properties": {"num": {"type":
"integer", "store": "true"},
"name": {"type": "keyword", "store": "true"},
"value": {"type": "keyword", "store": "true"}}},
"date": {"type": "date", "store": "true"},
"position": {"type": "integer", "store": "true"},
"name": {"type": "text", "store": "true", "term_vector":
"with_positions_offsets"}}}})
```

4. We retrieve the mapping:

```
mappings = es.indices.get_mapping(index_name, type_name)
```

5. We delete the index.

```
es.indices.delete(index_name)
```

How it works...

We have already seen the initialization of the client and the index creation in the previous recipe.

For creating a mapping, the method call is `<client>.indices.create_mapping`, giving the index name, the type name, and the mapping. The creation of the mapping is fully covered in the `Chapter 3`, *Managing Mappings*. It is easy to convert the standard Python types to JSON and vice versa:

```
es.indices.put_mapping(index_name, type_name, {...})
```

If an error is generated in the mapping process, an exception is raised. The `put_mapping` API has two behaviors: creation and updating.

In Elasticsearch, you cannot remove a property from a mapping. The schema manipulation, allows entering new properties with the `put_mapping` call.

To retrieve a mapping with the `get_mapping` API use the `<client>.indices.get_mapping` method, providing the index name and type name:

```
mappings = es.indices.get_mapping(index_name, type_name)
```

The `return` object is obviously the dictionary describing the mapping.

See also

- The *Putting a mapping in an index* recipe in `Chapter 4`, *Basic Operations* about applying a mapping to an index and the *Getting a mapping* recipe in `Chapter 4`, *Basic Operations* to check and retrieve an index mapping.

Managing documents

The APIs for managing a document (index, update, and delete) are the most important after the search ones. In this recipe, we will see how to use them in a standard way and in bulk actions to improve performances.

Getting ready

You need an up-and-running Elasticsearch installation, as we described in the *Downloading and installing Elasticsearch* recipe in `Chapter 2`, *Downloading and Setup*.

You also need the Python installed packages of *Creating a client* recipe of this chapter.

The full code for this recipe can be found in the `chapter_16/document_management.py` file.

How to do it...

The three main operations to manage the documents are as follows:

- `index`: This operation stores a document in Elasticsearch. It is mapped on the index API call.
- `update`: This allows updating some values in a document. This operation is composed internally (via Lucene) by deleting the previous document and re-indexing the document with the new values. It is mapped to the update API call.
- `delete`: This delete a document from the index. It is mapped to the delete API call.

With the Elasticsearch Python client, these operations can be done by performing the following steps.

1. We initialize a client and create an index with the mapping:

```
import elasticsearch
from datetime import datetime
es = elasticsearch.Elasticsearch()
index_name = "my_index"
type_name = "my_type"
if es.indices.exists(index_name):
    es.indices.delete(index_name)
from utils import create_and_add_mapping
create_and_add_mapping(es, index_name, type_name)
```

2. We index some documents (we manage the parent/child):

```
es.index(index=index_name, doc_type=type_name, id=1,
    body={"name": "Joe Tester", "parsedtext": "Joe Testere
    nice guy", "uuid": "11111", "position": 1,
    "date": datetime(2013, 12, 8)})
es.index(index=index_name, doc_type=type_name + "2", id=1,
    body={"name": "data1", "value": "value1"}, parent=1)
es.index(index=index_name, doc_type=type_name, id=2,
    body={"name": "Bill Baloney", "parsedtext": "Bill Testere
    nice guy", "uuid": "22222", "position": 2,
    "date": datetime(2013, 12, 8)})
es.index(index=index_name, doc_type=type_name + "2", id=2,
    body={"name": "data2", "value": "value2"}, parent=2)
es.index(index=index_name, doc_type=type_name, id=3,
    body={"name": "Bill Clinton", "parsedtext": """Bill is not
    nice guy""", "uuid": "33333", "position": 3, "date":
    datetime(2013, 12, 8)})
```

3. We update a document:

```
document=es.get(index=index_name, doc_type=type_name, id=2)
print(document)
```

4. We delete a document:

```
es.delete(index=index_name, doc_type=type_name, id=1)
```

5. We bulk-insert some documents:

```
from elasticsearch.helpers import bulk_index
bulk(es, [
    {"_index":index_name, "_type":type_name, "_id":"1",
"source":{"name": "Joe Tester", "parsedtext": "Joe Testere nice
guy", "uuid": "11111", "position": 1,
"date": datetime(2013, 12, 8)}},
    {"_index": index_name, "_type": type_name, "_id": "1",
    "source": {"name": "Bill Baloney", "parsedtext": "Bill Testere
    nice guy", "uuid": "22222", "position": 2,
    "date": datetime(2013, 12, 8)}}
])
```

6. We remove the index:

```
es.indices.delete(index_name)
```

How it works...

To simplify the example, after having instantiated the client, a function of the `utils` package, which sets up the index and puts the mapping, is called, as follows:

```
from utils import create_and_add_mapping
create_and_add_mapping(es, index_name, type_name)
```

This function contains the code for creating the mapping of the previous recipe.

To index a document, the method is `<client>.index` and it requires the name of the index, the type of the document, and the body of the document (if the ID is not given, it will be autogenerated):

```
es.index(index=index_name, doc_type=type_name, id=1,
         body={"name": "Joe Tester", "parsedtext": "Joe Testere nice guy",
 "uuid": "11111", "position": 1,
                "date": datetime(2013, 12, 8)})
```

It also accepts all the parameters that we have seen in the REST index API call in the *Indexing a document* recipe in Chapter 4, *Basic Operations*. The most common parameters passed to this function are as follows:

- `id`: This provides an ID to be used to index the document
- `routing`: This provides a shard routing to index the document in the specified shard
- `parent`: This provides a parent ID to be used to put the child document in the correct shard

To update a document, the method is `<client>.update` and it requires the following parameters:

- `index_name`
- `type_name`

- `id` of the document
- `script` or document to update the document
- `*` `lang` (optional): the language to be used, usually `painless`

If we want to increment a position by one, we will write a similar code:

```
es.update(index=index_name, doc_type=type_name, id=2, body=
{"script": 'ctx._source.position += 1')
```

Obviously, the call accepts all the parameters that we have discussed in the *Updating a document* recipe in Chapter 4, *Basic Operations*.

To delete a document, the method is `<client>.delete` and it requires the following parameters:

- `index_name`
- `type_name`
- `id` of the document

- If we want delete a document with `id=3`, we will write a similar code:

```
es.delete(index=index_name, doc_type=type_name, id=3)
```

> **TIP**
>
> Remember that all the Elasticsearch actions that work on documents are never seen instantly in the search. If you want to search without having to wait for the automatic refresh (every 1 second), you need to manually call the refresh API on the index.

To execute bulk indexing, the Elasticsearch client provides a `helper` function, which accepts a connection, an iterable list of documents, and the bulk size. The bulk size (the default is 500) defines the number of actions to send via a single bulk call. The parameters that must be passed to correctly control the indexing of the document are put in the document with the `_` prefix. The documents that are to be provided to the bulker must be formatted as a standard search result with the body in the `source` field:

```
from elasticsearch.helpers import bulk_index
bulk(es, [
    {"_index":index_name, "_type":type_name, "_id":"1", "source":
    {"name": "Joe Tester", "parsedtext": "Joe Testere nice guy",
    "uuid": "11111", "position": 1,
    "date": datetime(2013, 12, 8)}},

    {"_index": index_name, "_type": type_name, "_id": "1",
    "source": {"name": "Bill Baloney", "parsedtext": "Bill Testere
    nice guy", "uuid": "22222", "position": 2,
    "date": datetime(2013, 12, 8)}}
    ])
```

See also

- The *Indexing a document* recipe in `Chapter 4`, *Basic Operations*, about indexing a document in Elasticsearch
- The *Getting a document* recipe in `Chapter 4`, *Basic Operations*, about retrieving a document from Elasticsearch
- The *Deleting a document* recipe in `Chapter 4`, *Basic Operations*, about deleting stored documents in Elasticsearch
- The *Updating a document* recipe in `Chapter 4`, *Basic Operations*, about updating a document in Elasticsearch
- The *Speeding up atomic operations (Bulk operations)* recipe in `Chapter 4`, *Basic Operations*, about the advantages of using bulks for optimizing ingestion performances

Executing a standard search

After inserting documents, the most commonly executed action in Elasticsearch is the search. The official Elasticsearch client APIs for searching are similar to the REST API.

Getting ready

You need an up-and-running Elasticsearch installation, as we described in the *Downloading and installing Elasticsearch* recipe in `Chapter 2`, *Downloading and Setup*.

You also need the Python installed packages of the *Creating a client* recipe of this chapter.

The code of this recipe can be found in the `chapter_16/searching.py` file.

How to do it...

To execute a standard query, the client method `search` must be called by passing the `query` parameters, as we have seen in `Chapter 5`, *Search*. The required parameters are `index_name`, `type_name` and the query DSL. In this example, we show how to call a `match_all` query, a `term` query, and a `filter` query. We will perform the following steps:

1. We initialize the client and populate the index:

   ```
   import elasticsearch
   from pprint import pprint

   es = elasticsearch.Elasticsearch()
   index_name = "my_index"
   type_name = "my_type"

   if es.indices.exists(index_name):
       es.indices.delete(index_name)

   from utils import create_and_add_mapping, populate

   create_and_add_mapping(es, index_name, type_name)
   populate(es, index_name, type_name)
   ```

2. We execute a search with a `match_all` query and we will print the results:

   ```
   results = es.search(index_name, type_name, {"query":
   {"match_all": {}}})
   pprint(results)
   ```

3. We execute a search with a `term` query and we will print the results:

   ```
   results = es.search(index_name, type_name, {
       "query": {
       "query": {
           "term": {"name": {"boost": 3.0, "value": "joe"}}}
   }})
   pprint(results)
   ```

4. We execute a search with a `bool` filter query and we will print the results:

```
results = es.search(index_name, type_name, {"query": {
    "bool": {
        "filter": {
            "bool": {
                "should": [
                    {"term": {"position": 1}},
                    {"term": {"position": 2}}]}
        }}})
pprint(results)
```

5. We remove the index:

```
es.indices.delete(index_name)
```

How it works...

The idea behind Elasticsearch official clients is that they should offer a common API that is more similar to REST calls. In Python, it is very easy to use the query DSL, as it provides an easy mapping from the Python dictionary to JSON objects and vice versa.

In the preceding example, before calling the search, we need to initialize the index and put some data in it; this is done using the two helpers available in the `utils` package, available in `chapter_16` directory.

The two methods are:

- `create_and_add_mapping(es, index_name, type_name)`: This initializes the index and inserts the correct mapping to perform the search. The code of this function is taken from the *Managing mappings* recipe in this chapter.
- `populate(es, index_name, type_name)`: This populates the index with data. The code of this function is taken from the previous recipe.

After having initialized some data, we can execute queries against it. To execute a search, the method that must be called is `search` on the client. This method accepts all parameters described for REST calls in the *Searching* recipe in `Chapter 5`, *Search*.

The actual method signature for the `search` method is as follows:

```
@query_params('_source', '_source_exclude', '_source_include',
    'allow_no_indices', 'analyze_wildcard', 'analyzer', 'default_operator',
    'df', 'docvalue_fields', 'expand_wildcards', 'explain',
    'fielddata_fields', 'from_', 'ignore_unavailable', 'lenient',
    'lowercase_expanded_terms', 'preference', 'q', 'request_cache',
    'routing', 'scroll', 'search_type', 'size', 'sort', 'stats',
    'stored_fields', 'suggest_field', 'suggest_mode', 'suggest_size',
    'suggest_text', 'terminate_after', 'timeout', 'track_scores',
'version')
def search(self, index=None, doc_type=None, body=None, params=None):
```

The `index` value could be:

- An index name or an alias name
- A list of index (or alias) names as a string separated by commas (that is, `index1,index2,indexN`)
- `_all` is the special keyword that indicates all the indices

The `type` value could be:

- A `type_name`
- A list of type names as a string separated by a comma (that is, `type1,type2,typeN`)
- `None` to indicate all the types

The body is the search DSL, as we have seen in `Chapter 5`, *Search*. In the preceding example we have:

- A `match_all` query (see the *Matching all the documents* recipe in `Chapter 5`, *Search*) to match all the index-type documents:

    ```
    results = es.search(index_name, type_name, {"query":
    {"match_all": {}}})
    ```

- A `term` query that matches a name term `joe` with `boost 3.0` (for further details, see the *Quering for a single term* recipe in `Chapter 6`, *Text and Numeric Queries*):

    ```
    results = es.search(index_name, type_name, {
        "query": {
            "query": {
                "term": {"name": {"boost": 3.0, "value": "joe"}}}
        }})
    ```

- A filtered query with a query (`match_all`) and an `or` filter with two `term` filters matching `position` 1 and 2.

```
results = es.search(index_name, type_name, {"query": {
    "bool": {
        "filter": {
            "bool": {
                "should": [
                    {"term": {"position": 1}},
                    {"term": {"position": 2}}]]}
    }}}})
```

The returned result is a JSON dictionary, which we discussed in Chapter 5, *Search*.

If some hits are matched, they are returned in the hits field. The standard number of results returned is 10. To return more results, you need to paginate the results with the from and start parameters.

In Chapter 5, *Search*, there is a definition of all the parameters used in the search.

See also

- The *Executing a search* recipe in Chapter 5, *Search*, for a detailed description of some search parameters and the *Matching all the documents* recipe in Chapter 5, *Search*, for a description of the match_all query

Executing a search with aggregations

Searching for results is obviously the main activity for a search engine; thus a aggregations are very important because they often help to augment the results.

Aggregations are executed along the search by performing analytics on searched results.

Getting ready

You need an up-and-running Elasticsearch installation, as we described in the *Downloading and installing Elasticsearch* recipe in Chapter 2, *Downloading and Setup*.

You also need the Python installed packages of the *Creating a client* recipe of this chapter.

The code of this recipe can be found in the `chapter_16/aggregation.py` file.

How to do it...

To extend a query with the aggregations part, you need to define an aggregation section, as we have already seen in `Chapter 8`, *Aggregations*. In the case of the official Elasticsearch client, you can add the aggregation DSL to the search dictionary to provide aggregations. We will perform the following steps:

1. We initialize the client and populate the index:

```
import elasticsearch
from pprint import pprint

es = elasticsearch.Elasticsearch()
index_name = "my_index"
type_name = "my_type"

if es.indices.exists(index_name):
    es.indices.delete(index_name)

from utils import create_and_add_mapping, populate

create_and_add_mapping(es, index_name, type_name)
populate(es, index_name, type_name)
```

2. We can execute a search with a `terms` aggregation:

```
results = es.search(index_name, type_name,
    {
        "query": {"match_all": {}},
        "aggs": {
            "pterms": {"terms": {"field": "parsedtext", "size":
            10}}
        }
    })
pprint(results)
```

3. We can execute a search with a date histogram aggregation:

```
results = es.search(index_name, type_name,
    {
        "query": {"match_all": {}},
        "aggs": {
            "date_histo": {"date_histogram": {"field": "date",
            "interval": "month"}}
        }
    })
pprint(results)

es.indices.delete(index_name)
```

How it works...

As described in Chapter 8, *Aggregations*, the aggregations are calculated during the search in a distributed way. When you send a query to Elasticsearch with the aggregations defined, it adds an additional step in the query processing, allowing aggregation computation.

In the preceding example, there are two kinds of aggregations; the term aggregation and the date histogram aggregation.

The first one is used to count terms and it is often seen in sites that provide facet filtering on term aggregations of results such as producers, geographic locations, and so on:

```
results = es.search(index_name, type_name,
    {
        "query": {"match_all": {}},
        "aggs": {
            "pterms": {"terms": {"field": "parsedtext", "size": 10}}
        }
    })
```

The terms aggregation requires a field to count on. The default number of buckets for the field returned is 10. This value could be changed, defining the size parameter.

The second kind of aggregation calculated is the date histogram, which provides hits based on a `datetime` field. This aggregation requires at least two parameters; the `datetime` field to be used as the source and the `interval` to be used for computation:

```
results = es.search(index_name, type_name,
    {
        "query": {"match_all": {}},
        "aggs": {
            "date_histo": {"date_histogram": {"field": "date", "interval":
"month"}}
        }
    })
```

The search results are standard search responses that we have already seen in `Chapter 8`, *Aggregations*.

See also

- The *Executing the termsAggregation* recipe in `Chapter 8`, *Aggregations*, on aggregating terms values and the *Executing the date histogram aggregation* recipe in `Chapter 8`, *Aggregations*, on computing the histogram aggregation on datetime fields

17
Plugin Development

In this chapter we will cover the following recipes:

- Creating a plugin
- Creating an analyzer plugin
- Creating a REST plugin
- Creating a cluster action
- Creating an ingest plugin

Introduction

Elasticsearch is designed to be extended with plugins to improve its capabilities. In the previous chapters we installed and used many of them (new queries, REST endpoints, and scripting plugins).

Plugins are application extensions that can add many features to Elasticsearch. They can have several usages, such as:

- Adding new scripting language (that is, Python and JavaScript plugins)
  Adding new aggregation types
- Extending Lucene-supported analyzers and tokenizers
- Using native scripting to speed up computation of scores, filters and field manipulation
- Extending node capabilities, for example creating a node plugin that can execute your logic
- Monitoring and administering clusters

In this chapter, the Java language will be used to develop a the native plugin, but it is possible to use any JVM language that generates JAR files.

Creating a plugin

Native plugins allow several aspects of the Elasticsearch server to be extended, but they require a good knowledge of Java.

In this recipe we will see how to set up a working environment to develop native plugins.

Getting ready

You need an up-and-running Elasticsearch installation as we described in the *Downloading and installing Elasticsearch* recipe in `Chapter 2`, *Downloading and Setup*.

A Maven tool, or an IDE that supports Java programming, such as Eclipse or IntelliJ IDEA, is required.

The code to this recipe is available in the `chapter17/simple_plugin` directory.

How to do it...

Generally, Elasticsearch plugins are developed in Java using the Maven build tool and deployed as a ZIP file.

To create a simple JAR plugin, we will perform the following steps:

1. To correctly build and serve a plugin, some files must be defined:
    - `pom.xml` is used to define the build configuration for Maven.
    - `es-plugin.properties` defines the namespace of the plugin class that must be loaded.
    - `<name>plugin.java` is the main plugin class, which is loaded at startup and also initializes the action's plugin.
    - `plugin.xml` assemblies, which defines how to execute the assembly steps with Maven. It is used to build the ZIP file to deliver the plugin.

2. A standard `pom.xml` file is used for creating a plugin containing the following code:

    The Maven `pom.xml` header:

```xml
<?xml version="1.0" encoding="UTF-8"?>
<project xmlns="http://maven.apache.org/POM/4.0.0"
        xmlns:xsi="http://www.w3.org/2001/XMLSchema-instance"
        xsi:schemaLocation="http://maven.apache.org/POM/4.0.0
http://maven.apache.org/xsd/maven-4.0.0.xsd">
    <name>elasticsearch-simple-plugin</name>
    <modelVersion>4.0.0</modelVersion>
    <groupId>com.packtpub</groupId>
    <artifactId>simple-plugin</artifactId>
    <version>${elasticsearch.version}</version>
    <packaging>jar</packaging>
    <description>A simple plugin for Elasticsearch</description>
    <inceptionYear>2013</inceptionYear>
    <licenses>...   </licenses>
```

3. The parent `pom.xml` file is used to derive common properties or settings:

```xml
<parent>
    <groupId>org.sonatype.oss</groupId>
    <artifactId>oss-parent</artifactId>
    <version>7</version>
</parent>
```

4. Some properties are mainly used to simplify the dependencies:

```xml
<properties>
    <elasticsearch.version>5.1.1</elasticsearch.version>
    <maven.compiler.target>1.8</maven.compiler.target>
    <elasticsearch.assembly.descriptor>${project.basedir}
    /src/main/assemblies/plugin.xml
    </elasticsearch.assembly.descriptor>
    <elasticsearch.plugin.name>simple-plugin
    </elasticsearch.plugin.name>
    <elasticsearch.plugin.classname>
    org.elasticsearch.plugin.simple.SimplePlugin
    </elasticsearch.plugin.classname>
    <elasticsearch.plugin.jvm>true</elasticsearch.plugin.jvm>
    <tests.rest.load_packaged>false</tests.rest.load_packaged>
    <skip.unit.tests>true</skip.unit.tests>
</properties>
```

5. A list of JAR dependencies:

```xml
<dependencies>
    <dependency>
        <groupId>org.elasticsearch</groupId>
        <artifactId>elasticsearch</artifactId>
        <version>${elasticsearch.version}</version>
        <scope>compile</scope>
    </dependency>
    <dependency>
        <groupId>org.apache.httpcomponents</groupId>
        <artifactId>httpclient</artifactId>
        <version>4.5.2</version>
    </dependency>
    <dependency>
        <groupId>org.apache.logging.log4j</groupId>
        <artifactId>log4j-api</artifactId>
        <version>2.3</version>
    </dependency>
    <!- Testing dependencies -->
    <dependency>
        <groupId>org.hamcrest</groupId>
        <artifactId>hamcrest-core</artifactId>
        <version>1.3</version>
        <scope>test</scope>
    </dependency>
    <dependency>
        <groupId>org.hamcrest</groupId>
        <artifactId>hamcrest-library</artifactId>
        <version>1.3</version>
        <scope>test</scope>
    </dependency>
    <dependency>
        <groupId>junit</groupId>
        <artifactId>junit</artifactId>
        <version>4.12</version>
        <scope>test</scope>
    </dependency>
</dependencies>
```

6. A list of Maven plugins required is to build and deploy the artifact:

```
<build>
    <plugins>
        <plugin><!- for compiling -->
            <groupId>org.apache.maven.plugins</groupId>
            <artifactId>maven-compiler-plugin</artifactId>
            <version>3.1</version>
            <configuration>
                <source>1.7</source>
                <target>1.7</target>
            </configuration>
        </plugin>
        <plugin><!- optional for executing tests -->
            <groupId>org.apache.maven.plugins</groupId>
            <artifactId>maven-surefire-plugin</artifactId>
            <version>2.12.3</version>
            <configuration>
                <includes>
                    <include>**/*Tests.java</include>
                </includes>
            </configuration>
        </plugin>
        <plugin><!- optional for publishing the source -->
            <groupId>org.apache.maven.plugins</groupId>
            <artifactId>maven-source-plugin</artifactId>
            <version>2.3</version>
            <executions>
                <execution>
                    <id>attach-sources</id>
                    <goals>
                        <goal>jar</goal>
                    </goals>
                </execution>
            </executions>
        </plugin>
        <plugin>><!- for packaging the plugin -->
            <artifactId>maven-assembly-plugin</artifactId>
            <version>2.3</version>
            <configuration>
                <appendAssemblyId>false</appendAssemblyId>
                <outputDirectory>${project.build.directory}
                /releases/</outputDirectory>
                <descriptors>
                <descriptor>${basedir}/src/main/assemblies
                 /plugin.xml</descriptor>
                </descriptors>
            </configuration>
```

```
                    <executions>
                        <execution>
                            <phase>package</phase>
                            <goals><goal>single</goal></goals>
                        </execution>
                    </executions>
                </plugin>
            </plugins>
        </build>
    </project>
```

7. In the JAR, there must be a `src/main/resources/plugin-descriptor.properties` file, which defines the entry point class that must be loaded during plugin initialization. This file must be embedded in the final JAR; it is usually put in the `src/main/resources` directory of the Maven project. It's generally rendered with the data taken from the Maven properties. For example:

```
classname=${elasticsearch.plugin.classname}
version=${project.version}
```

8. The `src/main/java/org/elasticsearch/plugin/simple/SimplePlugin.java` class is an example of the basic (the minimum required) code that needs to be compiled for executing a plugin:

```
package org.elasticsearch.plugin.simple;

import org.elasticsearch.plugins.Plugin;

public class SimplePlugin extends Plugin {

}
```

9. To complete compiling and deploying the workflow, we need to define a `src/main/assemblies/plugin.xml` file used in the Maven assembly step. This file defines the resources that must be packaged into the final ZIP archive. Let's take a look:

```
<?xml version="1.0"?>
<assembly>
    <id>simple-plugin</id>
    <formats>
        <format>zip</format>
    </formats>
    <includeBaseDirectory>false</includeBaseDirectory>
    <dependencySets>
```

```
<dependencySet>
    <outputDirectory>/</outputDirectory>
    <useProjectArtifact>true</useProjectArtifact>
    <useTransitiveFiltering>true</useTransitiveFiltering>
      <excludes>
      <exclude>org.elasticsearch:elasticsearch</exclude>
    </excludes>
    </dependencySet>
  </dependencySets>
</assembly>
```

How it works...

Several parts make up the development life cycle of a plugin, such as designing, coding, building, and deploying. To speed up the build and deployment steps, which are common to all plugins, we need to create a Maven pom.xml file.

The preceding pom.xml file is a standard for developing Elasticsearch plugins. This file is composed of:

- Several section entries used to set up the current Maven project. In detail, we have:
- The name of the plugin (that is, elasticsearch-simple-plugin):

  ```
  <name>elasticsearch-simple-plugin</name>
  ```

- The groupId and artifactId used to define the plugin artifact name:

  ```
  <groupId>com.packtpub</groupId>
  <artifactId>simple-plugin</artifactId>
  ```

- The plugin version:

  ```
  <version>${elasticsearch.version}</version>
  ```

- The type of packaging:

  ```
  <packaging>jar</packaging>
  ```

- A project description with the starting year:

  ```
  <description>A simple plugin for Elasticsearch</description>
  <inceptionYear>2016</inceptionYear>
  ```

- An optional license section, in which we can define the license for the plugin. For the standard Apache one, the code should look like this:

```
<licenses>
    <license>
        <name>The Apache Software License, Version 2.0</name>
        <url>http://www.apache.org/licenses/LICENSE-2.0.txt</url>
        <distribution>repo</distribution>
    </license>
</licenses>
```

- A parent pom, used to inherit common properties. Generally for plugins, it is useful to inherit from the `sonatype` base pom.

```
<parent>
    <groupId>org.sonatype.oss</groupId>
    <artifactId>oss-parent</artifactId>
    <version>7</version>
</parent>
```

- Global variables set are typically in the `properties` section, the Elasticsearch version and other library versions are set. The properties are used to modularize the Maven strings (replace the properties variable value in different part of `pom.xml`). Here we can also define variables that will be resolved during Maven execution.

> It is very important that the Elasticsearch JAR version matches the Elasticsearch cluster version to prevent issues arising from changes between releases.

- A list of dependencies for compiling a plugin, the Elasticsearch JAR and the `log4j` library are required for the compile phase. If you need to test it, remember to add the test JAR as dependencies.
- The Maven plugin section contains a list of Maven plugins that execute several build steps. We have:

    The compiler section, which requires a source compilation. The Java version is fixed at 1.8:

```
<plugin>
    <groupId>org.apache.maven.plugins</groupId>
    <artifactId>maven-compiler-plugin</artifactId>
    <version>3.5.1</version>
    <configuration>
```

```
        <source>${maven.compiler.target}</source>
        <target>${maven.compiler.target}</target>
    </configuration>
</plugin>
```

The source section, which enables the creation of source packages that are to be released with the binary (useful for debugging):

```
<plugin>
    <groupId>org.apache.maven.plugins</groupId>
    <artifactId>maven-source-plugin</artifactId>
    <version>2.3</version>
        <executions>
        <execution>
            <id>attach-sources</id>
            <goals>
                <goal>jar</goal>
            </goals>
        </execution>
    </executions>
</plugin>
```

The assembly section, which builds a ZIP taking a configuration `plugin.xml` file and puts the output in the releases directory:

```
<plugin>
    <artifactId>maven-assembly-plugin</artifactId>
    <version>2.3</version>
    <configuration>
        <appendAssemblyId>false</appendAssemblyId>
        <outputDirectory>${project.build.directory}
        /releases/</outputDirectory>
        <descriptors>
<descriptor>${basedir}/src/main/assemblies/
plugin.xml</descriptor>
        </descriptors>
    </configuration>
    <executions>
        <execution>
            <phase>package</phase>
            <goals><goal>single</goal></goals>
        </execution>
    </executions>
</plugin>
```

Related to `pom.xml`, we have the `plugin.xml` file, which describes how to assemble the final ZIP file. This file is usually contained in the `/src/main/assemblies/` directory of the project.

The most important sections of this file are as follows:

- `formats`: Here the destination format is defined:

```
<formats><format>zip</format></formats>
```

- `excludes sets in dependencySet`: Contains the artifacts to exclude from the package. Generally, we exclude the Elasticsearch JAR as it's already provided in the server install:

```
<dependencySet>
    <outputDirectory>/</outputDirectory>
    <useProjectArtifact>true</useProjectArtifact>
    <useTransitiveFiltering>true</useTransitiveFiltering>
    <excludes>
        <exclude>org.elasticsearch:elasticsearch</exclude>
    </excludes>
</dependencySet>
```

- `includes sets in dependencySet`: Contains the artifacts to include into the package. They are mainly the required JAR files used to run the plugin:

```
<dependencySet>
    <outputDirectory>/</outputDirectory>
    <useProjectArtifact>true</useProjectArtifact>
    <useTransitiveFiltering>true</useTransitiveFiltering>
    <includes>... truncated ...</includes>
</dependencySet>
```

During plugin packaging, the `include` and `exclude` rules are verified and only files that are allowed to be distributed are put in the ZIP.

After having configured Maven, we can start to write the main plugin class.

Every plugin class must be derived from `Plugin` one and it must be public otherwise it cannot be loaded dynamically from the JAR:

```
import org.elasticsearch.plugins.Plugin;
public class SimplePlugin extends Plugin {
```

After having defined all files required to generate a ZIP release of our plugin it is enough to invoke the `maven package` command. This command will compile the code and create a `zip` package in the `target/releases` directory of your project: the final ZIP file can be deployed as a plugin on your Elasticsearch cluster.

In this recipe, we configured a working environment to build, deploy and test plugins. In the next recipes, we will reuse this environment to develop several plugin types.

There's more...

Compiling and packaging a plugin are not enough to define a good lifecycle for your plugin: a test phase for testing your plugin functionalities needs to be provided.

Testing the plugin functionalities with test cases reduces the number of bugs that can affect the plugin when its released.

It is possible to add a test phase in the Maven build `pom.xml`.

Firstly, we need to add the package dependencies required for testing Elasticsearch and Lucene. These dependencies must be added for the test:

```
<dependencies>
  <dependency>
    <groupId>org.apache.lucene</groupId>
    <artifactId>lucene-test-framework</artifactId>
    <version>${lucene.version}</version>
    <scope>test</scope>
  </dependency>
  <dependency>
    <groupId>org.elasticsearch.test</groupId>
    <artifactId>framework</artifactId>
    <version>${elasticsearch.version}</version>
    <scope>test</scope>
  </dependency>
</dependencies>
```

The order is very important, so make sure to put the `lucene-test-framework` at the top of your dependencies; otherwise problems with loading and executing tests may occur.

For the unit and integration test, the Elasticsearch community mainly uses the `hamcrest` library (`https://code.google.com/p/hamcrest/`). To use this, you need to add its dependencies in the `dependencies` section of the `pom.xml`:

```
<dependency>
    <groupId>org.hamcrest</groupId>
    <artifactId>hamcrest-core</artifactId>
    <version>1.3</version>
    <scope>test</scope>
</dependency>
```

```
<dependency>
    <groupId>org.hamcrest</groupId>
    <artifactId>hamcrest-library</artifactId>
    <version>1.3 </version>
    <scope>test</scope>
</dependency>
```

> Note that the compiling scope is `test`, which means that these are dependencies applied only during the test phase.

To complete the test part, we need to add a Maven plugin, which executes the tests:

```
<plugin>
    <groupId>org.apache.maven.plugins</groupId>
    <artifactId>maven-surefire-plugin</artifactId>
    <version>2.12.3</version>
    <configuration>
        <includes><include>**/*Tests.java</include></includes>
    </configuration>
</plugin>
```

The `includes` section lists all the possible classes that contain tests via the glob expression.

Creating an analyzer plugin

Elasticsearch provides, out-of-the-box, a large set of analyzers and tokenizers to cover general needs. Sometimes we need to extend the capabilities of Elasticsearch by adding new analyzers.

Typically you can create an analyzer plugin when you need:

- To add standard Lucene analyzers/tokenizers not provided by Elasticsearch
- To integrate third-part analyzers
- To add custom analyzers

In this recipe we will add a new custom English analyzer similar to the one provided by Elasticsearch.

Getting ready

You need an up-and-running Elasticsearch installation as we described in the *Downloading and installing Elasticsearch* recipe in Chapter 2, *Downloading and Setup*.

A Maven tool, or an IDE that supports Java programming, such as Eclipse or IntelliJ IDEA. The code for this recipe is available in the chapter17/analysis_plugin directory.

How to do it...

An analyzer plugin is generally composed of two classes:

- A Plugin class, which implements the org.elasticsearch.plugins.AnalysisPlugin class
- An AnalyzerProviders class, which provides an analyzer

For creating an analyzer plugin, we will perform the following steps:

1. The plugin class is similar to previous recipes, plus a method that returns the analyzers:

```
public class AnalysisPlugin extends Plugin implements
org.elasticsearch.plugins.AnalysisPlugin {
    @Override
    public Map<String, AnalysisModule.AnalysisProvider
    <AnalyzerProvider<? extends Analyzer>>>
    getAnalyzers() {
        Map<String, AnalysisModule.AnalysisProvider
        <AnalyzerProvider<? extends Analyzer>>>
analyzers = new HashMap();
        analyzers.put(CustomEnglishAnalyzerProvider.NAME,
        CustomEnglishAnalyzerProvider::
        getCustomEnglishAnalyzerProvider);
        return analyzers;
    }
}
```

2. The `AnalyzerProvider` class provides the initialization of our analyzer, passing parameters provided by the settings:

```
package org.elasticsearch.index.analysis;

import org.apache.lucene.analysis.en.EnglishAnalyzer;
import org.apache.lucene.analysis.util.CharArraySet;
import org.elasticsearch.common.settings.Settings;
import org.elasticsearch.env.Environment;
import org.elasticsearch.index.IndexSettings;

public class CustomEnglishAnalyzerProvider extends
AbstractIndexAnalyzerProvider<EnglishAnalyzer> {
    public static String NAME = "custom_english";

    private final EnglishAnalyzer analyzer;

    public CustomEnglishAnalyzerProvider(IndexSettings
    indexSettings, Environment env, String name, Settings
    settings, boolean useSmart) {
        super(indexSettings, name, settings);

        analyzer = new EnglishAnalyzer(
                Analysis.parseStopWords(env, settings,
                EnglishAnalyzer.getDefaultStopSet(), true),
                Analysis.parseStemExclusion(settings,
                CharArraySet.EMPTY_SET));
    }

    public static CustomEnglishAnalyzerProvider
    getCustomEnglishAnalyzerProvider(IndexSettings
    indexSettings, Environment env, String name, Settings
    settings) {
        return new CustomEnglishAnalyzerProvider(indexSettings,
        env, name, settings, true);
     }

    @Override
    public EnglishAnalyzer get() {
        return this.analyzer;
    }
}
```

After building the plugin and installing it on an Elasticsearch server, our analyzer is accessible as any native Elasticsearch analyzer.

How it works...

Creating an analyzer plugin is quite simple. The general workflow is:

- Wrap the analyzer initialization in a provider
- Register the analyzer provider in the plugin

In the preceding example, we registered a `CustomEnglishAnalyzerProvider` class, which extends the `EnglishAnalyzer` class.

```
public class CustomEnglishAnalyzerProvider extends
AbstractIndexAnalyzerProvider<EnglishAnalyzer>
```

We need to provide a name to `analyzer`:

```
public static String NAME="custom_english";
```

We instantiate a private scope Lucene analyzer to be provided on request with the GET method.

```
private final EnglishAnalyzer analyzer;
```

The `CustomEnglishAnalyzerProvider` constructor can be injected via Google Guice, with settings that can be used to provide cluster defaults, via index settings or `elasticsearch.yml`.

```
public CustomEnglishAnalyzerProvider(IndexSettings indexSettings,
Environment env, String name, Settings settings) {
```

To make it work correctly, we need to set up the parent constructor via the super call.

```
super(index, indexSettings, name, settings);
```

Now we can initialize the internal analyzer, which must be returned by the GET method:

```
analyzer = new EnglishAnalyzer(
Analysis.parseStopWords(env, settings, EnglishAnalyzer.getDefaultStopSet(),
true),
            Analysis.parseStemExclusion(settings,
CharArraySet.EMPTY_SET));
```

This analyzer accepts:

- A list of stopwords that can be loaded by settings or set by the default ones
- A list of words that must be excluded by the stemming step

To easily wrap the analyzer we need to create a `static` method that can be called to create the analyzer; and we'll use it in the plugin definition:

```
public static CustomEnglishAnalyzerProvider
getCustomEnglishAnalyzerProvider(IndexSettings indexSettings, Environment
env, String name, Settings settings) {
    return new CustomEnglishAnalyzerProvider(indexSettings, env, name,
settings, true);
}
```

Finally we can register our analyzer in the plugin. To do so our plugin must derive from `AnalysisPlugin` so that we can override the `getAnalyzers` method:

```
@Override
public Map<String, AnalysisModule.AnalysisProvider<AnalyzerProvider<?
extends Analyzer>>> getAnalyzers() {
    Map<String, AnalysisModule.AnalysisProvider<AnalyzerProvider<? extends
Analyzer>>> analyzers = new HashMap();
    analyzers.put(CustomEnglishAnalyzerProvider.NAME,
CustomEnglishAnalyzerProvider::getCustomEnglishAnalyzerProvider);
    return analyzers;
}
```

The `::` operator of Java 8 allows us to provide a function that will be used for the construction of our `AnalyzerProvider`.

There's more...

A plugin extends several Elasticsearch functionalities. To provide them with this requires extending the correct plugin interface. In Elasticsearch 5.x, the plugin interfaces are:

- `ActionPlugin`: This is used for REST and cluster actions
- `AnalysisPlugin`: This is used for extending all the analysis stuff, such as analyzers, tokenizers, tokenFilters, and charFilters
- `ClusterPlugin`: This is used to provide new deciders
- `DiscoveryPlugin`: This is used to provide custom node name resolvers
- `IngestPlugin`: This is used to provide new ingest processors
- `MapperPlugin`: This is used to provide new mappers and metadata mappers
- `RepositoryPlugin`: This allows the provision of new repositories to be used in backup/restore functionalities
- `ScriptPlugin`: This allows the provision of new scripting languages, scripting contexts or native scripts (Java based ones)

- `SearchPlugin`: This allows extending all the search functionalities: Highlighter, aggregations, suggesters, and queries

If your plugin needs to extend more than a single functionality, it can extend from several plugin interfaces at once.

Creating a REST plugin

In the previous recipe we read how to build an analyzer plugin that extends the query capabilities of Elasticsearch. In this recipe, we will see how to create one of the most common Elasticsearch plugins.

This kind of plugin allows the standard REST calls to be extended with custom ones to easily improve the capabilities of Elasticsearch.

In this recipe, we will see how to define a REST entry-point and create its action; in the next one, we'll see how to execute this action distributed in shards.

Getting ready

You need an up-and-running Elasticsearch installation as we described in the *Downloading and installing Elasticsearch* recipe in `Chapter 2`, *Downloading and Setup*.

A Maven tool, or an IDE that supports Java programming, such as Eclipse or IntelliJ IDEA. The code for this recipe is available in the `chapter17/rest_plugin` directory.

How to do it...

To create a REST entry-point, we need to create the action and then register it in the plugin. We will perform the following steps:

1. We create a REST `simple` action (`RestSimpleAction.java`):

```
...
public class RestSimpleAction extends BaseRestHandler {
    @Inject
    public RestSimpleAction(Settings settings, Client client,
    RestController controller) {
        super(settings);
        controller.registerHandler(POST, "/_simple", this);
```

```
        controller.registerHandler(POST, "/{index}/_simple",
        this);
        controller.registerHandler(POST, "/_simple/{field}",
        this);
        controller.registerHandler(GET, "/_simple", this);
        controller.registerHandler(GET, "/{index}/_simple",
        this);
        controller.registerHandler(GET, "/_simple/{field}",
        this);
    }

    @Override
    protected RestChannelConsumer prepareRequest(RestRequest
    request, NodeClient client) throws IOException {
        final SimpleRequest simpleRequest = new
        SimpleRequest(Strings.splitStringByCommaToArray
        (request.param("index")));
        simpleRequest.setField(request.param("field"));
        return channel -> client.execute(SimpleAction.INSTANCE,
        simpleRequest, new RestBuilderListener<SimpleResponse>
        (channel){
    @Override
    public RestResponse buildResponse(SimpleResponse
    simpleResponse, XContentBuilder builder) throws Exception {
                try {
                    builder.startObject();
                    builder.field("ok", true);
                    builder.array("terms",
                    simpleResponse.getSimple().toArray());
                    builder.endObject();

                } catch (Exception e) {
                    onFailure(e);
                }
                return new BytesRestResponse(OK, builder);
            }
        });
    }
}
```

2. We need to register it in the plugin with the following lines:

```
public class RestPlugin extends Plugin implements ActionPlugin {

    @Override
    public List<Class<? extends RestHandler>> getRestHandlers() {
        return singletonList(RestSimpleAction.class);
    }
```

```
        @Override
        public List<ActionHandler<? extends ActionRequest<?>, ?
        extends ActionResponse>> getActions() {
            return singletonList(new ActionHandler<>
            (SimpleAction.INSTANCE, TransportSimpleAction.class));
        }


    }
```

3. Now we can build the plugin via the `mvn package` and manually install the ZIP. If we restart the Elasticsearch server, we should see the plugin loaded:

```
[...][INFO ][o.e.n.Node                ] [es] initializing ...
[...][INFO ][o.e.e.NodeEnvironment     ] [es] using [1] data
paths, mounts [[/ (/dev/disk1)]], net usable_space [24.8gb],
net total_space [930.7gb], spins? [unknown], types [hfs]
[...][INFO ][o.e.e.NodeEnvironment     ] [es] heap size [1.9gb],
compressed ordinary object pointers [true]
[...][INFO ][o.e.n.Node                ] [es] version[5.0.2],
pid[46225], build[f6b4951/2016-11-24T10:07:18.101Z], OS[Mac OS
X/10.12.1/x86_64], JVM[Oracle Corporation/Java HotSpot(TM) 64-
Bit Server VM/1.8.0_101/25.101-b13]
[...][INFO ][o.e.p.PluginsService      ] [es] loaded module
[aggs-matrix-stats]
[...][INFO ][o.e.p.PluginsService      ] [es] loaded module
[ingest-common]
[...][INFO ][o.e.p.PluginsService      ] [es] loaded module
[lang-expression]
[...][INFO ][o.e.p.PluginsService      ] [es] loaded module
[lang-groovy]
[...][INFO ][o.e.p.PluginsService      ] [es] loaded module
[lang-mustache]
[...][INFO ][o.e.p.PluginsService      ] [es] loaded module
[lang-painless]
[...][INFO ][o.e.p.PluginsService      ] [es] loaded module
[percolator]
[...][INFO ][o.e.p.PluginsService      ] [es] loaded module
[reindex]
[...][INFO ][o.e.p.PluginsService      ] [es] loaded module
[transport-netty3]
[...][INFO ][o.e.p.PluginsService      ] [es] loaded module
[transport-netty4]
[...][INFO ][o.e.p.PluginsService      ] [es] loaded plugin
[simple-plugin]
[...][INFO ][o.e.n.Node                ] [es] initialized
[...][INFO ][o.e.n.Node                ] [es] starting ...
```

4. We can test out custom REST via `curl`:

```
curl 'http://127.0.0.1:9200/_simple?field=mytest&pretty'
```

5. The result will be something similar to:

```
{
  "ok" : true,
  "terms" : [
    "mytest_[test-index][0]",
    "mytest_[test-index][3]",
    "mytest_[test-index][4]",
    "mytest_[test-index][1]",
    "mytest_[test-index][2]"
  ]
}
```

How it works...

Adding a REST action is very easy: We need to create a `RestXXXAction` class that handles the calls.

The rest action is derived from the `BaseRestHandler` class and needs to implement the `handleRequest` method.

The constructor is very important. So let's start by writing:

```
@Inject
public RestSimpleAction(Settings settings, RestController controller)
```

Its signature usually `injects` via Guice (a lightweight dependency injection framework very popular in the Java ecosystem. See the library homepage for more details at https://code.google.com/p/google-guice/) with the following parameters:

- `Settings`, which can be used to load custom settings for your rest action
- `RestController`, which is used to register the REST action to the controller

In the constructor of the REST action, the list of actions that must be handled is registered in the `RestController`:

```
controller.registerHandler(POST, "/_simple", this);
...
```

To register an action, some parameters must be passed to the controller:

- The REST method (GET/POST/PUT/DELETE/HEAD/OPTIONS)
- The URL entry-point
- The RestHandler, usually the same class, which must answer the call

After having defined the constructor, if an action is fired, the class method prepareRequest is called:

```
@Override
protected RestChannelConsumer prepareRequest(RestRequest request,
NodeClient client) throws IOException {
```

This method is the core of the REST action. It processes the request and sends back the result. The parameters passed to the method are:

- RestRequest: The REST request that hits the Elasticsearch server
- RestChannel: The channel used to send back the response
- NodeClient: The client used to communicate in the cluster

The returned value is a RestChannelConsumer that is a FunctionalInterface that accepts a RestChannel– it's a simple Lambda.

A prepareRequest method is usually composed of these phases:

- Process the REST request and build an inner Elasticsearch request object
- Call the client with the Elasticsearch request
- If it is okay, process the Elasticsearch response and build the resulting JSON
- If there are errors, send back the JSON error response

In the preceding example, we created a SimpleRequest processing the request:

```
final SimpleRequest simpleRequest = new
SimpleRequest(Strings.splitStringByCommaToArray(request.param("index")));
simpleRequest.setField(request.param("field"));
```

As you can see, it accepts a list of indices (we split the classic comma-separated list of indices via the Strings.splitStringByCommaToArray helper) and we had the field parameter if available.

Now that we have a `SimpleRequest`, we can send it to the cluster and get back `SimpleResponse` via the Lambda closure:

```
return channel -> client.execute(SimpleAction.INSTANCE, simpleRequest, new
RestBuilderListener<SimpleResponse>(channel){
```

`client.execute` accepts an action, a request, and a `RestBuilderListener` class that maps a future response. We can now process the response via the definition of a `onResponse` method.

`onResponse` receives a `Response` object that must be converted in a JSON result.

```
@Override
public RestResponse buildResponse(SimpleResponse simpleResponse,
XContentBuilder builder) throws Exception {
```

The builder is the standard JSON `XContentBuilder` that we have already seen in `Chapter 14`, *Java Integration,*

After having processed the cluster response and built the JSON, we can send the REST response.

```
return new BytesRestResponse(OK, builder);
```

Obviously, if something goes wrong during the JSON creation, an exception must be raised.

```
try {/* JSON building*/
} catch (Exception e) {
    onFailure(e);
}
```

We will discuss `SimpleRequest` in the next recipe.

See also

- Google Guice is used for dependency injection at;
  see `https://code.google.com/p/google-guice/` for more information on the dependency injection system used by Elasticsearch

Creating a cluster action

In the previous recipe, we saw how to create a REST entry-point, but to execute the action at cluster level, we will need to create a cluster action.

An Elasticsearch action is generally executed and distributed in the cluster and in this recipe we will see how to implement this kind of action. The cluster action will be very bare; we send a string with a value to every shard and the shards echo a result string concatenating the string with the shard number.

Getting ready

You need an up-and-running Elasticsearch installation as we described in the *Downloading and installing Elasticsearch* recipe in `Chapter 2`, *Downloading and Setup*.

A Maven tool, or an IDE that support Java programming, such as Eclipse or IntelliJ IDEA. The code for this recipe is available in the `chapter17/rest_plugin` directory.

How to do it...

In this recipe we will see that a REST call is converted to an internal cluster action. To execute an internal cluster action, some classes are required:

- A `Request` and `Response` class to communicate with the cluster
- A `RequestBuilder` used to execute a request to the cluster
- An `Action` used to register the action and bound `Request`, `Response` and `RequestBuilder`
- A `Transport*Action` to bind the request and response to `ShardResponse`: it manages the reduce part of the query
- A `ShardResponse` to manage the shard results

We will perform the following steps:

1. We write a `SimpleRequest` class:

   ```
   ...
   public class SimpleRequest extends
   BroadcastRequest<SimpleRequest> {
       private String field;
   ```

```
        SimpleRequest() {
        }

        public SimpleRequest(String... indices) {
            super(indices);
        }

        public void setField(String field) {
            this.field = field;
        }

        public String getField() {
            return field;
        }

        @Override
        public void readFrom(StreamInput in) throws IOException {
            super.readFrom(in);
            field = in.readString();
        }

         @Override
        public void writeTo(StreamOutput out) throws IOException {
            super.writeTo(out);
            out.writeString(field);
        }
    }
```

2. The `SimpleResponse` class is very similar to the `SimpleRequest`.

3. To bind the request and the response, an action (`SimpleAction`) is required:

```
package org.elasticsearch.action.simple;

import org.elasticsearch.action.Action;
import org.elasticsearch.client.ElasticsearchClient;

public class SimpleAction extends Action<SimpleRequest,
SimpleResponse, SimpleRequestBuilder> {

    public static final SimpleAction INSTANCE = new
    SimpleAction();
    public static final String NAME = "custom:indices/simple";

    private SimpleAction() {
        super(NAME);
    }

    @Override
```

```
    public SimpleResponse newResponse() {
        return new SimpleResponse();
    }

    @Override
    public SimpleRequestBuilder
    newRequestBuilder(ElasticsearchClient elasticsearchClient)
    {
        return new SimpleRequestBuilder(elasticsearchClient,
        this);
    }
}
```

4. The `Transport` class is the core of the action. It's quite long so we'll present only the main important parts:

```
public class TransportSimpleAction
        extends TransportBroadcastByNodeAction<SimpleRequest,
        SimpleResponse, ShardSimpleResponse> {
...

    @Override
    protected SimpleResponse newResponse(SimpleRequest request,
    int totalShards, int successfulShards, int failedShards,
    List<ShardSimpleResponse> shardSimpleResponses,
    List<ShardOperationFailedException> shardFailures,
    ClusterState clusterState) {
        Set<String> simple = new HashSet<String>();
        for (ShardSimpleResponse shardSimpleResponse :
        shardSimpleResponses) {
            simple.addAll(shardSimpleResponse.getTermList());
        }

        return new SimpleResponse(totalShards,
        successfulShards, failedShards, shardFailures, simple);
    }

    @Override
    protected ShardSimpleResponse shardOperation(SimpleRequest
    request, ShardRouting shardRouting) throws IOException {
        IndexService indexService =
        indicesService.indexServiceSafe(shardRouting.shardId()
        .getIndex());
        IndexShard indexShard =
        indexService.getShard(shardRouting.shardId().id());
        indexShard.store().directory();
        Set<String> set = new HashSet<String>();
        set.add(request.getField() + "_" +
```

```
                    shardRouting.shardId());
                    return new ShardSimpleResponse(shardRouting, set);
              }
      ...
```

How it works…

In this example, we used an action that is executed in every cluster node and for every shard that is selected on that node.

As you have seen, to execute a cluster action many classes are required:

- A couple of `Request`/`Response` to interact with the cluster
- A task action on the cluster level
- A Shard `Response` to interact with the shards
- A `Transport` class to manage the map/reduce shard part that must be invoked by the REST call

These classes must extend one of the supported kinds of action:

- `TrasportBroadcastAction` for actions that must be spread across the all cluster.
- `TransportClusterInfoAction` for actions that need to read informations at cluster level.
- `TransportMasterNodeAction` for actions that must be executed only by the master node (such as index and mapping configuration). For simple acknowledge on the master, there are also `AcknowledgedRequest` response.
- `TransportNodeAction` for actions that must be executed on nodes (that is, all the node statistic actions).
- `TransportBroadcastReplicationAction`, `TransportReplicationAction`, `TransportWriteAction` for actions that must be executed by a particular replica, first on primary and then on secondary ones.
- `TransportInstanceSingleOperationAction` for actions that must be executed as a singleton in the cluster.
- `TransportSingleShardAction` for actions that must be executed only in a shard (that is, `GET` actions). If it fails on a shard, it automatically trys on the shard replicas.
- `TransportTasksAction` for actions that need to interact with cluster tasks.

In our example, we have defined an action that will be broadcasted to every node and for every node it collects its shard result and then it aggregates:

```
public class TransportSimpleAction
        extends TransportBroadcastByNodeAction<SimpleRequest,
SimpleResponse, ShardSimpleResponse> {
```

All the request/response classes extend a `Streamable` class, so two methods for serializing their content must be provided:

- `readFrom`, which reads from an `StreamInput`, a class that encapsulates common input stream operations. This method allows the deserialization of the data we transmit on the wire. In the preceding example, we read a string with the following code:

```
@Override
public void readFrom(StreamInput in) throws IOException {
    super.readFrom(in);
    field = in.readString();
}
```

- `writeTo`, which writes the contents of the class to be sent via the network. The `StreamOutput` provides convenient methods to process the output. In the preceding example, we serialized a string:

```
@Override
public void writeTo(StreamOutput out) throws IOException {
    super.writeTo(out);
    out.writeString(field);
}
```

In both actions, `super` must be called to allow the correct serialization of parent classes.

> **TIP**
>
> Every internal action in Elasticsearch is designed as a request/response pattern.

To complete the request/response action, we must define an action that binds the request with the correct response and a builder to construct it. To do so, we need to define an `Action` class.

```
public class SimpleAction extends Action<SimpleRequest, SimpleResponse,
SimpleRequestBuilder> {
```

This `Action` object is a singleton object: we obtain it by creating a default static instance and private constructors:

```
public static final SimpleAction INSTANCE = new SimpleAction();
public static final String NAME = "custom:indices/simple";
private SimpleAction() {super(NAME); }
```

The static string `NAME` is used to uniquely identify the action at the cluster level.

To complete the `Action` definition, two methods must be defined:

- `newResponse`, which is used to create a new empty response:

  ```
  @Override public SimpleResponse newResponse() {
      return new SimpleResponse();
  }
  ```

- `newRequestBuilder`, which is used to return a new request builder for the current action type:

  ```
  @Override
  public SimpleRequestBuilder
  newRequestBuilder(ElasticsearchClient elasticsearchClient) {
      return new SimpleRequestBuilder(elasticsearchClient, this);
  }
  ```

When the action is executed, the request and the response are serialized and sent to the cluster. To execute our custom code at cluster level, a transport action is required.

The transport actions are usually defined as map and reduce jobs. The map part consists of executing the action on several shards, and then reducing parts consisting of collecting all the results from the shards in a response that must be sent back to the requester. To speed up the process in Elasticsearch 5.x, all the shard's responses that belong in the same node are reduced in place to optimize the I/O and the network usage.

The transport action is a long class with many methods, but the most important ones are the `ShardOperation` (map part) and `newResponse` (reduce part).

The original request is converted in a distributed `ShardRequest` that is processed by the `shardOperation` method:

```
@Override
protected ShardSimpleResponse shardOperation(SimpleRequest request,
ShardRouting shardRouting) throws IOException {
```

To obtain the internal shard, we need to ask at the `IndexService` to return a shard-based on wanted index.

The shard request contains the index and the ID of the shard that must be used to execute the action:

```
IndexService indexService =
indicesService.indexServiceSafe(shardRouting.shardId().getIndex());
IndexShard indexShard = indexService.getShard(shardRouting.shardId().id());
```

The `IndexShard` object allows the execution of every possible shard operation (`search`, `get`, `index` and many others). By this method, we can execute every data shard manipulation that we want.

> Custom shard action can execute the application's business operation in a distributed and fast way.

In the preceding example, we have created a simple set of values:

```
Set<String> set = new HashSet<String>();
set.add(request.getField() + "_" + request.shardId());
```

The final step of our shard operation is to create a response to send back to the reduce step. In creating `ShardResponse`, we need to return the result plus information about the index and the shard that executed the action.

```
return new ShardSimpleResponse(request.shardId(), set);
```

The distributed shard operations are collected in the reduce step (`newResponse` method). This step aggregates all the shard results and sends back the result to the original `Action`.

```
@Override
protected SimpleResponse newResponse(
    SimpleRequest request,
    int totalShards, int successfulShards, int failedShards,
    List<ShardSimpleResponse> shardSimpleResponses,
    List<ShardOperationFailedException> shardFailures,
    ClusterState clusterState) {
```

Other than the shard's result, the methods receive the status of shard level operation and they are collected in three values: `successfulShards`, `failedShards` and `shardFailures`.

The request result is a set of collected strings, so we create an empty set to collect the term's results:

```
Set<String> simple = new HashSet<String>();
```

Then you collect the results, we need to iterate on the shard responses:

```
for (ShardSimpleResponse shardSimpleResponse : shardSimpleResponses) {
    simple.addAll(shardSimpleResponse.getTermList());
}
```

The final step is to create the response collecting the previous result and response status:

```
return new SimpleResponse(totalShards, successfulShards, failedShards,
    shardFailures, simple);
```

Creating a cluster action is required when there are low level operations that we want to execute very fast, such as special aggregations, server side join, or a complex manipulation that requires several Elasticsearch calls to be executed. Writing custom Elasticsearch actions is an advanced Elasticsearch feature, but it can create new business use scenarios that can level up the capabilities of Elasticsearch.

See also

- *Creating a REST plugin* in this chapter for how to interface the cluster action with a REST call

Creating an ingest plugin

Elasticsearch 5.x introduces the ingest node that allows the modification, via a pipeline, to the records before ingesting in Elasticsearch. We have already seen in `Chapter 13`, *Ingest* that a pipeline is composed by one or more processor action. In this recipe, we will see how to create a custom processor that store in a field the initial character of another one.

Getting ready

You need an up-and-running Elasticsearch installation as we described in the *Downloading and installing Elasticsearch* recipe in Chapter 2, *Downloading and Setup*.

A Maven tool, or an IDE that support Java programming, such as Eclipse or IntelliJ IDEA. The code for this recipe is available in the chapter17/ingest_plugin directory.

How to do it...

To create an ingest processor plugin, we need to create the processor and then register it in the plugin class. We will perform the following steps:

1. We create the processor and its factory:

```
...
public final class InitialProcessor extends AbstractProcessor {

    public static final String TYPE = "initial";

    private final String field;
    private final String targetField;
    private final boolean ignoreMissing;

    InitialProcessor(String tag, String field, String
    targetField, boolean ignoreMissing) {
        super(tag);
        this.field = field;
        this.targetField = targetField;
        this.ignoreMissing = ignoreMissing;
    }

    String getField() {
        return field;
    }

    String getTargetField() {
        return targetField;
    }

    boolean isIgnoreMissing() {
        return ignoreMissing;
    }

    @Override
```

```
public void execute(IngestDocument document) {
    if (document.hasField(field, true) == false) {
        if (ignoreMissing) {
            return;
        } else {
            throw new IllegalArgumentException("field [" +
            field + "] doesn't exist");
        }
    }
    if (document.hasField(targetField, true)) {
        throw new IllegalArgumentException("field [" +
        targetField + "] already exists");
    }

    Object value = document.getFieldValue(field,
    Object.class);
    if( value!=null && value instanceof String ) {
        String myValue=value.toString().trim();
        if(myValue.length()>1){
            try {
                document.setFieldValue(targetField,
                myValue.substring(0,1).toLowerCase());
            } catch (Exception e) {
         // setting the value back to the original field
         shouldn't as we just fetched it from that field:
                document.setFieldValue(field, value);
                throw e;
            }
        }
    }
}

@Override
public String getType() {
    return TYPE;
}

public static final class Factory implements
Processor.Factory {
@Override
public InitialProcessor create(Map<String,
Processor.Factory> registry, String processorTag,
                        Map<String, Object> config)
throws Exception {
String field = ConfigurationUtils.readStringProperty(TYPE,
processorTag, config, "field");
String targetField =
ConfigurationUtils.readStringProperty(TYPE, processorTag,
```

```
    config, "target_field");
    boolean ignoreMissing =
    ConfigurationUtils.readBooleanProperty(TYPE, processorTag,
    config, "ignore_missing", false);
    return new InitialProcessor(processorTag, field,
    targetField, ignoreMissing);
        }
    }
}
```

2. We need to register it in the `Plugin` class with the following lines:

```
public class MyIngestPlugin extends Plugin implements
IngestPlugin {
    @Override
    public Map<String, Processor.Factory>
    getProcessors(Processor.Parameters parameters) {
        return Collections.singletonMap(InitialProcessor.TYPE,
                (factories, tag, config) -> new
        InitialProcessor.Factory().create(factories, tag,
        config));
    }
}
```

3. Now we can build the plugin via `mvn package` and manually install the ZIP. If we restart the Elasticsearch server, we should see the plugin loaded:

```
...truncated
[][INFO ][o.e.p.PluginsService     ] [PARO] loaded module
[aggs-matrix-stats]
[][INFO ][o.e.p.PluginsService     ] [PARO] loaded module
[ingest-common]
[][INFO ][o.e.p.PluginsService     ] [PARO] loaded module
[lang-expression]
[][INFO ][o.e.p.PluginsService     ] [PARO] loaded module
[lang-groovy]
[][INFO ][o.e.p.PluginsService     ] [PARO] loaded module
[lang-mustache]
[][INFO ][o.e.p.PluginsService     ] [PARO] loaded module
[lang-painless]
[][INFO ][o.e.p.PluginsService     ] [PARO] loaded module
[percolator]
[][INFO ][o.e.p.PluginsService     ] [PARO] loaded module
[reindex]
[][INFO ][o.e.p.PluginsService     ] [PARO] loaded module
[transport-netty3]
[][INFO ][o.e.p.PluginsService     ] [PARO] loaded module
[transport-netty4]
```

```
[][INFO ][o.e.p.PluginsService      ] [PARO] loaded plugin
[my-ingest-plugin]
[][INFO ][o.e.p.PluginsService      ] [PARO] loaded plugin
[simple-plugin]
[...][INFO ][o.e.n.Node               ] [es] initialized
[...][INFO ][o.e.n.Node               ] [es] starting ...
```

4. We can test out custom ingest plugin via Simulate Ingest API with a curl:

```
curl -XPOST 'http://127.0.0.1:9200/_ingest/pipeline/_simulate?
verbose&pretty' -d '{
  "pipeline": {
     "description": "Test my custom plugin",
     "processors": [
       {
         "initial": {
           "field": "user",
           "target_field": "user_initial"
         }
       }
     ],
     "version": 1
  },
  "docs": [
    {
      "_source": {
        "user": "john"
      }
    },
    {
      "_source": {
        "user": "Nancy"
      }
    }
  ]
}'
```

5. The result will be something similar to:

```
{
  "docs" : [
    {
      "processor_results" : [
        {
          "doc" : {
            "_index" : "_index",
            "_type" : "_type",
            "_id" : "_id",
```

```json
            "_source" : {
              "user_initial" : "j",
              "user" : "john"
            },
            "_ingest" : {
              "timestamp" : "2016-12-10T17:04:07.032+0000"
            }
          }
        }
      }
    ]
  },
    {
      "processor_results" : [
        {
          "doc" : {
            "_index" : "_index",
            "_type" : "_type",
            "_id" : "_id",
            "_source" : {
              "user_initial" : "n",
              "user" : "Nancy"
            },
            "_ingest" : {
              "timestamp" : "2016-12-10T17:04:07.032+0000"
            }
          }
        }
      ]
    }
  ]
}
```

How it works...

First you need to define the class that will manage your custom processor which extends an
`AbstractProcessor`:

```
public final class InitialProcessor extends AbstractProcessor {
```

The `processor` needs to know the fields on which it operates. They are kept in the internal
state of the processor:

```
public static final String TYPE = "initial";

private final String field;
private final String targetField;
```

```
private final boolean ignoreMissing;

InitialProcessor(String tag, String field, String targetField,
boolean ignoreMissing) {
    super(tag);
    this.field = field;
    this.targetField = targetField;
    this.ignoreMissing = ignoreMissing;
}
```

The core of the processor is the `execute` function, which contains our processor login:

```
@Override
public void execute(IngestDocument document) {
```

The `execute` function is composed of the following steps:

1. Check if the `source` field exits:

```
if (document.hasField(field, true) == false) {
    if (ignoreMissing) {
        return;
    } else {
        throw new IllegalArgumentException
        ("field [" + field + "] doesn't exist");
    }
}
```

2. Check if the `target` field does not exist:

```
if (document.hasField(targetField, true)) {
    throw new IllegalArgumentException
    ("field [" + targetField + "] already exists");
}
```

3. We extract the value from document and check if it's valid:

```
Object value = document.getFieldValue(field, Object.class);
if( value!=null && value instanceof String ) {
```

4. Now we can process the value and set in the `target` field:

```
String myValue=value.toString().trim();
f(myValue.length()>1){
    try {
        document.setFieldValue(targetField,
        myValue.substring(0,1).toLowerCase());
    } catch (Exception e) {
```

```
        // setting the value back to the original field shouldn't as we
        just fetched it from that field:
                document.setFieldValue(field, value);
                throw e;
            }
        }
```

To be able to initialize the processor for its definition, we need to define a `Factory` object.

```
public static final class Factory implements Processor.Factory {
```

The `Factory` object contains the `create` method that receives the registered processors, the `processorTag`, and its configuration that must be read:

```
    @Override
    public InitialProcessor create(Map<String, Processor.Factory> registry,
    String processorTag,
                                    Map<String, Object> config) throws
    Exception {
            String field = ConfigurationUtils.readStringProperty(TYPE,
    processorTag, config, "field");
            String targetField = ConfigurationUtils.readStringProperty(TYPE,
    processorTag, config, "target_field");
            boolean ignoreMissing =
    ConfigurationUtils.readBooleanProperty(TYPE, processorTag, config,
    "ignore_missing", false);
```

After having recovered, we can initialize processor parameters it:

```
return new InitialProcessor(processorTag, field, targetField,
ignoreMissing);
    }
```

To be used as a custom processor, it needs to be registered in the plugin. This is done by extending the plugin as `IngestPlugin`.

```
public class MyIngestPlugin extends Plugin implements IngestPlugin {
```

Now we can register the `Factory` plugin in the `getProcessors` method.

```
@Override
public Map<String, Processor.Factory> getProcessors(Processor.Parameters
parameters) {
    return Collections.singletonMap(InitialProcessor.TYPE,
            (factories, tag, config) -> new
InitialProcessor.Factory().create(factories, tag, config));
}
```

Implementing an ingestion processor via a plugin is quite simple, and it's an incredibly powerful feature. With this approach a user can create custom enrichment pipelines.

18
Big Data Integration

In this chapter we will cover the following recipes:

- Installing Apache Spark
- Indexing data via Apache Spark
- Indexing data with meta via Apache Spark
- Reading data with Apache Spark
- Reading data using SparkSQL
- Indexing data with Apache Pig

Introduction

Elasticsearch has become a common component in big data architectures because it provides several features:

- It allows searching on massive amount of data in a very fast way
- For common aggregation operations, it provides real-time analytics on big data
- It's more easy to use an Elasticsearch aggregation than a spark one
- If you need to move on to a fast data solution, starting from a subset of documents after a query is faster than doing a full rescan of all your data

The most common big data software used for processing data is now Apache Spark (http://spark.apache.org/) that is considered the evolution of the obsolete Hadoop MapReduce moving the processing from disk to memory.

In this chapter, we will see how to integrate Elasticsearch in Spark both for write and read data. In the end, we will see how to use Apache Pig to write data in Elasticsearch in a simple way.

Installing Apache Spark

To use Apache Spark, first install it. The process is very easy, because its requirements are not the traditional Hadoop ones that require Apache Zookeeper and Hadoop HDFS.

Apache spark is able to work in a standalone node installation that is similar to an Elasticsearch one.

Getting ready

You need a Java Virtual Machine installed: generally version 8.x or above is used.

How to do it...

For installing Apache Spark, we will perform the following steps:

1. We will download a binary distribution from at
   `http://spark.apache.org/downloads.html`. For a generic usage, I suggest you to download a standard version via:

   ```
   wget http://d3kbcqa49mib13.cloudfront.net/spark-2.1.0-bin-
   hadoop2.7.tgz
   ```

2. Now we can extract the Spark distribution via:

   ```
   tar xfvz spark-2.1.0-bin-hadoop2.7.tgz
   ```

3. Now, we can test if Apache Spark is working by executing a test:

   ```
   cd spark-2.1.0-bin-hadoop2.7
   ./bin/run-example SparkPi
   ```

4. The result will be similar to the following screenshot:

   ```
   INFO SparkContext: Running Spark version 2.1.0
   WARN NativeCodeLoader: Unable to load native-hadoop library for
   your platform... using builtin-java classes where applicable
   INFO SecurityManager: Changing view acls to: alberto
   INFO SecurityManager: Changing modify acls to: alberto
   INFO SecurityManager: Changing view acls groups to:
   INFO SecurityManager: Changing modify acls groups to:
   INFO SecurityManager: SecurityManager: authentication disabled;
   ui acls disabled; users  with view permissions: Set(alberto);
   ```

```
groups with view permissions: Set();
...
Pi is roughly 3.1365756828784144
...
INFO BlockManagerMaster: BlockManagerMaster stopped
INFO OutputCommitCoordinator$OutputCommitCoordinatorEndpoint:
OutputCommitCoordinator stopped!
INFO SparkContext: Successfully stopped SparkContext
INFO ShutdownHookManager: Shutdown hook called
INFO ShutdownHookManager: Deleting directory
/private/var/folders/gq/v7rky81s6d13m81zr9dzq9mm0000gn/T/spark-
27d64c52-04c9-4a89-a1e6-42d2c237d819
```

How it works...

Apache Spark as a standalone node is very easy to be installed. Similar to Elasticsearch, it requires only a Java Virtual Machine installed in the system.

The installation process is very easy, you only need to unpack the archive and there is a complete working installation.

In the preceding steps we also tested whether the spark installation was working.

Spark is written in Scala and the default binaries are targeting version 2.11.x. Scala major versions are not compatible, so you need to pay attention to make sure that both Spark and Elasticsearch Hadoop are using the same version.

When executing a Spark job, the simplified steps are as follows:

1. The Spark environment is initialized.
2. Spark MemoryStore and BlockManager master are initialized.
3. A SparkContext for the execution is initialized.
4. SparkUI is activated at `http://0.0.0.0:4040`.
5. The job is taken.
6. An execution graph **Direct Acyclic Graph (DAG)** is created for the job.
7. Every vertex in the DAG is a stage and a stage is split in tasks that are executed in parallel.
8. After executing the stages and tasks, the processing ends.
9. The result is returned.
10. The SparkContext is stopped.
11. The Spark system is shut down.

There's more…

One of the powerful tools of Spark is the shell (Spark shell). It allows you to enter commands and execute directly on the Spark cluster.

To access Spark shell, you need to invoke it via `./bin/spark-shell`.

When invoked, the output will be something like this:

```
Spark context Web UI available at http://192.168.1.230:4040
Spark context available as 'sc' (master = local[*], app id = local-
1483719015121).
Spark session available as 'spark'.
Welcome to
      ____              __
     / __/__  ___ _____/ /__
    _\ \/ _ \/ _ `/ __/  '_/
   /___/ .__/\_,_/_/ /_/\_\   version 2.1.0
      /_/

Using Scala version 2.11.8 (Java HotSpot(TM) 64-Bit Server VM, Java
1.8.0_101)
Type in expressions to have them evaluated.
Type :help for more information.
scala>
```

Now, it's possible to insert the command-line commands that are to be executed in the cluster.

Indexing data via Apache Spark

After having installed Apache Spark, we can configure it to work with Elasticsearch and write some data in it.

Getting ready

You need an up-and-running Elasticsearch installation as we described in the *Downloading and installing Elasticsearch* recipe in `Chapter 2`, *Downloading and Setup*.

You also need a working installation of Apache Spark.

How to do it...

To configure Apache Spark to communicate with Elasticsearch, we will perform the following steps:

1. We need to download the ElasticSearch Spark JAR:

   ```
   wget http://download.elastic.co/hadoop/elasticsearch-hadoop-
   5.1.1.zip
   unzip elasticsearch-hadoop-5.1.1.zip
   ```

2. A quick way to access the Spark shell in Elasticsearch is to copy the Elasticsearch Hadoop required file in Spark's `.jar` directory. The file that must be copied is `elasticsearch-spark-20_2.11-5.1.1.jar`.

   > The version of Scala used by both Apache Spark and Elasticsearch Spark must match!

For storing data in Elasticsearch via Apache Spark, we will perform the following steps:

1. We need to start the Spark shell:

   ```
   ./bin/spark-shell
   ```

2. We can apply the Elasticsearch configuration:

   ```
   val conf = sc.getConf
   conf.setAppName("ESImport")
   conf.set("es.index.auto.create", "true")
   ```

3. We import Elasticsearch Spark implicits:

   ```
   import org.elasticsearch.spark._
   ```

4. We create two documents to be indexed:

   ```
   val numbers = Map("one" -> 1, "two" -> 2, "three" -> 3)
   val airports = Map("arrival" -> "Otopeni", "SFO" -> "San Fran")
   ```

5. Now we can create a RDD and save the document in Elasticsearch:

   ```
   sc.makeRDD(Seq(numbers, airports)).saveToEs("spark/docs")
   ```

How it works...

Storing documents in Elasticsearch via Spark is quite simple.

After having started a Spark shell, in the shell context an `sc` variable is available that contains the SparkContext. If we need to pass values to the underlying Elasticsearch configuration, you need to set them in the Spark configuration.

There are several configurations that can be set; the most commonly used ones are:

- `es.index.auto.create`: This is used to create indices if they do not exist
- `es.nodes`: This is used to define a list of nodes to connect with (default `localhost`)
- `es.port`: This is used to define the HTTP Elasticsearch port to connect with (default `9200`)
- `es.ingest.pipeline`: This is used to define an ingest pipeline to be used (default `none`)
- `es.mapping.id`: This is used to define a field to extract the ID value (default `none`)
- `es.mapping.parent`: This is used to define a field to extract the parent value (default `none`)

Simple documents can be defined as `Map[String, AnyRef]` and they can be indexed via **Resilient Distributed Dataset** (**RDD**), a special Spark abstraction on a collection.

Via the implicits available in the `org.elasticsearch.spark` RDD has a new method called `saveToEs` that allows you to define the pair index/document to be used for indexing.

See also

- To download the latest version of Elasticsearch Hadoop, the official page is at `https://www.elastic.co/downloads/hadoop`.
- The official documentation on installing Elasticsearch Hadoop `https://www.elastic.co/guide/en/elasticsearch/hadoop/current/install.html`. This page also provides some `border` cases.
- For a quickstart on using Spark, I suggest the Spark documentation at `http://spark.apache.org/docs/latest/quick-start.html`.

- For a detailed list of configuration parameters that can be set in Spark Config look at `https://www.elastic.co/guide/en/elasticsearch/hadoop/5.x/configuration.html`.

Indexing data with meta via Apache Spark

Using a simple map for ingesting data is not good for simple jobs. The best practice in Spark is to use the `case` class so that you have fast serialization and you are to manage complex type checking. During indexing, providing custom IDs can be very handy. In this recipe, we will see how to cover these issues.

Getting ready

You need an up-and-running Elasticsearch installation as we described in the *Downloading and installing Elasticsearch* recipe in `Chapter 2`, *Downloading and Setup*.

You also need a working installation of Apache Spark.

How to do it...

To store data in Elasticsearch via Apache Spark, we will perform the following steps:

1. We need to start the Spark shell:

   ```
   ./bin/spark-shell
   ```

2. We will import the required classes:

   ```
   import org.apache.spark.SparkContext
   import org.elasticsearch.spark.rdd.EsSpark
   ```

3. We will create a `case class Person`:

   ```
   case class Person(username:String, name:String, age:Int)
   ```

4. We create two documents that are to be indexed:

   ```
   val persons = Seq(Person("bob", "Bob",19),Person("susan",
   "Susan",21))
   ```

5. Now we can create a RDD:

```
val rdd=sc.makeRDD(persons)
```

6. We can index them via `EsSpark`:

```
EsSpark.saveToEs(rdd, "spark/persons", Map("es.mapping.id" ->
"username"))
```

7. In Elasticsearch, the indexed data will be as follows:

```
{
  ...,
  "hits": {
   "total": 2,
   "max_score": 1,
    "hits": [
      {
        "_index": "spark",
        "_type": "persons",
        "_id": "susan",
        "_score": 1,
        "_source": {
          "username": "susan",
          "name": "Susan",
          "age": 21
        }
      },
      {
        "_index": "spark",
        "_type": "persons",
        "_id": "bob",
        "_score": 1,
        "_source": {
          "username": "bob",
          "name": "Bob",
         "age": 19
        }
      }
    ]
  }
}
```

How it works...

To speed up computation, in Apache Spark, the `case` class is used to better describe the domain object we used during job processing. It has fast serializators and deserializators that allow easy conversion of the `case` class to JSON and vice versa.

Using `case` class the data is strong typed modeled.

In the preceding example, we have created a `Person` class that designs a standard person. Nested `case` class are automatically managed.

After having instantiated some `Person` objects, we need to create a RDD that will be saved in Elasticsearch.

In this example, we have used a special class `EsSpark` that provides helpers to pass metadata used for indexing. In our case, we have provided information in how to extract the id from the document via `Map("es.mapping.id" -> "username")`.

There's more...

Often the ID is not a field of your object, but it's a complex value computed on the document. In this case you can manage to create an RDD with a tuple (ID, document) to be indexed.

For the preceding example, we can define the function that does the ID computation on the `Person` class:

```
import org.elasticsearch.spark._
case class Person(username:String, name:String, age:Int) {
def id=this.username+this.age
}
```

When we can use it to compute our new RDD:

```
val persons = Seq(Person("bob", "Bob",19),Person("susan", "Susan",21))
val personIds=persons.map(p => p.id -> p)
val rdd=sc.makeRDD(personIds)
```

Now we can index them:

```
rdd.saveToEsWithMeta("spark/person_id")
```

In this case the stored documents will be:

```
{
   ...
   "hits": {
     "total": 2,
     "max_score": 1,
     "hits": [
       {
         "_index": "spark",
         "_type": "person_id",
         "_id": "bob19",
         "_score": 1,
         "_source": {
           "username": "bob",
           "name": "Bob",
           "age": 19
         }
       },
       {
         "_index": "spark",
         "_type": "person_id",
         "_id": "susan21",
         "_score": 1,
         "_source": {
           "username": "susan",
           "name": "Susan",
           "age": 21
         }
       }
     ]
   }
}
```

Reading data with Apache Spark

In Spark you can read data from a lot of sources, but in general NoSQL datastores such as HBase, Accumulo, and Cassandra you have a limited query subset and you often need to scan all the data to read only the required data. Using Elasticsearch you can retrieve a subset of documents that match your Elasticsearch query.

Getting ready

To read an up-and-running Elasticsearch installation as we described in the Downloading and installing Elasticsearch recipe in `Chapter 2`, *Downloading and Setup*.

You also need a working installation of Apache Spark and the data indexed in the previous example.

How to do it...

For reading data in Elasticsearch via Apache Spark, we will perform the steps given as follows:

1. We need to start the Spark Shell:

   ```
   ./bin/spark-shell
   ```

2. We import the required classes:

   ```
   import org.elasticsearch.spark._
   ```

3. Now we can create a RDD by reading data from Elasticsearch:

   ```
   val rdd=sc.esRDD("spark/persons")
   ```

4. We can watch the fetched values using:

   ```
   rdd.collect.foreach(println)
   ```

5. The result will be the following:

   ```
   (susan,Map(username -> susan, name -> Susan, age -> 21))
   (bob,Map(username -> bob, name -> Bob, age -> 19))
   ```

How it works...

The Elastic team has done a good job in allowing the use of the simple API to read data from Elasticsearch.

You need to only import the implicit that extends the standard RDD with the `esRDD` method to allow retrieving data from Elasticsearch.

The `esRDD` method accepts several parameters such as:

- `resource`: This is generally an index/type tuple.
- `query`: This is a query that is used to filter the results. It's in the query args format (an optional string).
- `config`: This contains extra configurations to be provided to Elasticsearch (an optional `Map[String, String]`).

The returned value is a collection of tuples in the form of the ID and `Map` objects.

Reading data using SparkSQL

Spark SQL is a Spark module for structured data processing. It provides a programming abstraction called DataFrames and can also act as distributed SQL query engine. Elasticsearch Spark integration allows us to read data via SQL queries.

> Spark SQL works with structured data; in other words, all entries are expected to have the same structure (the same number of fields, of the same type and name). Using unstructured data (documents with different structures) is not supported and will cause problems.

Getting ready

You need an up-and-running Elasticsearch installation as we described in the *Downloading and installing Elasticsearch* recipe in Chapter 2, *Downloading and Setup*.

You also need a working installation of Apache Spark and the data indexed in the *Indexing data via Apache Spark* recipe of this chapter.

How to do it...

To read data in Elasticsearch via Apache Spark SQL and via DataFrame, we will perform the steps given as follows:

1. We need to start the Spark shell.

```
./bin/spark-shell
```

2. We create a DataFrame in the format `org.elasticsearch.spark.sql` and load data from `spark/person_id`:

```
val df =
spark.read.format("org.elasticsearch.spark.sql").load
("spark/person_id")
```

3. If we want to check the schema, we are able to inspect it via `printSchema`:

```
df.printSchema
root
 |-- age: long (nullable = true)
 |-- name: string (nullable = true)
 |-- username: string (nullable = true)
```

4. We can watch fetched values using:

```
df.filter(df("age").gt(20)).collect.foreach(println)
[21,Susan,susan]
```

For reading data in Elasticsearch via Apache Spark SQL via SQL queries, we will perform the steps given as follows:

1. We need to start the Spark shell:

```
./bin/spark-shell
```

2. We create a view for reading data from `spark/person_id`:

```
spark.sql(
   "CREATE TEMPORARY VIEW persons USING
    org.elasticsearch.spark.sql OPTIONS (resource
   'spark/person_id', scroll_size '2000')" )
```

3. We can now execute a SQL query against the previous created view:

```
val over20 = spark.sql("SELECT * FROM persons WHERE age >= 20")
```

4. We can watch fetched values using:

```
over20.collect.foreach(println)
[21,Susan,susan]
```

How it works…

The core of data management in Spark is the DataFrame that allows fetching values from different datastores.

You can use SQL query capabilities at the top of DataFrames and depending of the driver used (`org.elasticsearch.spark.sql` in our case) the query can be pushed down at driver level (a native query in Elasticsearch). For example, in our preceding example, the query is converted in a Boolean filter with a range that is executed natively by Elasticsearch.

The Elasticsearch Spark driver is able to do inference reading information from the mappings and to manage the datastore as a standard sql datastore.

The SQL approach is very power and allows to re-use SQL expertise that is very common.

A good approach in using Elasticsearch with Spark is to use the Spark Notebooks: interactive web based interfaces that speed up the testing phases of application prototype. The most famous ones are Spark Notebook available at `http://spark-notebook.io` and Apache Zeppelin available at `https://zeppelin.apache.org`.

Indexing data with Apache Pig

Apache Pig (`https://pig.apache.org/`) is a tool frequently used to store/manipulate data in datastores. It can be very handy if you need to import some CSV in Elasticsearch in a very fast way.

Getting ready

You need an up-and-running Elasticsearch installation as we described in *Downloading and installing Elasticsearch* recipe in `Chapter 2`, *Downloading and Setup*.

You need a working Pig installation. Depending on your operating system you should follow the instruction at `http://pig.apache.org/docs/r0.16.0/start.html`.

If you are using Mac OS X with Homebrew you can install it with `brew install pig`.

How to do it...

We want read a CSV and write the data in Elasticsearch. We will perform the steps given as follows:

1. We will download a CSV dataset from geonames site: all the geoname locations of Great Britain. We can fast download them and unzip them via:

```
wget http://download.geonames.org/export/dump/GB.zip
unzip GB.zip
```

2. We can write `es.pig` that contains the Pig commands to be executed:

```
REGISTER /Users/alberto/elasticsearch/elasticsearch-hadoop-
5.1.1/dist/elasticsearch-hadoop-pig-5.1.1.jar;

SET pig.noSplitCombination TRUE;

DEFINE EsStorage org.elasticsearch.hadoop.pig.EsStorage();

-- launch the Map/Reduce job with 5 reducers
SET default_parallel 5;

--load the GB.txt file
geonames= LOAD 'GB.txt' using PigStorage('\t') AS
(geonameid:int,name:chararray,asciiname:chararray,
alternatenames:chararray,latitude:double,longitude:double,
feature_class:chararray,feature_code:chararray,
country_code:chararray,cc2:chararray,admin1_code:chararray,
admin2_code:chararray,admin3_code:chararray,
admin4_code:chararray,population:int,elevation:int,
dem:chararray,timezone:chararray,modification_date:chararray);


STORE geonames INTO 'geoname/gb' USING EsStorage();
```

3. Now we can execute the `pig` command:

```
pig -x local es.pig
```

The output will be similar to the following:

```
...
2017-01-07 16:13:37,965 [main] INFO
org.apache.pig.backend.hadoop.executionengine.mapReduceLayer.MapReduceLaunc
her - 100% complete
2017-01-07 16:13:37,966 [main] INFO
```

```
org.apache.pig.tools.pigstats.mapreduce.SimplePigStats - Script Statistics:

HadoopVersion  PigVersion  UserId  StartedAt  FinishedAt  Features
1.0.4  0.16.0  alberto  2017-01-07 16:13:28  2017-01-07 16:13:37  UNKNOWN

Success!

Job Stats (time in seconds):
JobId  Maps  Reduces  MaxMapTime  MinMapTime  AvgMapTime  MedianMapTime
MaxReduceTime  MinReduceTime  AvgReduceTime  MedianReducetime  Alias
Feature  Outputs
job_local_0001  1  0  n/a  n/a  n/a  n/a  0  0  0  0  geonames  MAP_ONLY
geoname/gb,

Input(s):
Successfully read 61021 records from:
"file:///Users/alberto/elasticsearch/GB.txt"

Output(s):
Successfully stored 61021 records in: "geoname/gb"

Counters:
Total records written : 61021
Total bytes written : 0
Spillable Memory Manager spill count : 0
Total bags proactively spilled: 0
Total records proactively spilled: 0

Job DAG: job_local_0001

2017-01-07 16:13:37,967 [main] INFO
org.apache.pig.backend.hadoop.executionengine.mapReduceLayer.MapReduceLaunc
her - Success!
2017-01-07 16:13:37,978 [main] INFO  org.apache.pig.Main - Pig script
completed in 10 seconds and 469 milliseconds (10469 ms)
```

After a few seconds, all the CSV data is indexed in Elasticsearch.

How it works...

Apache Pig is a very handy tool. With a small number of code lines, it's able to read/transform/store data in different datastores.

It has a shell, but it's very common to write a Pig script with all the commands to be executed.

For using Elasticsearch in Apache Pig, you need to register the library that contains `EsStorage`. This is done via the register script: the JAR position depends on your installation:

```
REGISTER /Users/alberto/elasticsearch/elasticsearch-
hadoop-5.1.1/dist/elasticsearch-hadoop-pig-5.1.1.jar;
```

By default, Pig splits the data in blocks and then combines it before sending it to Elasticsearch. To maintain maximum parallelism, you need to disable this behavior via `SET pig.noSplitCombination TRUE`.

To prevent typing the full path for the `EsStorage`, we define a shortcut:

```
DEFINE EsStorage org.elasticsearch.hadoop.pig.EsStorage();
```

By default, the Pig parallelism is set to `1`. If we want to speed up the process, we need to increase this value:

```
-- launch the Map/Reduce job with 5 reducers
SET default_parallel 5;
```

Reading a CSV in Pig is very simple; we define a file, the `PigStorage` with the field separator and the format of the fields:

```
--load the GB.txt file
geonames= LOAD 'GB.txt' using PigStorage('\t') AS
(geonameid:int,name:chararray,asciiname:chararray,alternatenames:chararray,
latitude:double,longitude:double,feature_class:chararray,feature_code:chara
rray,country_code:chararray,cc2:chararray,admin1_code:chararray,admin2_code
:chararray,admin3_code:chararray,admin4_code:chararray,population:int,eleva
tion:int,dem:chararray,timezone:chararray,modification_date:chararray);
```

After having read the CSV file, the lines are indexed as objects in Elasticsearch:

```
STORE geonames INTO 'geoname/gb' USING EsStorage();
```

As a reader can see, all the complexity in using Pig is to manage the format of input and output. The key winning of Apache Pig is the ability to load different datasets, join them, and store them in few lines of code.

Index

Y